The Royal Remains

The Royal Remains

The People's Two Bodies and the
Endgames of Sovereignty

ERIC L. SANTNER

The University of Chicago Press   Chicago and London

ERIC L. SANTNER is the Philip and Ida Romberg Professor in Modern Germanic Studies, professor of Germanic studies, and a member of the Committee on Jewish Studies at the University of Chicago. He is the author of several books, most recently including *On Creaturely Life: Rilke, Benjamin, Sebald*, also published by the University of Chicago Press.

The University of Chicago Press, Chicago 60637
The University of Chicago Press, Ltd., London
© 2011 by The University of Chicago
All rights reserved. Published 2011
Printed in the United States of America
20 19 18 17 16 15 14 13 12 11   1 2 3 4 5

ISBN-13: 978-0-226-73535-1 (cloth)
ISBN-13: 978-0-226-73536-8 (paper)
ISBN-10: 0-226-73535-4 (cloth)
ISBN-10: 0-226-73536-2 (paper)

Library of Congress Cataloging-in-Publication Data
Santner, Eric L., 1955–
      The royal remains : the people's two bodies and the endgames
   of sovereignty / Eric L. Santner.
         p. cm.
      Includes index.
      ISBN-13: 978-0-226-73535-1 (cloth : alk. paper)
      ISBN-10: 0-226-73535-4 (cloth : alk. paper)
      ISBN-13: 978-0-226-73536-8 (pbk. : alk. paper)
      ISBN-10: 0-226-73536-2 (pbk. : alk. paper)
      1. Political theology. 2. Sovereignty—Religious aspects.
      3. Kings and rulers—Religious aspects. 4. Rilke, Rainer Maria,
      1875–1926. Aufzeichnungen des Malte Laurids Brigge.   I. Title.
   BT83.59.S26 2011
   201'.72—dc22   2010035081

♾ The paper used in this publication meets the minimum requirements of the American National Standard for Information Sciences— Permanence of Paper for Printed Library Materials, ANSI Z39.48-1992.

For Marcia Adler, in loving memory

Contents

Preface

I

Some years ago I wrote a small book about the famous case of Daniel Paul Schreber, the Saxon jurist whose autobiographical account of mental illness and psychiatric confinement provided Freud with crucial material for elaborating a theory of paranoia and psychotic formations more generally.[1] There I suggested—all too casually—that Schreber's delusional system, which was largely organized around the religious and political meanings of a series of spectacular somatic symptoms, could be understood as a uniquely modern and even modernist mutation of the political theological tradition of the "king's two bodies," a tradition elaborated in extraordinary detail by Ernst Kantorowicz in his famous study on the subject.[2] I also suggested that one ultimately needed to insert the "body of the analyst" within that same tradition, to discern in the agency, figure, and corporeal presence of this new kind of healer a countervailing remnant of that very tradition. The present study represents an attempt to "flesh out" these intuitions with regard to the modern afterlives of the king's body, the ways in which something of the royal remains. As I will argue, one can do so only by way of a theory of "the flesh" as the sublime substance that the various rituals, legal and theological doctrines, and literary and social fantasies surrounding

---

1. Eric Santner, *My Own Private Germany: Daniel Paul Schreber's Secret History of Modernity* (Princeton, NJ: Princeton University Press, 1996).

2. Ernst Kantorowicz, *The King's Two Bodies: A Study in Medieval Political Theology* (Princeton, NJ: Princeton University Press, 1981).

the monarch's singular physiology (the arcana that fill the pages of Kantorowicz's now-canonical study) originally attempted to shape and manage.

One might, in this context, recall that at one of the key moments in Schreber's account of his own experience of divine election, his delusional mutation into God's concubine, he reports that on a particular day one of the divine voices that at various times spoke to and through him (and to which he refers by way of the Zoroastrian names of God's dual aspects) used a special term of address that produced in him (or, at the very least, was correlated with) a series of special effects to which his body was subject. Among other things, the word, a cross between a curse and a title that functions as a kind of debased *laudes regiae*, seemed to posit Schreber as the abject bearer of rotting flesh, as if the official identity he was unable to inhabit (he had been invested with the office of president of the Sachsen Supreme Court) had melted down into so much putrescence:

I believe I may say that at that time and at that time *only*, I saw God's omnipotence in its complete purity. During the night . . . the lower God (Ariman) appeared. The radiant picture of his rays became visible to my inner eye . . . that is to say he was reflected on my inner nervous system. Simultaneously I heard his voice; but it was not a soft whisper—as the talk of the voices always was before and after that time—it resounded in a mighty bass as if directly in front of my bedroom window. The impression was intense, so that anybody not hardened to terrifying miraculous impressions as I was, would have been shaken to the core. Also *what* was spoken did not sound friendly by any means: everything seemed calculated to instil fright and terror into me and the word "wretch" [*Luder*] was frequently heard—an expression quite common in the basic language to denote a human being destined to be destroyed by God and to feel God's power and wrath.[3]

The word singled out by Schreber, "Luder," has especially rich connotations in the context of the judge's torments. It can indeed mean wretch, in the sense of a lost and pathetic figure, but can also signify a cunning swindler or scoundrel; a whore, tart, or slut; and finally, the dead, rotting flesh of an animal, especially in the sense of carrion used as bait in hunting.[4] The last two significations capture Schreber's fear of being

3. Daniel Paul Schreber, *Memoirs of My Nervous Illness*, trans. Ida Macalpine and Richard A. Hunter (Cambridge, MA: Harvard University Press, 1988), 124.

4. Jacques Lacan, in his seminar on the Schreber case, notes that the French translation of this word is *charogne*, which also happens to be the title of one of Baudelaire's most famous poems. In this context one might also recall that critics responded to the initial display of Manet's *Olympia* as if confronted by a *Luder* in all the meanings conveyed by the word. T. J. Clark summarizes some

turned over to others for the purposes of sexual exploitation as well as his delusions, which would seem to flow from such abuse, about putre-faction, about having been abandoned and left to rot or waste away. These delusions merge at times with a preoccupation about being sick with the plague, leprosy, or syphilis. What I want to emphasize here is that the transformation of Schreber's body—its decomposition and feminization—is at least in part precipitated by the "revelation" of a word that itself signifies the effects that its forceful accusative utterance seems directly to provoke in Schreber's body. We are faced here with a radical concretization or materialization of the operations of a performative ut-terance. It is as if the meeting of this "acclamation" *Luder!* with this body had produced or deposited at its point of contact the nervously agitated flesh Schreber was enjoined to bear and even *to enjoy*.[5]

Over the course of this study, I track the vicissitudes of the flesh in a se-ries of readings of literature, philosophy, painting, and political thought. I focus on works produced, for the most part, in the twentieth century, works that are representative of or profoundly engaged with that sweep of cultural history referred to as "modernism." The premise of these read-ings is that one will get hold of what distinguishes this chapter of cultural history only if one grasps the ways it has labored under what could be characterized as the *biopolitical pressures* generated by the transition from royal to popular sovereignty in the wake of the French Revolution and the long struggle to reconstitute the "physiology" of the body politic over the course of the nineteenth century. To put it in a formula, my thesis is that crucial features of modernity can be grasped by following the trans-formation of the complex tensions belonging to the political theology of royal sovereignty into the biopolitical pressures of popular sovereignty. My claim is that biopolitics assumes its particular urgency and expansive-ness in modernity because what is at issue in it is not simply the biologi-cal life or health of populations but the "sublime" life-substance of the

---

of the critics' responses: "There was something about *Olympia* which eluded their normal frame of reference, and writers were almost fond of admitting they had no words for what they saw. *Olympia* was 'informe,' 'inconcevable,' 'inqualifiable,' 'indéchiffrable.'. . . 'The least handsome of women has bones, muscles, skin, form, and some kind of color,' whereas Olympia had none; she was 'neither true nor living nor beautiful.'" T. J. Clark, *The Painting of Modern Life: Paris in the Art of Manet and His Followers* (Princeton, NJ: Princeton University Press, 1984), 92. Various critics explicitly underlined the cadaverous aspect of her body. One Victor de Jankovitz wrote, "The expression of her face is that of being prematurely aged and vicious; her body, of a putrefying colour, recalls the horror of the morgue" (cited ibid., 96).

5. Schreber famously insisted that "God demands *constant enjoyment*. . . . It is my duty to pro-vide Him with it in the form of highly developed soul-voluptuousness, as far as this is possible in circumstances contrary to the Order of the World." He then added that in his "relation to God . . . voluptuousness has become 'God-fearing.'" Schreber, *Memoirs of My Nervous Illness*, 208–9, 210.

People, who, at least in principle, become the bearers of sovereignty, assume the dignity of the *prince*. Indeed, I think the case of Daniel Paul Schreber, whose delusions capture what I have referred to as a "secret history of modernity," have become such a lure—such *Luder*—for thinkers of modernity such as Freud, Benjamin, Canetti, Deleuze, Foucault, Certau, Lacan, and Kittler, among many others, because Schreber himself appeared to grasp these pressures and their "fleshly" materiality as the basis for a rethinking of the political theological (or perhaps better, the *biocratic*) constitution of modern life. These pressures pertain not only to questions concerning the foundation and constitution of political authority but also more generally to those concerning the patterns and procedures whereby human beings come to be vested with the authority of the various "offices" they occupy and the ways in which such procedures of investiture, such transferences of symbolic authority, are ultimately legitimated. Schreber's difficulties in metabolizing such pressures (in my study of the case I characterized these difficulties as a chronic "crisis of investiture") can be measured by his fundamental uncertainty as to the proper addressee or audience for his memoirs. It was, in a word, unclear whether they concerned medical science, the law, the world of religious thought and experience, the realm of politics, or some new sort of science or mode of knowledge yet to come. As we shall see, such uncertainty belongs to the phenomena at issue.

It should be noted that the concept "political theology" is itself already highly overdetermined, the bearer of multiple and at times conflicting semantic and ideological values. At one level, the notion of political theology conveys the expansion of the reach of religious meanings and values into the sphere of political life, the investment of political institutions and actors with the trappings and charisma of sacred authority. But it thereby also signifies a contraction of the domain of religious life and practices into what eventually became the "private sphere" of citizens. Political theology can thus be seen to function as an operator of secularization—the displacement of religion by politics as the central organizing force of sociality and collective identifications—but only insofar as this "elevation" of politics above the confessional affiliations and practices of subjects is itself sustained by theological values and concepts. As we shall see, the further shift from the political theology of royal sovereignty to ostensibly de-theologized, fully secularized political theories of popular sovereignty (and the forms of life framed by them) brings such complexities and ambiguities ever more to the fore, though in new guises and modalities.

II

The following reflections orbit to a very large extent around a single question that first emerged for me in the context of my engagement with the Schreber material but that has at some level persisted throughout all my subsequent work. It is a version of the great question concerning the relation between mind and brain, the space of meaning and the chemistry and machinery of neurological functioning. As I understand it, the question Schreber himself raises is this: How is it that a disturbance in *the space of representation*—the space in which we engage with one another by way of offices, titles, symbolic roles and mandates, generic predicates of all kinds—can generate (or more cautiously, be correlated to) *a nervous disorder*? In other words, what is the relation between *representations* (in Lacan's terms, the signifiers subjects are compelled to contract or take on as "members" of a symbolic order to represent them to other signifiers) and *nerves*? That fundamental relation was the focus of Freud's famous *Project for a Scientific Psychology*, a work that, however, remained fragmentary. And no doubt part of what makes Lacan's "return to Freud" so compelling is that he in some sense tried to read all of Freud as so many attempts to return to and elaborate the intuitions of that early project. This book represents yet a further effort in the same direction, though I try to approach it from a new perspective. Perhaps the most provocative way of introducing this perspective—one I will elaborate in some detail—would be to claim that Foucault's investigation of the proliferation of new kinds of political power and authority in modernity (what he ultimately characterized as the birth of biopolitics) should itself be understood as a crucial contribution to the original Freudian research paradigm concerning the relation between representations and nerves. In a sense, I am putting Freud and Foucault on the same team (over the course of this study I recruit other perhaps equally surprising team members). Both are concerned with the ways in which a certain "intensification" of the body can be correlated with disorders or shifts in the resources of representation available to subjects and in the capacities of subjects to use those resources, to discharge the normative pressures they introduce into the life of subjects.[6]

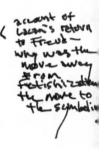

account of Lacan's return to Freud — why was the move away from fetishization the move to the symbolic

---

6. The psychoanalytic dimension of "normative pressure," a concept largely used in the social sciences to identify various forms of the pressure to conform, has been nicely developed by Candace Vogler and Jonathan Lear in the context of seminar presentations at the University of Chicago in recent years. In my study of Schreber I characterized this pressure as the *drive dimension of signification*, as the *signifying stress* that supplements every act of symbolic investiture, of being invested with

What Schreber discovered was that an inability to inhabit and to feel *libidinally implicated* in the space of representations had the effect of transforming his entire being into a bundle of excitable flesh that had then to be entrusted to the care of psychiatry, one of the key institutions of the biopolitical regime investigated by Foucault and one that was already committed to a largely neurological understanding of mental disease.[7] We are very fortunate that Schreber was smart enough and aware enough to grasp that his condition and fate were *denkwürdig*, "worthy of thought" (his memoir was entitled *Denkwürdigkeiten eines Nervenkranken*). That is, he grasped that his "metamorphosis" into an agitated *Luder* had something to do with larger social transformations pertaining, above all, to the realms of *politics and religion*, and that it was these transformations that attenuated his capacity to cathect to—to inhabit, occupy, erotically invest in—the signifiers representing him in the world, the ways he had been "vested" in "the field of the Other." That is, he grasped that his metamorphosis was connected to the history of political theology and its link to what Freud theorized as the libidinal economy of human mindedness. What is at issue here is, as I have suggested, not simply the question of the sources of legitimate political rule but, more profoundly, our capacity to feel represented in the social field, to experience those representations as *viable facilitations of our vitality*. The Schreber case demonstrates that the more attenuated this capacity becomes, the more such vitality comes to be registered as an invasive excitation of nerves. For Schreber, the normative pressures injected into human life by way of one's inscription into a symbolic order are imagined to return as real bodily impingements and violations. Schreber, for his part, attempted to grasp this state as a sort of neurotheological revelation, to discover traces of transcendence in the radical immanence of agitated nerve tissue. It is just such a collapse or contraction of the space of representation into that of the overstimulated flesh that generates the ultimate lure or *Luder* for the biopolitical operations of modernity. As it turns out, the more one becomes the object of such operations, the more attenuated, the more (un)deadening the space of representation becomes.

---

some sort of social status that places one in relation to the normative authority regulating the enjoyment of the incumbency of that "office." Vogler and Lear above all emphasize the potential for anxiety in normative pressure, *the threat of being found wanting* with respect to some representative of normative authority. My argument here is that at the core of *this* anxiety is the far more terrifying one of *not being found at all*, that is, of being reduced to a state in which one does not even get to experience the first form of anxiety.

7. Schreber's psychiatrist, Paul Flechsig, had famously declared that the age of the brain had finally displaced that of the *soul* (see my discussion of Flechsig in *My Own Private Germany*).

III

The space of representation has always been one in which the dimension of the flesh has been implicated. Indeed, I will argue that the crucial thought at the heart of the doctrine of the King's Two Bodies is that within the framework of the political theology of sovereignty, the signifiers that represent the subject for other signifiers are, so to speak, "backed" or "underwritten" by the sublime flesh, the sacral soma, of the monarch. With the demise of the political theology of kingship, this "personal" source of libidinal credit disappears. Postmonarchical societies are then faced with the problem of *securing the flesh* of the new bearer of the principle of sovereignty, the People. Biopolitics—and its near relative disciplinary power—can be grasped as the strategies deployed by modern societies to secure this new underwriting arrangement, this new backing for the signs and values circulating across new kinds of networks and relays. It is against this background that we should read Foucault's characterization of the transition from classical sovereignty to the forms of power and governmentality that emerge at the threshold of modernity: "The body of the king, with *its strange material and physical presence*, with the *force* that he himself deploys or transmits to some few others, is at the opposite extreme of *this new physics of power* . . . : a physics of a relational and multiple power, which has its maximum intensity *not in the person of the king, but in the bodies that can be individualized by these relations*."[8] But here we need to add that insofar as the agents of this new physics imagine themselves to be addressing the care and discipline of living bodies and the biological life and health of populations rather than securing the strange materiality of the "flesh"—the bit of the real that underwrites the circulation of signs and values—they do not and cannot fully grasp the urgency of their tasks. In a word, *they know not what they do.*

In my study of the Schreber case, I cited the work of an author who, although her immediate concerns were far from mine, helped me to find my initial orientation in the material. I would like to cite, once more, several brief passages that have taken on further resonance in light of the considerable work that has been done over the intervening years—above all, by Giorgio Agamben—on the concept of the state of exception and its relation to biopolitics, a connection that also plays a significant role in the following chapters. The passages in question pertain precisely to the

---

8. Michel Foucault, *Discipline and Punish. The Birth of the Prison*, trans. Alan Sheridan (New York: Vintage, 1977), 208; my emphasis.

status of the flesh in the constitution of viable resources of representation. They are addressed to the "gap" in knowledge to which I have just alluded, to just what it is that the agents of biopolitical operations are *really doing*.

In her groundbreaking book *The Body in Pain*, Elaine Scarry explored the ways in which, above all in the practices of torture and war, human pain (what she so poignantly characterized as the "obscenely . . . alive tissue" of the human body) is enlisted as a source of verification and substantiation of the symbolic authority of institutions and the social facts they sponsor.[9] This bottoming out of symbolic function on what I am calling the flesh becomes urgent, Scarry argues, when there is a crisis of belief or legitimation in a society: "At particular moments when there is within society a crisis of belief—that is, when some central idea or ideology or cultural construct has ceased to elicit a population's belief either because it is manifestly fictitious or because it has for some reason been divested of ordinary forms of substantiation—the sheer material factualness of the human body will be borrowed to lend that cultural construct the aura of 'realness' and 'certainty'" (14). Speaking more specifically of the structure of war, Scarry argues that "injuring is relied on as a form of legitimation because, though it lacks interior connections to the issues, wounding is able to open up a source of reality that can give the issue force and holding power. That is, the outcome of war has its substantiation not in an absolute inability of the defeated to contest the outcome but in a process of perception that allows extreme attributes of the body to be translated into another language, to be broken away from the body and relocated elsewhere at the very moment that the body itself is disowned" (124). This conception of the injured body as an unspeakable piece of the real that provides the ultimate support or backing of a symbolic order, that (unconsciously) helps to make the social facts constituted within the space of representation feel real rather than fictional, allows Scarry, in effect, to recast the psychoanalytic concept of *transference* in more social and political terms. It comes to signify, for Scarry, the "intricacies of the process of transfer that make it possible for the *incontestable reality of the physical body to now become an attribute of an issue that at that moment has no independent reality of its own*" (124–25). What becomes painfully manifest in both war and torture "is the process by which a made world of culture acquires the characteristics of 'reality,' the process of percep-

9. Elaine Scarry, *The Body in Pain: The Making and Unmaking of the World* (New York: Oxford University Press, 1985), 31. Subsequent references are made in the text.

tion that allows invented ideas, beliefs, and made objects to be accepted and entered into as though they had the same ontological status as the naturally given world" (125).

IV

The following chapters represent a further attempt to fill in the "gap" in knowledge that haunts the practices—and theorizations—of biopolitics, to get clear about what is "really" going on there. I have divided the project into two parts, the first addressing theoretical and historical concerns pertaining to the notion and vicissitudes of the flesh at the point of its reorganization in the transition from royal to popular sovereignty. Chapter 1 attempts to locate the topic of the flesh in current theories of biopolitics and to suggest ways in which it can be brought more productively into view. My primary "interlocutor" in this discussion is Roberto Esposito, who, next to Agamben, has provided what I consider to be the most comprehensive and original elaboration of biopolitics after Foucault. In chapter 2 I engage directly with the work of Ernst Kantorowicz, whose groundbreaking book *The King's Two Bodies* provides us with an opportunity to articulate more precisely the ways in which the topic of biopolitics can be traced to issues that already animate the complex history of the political theology of sovereignty in Europe. From there one comes, I think, to a far better grasp and appreciation of the work done by both Hannah Arendt and Giorgio Agamben on how issues of sovereign power and authority persist even within more directly biopolitical modes of modern governmentality. In chapter 3 I turn to the work of Freud, Lacan, and other psychoanalytic thinkers to develop a more general theory of what I am calling the flesh precisely by acknowledging the historical pressures under which this new and strange science emerged. The strange self-reflexivity at work here is that only with psychoanalytic theory can one truly grasp the nature of the historical context in which that theoretical paradigm emerged.

In part 2 I turn to the ways in which the biopolitical pressures that constitute the flesh make themselves felt in the field of aesthetic experience. In chapter 4 I focus on the vicissitudes of the flesh in visual modernism. Here I engage above all with the work of a series of art historians, critics, and philosophers who, in their efforts to grasp the specificity of modernist aesthetic practices, have placed issues of embodiment and corporeality at the center of their analyses. Chapter 5 is something of a hybrid. It begins with a discussion of Carl Schmitt's provocative essay on Shakespeare's *Hamlet*. In this essay Schmitt gives us a feel as to how his profoundly influential views on sovereignty (views discussed at some length in my first three chapters) extend into and borrow from the realm of aesthetic experience. Schmitt's essay also turns out to be an extremely helpful introduction to the work of Hugo von Hofmannsthal, the great Austrian writer who first (quite sympathetically) characterized the cultural movement now inextricably linked to Carl Schmitt's name as a "conservative revolution." Chapter 6 offers a comprehensive reading of Rainer Maria Rilke's great modernist novel *The Notebooks of Malte Laurids Brigge*. Here I argue that this groundbreaking work achieves its force and legibility only against the background of the right understanding of the vicissitudes of the flesh, of the epochal shift from the King's Two Bodies to the People's Two Bodies. In the epilogue I try to point the way toward further avenues of research on the legacies of the "royal remains" in modernity.

There is, of course, a considerable degree of contingency at work in the choice of examples for the elaboration of an argument such as the one I am putting forth in this study. I would say, however, that for me the examples taken above all from art and literature represent not simply ideal cases for the presentation of my claims (there are no doubt many other works of art that could function just as well); they have served not so much as testing grounds for a freestanding theory but rather as the objects that caused me to undertake this labor of theory-building in the first place. They are works that got "under my skin" in such a way that they allowed me to grasp just what that expression really means, what *it* is, exactly, that lies beneath the skin and how it is that words and images can lodge themselves there. This is most emphatically the case with the work I discuss at greatest length, Rainer Maria Rilke's *Notebooks of Malte Laurids Brigge*, a novel I read for the first time more than thirty years ago and one to which I found myself returning again and again. At some level this entire project represents an effort to understand better just why Rilke's work has haunted me, why it has stuck with and to me for so long. Over the course of this project I have, I think, finally learned how to enjoy the enjoyment embedded in this particular "symptom."

My own history with *Malte* has not been without influence on the rest of the project. What I have come to realize is that my own use of historical figures, documents, and events in the construction of my argument (an argument that serves, in the end, to frame a reading of Rilke's novel) was to some degree reenacting Rilke's own idiosyncratic mode of engagement with history. Rilke tried to explain his "historical methodology" in a letter to the Polish translator of his novel, Witold Hulewicz. In his response to Hulewicz's series of queries concerning various historical references and allusions in the novel, Rilke underlined the value such references had *for Malte* in the context of the protagonist's existential crisis and sense of psychic endangerment (Rilke speaks of the *Notzeit*, the time of distress, even emergency, of his protagonist). In the novel, Rilke writes, "There can be no question of specifying and detaching [*zu präzisieren und zu verselbstständigen*] the manifold evocations. The reader should not be in communication with their historical or imaginary reality, but through them with Malte's experience: who is himself involved with them only as, on the street, one might let a passer-by, might let a neighbor, say, impress one. The connection," Rilke continues, "lies in the circumstance that the particular characters conjured up *register the same vibration-rate of vital intensity* [*Schwingungszahl der Lebensintensität*] *that vibrates in Malte's own nature.*"[10] What I have attempted to do in this study is also, in some sense, to bring together texts and figures that exhibit similar "frequencies" of vital intensity, with the aim, however, of clarifying just *what it is* that is vibrating, just *what sort of vital intensity* is at issue. This no doubt leads, in some instances, to a certain loss of specificity with regard to the more local historical settings of the texts and figures in question, and I apologize to the reader in advance for this sacrifice.

Another way I would characterize Rilke's method in *Malte* as well as my own mode of engagement with historical texts, figures, and events in this study would be in terms proposed by Walter Benjamin in his reflections on the "mimetic faculty" and the "doctrine of similarities."[11] For Benjamin, too, the task of reading, of the critical engagement with history and with cultural texts of any kind, involves the seizing of a moment in which a constellation of what he refers to as "nonsensuous similarities" comes into focus, or, to use Rilke's acoustic figure, a moment in which the frequencies of vital intensity dispersed across historical epochs become synchronized. For Benjamin, it is, in the end, language itself that provides what he refers to as "the most perfect archive of nonsensuous similarity."[12] Benjamin goes on to characterize language as "the highest application of the mimetic faculty—a medium into which the earlier perceptual capacity for recognizing the similar had, without residue, entered

10. Letter of November 10, 1925, in *Letters of Rainer Maria Rilke, 1910–1925*, trans. Jane Bannard Greene and M. D. Herter Norton (New York: Norton, 1972), 371; my emphasis.

11. Walter Benjamin, "Doctrine of the Similar" and "On the Mimetic Faculty," both in Walter Benjamin, *Selected Writings*, vol. 2, *1927–1934*, ed. Michael W. Jennings, Howard Eiland, and Gary Smith (Cambridge, MA: Harvard University Press, 1999).

12. Benjamin, "Doctrine of the Similar," 697.

to such an extent that language now represents the medium in which objects encounter and come into relation with one another. No longer directly, as they once did in the mind of the augur or priest, but in their essences, *in their most transient and delicate substances.*"[13] In the following I argue—or better, try *to demonstrate*—that what Benjamin has in mind here is that language provides the archive and resonance chamber for the vibrations and twitches of that most transient and delicate substance that I have been calling the flesh.[14] The task of bringing off such a demonstration imposes its own forms of using and, perhaps, abusing history.

V

In concluding this preface, I will quickly summarize the core argument of the book and what I take to be its implications for understanding crucial aspects of modernity and modernism. *The Royal Remains* develops a kind of philosophical anthropology that locates what animates, deadens, and "undeadens" human life in the vicissitudes of the normative pressures that human beings take on by virtue of being subjects of symbolic systems. Because for human beings the enjoyment of life and goods is always intertwined with processes and procedures of symbolic entitlement or investiture, the very value of human life—what makes life worth living, what causes it to matter—is subject to enormous fluctuation. Sigmund Freud first elaborated the laws of such fluctuation by means of the concepts of libido and libidinal economy, suggesting, ultimately, that being a human subject just *is* to be subject to such fluctuations. *The Royal Remains* argues that Freud's crucial insight needs to be placed within a larger history of the ways in which early modern and modern societies have attempted to organize, manage, and administer such fluctuations by means of the logic of sovereignty, according to which, to use Lacan's (distinctly Hobbesian) formulation once more, a master "signifier" comes to represent the subject for all other signifiers, all other bearers of symbolic value.

13. Ibid., 697–98; my emphasis. To put it in terms introduced into psychoanalytic theory and practice by Melanie Klein, we might say that all human projects are not only haunted by but also to some extent sustained by the persistence of archaic forms of projective identification that are now transmitted in and through language.

14. I think this is also what Benjamin had in mind when, in his essay on surrealism several years earlier, he spoke of the "innervations" that gather in the "body and image space" [*Leib und Bildraum*] of collectives, charging them with potentially revolutionary energy. Walter Benjamin, "Surrealism: The Last Snapshot of the European Intelligentsia," in *Selected Writings*, 2:217.

Because this logic of representation can never absolve itself of its own ultimate groundlessness—its lack of an anchoring point in the real—the normative pressures it generates for its members, the pressures to be recognized as *fit* and *fitting* for the symbolic system in question, are always in excess of what could ever be satisfied. Among the crucial tasks of the *figure* of the sovereign is to take up not the "slack" but rather this excess of pressure produced by the very logic of sovereignty. It is this excess that, I argue, constitutes the "flesh" of the king's sublime body, that curious physiological entity that was the topic of Kantorowicz's famous study of the political theology of medieval and early modern Europe, *The King's Two Bodies*.[15]

In the following chapters I attempt to track the remainders of this figure in the symbolic space opened by the shift from royal to popular sovereignty. The project aims, in effect, to track the remainders of a figure who already served as the imaginary site of a remainder or surplus produced by the logic of sovereign representation. With this shift, however, a figure whose sacral soma was seen to embody a "vertical" link to a locus of transcendence—to divine authorization—comes to be dispersed "horizontally" among the "people," who now come to be both blessed and plagued by a *surplus of immanence*. The new bearers of the principle of sovereignty are in some sense stuck with an excess of flesh that their own bodies cannot fully close in upon and that must be "managed" in new ways.

I try to elaborate this intuition by exploring three intersecting developments and domains associated with modernity. The first area of investigation concerns the emergence of biopolitics as the new site for the administration of what was previously concentrated and localized in the strange material presence of the king, one that precisely called forth the peculiar doctrine of the King's Two Bodies. The second domain is made up of modernist aesthetic practices in the visual and literary arts that gather at the unstable boundaries between figuration and abstraction. The third large area of investigation concerns Freud's own efforts to

15. In a personal communication, Kenneth Reinhard has suggested—and I think he is right—that the book's argument could be fruitfully mapped onto the mutations of the concept of *will* in political and social thought. The story would take us from classical notions of sovereign will, to Rousseau's concept of the general will, to Schopenhauer's metaphysical understanding of will (in contrast to representation), to Nietzsche's notion of will to power, and, finally, to the ways in which Foucault's work assumes and transforms Nietzsche's legacy in his own analyses of power. In my view, one would have to execute this remapping in light of the complexity introduced into the concept of the will by the psychoanalytic theory of desire, the drives, and sexual difference (recall Freud's famous perplexity as to the question *Was will das Weib?*). The work done in this volume could thus be seen as the necessary groundwork for any attempt to tell the history of political thought in the West in light of shifts in the semantic field of the concept "will."

invent a new science, one that attempts, precisely, to *separate out* the element of the flesh as the virtual yet unnervingly visceral substance of the fantasies that both constrain and amplify the lives of modern subjects. Psychoanalysis is thereby shown to offer the general concepts that allow us to grasp its own historicity, its place, that is, among the endgames of the political theology of sovereignty.[16]

16. Unless otherwise noted, translations cited in this volume are my own.

Acknowledgments

A good deal of the material in this book was first presented in the form of lectures and seminars and at workshops. I am deeply grateful to those friends, colleagues, and students who in these various contexts and settings helped me to get a better grip on this project. I think especially of Dieter Mersch, Kenneth Reinhard, Michael Minden, Andrew Webber, Rebecca Comay, Bronwen Wilson, Andrew Benjamin, Jessica Whyte, Nicholas Heron, Carter Smith, and Christian Sorace, among others I am no doubt forgetting. I owe a special debt of gratitude to Klaus Mladek and George Edmondson for allowing me to participate in a wonderful workshop they conducted at the Leslie Center for the Humanities at Dartmouth College in the spring quarter of 2009 on the topic "States of Exception: Sovereignty, Security, Secrecy." Klaus and George were crucial interlocutors for me as I was getting into the thick of this book. I also want to give special thanks to another participant in the workshop, Adam Sitze, who introduced me not only to new texts and writers but also to new problems, questions, and ways of thinking. I am deeply grateful to Fiona Jenkins and Debjani Ganguly for inviting me to their conference on the "Limits of the Human" at the Australian National University. I can't quite imagine how this book would have turned out had I not had the chance to learn from the participants at that event. Fiona's work, in particular, had a formative influence on my understanding of the concept and of the real consequences of states of exception in the past and the present. In Australia I also had the great good fortune to get to know William McClure, a philosopher and artist who has become a significant partner in thinking about the interconnections of aesthetics, ethics, and politics. As will become clear to the reader, my intellectual debts to Mladen Dolar, Slavoj Žižek, Jonathan Lear, and Alenka Zupančič just continue to grow. It was extremely helpful to me to be working on this project while Robert Buch, a friend and colleague at the University of Chicago, was working on his own study of what he calls the *pathos of the real*; in these past years, our intellectual trajectories have overlapped and intersected in significant and fruitful ways. I feel extremely lucky that my manuscript landed with such generous and attentive readers. Julia Lupton, whose work I have admired for years, along with a second reader who has remained anonymous, gave me a clear and forceful sense of how to refine and amplify the book's argument at structural and local levels. I continue to thank my lucky stars that Alan Thomas at the University of Chicago Press has been willing to work with me on project after project. I think we make good books together. Lois Crum's precise copyediting and Michael Koplow's keen eye for detail have surely made this a better book, and for that I am most grateful. My gratitude to Pamela Pascoe is without measure; among many other things, I continue to learn from her how works of art *think* and how to follow the tracks of that thinking. Finally, I wish I could express the depth of my gratitude to the marvelous Marcia Adler, whose passing I still cannot quite take in. I know it will be years before I fully grasp what I have learned from her about what it means to be alive to the world.

PART ONE

ONE

Sovereignty and the Vital Sphere

I

One of the most influential recent reflections on the transition from royal to popular sovereignty and the fundamental sorts of political, social, and existential questions it raises is Claude Lefort's essay "The Permanence of the Theologico-Political?" In his essay, which, like every intervention into this field of inquiry, cites Kantorowicz's work as a primary point of reference, Lefort makes very clear that his main concern is precisely in differentiating what he calls "the symbolic dimension of the political" from what political science typically characterizes as its object of study.[1] His focus is not so much the narrowly conceived "regional ontology" of political science as it is the dimension or element in which politics touches on the intelligibility of the social world more generally, on one's sense of the coherence, continuity, and vibrancy of the form of life into which one is inscribed and from which one derives one's most basic sense of orientation in the world. What is at issue here is the authoritative grip of how "things are done" as well as one's own sense of *existential legitimacy*: that one has a place in the world that entitles one to enjoy a modicum of recognition of one's words and actions. This *entitlement to enjoyment/*

---

1. Claude Lefort, *Democracy and Political Theory*, trans. David Macey (Minneapolis: University of Minnesota Press, 1988), 215. Subsequent references are made in the text.

enjoyment of entitlement points, as Lefort puts it, to "a hidden part of social life, namely the processes which make people consent to a given regime—or, to put it more forcefully, which determines *their manner of being in society*—and which guarantee that this regime or mode of society has a permanence in time, regardless of the various events that may affect it" (214–15). In his critique of what he sees as liberal thought's attempts to reduce power to an instrumental function and the people to "a fiction which simply masks the efficacy of a contract thanks to which a minority submits to a government formed by a majority," Lefort puts it even more starkly by suggesting that such reductions amount to erasing "both the question of sovereignty and that of the meaning of the institution, which are always bound up with *the ultimate question of the legitimacy of that which exists*" (232; my emphasis).

Very early in the essay, Lefort, the editor of Maurice Merleau-Ponty's posthumous works, appropriates his former teacher's difficult and evocative notion of the "flesh of the world" to characterize this "primal dimensionality of the social" that in turn implies "an idea of its primal *form*, of its political *form*" (218). "Flesh," in this context, refers not to the corporeal matter beneath the skin that normally remains hidden from view, but rather to the semiotic—and somatic—vibrancy generated by the inscription of bodies into a normative social space in the first place, by this interlacing of entitlement and enjoyment that opens up the possibilities of distinctively human forms of wretchedness and joy, of misery and *jouissance*. As I have stated, my goal is to explore some of the modes of appearance of the "flesh of the world" at the point where the *body of the king* is no longer able to give some measure to, no longer able to figure, form, and distribute, this sublime somatic materiality that, as Lefort suggests, serves as the very "stuff" that binds subjects to that space of representation that is the "body politic."

The editors of a recent volume of essays on the "Republican Body" have put the problem quite succinctly: "With democracy the concept of the nation replaced the monarch and sovereignty was dispersed from the king's body to all bodies. *Suddenly every body bore political weight.* . . . With the old sartorial and behavioral codes gone, bodies were less legible, and a person's place in the nation was unclear."[2] My own interest is less about the transformation of social codes than about the agitations of the "flesh" brought about by this shift, the nature of the "matter" that accounts for

---

2. Sara Melzer and Kathryn Norberg, eds., *From the Royal to the Republican Body: Incorporating the Political in Seventeenth- and Eighteenth-Century France* (Berkeley: University of California Press, 1998), 10–11; my emphasis.

the new "political weight" of every citizen. To put it in terms suggested by Lefort, the reference to power as an "empty place," as an absent center that is ostensibly the defining feature of democratic societies, does not get rid of the problem of the carnal or corporeal dimension of representation. It does, however, make it much harder to delimit and locate. My hunch is that a great deal of modernist art and literature can help us in these efforts. And as we shall also see, it was not for nothing that Merleau-Ponty characterized Freud as, above all, a *philosopher of the flesh.*

In a first approach, I would propose that the notion of the "flesh" refers to the substantial pressures, the semiotic and somatic stresses, of what I have elsewhere characterized as "creaturely life."[3] By "creaturely" I do not simply mean nature or living things or sentient beings, or even what the religiously minded would think of as the whole of God's creation, but rather a dimension specific to human existence, albeit one that seems to push thinking in the direction of theology.[4] It signifies a mode of *exposure* that distinguishes human beings from other kinds of life: not exposure simply to the elements or to the fragility and precariousness of our mortal, finite lives, but rather to an ultimate lack of foundation for the historical forms of life that distinguish human community. This lack, this crucial *missing piece of the world*, to which we are ultimately and intimately exposed as social beings of language is one that we thus first *acquire* by way of our initiation into these forms of life, not one already there in the bare fact of our biological being (and, thus, one not readily accessible to the biological sciences). We could say that the precariousness, the fragility—the "nudity"—of biological life becomes potentiated, amplified, by way of exposure to the radical contingency of the forms

3. See Eric Santner, *On Creaturely Life: Rilke, Benjamin, Sebald* (Chicago: University of Chicago Press, 2006).

4. What the great German-Jewish philosopher Franz Rosenzweig called "the new thinking" is precisely a mode of philosophical thought that tries to remain open to this pressure. See my *On the Psychotheology of Everyday Life: Reflections on Freud and Rosenzweig* (Chicago: University of Chicago Press, 2001). As Lefort puts it in his reflections on political theology, "Every religion *states* in its own way that human society can only open on to itself by being held in an opening it did not create. Philosophy says the same thing, but religion said it first, albeit in terms which philosophy cannot accept. . . . What philosophy discovers in religion is a mode of portraying or dramatizing the relations that human beings establish with something that goes beyond empirical time and the space within which they establish relations with one another" (222–23). That is, human beings fill in, populate this "opening" with objects, figures, and stories based on "the most general conditions of their lives," "invent a time that exists before time, organize a space that exists behind their space" (223). What philosophy above all needs to remain mindful of, Lefort suggests, is that the experience of the difference in question—the minimal difference that allows human beings to relate to their humanity—"bears the marks of an *ordeal*" (223), one staged in staggering fashion in the narratives and image-world of Christianity. What Lefort calls, borrowing from Merleau-Ponty, the *flesh* of the sociopolitical link is the element produced and sustained in this ordeal.

of life that constitute the space of meaning within which human life unfolds, and that it is only through such "potentiation" that we take on the flesh of creaturely life. Creatureliness is thus a dimension not so much of biological as of *ontological vulnerability*, a vulnerability that permeates human being as that being whose essence it is to exist in forms of life that are, in turn, contingent, fragile, susceptible to breakdown.[5] But here we need to go a step further. For as we shall see, the very ways in which human communities attempt to shelter—to immunize—their lives from such vulnerability effectively serve to intensify it. The paradox at work here is, in short, that the defense mechanisms cultures use to protect against a primordial exposure—to "cover" our nudity—serve in the end to redouble this exposure and thereby to "fatten" the flesh of creaturely life. It thus becomes next to impossible to isolate definitively an "original" condition from one co-constituted by the very efforts aimed at managing or defending against it.

At first glance it would seem that we are dealing here with a rather straightforward dialectic familiar to any parent who has struggled with balancing the interests of protecting his or her child from harm with those of fostering the child's growth and vitality. The danger is that too much protection, that is, a too vigorous attempt to immunize the child against risk, can end up arresting the child's development: the protective shelter becomes a sterile enclosure, the immune response becomes a kind of autoimmunity, attacking the vitality at issue. By failing to see that human flourishing includes *the capacity to be unwell*, the parent bent on protecting the child from anything that might threaten her well-being ends up isolating her from what might stimulate her own vital resources of self-preservation and development, her robustness. One can, of course, make the same observation with respect to a democratic state that is tempted

---

5. I take the term "ontological vulnerability" from Jonathan Lear's *Radical Hope: Ethics in the Face of Cultural Devastation* (Cambridge, MA: Harvard University Press, 2006). There Lear presents a philosophical anthropology meant to make sense of the enigmatic utterance of the last great chief of the Crow nation, Plenty Coups, who said that after the disappearance of the buffalo, "nothing happened." Lear writes that the "question is what it would be for Plenty Coups to be a witness to a peculiar form of human vulnerability. If there is a genuine possibility of happenings' breaking down, it is one with which we all live. We are familiar with the thought that as human creatures we are by nature vulnerable: to bodily injury, disease, ageing, death—and all sorts of insults from the environment. But the vulnerability we are concerned with here is of a different order. We seem to acquire it as a result of the fact that we essentially inhabit a way of life. Humans are by nature cultural animals: we necessarily inhabit a way of life that is expressed in a culture. But our way of life—whatever it is—is vulnerable in various ways. And we, as participants in that way of life, thereby inherit a vulnerability. Should that way of life break down, that is *our* problem" (6). Lear goes on to suggest that Plenty Coups served as a special kind of witness to the breakdown of the Crow way of life, as its "designated mourner." In *On Creaturely Life*, I argue that W. G. Sebald's work has functioned in much the same way with regard to various aspects of modern European life.

to limit the freedoms of its citizens in the name of protecting lives during periods of heightened risk. At a certain point the measures designed to immunize the population against risk begin to destroy the vibrancy of the community and the values on which its civic life is based.[6] In numerous spheres of activity, strategies of self-preservation can, in short, become a form of mortification; in each case, out of a fear of breakdown or dying, of exposing oneself to what is perceived to be mortal risk, one preemptively deadens oneself.

I will argue, however, that this conception of an "immunological dialectic" whereby shelter becomes its own kind of life-threatening exposure, immunity becomes autoimmunity, self-preservation becomes a mode of mortification, life drive becomes a kind of death drive, fails to capture the full complexity of the phenomena in question. Something falls through the cracks of the dialectic and keeps returning to its place to initiate the whole process again, indeed to endow it with the aspect of a *repetition compulsion*; this something is the dimension I am trying to capture with the notion of the flesh that both does and does not belong to the life at issue in the efforts at immunization it seems to call forth over and over again.

II

In recent work, the Italian philosopher Roberto Esposito has focused on the concept of immunization as the key to grasping the biopolitical turn of modernity as first theorized by Michel Foucault. Esposito even suggests that it has greater explanatory value for understanding modernity than more familiar notions such as rationalization, secularization, or (the crisis of) legitimation.[7] In what follows I try to develop a feel for the immunological dialectic—and, just as importantly, *what both escapes and drives it*—by way of an extended "conversation" with Esposito's work, which represents, next to Agamben's writings, the most comprehensive and compelling engagement with the subject of biopolitics I know.

Esposito develops his conception of the immunization paradigm apropos of a perceived equivocation in Foucault's writings and lectures concerning the status of the concept of sovereignty in the passage from the

---

6. This dialectic is, of course, also at the heart of much libertarian opposition to the regulation of economic activity in the so-called free market.

7. Roberto Esposito, *Bios: Biopolitics and Philosophy*, trans. Timothy Campbell (Minneapolis: University of Minnesota Press, 2008). Subsequent references are made in the text.

ancien régime to modernity, the passage that I have proposed to analyze by way of the "metamorphosis" of the King's Two Bodies into the People's Two Bodies. In some of his writings, it would appear as if Foucault was committed to the view that the displacement of royal by constitutional forms of governmental power and authority in European nation-states over the course of the seventeenth, eighteenth, and nineteenth centuries signaled the emergence of a radically new form of power and set of power relations between states and subjects that could no longer be understood with the conceptual tools of the classical theories of sovereignty and indeed that such power relations more or less completely superseded the dynamics of sovereignty in the actual regulation of the lives of modern citizens; if the concept and figure of sovereign power lived on at all, they survived merely as an ideological phantasm that had outlived its true historical space and moment. The sovereign had long been dead, but it took Foucault to remind him of that on behalf of the rest of us.

On this view, what Foucault referred to as "disciplinary power" and "biopower" thus represents forms of governmentality that *follow upon* the demise of sovereign power, a demise that could more or less be correlated with the effective end of monarchy in Europe. Sovereign power, Foucault argues, was power based on the principle of *deduction*: "Power in this instance was essentially a right of seizure: of things, time, bodies, and ultimately of life itself; it culminated in the privilege to seize hold of life in order to suppress it."[8] But, as he continues, "since the classical age the West has undergone a very profound transformation of these mechanisms of power. 'Deduction' has tended to be no longer the major form of power but merely one element among others, working to incite, reinforce, control, monitor, optimize, and organize the forces under it: a power bent on generating forces, making them grow, and ordering them, rather than one dedicated to impeding them, making them submit, or destroying them" (136). Very simply, "the old power of death that symbolized sovereign power was now carefully supplanted by the administration of bodies and the calculated management of life" (139–40).

Foucault goes on to argue that a crucial consequence of this shift in modes of governmental power and authority "was the growing importance assumed by the action of the norm, at the expense of the juridical system of the law. . . . The law always refers to the sword. But a power whose task is to take charge of life needs continuous regulatory mechanisms. It is no longer a matter of bringing death into play in the field of

8. Michel Foucault, *The History of Sexuality*, vol. 1, *An Introduction*, trans. Robert Hurley (New York: Vintage, 1990), 136. Subsequent references are made in the text.

sovereignty, but of distributing the living in the domain of value and utility" (144). "I do not," he adds, "mean to say that the law fades into the background or that the institutions of justice tend to disappear, but rather that the law operates more and more as a norm, and that the juridical institution is increasingly incorporated into a continuum of apparatuses (medical, administrative, and so on) whose functions are for the most part regulatory. A normalizing society is the historical outcome of a technology of power centered on life" (144). He famously summarizes this shift in the semantics and dynamics of governmental power and authority:

For the first time in history, no doubt, biological existence was reflected in political existence; the fact of living was no longer an inaccessible substrate that only emerged from time to time. . . . part of it passed into knowledge's field of control and power's sphere of intervention. Power would no longer be dealing simply with legal subjects over whom the ultimate dominion was death, but with living beings, and the mastery it would be able to exercise over them would have to be applied at the level of life itself; it was the taking charge of life, more than the threat of death, that gave power its access even to the body. If one can apply the term *bio-history* to the pressures through which the movements of life and the processes of history interfere with one another, one would have to speak of *bio-power* to designate what brought life and its mechanisms into the realm of explicit calculations and made knowledge-power an agent of transformation of human life. (142–43)

One can take the real measure of such transformations in the changing status of the criminal and his act at this threshold of modernity. As Esposito puts it, "In the moment in which the criminal act is no longer to be charged to the will of the subject, but rather to a psychopathological configuration, we enter into a zone of indistinction between law and medicine in whose depths we can make out a new rationality centered on the question of life—of its preservation, its development, and its management." This new chapter in the "governmentalization of life" does not imply, Esposito continues, "a withdrawal or contraction of the field that is subjected to the law. Rather, it is the latter that is progressively transferred from the *transcendental level* of codes and sanctions that essentially have to do with subjects of will to the *immanent level* of rules and norms that are addressed instead to bodies" (28; my emphasis).

In some of his writings, Foucault has correlated this process of *immanentization* to a kind of *agon* that at a certain point begins to agitate the law from within, to something like a chronic state of emergency within the domain of law itself. In one of many discussions of "disciplinary power," Foucault traces a sort of ascending scale of perturbations within the realm of law:

In appearance, the disciplines constitute nothing more than *an infra-law*. They seem to extend the general forms defined by law to the infinitesimal level of individual lives; or they appear as methods of training that enable individuals to become integrated into these general demands. They seem to constitute the same type of law on a different scale, thereby making it more meticulous and more indulgent. The disciplines should be regarded as *a sort of counter-law*. They have the precise role of introducing insuperable asymmetries and excluding reciprocities. . . . Moreover, whereas the juridical systems define juridical subjects according to universal norms, the disciplines characterize, classify, specialize; they distribute along a scale, around a norm, hierarchize individuals in relation to one another and, if necessary, disqualify and invalidate. In any case, in the space and during the time in which they exercise their control and bring into play the asymmetries of their power, they effect *a suspension of the law* that is never total, but is never annulled either.[9]

What is particularly striking is that Foucault sets this self-splitting, self-supplementation, and even (partial) self-suspension of the law over against *the body of the king*, that remarkable, quasi-human thing that, as Foucault had learned from Kantorowicz, was itself the product of a process of gemination, doubling, or self-supplementation. Here I would like to return to a passage already cited in the preface: "The body of the king, with *its strange material and physical presence*, with the *force* that he himself deploys or transmits to some few others, is at the opposite extreme of *this new physics of power* . . . : a physics of a relational and multiple power, which has its maximum intensity *not in the person of the king, but in the bodies that can be individualized by these relations*."[10] What I believe Foucault has drawn attention to here without being fully able to name it is, precisely, the mutation of the King's Two Bodies into the People's Two Bodies: the migration of the *royal flesh*—that "strange material and physical presence" endowed with a peculiar force—that supplants the merely mortal body of the king into the bodies and lives of the citizens of modern nation-states. This mutation calls to the scene the "experts" charged with managing the sublime somatic substance of the new bearer of the principle of sovereignty. And if, as Foucault suggests, such management can be characterized as a kind of "physics," it is one that is deployed with

9. Michel Foucault, *Discipline and Punish: The Birth of the Prison*, trans. Alan Sheridan (New York: Vintage, 1977), 222–23; my emphasis.
10. Ibid., 208; my emphasis.

respect to a materiality the real strangeness of which we have yet to fully appreciate. What remains clear, however, is that the transmission of the force associated with it is no longer limited to "some few others."

It might help at this point to note, briefly, Jacques Lacan's take on the issue at hand, that is, the difficulty of conceptualizing and historicizing the relation between doctrines and practices of sovereignty based on the political theology of the monarch or "master," on the one hand, and new kinds of power and authority wielded at least to a very large extent by medical and social-scientific "experts" authorized according to secular protocols of knowledge production, on the other. Lacan's perspective on this question can be discerned in his theory of discourses as formal matrices of sociality. Lacan posited the emergence, in the long nineteenth century, of a new kind of social bond and discourse—the "discourse of the university"—which, he suggested, supplanted the dominance of the "discourse of the master." Lacan's understanding of the new discourse corresponds closely to what Foucault was aiming at with the notions of the *disciplines* as the *"anatomo-politics of the human body"* and *regulatory controls* as the *"biopolitics of the population."*[11] Indeed, Lacan's formula or "matheme" of the university discourse suggests that the new paradigm whereby knowledge aims at grasping and controlling directly some *real* of the human body (and perhaps of nature more generally)—in his notation $S2 \rightarrow a$—represents the flip side of what I have referred to as a generalized investiture crisis in society at large, the difficulty of the subject (\$) in locating himself with respect to a master signifier (S1). By that I mean a crisis whereby the symbolic authority regulating status and social roles—one's *dignitas*—has become radically attenuated, where the distribution of symbolic authority is no longer grounded in the person and charisma of a master. The new "master" is one who commands a "new physics of power," to use Foucault's phrase.[12] If there is a distribution of *dignitas* here, it is, so to speak, a *biocratic* one.[13]

I do not want to claim that Lacan's formalization of the issues we have noted with respect to Foucault's work resolves the questions at hand. Indeed, there remains considerable uncertainty as to the conceptual and historical relations among the discourses in Lacan's "theory." What Lacan does make clear, however, is that the "object" of the university

---

11. Foucault, *History of Sexuality*, 1:139.

12. See Jacques Lacan, *The Other Side of Psychoanalysis: The Seminar of Jacques Lacan, Book XVII*, trans. Russell Grigg (New York: Norton, 2007).

13. Contemporary debates on such matters as obesity bring home just how much our understanding of social status now almost fully orbits around the body and its health. The preoccupation with obesity is, I am suggesting, one that pertains not simply to "fat" but also to the "flesh."

discourse and so what is at issue in the disciplines and biopolitics, cannot be captured by an accumulation and deployment of knowledge concerning *bodily life*. With the notion of the *objet a*, Lacan attempts to hold the place of the dimension that accounts for the "*strange material and physical presence*" that Foucault located in the body of the king. This is precisely the dimension I am trying to develop with the notion of the flesh; it is, we might say, that "thing" in the king that cannot be contained in his natural life and body but only—and indeed *only barely*—in a second one. We need, in other words, to introduce a slight but crucial adjustment into Foucault's terms and insist that the real object of the new physics of power is not simply the body or life but rather the flesh that has become separated from the body of the king and has entered, like a strange alien presence, into that of the people (as we shall see, science fiction, horror, and political theory are not as far apart as one might think). But rather than simply insist on this point, I would like to show how it emerges from Esposito's compelling account of the immunological paradigm of sovereign power and its persistence in the biopolitics of modern states.

III

As I have indicated, Esposito spends considerable time and effort tracking the ambiguities and potential inconsistencies that haunt Foucault's formulations of the narrative according to which biopolitics represents a genuine historical break with and displacement of the political theology and juridico-institutional framework of sovereignty. These ambiguities can be grouped under a series of fundamental questions:

How are sovereignty and biopolitics to be related? Chronologically or by a differing superimposition? It is said that one emerges out of the background of the other, but what are we to make of such a background? Is it the definitive withdrawal of a preceding presence, or rather is it the horizon that embraces and holds what newly emerges within it? And is such an emergence really new or is it already inadvertently installed in the categorical framework that it will also modify? On this point . . . Foucault refuses to respond definitively. He continues to oscillate between the two opposing hypotheses without opting conclusively for either one or the other. Or better: he adopts both with that characteristic, optical effect of splitting or doubling that confers on his text the slight dizziness that simultaneously seduces and disorients the reader. (34)

What Esposito has identified here is the status of "biopolitics" as an *enigmatic signifier*, a term that induces transference in the reader by promising a kind of ultimate clarity while remaining at some fundamental level obscure. And the chapter in which Esposito addresses Foucault's writings on this topic is called "The Enigma of Biopolitics." I would submit, however, that this is not simply one enigma among others in the history of philosophy (and the philosophy of history) but is in some sense the paradigmatic enigma, namely the one pertaining to the jointure of nature and culture, the inscription of biological life into historical forms of life, the enigma, that is, of what constitutes the specificity of human *forms of life* as distinct from *life forms* that, to use Heidegger's terms, are ostensibly not charged with the understanding of Being, with *being-there*. The "slight dizziness" Esposito notes becomes a full-fledged vertigo at the point at which one tries to think through, in Foucauldian terms, what would appear to be the ultimate biopolitical project of modernity, the so-called final solution of the Jewish question in Europe. For there the biopolitical task of optimizing life—of *making live*—comes to be expressed almost exclusively in the ostensibly sovereign mode of *deciding on death*.[14] In a word, the peculiar way in which Nazism pushed biopolitical discourses and practices in a radically *thanato-political* direction would seem to call into question the entire narrative frame articulating the historical relations of the two paradigms of governmentality in Foucault's work. As Esposito puts it,

How do we explain that the culmination of a politics of life generated a lethal power that contradicts the productive impulse? This is the paradox, the impassable stumbling block that not only twentieth-century totalitarianism, but also nuclear power asks philosophy with regard to a resolutely affirmative declension of biopolitics. How is it possible that a power of life is exercised against life itself? Why are we not dealing with two parallel processes or simply two simultaneous processes? . . . Once again we are faced with that enigma, that terrible unsaid, that the "bio" placed before politics holds for the term's meaning. Why does biopolitics continually threaten to be reversed into thanatopolitics? Here too the response to such an interrogative seems to reside in the problematic point of intersection between sovereignty and biopolitics. (39)

For Esposito, these questions are ultimately irresolvable within the framework of Foucault's conceptual universe. The two paradigms are intertwined in an "aporetic knot that prevents us from interpreting the association of sovereignty and biopolitics in a monolinear form or in the

---

14. Foucault tries, in part, to resolve this tension by way of recasting the sovereign decision: "One might say that the ancient right to *take* life or *let* live was replaced by a power to *foster* life or *disallow* it to the point of death." *History of Sexuality*, 138.

sense of contemporaneity or succession" (40). With respect to the Shoah, this aporia makes itself felt as a vertiginous series of chiasmic borrowings and reversals between sovereignty and biopolitics: "If we consider the Nazi state, we can say indifferently, as Foucault himself does, that it was the old sovereign power that adopts biological racism for itself, a racism born in opposition to it. Or, on the contrary, that it is the new biopolitical power that made use of the sovereign right of death in order to give life to state racism. If we have recourse to the first interpretive model, biopolitics becomes an inner articulation of sovereignty; if we privilege the second, sovereignty is reduced to a formal schema of biopolitics" (41).

The fundamental question seems to be whether the thanato-political turn of modern politics as manifest in the Nazi project of extermination could be understood as a return of the repressed (sovereign power), as an essentially atavistic exercise of the sovereign decision of life and death, or rather as the explosive and self-destructive force of biopower at the very point at which the sovereign master finally disappears from the stage, indeed as if his disappearance or, at the very least, complete impotence, is what let loose the paroxysm of violence aimed above all at the destruction of European Jewry:

On the one hand, [Foucault] hypothesizes something like a return to the sovereign paradigm within a biopolitical horizon. In that case, we would be dealing with a literally phantasmal event, in the technical sense of a reappearance of death—of the destitute sovereign decapitated by the grand revolution—on the scene of life; as if a tear suddenly opened in the reign of immunization (which is precisely that of biopolitics), from which the blade of transcendence once again vibrates, the ancient power of taking life. On the other hand, Foucault introduces the opposing hypothesis, which says that it was precisely the final disappearance of the sovereign paradigm that liberates a vital force so dense as to overflow and be turned against itself. (41)

IV

Esposito's own project proposes to rearticulate the relations of biopolitics and sovereignty as declensions of a single, though historically variable, paradigm concerning the relation of politics and life, that of *immunization*, according to which politics, including the institution of sovereignty, is, at a fundamental level, "nothing other than the possibility or the instrument for keeping life alive" (46). Especially important in this context is the intimate link of the semantics of immunization to what appears to be its opposite, a connection that will ultimately hold open the door for an affirmative biopolitics in a community to come: "Tracing it back to its etymological roots, *immunitas* is revealed as the negative or lacking form of *communitas*. If *communitas* is that relation, which in binding its members to an obligation of reciprocal donation, jeopardizes individual identity, *immunitas* is the condition of dispensation from such an obligation and therefore the defense against the expropriating features of *communitas*. . . . One can say that generally *immunitas*, to the degree it protects the one who bears it from risky contact with those who lack it, restores its own borders that were jeopardized by the common" (50). The relation between *immunitas* and *communitas* would seem to return us to the tense dialectic noted earlier whereby the defense of the life of individuals and communities *takes on a life of its own* that, in turn, depletes and constrains the life it is designed to protect and preserve, becoming a kind of *autoimmune* response. The very means of sheltering a community gives birth to a sort of demonic *Doppelgänger* that stalks that selfsame community:

What is immunized . . . is the same community in a form that both preserves and negates it, or better, preserves it through the negation of its original horizon of sense. From this point of view, one might say that more than the defensive apparatus super-imposed on the community, immunization is its internal mechanism: the fold that in some way separates community from itself, sheltering it from *an unbearable excess*. The differential margin that prevents the community from coinciding with itself takes on the deep semantic intensity of its own concept. To survive, the community, every community, is forced to introject the negative modality of its opposite. (52; my emphasis)

I will return to this "unbearable excess" shortly, for I do not think that Esposito's own terms can sufficiently account for it. It is, once again, the question of the cause of the compulsive aspect of the immunization paradigm, something I do not think can be fully grasped by way of the internal tensions within any system between the need for stability, persistence over time, and the need for growth and innovation. To refer to a familiar domain of popular culture, I am arguing that some additional dimension, some other kind of cause or object, is needed to elevate such tensions to the level at which they function in so many science fiction fantasies. The plot is familiar: the technologies created to secure the protection and flourishing of the human world—robots, computers, replicants—"come alive" and turn against that world; the *means* of self-preservation, of individual and communal immunization, themselves become infected with their own drive of self-preservation and begin, in the manner of compulsive *Doppelgänger*, to attack the life at issue. As Esposito himself provocatively

15

suggests, one of the most fully formed visions of such an immunological monstrosity—or at least of its potential—turns out to be not a piece of science fiction but rather the most famous early modern theory of sovereignty, Hobbes's *Leviathan*.

What accounts for the (early) *modernity* of this work is that, according to Esposito, the project of immunization begins to serve as the "most intimate essence" (55) of society, to function not simply as a more or less dependable means toward achieving the good—the flourishing of a historical culture with its particular conception of what constitutes excellence and living well—but *as* the highest good, as what life in society is fundamentally about. That is not quite the same thing as positing the mere survival of the population as the highest good; it is rather elevating the project of immunization to that status, which thereby comes to be the locus of the community's "life drive." We might say that immunization thereby acquires the status of an ethical principle, that modern societies are governed by a *bioethics of immunization*, one undergirded by a theory of sovereignty. For Esposito, this modern inflection of the immunization paradigm is the key to the political theology of sovereignty as envisioned by Hobbes. Rising from the ruins of theological crisis, it forms the nodal point that ties together the three other major aspects of modernization (secularization, rationalization, legitimation):

One might come to affirm that it wasn't modernity that raised the question of the self-preservation of life, but that self-preservation is itself raised in modernity's own being, which is to say it invents modernity as a historical and categorical apparatus able to cope with it. . . . This occurred when natural defenses were diminished; when defenses that had up to a certain point constituted the symbolic, protective shell of human experience were lessened, none more important than the transcendental order that was linked to the theological matrix. *It is the tear that suddenly opens in the middle of the last millennium in that earlier immunitarian wrapping that determines the need for a different defensive apparatus of the artificial sort that can protect a world that is constitutively exposed to risk.* (55, my emphasis)[15]

Hobbes's conception of the social contract, in and through which the sovereign qua *artificial person* is installed in his exceptional place apart as the bearer of the right over the life and death of his subjects, becomes legible as an attempt to respond to just such exigencies in the wake of

15. As I indicated earlier, this suggests that the very concept of political theology would ultimately have to be grasped as "political ~~theology~~," that is, with *theology* written "under erasure," as *aufgehoben*.

a "tear" in a prior "immunitarian wrapping." In order to overcome the chronic threat to life represented by the conflicts among men, generated, as Hobbes sees it, by the natural liberty each man by nature enjoys to preserve his life by any means necessary and to pursue the dictates of his needs and desires (conflicts made all too palpable by *religious schism* and *civil war*), men establish the artifice of the sovereign ruler who thereby becomes delegated with the task of immunizing the group against internal and external threats. As Esposito puts it, "in order to save itself, *life needs to step out from itself and constitute a transcendental point* from which it receives orders and shelter" (58; my emphasis).

At a certain point, then, an immunological dynamic immanent to life itself generates the pressures that culminate in the "social contract," what we might call *the forced choice of sovereignty*. *Leviathan* proves, in this way, to be the crucial precursor text to Lacan's writings on the logic of the signifier, according to which a (master) signifier comes to represent the subject for all other signifiers. This logic can be grasped, that is, as a formalization of the dynamic structure of the sovereign immunization elaborated in Hobbes's monumental work. Esposito nicely summarizes this dynamic whereby nature exceeds itself and, as it were, *grows its own prosthetic extension*, one that enjoys its own autonomy, indeed its own automatism. This peculiar "growth" or mutation that seems to bridge the divide between nature and culture involves a series of well-known spatial and temporal—call them *chrono-topological*—paradoxes:

It can be defined as an immanent transcendence situated outside the control of those that also produced it as the expression of their own will. This is precisely the contradictory structure that Hobbes assigns to the concept of representation: the one representing, that is, the sovereign, is simultaneously identical and different with respect to those that he represents. He is identical because he takes their place, yet different from them because that "place" remains outside their range. The same spatial antinomy is seen temporally, that is, that which the instituting subjects declare to have put in place eludes them because it logically precedes them as their own same presupposition. From this point of view, one could say that the immunization of the modern subject lies precisely in this exchange between cause and effect: he, the subject, can be presupposed . . . because he is already caught in a presupposition that precedes and determines him. (60)

The logic of sovereign immunization is essentially one of exchange and substitution: the fears each person has with regard to every other are exchanged for the fear *all* now have for the sovereign who represents them qua *subject* of the state. According to this "contract" whereby one "contracts" a signifier (one now enjoys the entitlement to be recognized as a member of the commonwealth), "the subject finds himself vis-à-vis a sovereign who preserves the natural right deposited by all the other moments of the entrance into the civil state. What occurs from this, as a result, is the necessary linking of the preservation of life with the possibility—always present even if rarely utilized—of the taking away of life by the one who is charged with insuring it" (62).[16]

V

As I have indicated, what is still missing from Esposito's story is a focused engagement with what I earlier characterized as a "missing piece" of the world, that element on account of which the dialectic of immunization takes on a compulsive, not to say demonic, aspect. This element, this bit of flesh, holds—we might even say *insists on*—the place of the ontological difference between ontic and ontological vulnerability: the bareness, nakedness, and vulnerability pertaining to the precariousness of our organic, mortal lives; the bareness, nakedness, and vulnerability pertaining to the fact that the historical forms of life in which we dwell are susceptible to breakdown.[17] In the context we have been exploring here, the flesh is the bit that goes missing—not once and for all but over and over

16. In his seminar on the psychoses—the one that deals largely with the case of Daniel Paul Schreber—Lacan laid out this same logic of exchange apropos of another early modern treatment of sovereign authority. In his presentation of the concept of the master signifier qua "quilting point" of a discursive field, Lacan closely follows Hobbes's reasoning regarding the effects of the *fear of God* in Racine's play *Athaliah*. We might say that Lacan is after the more purely theological dimension of the logic of the signifier, while Hobbes's treatment pertains to the realm of political theology: "The fear of God isn't a signifier that is found everywhere. Someone had to invent it and propose to men, as the remedy for a world made up of manifold terrors, that they fear a being who is, after all, only able to exercise his cruelty through the evils that are there, multifariously present in human life. To have replaced these innumerable fears by the fear of a unique being who has no other means of manifesting his power than through what is feared behind these innumerable fears, is quite an accomplishment. . . . This famous fear of God completes the sleight of hand that transforms from one minute to the next, all fears into perfect courage. All fears—*I have no other fear*—are exchanged for what is called the fear of God, which, however constraining it may be, is the opposite of fear." Jacques Lacan, *The Seminar of Jacques Lacan: Book III, The Psychoses, 1955–56*, trans. Russell Grigg (New York: Norton, 1993), 266–67.

17. This difference is what accounts for the notion of "two deaths," that is, that a human being not only dies but also dies to a form of life, which, in turn, generates the pressure among the survivors to acknowledge, register, and mourn the death, that is, to establish the fact of the death by way of some sort of symbolic action. The other side of this phenomenon is that a person or group might survive the death of the form of life that constituted the horizon of meaning for everything they did, everything that counted as a "doing." At such a point, the space of representations can no longer viably facilitate the vitality of its members.

again—once the sovereign operation is under way, once the subject has contracted the "master" signifier that represents it for other signifiers in the space of human action that Lacan referred to as the "symbolic order." As we shall explore in more detail, the work of fantasy is the way in which forms of life find and elaborate their imaginary access to this bit of the real that sustains the vibrancy of its resources of representation.

I am suggesting, then, that without taking into account this errant bit of flesh, we cannot really make sense of the automatism that comes to inform that strange instrument of biopolitical technology—or political biotechnology—that we call the sovereign, the agency to which the subject qua subject is subjected. My worry is that Esposito's analysis largely remains at the conceptual level of the dialectic I have noted, one according to which the defensive measures established by a community to shelter itself from risk end up depleting the vitality and vibrancy of the communal life that require precisely exposure, risk, contact, even a certain decadence and degeneration.[18] The concept of immunization alone, even along with its attendant dialectic, is, I am suggesting, not able fully to account for the source of the internal pressure, for what Esposito himself refers to as the "unbearable excess" that is constantly being suppressed and generated within the same system. The flesh is, I am arguing, the source of the strange life that the immunological apparatus itself assumes once it is installed, of its destiny as a sort of spectral *Doppelgänger* of the life it is established to shelter. It is, in a word, the peculiar substance that ultimately *drives* the political theologies of sovereignty and the science fictions of immunological monstrosities, two seemingly disparate traditions that in some sense converge in Hobbes's *Leviathan*.

Esposito, for his part, comes very close to identifying the blindness at issue—and the beginnings of a more fulsome and complex insight— precisely where he seeks to locate a significant inhibition in Hobbes's work: "There is something else that Hobbes doesn't say explicitly, as he limits himself to letting it emerge from the creases or the internal shifts of the discourse itself. It concerns a *remnant of violence* that the immunitary apparatus cannot mediate because it has produced it itself" (61; my

18. This point becomes crucial to Esposito's efforts to discern in Nietzsche's writings an affirmative biopolitical strain of thought, one that demands "immunity's opening to its own communal reversal, to that form of self-dissolving gift giving that *communitas* names" (105). What is new in this relation between life and danger, shelter and exposure, is that "the logic that underpins it is not directed to preserving identity or to simple survival, but rather to innovation and alteration. . . . From this perspective, the negative . . . is affirmed as such: as what forms an essential part of life, even if, indeed precisely because, it continually endangers it, pushing it on to a problematic fault line to which it is both reduced and strengthened" (106).

emphasis). When Esposito begins to unpack this notion of an uncanny remnant that, as it were, sticks to the apparatus that produced it, a remnant that can neither be metabolized nor be left behind, he makes use of the language favored by his better-known Italian colleague Giorgio Agamben, who has, of course, dedicated much of his career to carrying forward in his own way Foucault's intellectual project concerning the conceptual and historical articulation of sovereignty and biopolitics.[19] What Esposito discovers with regard to this remnant that persists as a liminal feature of the Hobbesian construction turns out to be what Carl Schmitt characterized as the key *Grenzbegriff*—we might say *central liminal concept*—of political theology, the very one that Agamben has placed at the heart of his own project: *the state of exception*.[20]

The decision on the state of exception that Schmitt proposes as the defining feature of sovereign power and authority refers to the paradoxical entitlement of a sovereign to suspend the protections of law in the name of protecting the state and its population from sudden or excessive risk.[21] As Agamben has repeatedly emphasized in his work, in the state of exception the inhabitants of a state are addressed or interpellated not in their legal personhood but in their "bare life," as, so to speak, worthy only of living. They are thus not so much subjects of a state or of an "ideological state apparatus," to use Althusser's term, but rather of a purely immunological operation. The measures taken by sovereign power in the state of exception thus protect life by reducing it to a bare minimum of the entitlements afforded by rule of law. "Bare life" is, we might say, the uncanny remainder that is left over once such entitlements are stripped down to a kind of zero-degree, the minimal entitlement *to enjoy life*.[22] In the state of exception, sovereign power protects its people by subjecting them to the pure force of law before which their worth or dignity contracts into the fact of bare life. At this point the biopolitical and the juridical meanings

19. Agamben's work, against which Esposito is very clearly trying to position himself, is mentioned only once in a brief footnote in *Bios*.

20. The reader will recall that Foucault had already characterized the new physics of power as a kind of "infra-law," "counter-law," or even chronic "suspension of law" that permeates modern forms of governmentality. This amounts to claiming that this new physics represents a kind of normalization of a state of exception, a view that has, of course, been elaborated in compelling detail by Agamben.

21. The German language has a word that nicely captures the strangeness of this peculiar entitlement. It can be understood as a *Vorrecht*, a "right" that in some sense comes before and takes precedence over all other rights.

22. The ambiguity of this expression is, of course, significant. It suggests that there is a deep connection between the state of exception and the culture of enjoyment/consumption. It is beyond the scope of this study to explore that connection.

of immunity would seem to converge: to "enjoy" bare life means, in a word, to "enjoy" immunity from (the protections of) law.

Concerning the sovereign's right over the life and death of his subjects, Esposito speaks of the "normal character of the exception (because anticipated by the same order that seems to exclude it)" and describes it as "the liminal coincidence of preservation and capacity to be sacrificed of life." It represents "a remainder that cannot be mediated and the structural antinomy on which the machine of immunitary mediation rests"; it marks *"the residue of transcendence that immanence cannot reabsorb."* As Esposito glosses it, Hobbes's model of sovereign immunization is, thus, structured "as if the negative, keeping to its immunitary function of protecting life, suddenly *moves outside the frame and on its reentry strikes life with uncontrollable violence"* (62–63; my emphasis).

I will have more to say in chapter 2 about the concept of the state of exception and Agamben's use of it in his work. But already here we can discern some of the features that make it relevant to any effort to grasp the chiasmus we have been tracking that turns sovereignty toward biopolitics and biopolitics toward the institution of sovereignty. Indeed, we might say that this chiasmus—this "X"—marks the spot occupied by the state of exception as the key point of relay or transfer between politics and life, as, so to speak, that state in which the "experimental conditions" obtain under which nature exceeds itself and "grows" a commanding symbolic prosthesis, that biotechnical mutation called sovereignty. More accurately, we should say that the state of exception is the way in which sovereign power attempts to *appropriate* the site of a mutation "proper" to human life as such and to stand in as its *creator*.[23] This is a mutation that, as we have seen, bears the features of a radical *expropriation* constitutive of human life: the *forced choice* of a signifier that represents it for other signifiers. The one who gets caught up in such a biopolitical experiment—in essence, *the attempt to enforce what is already a forced choice*—thus becomes a "creature" in an emphatic sense. In the state of exception, the forced contraction of a signifier no longer opens out onto a field of symbolic agency—the space of possibilities in the "field of the Other"—but rather rivets one to a place of pure *suspense*. The entitlements that come with entering the space of representation are reduced to the minimal one: the

---

23. To use Heideggerian terms, we might say that the sovereign is the one who, by deciding on the state of exception, by pretending to occupy and rule from this paradoxical point that is both inside and outside the law, "ontically" claims responsibility for what is in fact an ontological dimension of human life.

entitlement to enjoy (bare) life. To put it in terms made famous by Franz Kafka, one remains stuck at an uncanny place "before the Law."[24]

VI

We began this excursus on the state of exception—the state or zone in which the *force* of law in some sense consumes the *rule* of law—with Esposito's characterization of it as a "residue of transcendence that immanence cannot reabsorb," which then "strikes life with uncontrollable violence" from the outside. What Esposito has discovered in "the creases or . . . internal shifts" of Hobbes's discourse is that in the state of exception, the symbolic agency that, by right of the social contract, ought to entitle the subject to expand out into a space of recognition returns as "a real" that presses it back into a kind of radical contraction and destitution, rivets it to that (non)place "before the law," the locus of what I have characterized as a bare or "creaturely" enjoyment of life. At this point, the "flesh of the world" appears to contract into the agitated, fleshly cringe that for Schreber marked the point of his becoming-*Luder*. What has become apparent here is the close proximity of the state of exception to the structural dynamics of *psychosis*, a dynamics I would like to pursue very briefly.

Commenting on the various delusions of world destruction that fill Schreber's memoir, Freud argues that its author indeed suffered something akin to the end of the world by withdrawing his libido from all internal representations of it: "The patient has withdrawn from the people in his environment and from the external world generally the libidinal cathexis which he has hitherto directed on to them. . . . The end of the world is the projection of this internal catastrophe; his subjective world has come to an end since his withdrawal of his love from it." This

---

24. The nature of this stuckness was the subject of considerable debate between Walter Benjamin and his friend Gershom Scholem. In a formulation that has become canonical in the scholarship on Kafka, Scholem characterizes this space "before the Law" as one in which the subject finds himself exposed to the "nothingness of revelation," its being in force, its persistence as "valid," in the absence of any livable meaning. As he puts in a letter of September 20, 1934, "You ask what I understand by the 'nothingness of revelation'? I understand by it a state in which revelation appears to be without meaning, in which it still asserts itself, in which it has *validity* but *no significance* [*in dem sie gilt, aber nicht bedeutet*]. A state in which the wealth of meaning is lost and what is in the process of appearing (for revelation is such a process) still does not disappear, even though it is reduced to the zero point of its own content, so to speak." *The Correspondence of Walter Benjamin and Gershom Scholem, 1932–1940*, trans. Gary Smith and Andre Lefevre (Cambridge, MA: Harvard University Press, 1992), 142.

leads Freud to conclude that the delusions of persecution that Schreber elaborates in often mind-numbing detail represent the judge's attempt to recreate the world ex nihilo, that is, out of *the nothingness of the erotic void* to which he previously consigned it: "And the paranoiac builds [the world] again, not more splendid, it is true, but at least so that he can once more live in it. He builds it up by the work of his delusions. *The delusion-formation, which we take to be the pathological product, is in reality an attempt at recovery, a process of reconstruction.*" This insight forms the crux of Freud's understanding of the work of projection in the symptom formation proper to paranoia: "What forces itself so noisily upon our attention is the process of recovery, which undoes the work of repression and brings back the libido again on to the people it had abandoned. In paranoia this process is carried out by the method of projection. . . . the truth is . . . as we now see, that *what was abolished internally returns from without.*"[25]

In his own efforts at analyzing the material, Lacan picks up on this formulation and adapts it to his own theory of "foreclosure," a profound mode of negation that forever disturbs the subject's relation to reality, his ability to distinguish inside and outside, dreams and hallucinations from objects *out there*. It is, in a word, a form of disorder that troubles the constitution of an "out there" in the first place as a field open to the circulation—the facilitations—of one's erotic investments.[26] For Lacan, foreclosure or *Verwerfung* (as opposed to the repression or *Verdrängung* that transpires within an established capacity to relate to the world, to "play" in this field of the Other, according to the pleasure and reality principles) involves the rejection, refusal, or attempt to dispose of the signifier whose introjection would facilitate such facilitations by first representing the subject for other signifiers and so putting the subject's desire into symbolic circulation. For Lacan, then, foreclosure is the name for a profound and irresolvable struggle with that inaugural "contraction" of a master or sovereign signifier that would, ideally, entitle the subject to enjoy her or his existential entitlement in the world, in *a commonwealth of symbolic values*. What Schreber's memoirs suggest, among other things, is that when a subject is "in foreclosure," the shelter of the symbolic order—its system of credits and accreditations—collapses in on him

25. Sigmund Freud, *The Standard Edition of the Complete Psychological Works of Sigmund Freud*, trans. James Strachey (London: Hogarth Press, 1953–74), 12:70, 71; my emphasis.

26. "Facilitation" is the English translation of Freud's term *Bahnung*. It signifies the movement of psychic energy along neuronal pathways formed as networks of *representations* or *signifiers*.

as a series of intrusive somatic impingements, as so many *disturbances of the flesh*. To put it somewhat differently, in psychosis the normative pressures injected into human life by way of one's inscription into a symbolic order are imagined to return as real bodily impingements and violations. Among his many formulations of the process of foreclosure, Lacan writes, "At issue is the rejection of a primordial signifier into the outer shadows, a signifier that will henceforth be missing at this level. Here you have the fundamental mechanism that I posit as being at the basis of paranoia. It's a matter of a primordial process of exclusion of an original within, which is not a bodily within but that of an initial body of signifiers. . . . It's *inside this primordial body* that Freud posits the constitution of a world of reality, which is already punctuated, already structured, in terms of signifiers."[27]

But if sovereignty is structurally linked to the state of exception, the capacity, that is, to suspend the rule of law, to invoke, by way of a paradoxical legal action, a certain *nothingness of the law*, of all juridical entitlements—law at its zero-degree of meaning—then sovereignty itself would seem to operate by way of a kind of immanent process of foreclosure or *Verwerfung*, one encamped, so to speak, within its very logic. To return to Freud's formula for the mechanism of projection, we might say that what is abolished internally, the *shelter* of the rule of law, returns in the real of the exception as *exposure* to the pure force of law. Apropos of Schreber's foreclosure of the master signifier in the oedipal organization of psychic structure, Lacan writes that it is "the lack of the Name-of-the-Father in that place which, by the hole that it opens up in the signified, sets off a cascade of reworkings of the signifier from which the growing disaster of the imaginary proceeds, until the level is reached at which signifier and signified stabilize in a delusional metaphor."[28] I am suggesting that one of the forms in which such a "delusional metaphor" appears in our collective political life is that remarkable convergence of political theology and science fiction that Hobbes called the "Leviathan." To return to Esposito's terms, the bit of transcendence that immanence cannot reabsorb is not simply the figure of the sovereign qua bearer of political authority, but one, precisely, whose presence—whose flesh—has been amplified by way of a psychotic dynamic at the heart of sovereign immunization: the re-

27. Lacan, *The Psychoses*, 150; my emphasis.

28. Jacques Lacan, "On a Question Prior to Any Possible Treatment of Psychosis," in *Ecrits: A Selection*, trans. Bruce Fink (New York: Norton, 2002), 207.

turn in the real of the law that is, at some level, always already foreclosed, always already suspended, in (the possibility of) the state of exception.

VII

Another way to grasp the relation between the sovereign who, under normal circumstances, represents the rule of law and the state of exception in which the sovereign suspends the law while still embodying its force, is to link it to the psychoanalytic distinction between ego-ideal and superego. Lacan, for his part, suggests just such a link in one of his very early remarks on the superego, remarks that can easily be read as commentary on one of Kafka's novels:

> The super-ego is an imperative. As is indicated by common sense and by the uses to which it is put, it is consonant with the register and the idea of the law, that is to say with the totality of the system of language, in so far as it defines the situation of man as such, that is to say in so far as he is not just a biological individual. On the other hand, one should also emphasize, as a counter to this, its senseless, blind character, of pure imperativeness and simple tyranny. . . . The super-ego has a relation to the law, and is at the same time a senseless law, going so far as to become a failure to recognize the law. . . . The super-ego is at one and the same time the law and its destruction. As such, it is speech itself, the commandment of law, in so far as nothing more than its root remains. The law is entirely reduced to something, which cannot even be expressed, like the *You must*, which is speech deprived of all its meaning. It is in this sense that the super-ego ends up by being identified with only what is most devastating, most fascinating, in the primitive experiences of the subject. It ends up being identified with what I call *the ferocious figure*, with the figures which we can link to primitive traumas the child has suffered, whatever these are.[29]

It was Freud, of course, who tried to ground the dynamics of the superego in a kind of scientific myth about the origins of human culture. What returns in the real of the state of exception is, in the framework of Freud's speculative writings on these matters, the spectral figure of the "primal father," whose murder by a "band of brothers" marks, for Freud, the true

---

29. Jacques Lacan, *The Seminar of Jacques Lacan: Book I, Freud's Papers on Technique, 1953–1954*, trans. John Forrester (New York: Norton, 1991), 102. As I have argued, this ferocious figure in some sense issues only one command: *Enjoy (bare) life!*

beginnings of human civilization.[30] As Freud sees it, civilization is born with a passage from spontaneous, unmediated enjoyment of objects of appetite to one mediated by systems of entitlement. This passage became possible, Freud thought, only by way of the elimination of the primal father, the embodiment of full and unmediated enjoyment. After murdering this figure and collectively placing a ban on the kind of enjoyment he embodied, the band of brothers establish, as an ambivalent testimony to their deed, the dead father as a sort of totemic or symbolic figure—the first "artificial person," to use Hobbes's formulation—who thenceforth sponsors, authorizes, entitles their destinies as desiring (rather than immediately and fully enjoying) subjects. The institution of the symbolic (and so, *dead*) father serves to immunize the group from attempts to usurp the place of the primal father and his full, unmediated—in a word, incestuous—enjoyment. We might say, then, that the *fiction* of the father as symbolic agency, as sovereign enforcer of the social contract of reciprocity established by the band of brothers, is forever shadowed by the *fantasy* of a ferocious father whose murder continues to clear the path for and facilitate the psychic growth of beings of language, beings endowed with the capacity for symbolic and "contractual" action. The flip side of the *forced choice* of being represented by the signifier for other signifiers, is, then, the *forced guilt* of a murder that is, at some level—that is to say, at the level of unconscious mental activity—*unceasing*. And as Freud further insisted, one of the crucial acts of this primal scene, this theater of origins, was the so-called *totem meal*, in which the brothers ostensibly consumed the sublime flesh of the all-powerful primal father (and his later, ritualized substitutions). The state of exception would seem, then, to mark a space of indistinction between *symbolic fiction* and *fundamental fantasy*, a space where the primal father *refuses to be refused* and returns in all his fleshy excess and overproximity. This would be the mythic way of characterizing the refusal at issue in the notion of foreclosure or *Verwerfung*. It represents one of Freud's mythico-anthropological efforts to capture what Esposito characterized as the destructive paradox of sovereign immunization according to which a "residue of transcendence that

30. The notion of "true beginnings" is, of course, a highly problematic one. Suffice it to say that Freud struggled his entire life with developing a concept of "historical truth," by which he meant to capture the eventful emergence of what is considered to be a *structural* feature of a form of life or even of human mindedness. In essence, Freud thought that the human mind cannot avoid positing the mythic presuppositions of its own functioning. For an extended discussion of the conceptual articulation of Freud's scientific myth of the primal father and the theory of the state of exception, see Kenneth Reinhard, "Toward a Political Theology of the Neighbor," in Slavoj Žižek, Eric Santner, and Kenneth Reinhard, *The Neighbor: Three Inquiries in Political Theology* (Chicago: University of Chicago Press, 2005), 11–75.

immanence cannot reabsorb . . . suddenly moves outside the frame and on its reentry strikes life with uncontrollable violence" (62–63).[31]

VIII

Against the backdrop of these reflections, it makes sense that the deeper Esposito gets into the complexity of the dialectic of immunization, the more he is pushed toward an encounter with the peculiar materiality that I have been calling the flesh. Already in his detailed discussion of the thanato-political kernel of the Nazi project of territorial and racial expansion, he marks the spot of the flesh by means of the chiasmus that, as we have seen, facilitates the relays of productive and destructive forces between the juridico-political institutions of sovereignty and the regulatory practices of biopower. Addressing the much-researched medicalization of politics that goes hand-in-hand with the biological racism that permeated the Nazi movement at all levels, Esposito writes, "It is as if medical power and political-juridical power are mutually superimposed over each other through alternating points that are ultimately destined to completely overlap: this is the claim that life is supreme, which provokes its absolute subordination to politics" (140). He then adds, "The concentration and later the extermination camps constitute the most symptomatic figure of such a chiasmus" (140). But if the goal of the camps was, ultimately, to secure the immunizing enclosure of the German national body upon itself while also enclosing each individual body upon its own biological constitution, it could do so only by, as it were, spiriting into the soma a kind of soul-substance, creating something like a surplus of immanence within immanence. What we encounter here is an extreme version of what I am calling "the People's Two Bodies":

In none of the writings of its theoreticians does Nazism deny what is commonly defined as "soul" or spirit—only it made out of these the means not to open the body toward transcendence, but rather to a further and more definitive enclosing. In this sense, the soul is the *body of the body*, the enclosing of its closing, what from a subjective point

---

31. One might think here of Kafka's famous story "The Judgment," in which an otherwise weak and impotent father suddenly takes on an imposing, carnal presence that issues his son's order of execution. Certainly one of the crucial moments in the story can be characterized as the revelation of the flesh that at some level sustains the final, lethal judgment: "'Ah, Georg,' his father said and immediately went toward him. His heavy robe fell open as he walked, the sides flapping around him—'My father is still a giant,' thought Georg to himself." Cited in *Kafka's Selected Stories*, trans. Stanley Corngold (New York: Norton, 2007), 6.

of view binds us to our objective imprisonment. It is the point of absolute coincidence of the body with itself, the consummation of every interval of difference within, the impossibility of any transcendence. In this sense, more than a reduction of *bios* to *zoē* or to "bare life" . . . we need to speak of the spiritualization of *zoē* and the biologization of the spirit. (141–42)

In Nazi ideology, the name for this surplus immanence that "confers meaning on the identity of the body with itself, a meaning that exceeds the individual borders from birth to death" (142), was, of course, *race*. The term used by the French eugenic thinker whom Esposito cites in this context, Vacher de Lapouge, actually evokes more powerfully the dimension at issue here, namely something in the body that is more than the body and yet is not simply spirit: "What is immortal isn't the soul, a dubious and probably imaginary character: it is the body, *or rather, the germinative plasma*" (142; my emphasis). The difficulties of isolating this sublime substance that would seem to figure the downward displacement of transcendence into a *too much of immanence* leads to a splitting of racial policy into the two opposing biopolitical projects of the Nazi movement: *eugenics*, the cultivation of the healthy flesh, and *genocide*, the elimination of precisely what represents a *too much of too much*, that purulent flesh that, as we saw, Judge Schreber imagined himself to have been singled out to embody and enjoy.[32]

In the final chapter of his study, Esposito dedicates an entire section to the topic of the flesh, which he even comes to see as a possible resource for imagining a new form of *communitas* in the aftermath of this radical thanato-political turn of *immunitas*. Seizing on Merleau-Ponty's suggestive use of the term, Esposito proposes that it might best capture the dimension that is truly at issue in this turn, that it names the "substance" among whose crucial properties is, as we have seen, the capacity to split into sublime and abject, intoxicating and merely toxic, modalities. Commenting on Merleau-Ponty's claim that the flesh "has no name in philosophy," Esposito writes that "no philosophy has known how to reach that undifferentiated layer (and . . . for this reason exposed to difference), in which the . . . notion of body, anything but enclosed, is now turned outside in an irreducible heterogeneity" (159). He goes on to suggest that the crucial blind spot in Heidegger's analysis of life can be traced to a

---

32. In my study of the case, I show in detail that in the context of fin-de-siècle Germany, such chosenness, which I see as a by-product of a chronic crisis of symbolic investiture, led to Schreber's metamorphosis into a feminized Wandering Jew.

failure to take the concept of the flesh into account in his thinking. In all of this Esposito fails to recall Merleau-Ponty's claim that it was, in fact, Freud who was the singular philosopher of the flesh.

Be that as it may, Esposito's discussion of the concept turns out to be quite productive on its own terms, terms that compel him to return to the canonical formulations of the crucial distinction between the flesh and the body in the letters of Saint Paul. In Paul's writings on these matters, we find some of the first statements that inaugurate in the West the political theology of sovereignty, the biopolitics of states, and the rhetorical figures that organize their reciprocal exchange of properties and energies. They have, of course, also set the pattern for the ways in which Jewish-Christian relations have been configured over the last two millennia, up to and including the thanato-political consignment of the Jews to the ways of all *abject* flesh, their identification as the primary bearers of *too much of a too much* that already troubles any "immunitarian" attempt to stabilize the borders of bodies and territories.

The crucial Pauline operation, Esposito says, concerns the transfiguration of the *flesh* into the animating principle of *corporate* integrity and unity: "More than an expulsion of the flesh, this concerns its incorporation into an organism that is capable of domesticating flesh's centrifugal and anarchic impulses. Only the spiritualization of the body (or better, the incorporation of a spirit that is capable of redeeming man from the misery of his corruptible flesh) will allow him entrance into the mystical body of the church" (164). The crucial "technology" of such a conversion was, of course, the sacrament of the Eucharist that facilitated "this salvific passage from flesh to body" (164). The fundamental paradox of the Christian conception of the incarnation is, then, that man can achieve this miraculous *sublimation* of the flesh only if God Himself undergoes a radical act of *desublimation*, entering fully into the plane of immanence, the ways of all flesh, and then, as it were, reabsorbing this surplus immanence into his mystical body. Esposito's rapid summary of the political theological aftermath of the Pauline codification of these transformations makes it abundantly clear that what is fundamentally at issue in the immunitary paradigm is not so much the protection of life from death but of the body from the flesh: "With all the variants as well as the conflicts that are derived from an initial competition, we can say that first the empire and then the nascent nation-states activated and secularized the same theological-political mechanism; but also here they did so in order to save themselves from the risk associated with 'bare life,' which is implicit in that extralegal condition defined as the 'state of nature'—namely, the 'flesh' of a plural and potentially rebellious multitude that needed to be integrated in a unified body at the command of the sovereign" (164–65). Esposito's characterization of the "flesh"—what he earlier referred to as an "unbearable excess"—as a potentially rebellious "multitude," comes far too quickly and in the end, I think, actually domesticates the intuition at work here. We will, in the following chapters, have a chance to explore further the link between the flesh and the "multitude," a link to some extent already inscribed in the semantic oscillations of the word *mass*. For the moment I would simply like to emphasize the perpetuation of the *agon* of flesh and body in the history of the corporative metaphor, of the "body politic," in the West.[33]

One of the key factors in perpetuating the semantics of the body politic in modernity was the attempt to locate, in the wake of the French Revolution, the new source of legitimate political membership in the concept of the *national community*, a political collectivity united by the fact of birth and so by way of a kind of *somatic distinction* or *dignitas*. I discuss this crucial transition in chapter 2. What I hope, above all, to have made clear, is that the persistence of the metaphor of the political body, of "corporate" conceptions of community and belonging, cannot be fully understood without grasping the nature of the substance that always seems to threaten the integrity and "organicity" of its composition and that at both an individual and a collective level represents a dimension of, as Esposito has put it, "unbearable excess." To express it in more psychoanalytic terms, what threatens the integrity of the corporate body is not the proliferation of *parts* but the agitation of *partial objects*.

Because it represents a kind of too-muchness that can never be fully contained by corporatist wrappings or expelled by immunological procedures, and because such defensive maneuvers would seem to have grown obsolete in the face of the dynamics of globalization, it would appear as if this unbearable excess could now become the site for a new thinking of politics and community. And because this surplus immanence results from a dynamic of incarnation not so much of God as of the place of God in human life, this new thinking offers itself as a profoundly reimagined messianism that would seek not to overcome but rather to *pro-*

---

33. For readers of German, the two single most important recent studies of corporative metaphors in the history of Western political theory and practice are Susanne Lüdemann, *Metaphern der Gesellschaft: Studien zum soziologischen und politischen Imaginären* (Munich: Wilhelm Fink, 2004), and a group effort in which Lüdemann was joined by Albrecht Koschorke, Thomas Frank, and Ethel Matala de Mazza, *Der fiktive Staat: Konstruktionen des politischen Körpers in der Geschichte Europas* (Frankfurt am Main: Fischer, 2007). My thinking on these matters has been very much enriched by both of these studies.

liferate and elaborate the carnal materiality of this surplus immanence. As Esposito puts it in one of the more rapturous passages in his study, one in which he joins the chorus of thinkers who have returned to the Pauline legacy in the hopes of deconstructing and reconstructing it, of deploying it for reimagining politics, community, and human sociality more generally,

Certainly, the fact that for the first time the politicization of life doesn't pass necessarily through a semantics of the body (because it refers to a world material that is antecedent to or that follows the constitution of the subject of law) opens up a series of possibilities unknown until now. What political form can flesh take on, the same flesh that has always belonged to the modality of the impolitical? And what can be assigned to something that is born out of the remains of anomie? Is it possible to extract from the cracks of *immunitas* the outlines of a different *communitas*? Perhaps the moment has arrived to rethink in nontheological terms the event that . . . two thousand years ago appeared under the enigmatic title "the resurrection of the flesh." To "rise again," today, cannot be the body inhabited by the spirit, but the flesh as such: a being that is both singular and communal, generic and specific, and undifferentiated and different, not only devoid of spirit, but a flesh that doesn't even have a body. (166–67)[34]

There is, I think, still a great deal of work to be done before one can attach any sort of radical hope, let alone messianism, to a new thinking of the flesh. At the very least I hope to have made clear just why Daniel Paul Schreber, who in some sense experienced himself as a first apostle of this new thinking, continues to command and deserve our attention. I also hope that I have persuaded the reader that this new thinking ultimately requires the intellectual resources provided by the figure whom Merleau-Ponty himself referred to as a philosopher of the flesh, Sigmund Freud. Indeed, I think that one of the shortcomings of Esposito's work—and also of the work on the same set of issues by Hannah Arendt and Giorgio Agamben to which I will turn in the next chapter—is that it neglects the conceptual tools that could facilitate a more precise attunement to the ways of the flesh. I also hope to have provided some additional context for the preoccupation with Saint Paul in contemporary philosophy and political theory. Any effort to track the mutations of the body politic in its relation to the dimension of the flesh is compelled to reckon with the legacy of Paul in the political theology of Europe. In the next chapter I will try to deepen the analysis of the modern mutations of these relations

34. I will address the Deleuzian echoes of such language when I turn to the work of the artist whom Esposito himself cites as a crucial witness to the possibilities he invokes here: Francis Bacon.

as they take shape in the passage from the ancien régime to the space of democratic nation-states. To grasp that transition we will, however, first have to acquire a bit more fluency in the doctrine of the King's Two Bodies that Ernst Kantorowicz elaborated in such painstaking detail in his monumental study of the topic.

TWO

Of Kings and
Other Creatures

I

In this chapter I address more directly the changing status of the flesh (and its cultural locations) that comes with the passage from royal to popular sovereignty in European states, a passage typically dated with the French Revolution and its aftermath. And as I have noted, one of my key guides for grasping the stakes of this transition has been Ernst Kantorowicz's deservedly famous study *The King's Two Bodies: A Study in Medieval Political Theology*. My hypothesis is that the complex symbolic structures and dynamics of sovereignty described by Kantorowicz in the context of medieval and early modern European monarchies do not simply disappear from the space of politics once the body of the king is no longer available as the primary incarnation of the principle and functions of sovereignty; rather, these structures and dynamics—along with their attendant paradoxes and impasses—"migrate" into a new location that thereby assumes a turbulent and disorienting semiotic density previously concentrated in the "strange material and physical presence" of the king. A central problem for secular modernity is how to account for the flesh once it no longer functions as that which, so to speak, "fattens" the one who occupies the place of power and authority, elevating the body that thereby comes to figure as its naturally—because supernaturally—appointed caretaker, the one charged with guaranteeing the health of this element for all the others (who thereby become his subjects). As I have been arguing, the discourses and practices that we now group under the heading of "biopolitics" come to be charged with these duties, with the caretaking of the sublime (but also potentially abject) flesh of the new bearer of the principle of sovereignty, the People. The dimension of the flesh comes, in a word, to be assimilated to the plane of the health, fitness, and wellness of bodies and populations that must, in turn, be obsessively measured and tested. But if my hunch is right, that would mean that before biopolitics emerged as such, it was, in some sense, already on the scene *as the political theology of kingship.* And as Kantorowicz has amply shown, those premodern practices that, as it were, limited their biopolitical reach to the body of the king as the singular locus of the principle of sovereign power and authority were equally troubled by the paradoxical status of the element I have been calling the flesh.

II

At this point it would perhaps be helpful to take stock of some of the crucial aspects of the institutions of kingship whose (biopolitical) end-game informs, as I will argue, a great deal of modern culture broadly conceived. What is above all at issue here, as in every political formation, is the nature of the linkage between questions of legitimate rule, the symbolic dynamics of "incorporation"—the constitution and delimitation of a recognizable "body politic"—and the endurance and flourishing of the thereby constituted political collective across time, along with the question as to what flourishing as well as collective self-identity across time actually means. What has to be linked here are thus at the very least four distinct matters: (1) the relation of parts to whole within a social formation; (2) the way in which the functionality, vitality, or flourishing of the formation is conceived; (3) the successful survival of the formation as self-identical across time, its organization of temporal *succession*; and (4) the sources of legitimacy of the formation: what justifies its existence, makes it more than utterly contingent? Or perhaps better, how does its elaboration of the question of legitimacy serve to "metabolize" its contingency?

In the period he studies—primarily from the High Middle Ages to the late Renaissance—Kantorowicz shows that this complex set of linkages was largely, if often unstably, secured by the peculiar doctrine that the royal personage had two bodies, one natural and subject to the fate of all mortal flesh and one supernatural, whose representational or official corporeality gave quasi-divine legitimacy, presence, and enduring substance to governmental authority—to *Herrschaft*—across the succession of generations. Put somewhat differently, what Kantorowicz apparently discovered was that if the king was to function as the general equivalent of subjects in his realm—and thereby help to sustain the realm in its symbolic efficiency as a locus of subject-formation—his being had to undergo, as if by some necessity in the logic of symbolic authority, a kind of doubling or "gemination" resulting in the production of the abstract physiological fiction of a sublime, quasi-angelic body, a body of immortal flesh that was thereby seen to enjoy both juridical and medical immunity, to stand above the laws of men and the laws of perishable nature. This view achieves its fullest formulation in the writings of English jurists of the sixteenth century. There one reads, for example, the following:

For the King has in him two Bodies, *viz.*, a Body natural, and a Body politic. His Body natural . . . is a Body mortal, subject to all Infirmities that come by Nature or Accident, to the Imbecility of Infancy or old Age, and to the like Defects that happen to the natural Bodies of other People. But his Body politic is a Body that cannot be seen or handled, consisting of Policy and Government, and constituted for the Direction of the People, and the Management of the public weal, and this Body is utterly void of Infancy, and old Age, and other natural Defects and Imbecilities, which the Body natural is subject to, and for this Cause, what the King does in his Body politic, cannot be invalidated or frustrated by any Disability in his natural Body.

Or further:

These two Bodies are incorporated in one Person, and make one Body and not divers, that is the Body corporate in the Body natural, *et e contra* the Body natural in the Body corporate. So that the Body natural, by this conjunction of the Body politic to it, (which Body politic contains the Office, Government, and Majesty royal) is magnified, and by the said Consolidation hath in it the Body politic.[1]

The bulk of Kantorowicz's magisterial study is taken up with tracing the complex genealogy of this peculiar and potent fiction across several centuries of tense and shifting relations between secular and ecclesiastical powers. The story begins with—and in a certain sense never fully

1. Edmund Plowden's *Reports*, cited in Ernst Kantorowicz, *The King's Two Bodies: A Study in Medieval Political Theology* (Princeton, NJ: Princeton University Press, 1981), 7, 9. Subsequent references are made in the text.

leaves behind—a conception of "Christ-centered kingship" in which the sovereign's double nature is modeled on the logic of the incarnation. The two natures of Christ are transferred to the king, who is thus seen to have not only his own mortal body but to enjoy by grace—made manifest and effective in the liturgical practices of consecration—a sublime body in and through which he appears as the "type and image of the Anointed in heaven and therewith of God" (48). As Kantorowicz puts it, here "the vision of the king as a *persona geminata* is ontological and, as an effluence of a sacramental and liturgical action performed at the altar, it is liturgical as well" (59).

The next chapter of the story is dominated by a gradual shift pursued in dizzying detail through the later Middle Ages, in which "the king's new relationship to Law and Justice" comes to overshadow his "former status with regard to Sacrament and Altar" (94). If "the anointed king appeared as a 'twinned person' because *per gratiam* this king reflected the two natures of the God-man," in this new "Law-centered era . . . and in the language of the jurists, the Prince no longer was 'god by grace' or the living image of Grace; he was the living image of Justice, and *ex officio* he was the personification of an Idea which likewise was both divine and human" (141–42).[2] Although what he characterizes as the "whiff of incense" (210) continues to permeate all the transformations traced throughout the study, Kantorowicz argues that at a certain point the idioms and practices of *juridical* speech come to displace those of *liturgical* speech as the locus of the performative magic whereby kingship comes to be endowed with its sublime aura. Summarizing this semantic shift pertaining to the king's dual nature, Kantorowicz writes,

The Prince as the animate Law or living Justice shared with *Iustitia* the duality which inheres in all Universals or "Ideas." It was this double aspect of Justice, human and

---

2. Among the peculiarities of this phase, we find the concept of the king as a *lex animata* or living law. Along with other sources, Kantorowicz cites an address to Barbarossa at the Diet of Roncaglia in 1158, attributed to the Four Doctors of Bologna: "You, being the living Law, can give, loosen, and proclaim laws; dukes stand and fall, and kings rule while you are the judge; anything you wish, you carry on as the animate Law" (129). He also cites the emperor Frederick II (the subject of Kantorowicz's most famous work prior to *The King's Two Bodies* and written while he was still part of the cultlike circle around the poet Stefan George), who characterized his own person as "the majesty which is the animate Law on earth and from which the civil laws originate" (131). The theory of the ruler as the living law was, Kantorowicz claims, brought to a kind of canonical conclusion in a work by one of Aquinas's pupils, Aegidius Romanus, who integrated the legal scholarship with Aristotelian philosophy. As Romanus puts it, "the king or prince is a kind of Law, and the Law is a kind of king or prince. For the Law is a kind of inanimate prince; the prince, however, a kind of animate Law. *And in so far as the animate exceeds the inanimate the king or prince must exceed the Law*" (134; my emphasis).

divine, which was mirrored by her imperial vicar on earth who, in his turn, was mainly through *Iustitia* also the vicar of God. Justice herself, at least in the language of learned jurisprudence, no longer was quite identical with the God of the altar, though still inseparable from God the Father; nor was she as yet subordinated to an absolute or deified State: she was, for that short period of transition, a living *Virtus* in her own right, the goddess of the age in which jurisprudence took the lead and became intellectually the great vivifier of almost every branch of knowledge. By analogy, the Prince no longer was the *christomimetes*, the manifestation of Christ the eternal King; nor was he, as yet, the exponent of an immortal nation; he had his share in immortality because he was the hypostasis of an immortal Idea. A new pattern of *persona mixta* emerged from the Law itself, with *Iustitia* as the model deity and the Prince as both her incarnation and her *Pontifax maximus*. (143)

In the next chapter of the story, the center of auratic gravity shifts more and more from "the ruling personages to the ruled collectives, the new national monarchies, and other political aggregates of human society" (193). It is in this phase of the ongoing exchanges of properties between Church and State, which had all the while produced hybridizations on both sides of the border such that, as Kantorowicz puts it, "the *sacerdotium* had an imperial appearance and the *regnum* a clerical touch" (193), that the Pauline background of the story becomes absolutely central. In this new phase of "polity-centered kingship," the Pauline conception of the Church as the *corpus Christi* is transformed and adapted to "the all-encompassing spiritual prototype of corporational concepts, the *corpus mysticum* of the Church" (194).

The crucial Pauline text in this genealogy is the twelfth chapter of 1 Corinthians, which itself takes up and revises the fable that provides one if not the central *Urtext* of organological conceptions of political formations in the West, of the political collective as a *body politic*: Menenius Agrippa's fable of the revolt of the body's members related in Livy's *Early History of Rome*.[3] It was, however, Paul's version of the allegory that

3. In order to prevent an all-out civil war between the commoners and the governing class (Livy is referring to an uprising of the plebeians in 494 B.C.), the "senatorial party . . . decided to employ Menenius as their spokesman to the commons on the Sacred Mount—he was a good speaker, and the commons liked him as he was one of themselves. Admitted to the deserters' camp, he is said to have told them, in the rugged style of those far-off days, the following story. 'Long ago when the members of the human body did not, as now they do, agree together, but had each its own thoughts and the words to express them in, the others resented the fact that they should have the worry and trouble of providing everything for the belly, which remained idle, surrounded by its ministers, with nothing to do but enjoy the pleasant things they gave it. So the discontented members plotted together that the hand should carry no food to the mouth, and that the mouth should take nothing that was offered it, and that the teeth should accept nothing to chew. But alas! while they sought in their resentment to subdue the belly by starvation, they themselves and the whole body

became the crucial proof text for political theological thinking in Europe. It is thus worth quoting the letter at length:

For just as the body is one and has many members, and all the members of the body, though many, are one body, so it is with Christ. For by one Spirit we were all baptized into one body—Jews or Greeks, slaves or free—and were all made to drink of one Spirit. For the body does not consist of one member but of many. If the foot should say, "Because I am not a hand, I do not belong to the body," that would not make it any less a part of the body. And if the ear should say, "Because I am not an eye, I do not belong to the body," that would not make it any less a part of the body. If the whole body were an eye, where would be the hearing? If the whole body were an ear, where would be the sense of smell? But as it is, God arranged the organs in the body, each one of them, as he chose. If all were a single organ, where would the body be? As it is, there are many parts, yet one body. The eye cannot say to the hand, "I have no need of you," nor again the head to the feet, "I have no need of you." On the contrary, the parts of the body which seem to be weaker are indispensable, and those parts of the body which we think less honorable we invest with the greater honor, and our unpresentable parts are treated with greater modesty, which our more presentable parts do not require. But God has so adjusted the body, giving the greater honor to the inferior parts, that there may be no discord in the body, but that the members may have the same care for one another.[4]

In Ephesians 4:15–16, this democratically constituted body is somewhat rearticulated to emphasize the paradoxical status of Christ as both the body in its entirety *and* the head that stands at its apex: "Rather, speaking the truth in love, we are to grow up in every way into him who is the head, into Christ, from whom the whole body, joined and knit together

---

wasted away to nothing. By this it was apparent that the belly, too, has no mean service to perform: it receives food, indeed; but it also nourishes in its turn the other members, giving back to all parts of the body, through all its veins, the blood it has made by the process of digestion; and upon this blood our life and our health depend.'" Livy, *The Early History of Rome*, trans. Aubrey de Sélincourt (London: Penguin, 2002), 146–47. As I have already noted, among the best studies of organological conceptions of political collectivities in the West is Albrecht Koschorke, Susanne Lüdemann, Thomas Frank, and Ethel Matala de Mazza, *Der fiktive Staat: Konstruktionen des politischen Körpers in der Geschichte Europas* (Frankfurt am Main: Fischer, 2007).

4. *The Writings of St. Paul*, ed. Wayne A. Meeks (New York: Norton, 1972), 40–41. One finds an extended discussion of Paul in *Der fiktive Staat* as well as in Susanne Lüdemann's separate volume *Metaphern der Gesellschaft: Studien zum soziologischen und politischen Imaginären* (Munich: Wilhelm Fink, 2004), 88–100. As we shall see, where I differ with these exemplary studies is largely a matter of focus. While Koschorke, Lüdemann, and coauthors attend for the most part to the part-whole logic of social and political figures and concepts deriving from the *image of the body*, I am more interested in the *real of the flesh*, which, again, refers not to the tissues beneath the skin but rather to an excessive element that both separates and joins nature and culture, bodies and political formations, however their logic might be figured.

by every joint with which it is supplied, when each part is working properly, makes bodily growth and upbuilds itself in love."[5] I have noted
earlier the ways in which Paul's thinking about the flesh in relation to the
body already troubles, from within, his organological thinking. Indeed,
we might say that for Paul, *the flesh is the thorn in the body*, the dimension of embodied subjectivity that registers an excess of the normative
pressures that inform and potentially "deform" a life lived in relation to
agencies of authority and authorization. The complex symbolic dynamic
of the constitution of kingship itself comes "to a head" precisely when
the *body* of the king is posited as the *head* of the body politic.[6]

III

Kantorowicz shows that medieval theological doctrine was able to transform Paul's notion of the *corpus Christi* into a more flexible and plastic
concept of the *corpus mysticum*, which then became the master trope
that allowed for the aggregation and sacramentalization of all manner
of secular entities, including, above all, the state and its various offices
and institutions. The transmutation takes place precisely by way of the
medium of the sacraments. In the course of the twelfth century, *corpus
mysticum*, a term with no biblical tradition, shifted from its liturgical and
sacramental meaning—"mystical body," in the sense of the consecrated
host—to a sociological one identifying "the Church as the organized
body of Christian society united in the Sacrament of the Altar"—the very
meaning Paul had reserved for the term *corpus Christi*. That Pauline term
came, in its turn, to signify the consecrated bread—also called the *corpus
verum* or *corpus naturale*—as well as the feast instituted in the Western
Church in 1264 (196). Kantorowicz emphasizes that these shifts were
consolidated in the wake of the Investiture Dispute, that is, a kind of
self-reflexive struggle as to which entity—Church or Empire—was primarily invested with the capacity to invest German bishops. This was a
time when the Church was beginning to hallow in a more juridical and
political mode its own administrative and institutional apparatus—its

---

5. *Writings of St. Paul*, 128.

6. If I am right that Freudian thought is in many ways an attempt to think through the shadowy,
largely biopolitical afterlife of (an originally Pauline) political theology in the psychic, political, and
cultural life of modernity—this is what I have elsewhere called the "psychotheology of everyday
life"—we might say that the problem Freud discovered was not so much that the body has a mind
of its own but rather that *the head has a body of its own*, one charged precisely with administering
the flesh.

"corporational" aspects—and secular political entities were beginning to assert their Church-independent political theological status. As Kantorowicz summarizes this development,

> While the lofty idea of the Church as *corpus mysticum cuius caput Christi* was inflated with secular contents, corporational as well as legal, the secular state itself—starting, as it were, from the opposite end—strove for its own exaltation and quasi-religious glorification. The noble concept of the *corpus mysticum*, after having lost much of its transcendental meaning and having been politicized and, in many respects, secularized by the Church itself, easily fell prey to the world of thought of statesmen, jurists, and scholars who were developing new ideologies for the nascent territorial and secular states. Barbarossa . . . hallowed his empire by the glorifying title *sacrum imperium*—a perfectly legitimate para-ecclesiastical term which he borrowed from the vocabulary of Roman Law, and not from that of the Church. The efforts, however, to provide the state institutions with some religious aureole, as well as the adaptability and general usefulness of ecclesiastical thought and language, led the theorists of the secular state very soon to a more than superficial appropriation of the vocabulary not only of Roman Law, but also of Canon Law and Theology at large. The new territorial and quasi-national state, self-sufficient according to its claims and independent of the Church and the Papacy, quarried the wealth of ecclesiastical notions, which were so convenient to handle, and finally proceeded to assert itself by placing its own temporariness on a level with the sempiternity of the militant Church. In that process the idea of the *corpus mysticum*, as well as other corporational doctrines developed by the Church were to be of major importance. (207)[7]

Certainly one of the most far-reaching results of this development was that it became possible to posit the death of a soldier in battlefield as *martyrdom* for the state; "*pro patria mori*, death for the sake of that mystico-political body, made sense; it became meaningful, as it was considered equal in value and consequence to the death for the Christian faith, for the Church, or for the Holy Land" (268).

At this point in his genealogy, Kantorowicz returns to the strange symbolico-anatomical feature already formulated by Paul apropos of Christ and brought to a terse formulation by Gregory of Bergamo: "One body of Christ which is he himself, and another body of which he is the

---

7. In all of this, Kantorowicz does not neglect the impact of Aristotelian thought on the development of the concept of corporate bodies. After Aquinas had "ecclesiasticized the Philosopher," Kantorowicz writes, "a new halo descended from the works of Aristotle upon the corporate organism of human society, a halo of morals and ethics different from that of the ecclesiological *corpus mysticum*, yet by no means incompatible with it; in fact, *corpus mysticum* and *corpus morale et politicum* became almost interchangeable notions" (211–12).

head" (cited in Kantorowicz, 268). Kantorowicz argues that as tempting as the thought might be, the historical sources do not support the view of a straightforward analogy between the *duplex corpus Christi* and an ostensibly *duplex corpus regis*: "Nowhere do we find, merely on the basis of the organic concept of the state, the idea expressed that the king as the head of the body politic has two bodies" (269). What makes things less straightforward is the dimension of *time*, the temporal dimension of the state qua *corpus mysticum* and of the body that serves as its "head." For the Church, this was not a dilemma at all; "the head of the mystical body of the Church was eternal, since Christ was both God and man" (271). Christ could, in a word, function as *the body of the head of his own mystical body* because of his own double or split nature qua God-man. The political theology of kingship needed not only a synchronic, *organological* dimension—the "organic" relations of parts to whole—but also a diachronic dimension of temporal persistence, if not of eternity then of a kind of *undying life* across the critical breaks of inevitable interregnum. The *body of the head* of the political *corpus mysticum* would, in a word, have to take on the properties if not exactly of eternal life then those of the *undead*, of a being whose body is charged with representing eternity in the space of secular, political life, one whose corporeality is elevated to the sublime dignity of an eternal Thing:

That is to say, before the king could represent (as in the language of the Tudor jurists) that strange being which, like the angels, was immortal, invisible, ubiquitous, never under age, never sick, and never senile, he had either to stop being a simple mortal or to acquire somehow a value of immortality; the eternity which Christ, in the language of theology, owned "by nature," had to accrue to the king from another source. Without some *character aeternitatis* he could not have his *character angelicus*, and without some inherent value of eternity he could not have "two bodies" or have a super-body distinct from his natural mortal body. (271–72)

The problem of the continuity of corporations—of the body politic—had to be in some way folded into and elaborated as a problem internal to the complex physiology of kingship, a physiology that was seen to include within its inner constitution enduring values. The flesh of the royal "super" or "surplus" body was grasped as the locus of a series of *virtual realities*: "The value of immortality or continuity upon which the new polity-centered rulership would thrive, was vested in the *universitas* 'which never dies,' in the perpetuity of an immortal people, polity, or *patria*, from which the individual king might easily be separated, *but not the Dynasty, the Crown, and the Royal Dignity*" (272; my emphasis).

41

Much of the rest of Kantorowicz's study focuses on the ways these various virtual realities—dynasty, crown, dignity—were seen to enter into the constitution of the "royal physiology," which could then serve as the linchpin and focal point guaranteeing the consistency and *undying nature* of the body politic.[8] It is no surprise that this physiology would come to the fore in especially emphatic ways on the occasion of royal funerals, events meant to preserve the vitality of the King's *physis* beyond that of the mortal king. In his account of the funeral of Edward II in 1327, Kantorowicz describes the introduction of effigies into the theater of royal mortuary ritual. These wooden or leather representations of the deceased sovereign, placed on top of the coffin, were typically dressed in coronation garments and displayed the insignia of sovereignty; they thus served not as doubles of the king but rather of the King—as doubles of his undying *Doppelgänger*: "Wherever the circumstances were not to the contrary, the effigies were henceforth used at the burials of royalty: enclosed in the coffin . . . there rested the corpse of the king, his mortal and normally visible—though now invisible—body natural; whereas his normally invisible body politic was on this occasion visibly displayed by the effigy in its pompous regalia: a *persona ficta*—the effigy—impersonating a *persona ficta*—the *Dignitas*" (421).[9] Here, as in numerous other passages, one might detect in Kantorowicz's emphasis on the artificial, fictive, manmade character of the king's second body his own struggle to distance himself from the nationalist "fictions" that had, during the Weimar period, so gripped his own imagination. But even if that is true,

8. The longest section in this discussion is dedicated to the notion that *dignitas non moritur*. About this concept Kantorowicz writes, "The Dignity . . . referred chiefly to the singularity of the royal office, to the sovereignty vested in the king by the people, and resting individually in the king alone" (384). In this context, Kantorowicz also refers to the importance of the metaphor of the Phoenix in the elaboration of the royal physiology: "The Phoenix metaphor fitted not badly to illustrate the nature of the *Dignitas quae non moritur*: the *Dignitas* of abbot, bishop, pope, or king appeared as a Phoenix-like *species* which coincided with the individual because it reproduced no more than one individuation at a time, the incumbent. Moreover, the Phoenix was, so to speak, a 'natural' one-individual corporation, and thus there arose from the ashes of the Phoenix metaphor the prototype of that spectre called the 'Corporation sole' which was at once immortal species and mortal individuation, collective *corpus politicum* and individual *corpus naturale*" (394).

9. Kantorowicz sees in such practices what he refers to as the "late Gothic" preoccupation with death and transience: "The jurists . . . discovered the immortality of the Dignity; but by this very discovery they made the ephemeral nature of the mortal incumbent all the more tangible. We should not forget that the uncanny juxtaposition of a decaying corpse and an immortal Dignity as displayed by the sepulchral monuments, or the sharp dichotomy of the lugubrious funeral train surrounding the corpse and the triumphant float of an effigy-dummy wrapped in regalia . . . evolved in the same intellectual climate, in which the juridical tenets concerning the 'King's two Bodies' achieved their final formulation. In both instances, there was a body mortal, God-made and therefore 'subject to all Infirmities that come by Nature or Accident,' set against another body, man-made and therefore immortal, which is 'utterly void of Infancy and old Age and other Defects and Imbecilities'" (436).

what is missed in such claims and, I would suggest, in all efforts to deflate the force of political metaphors by "deconstructing" their metaphoricity, their status as fictions or rhetorical figures, is the difference between symbolic fiction and fantasy. What is missed is precisely the fact that such fictions get a grip on the imagination of individuals and collectives because they are ultimately sustained by the "real stuff" of fantasy, by the dimension I have been calling the flesh.

IV

In the final chapter of Kantorowicz's study, the authority shaping the concept and image of kingship previously held by theologian, jurist, and political theorist passes to the poet. In Dante, Kantorowicz finds the resources for a new conception of kingship, one modeled on a scene of investiture staged by the poet himself in the twenty-seventh canto of the *Purgatory*. This scene, in which Dante is "crowned and mitred" by Virgil, represents for Kantorowicz a kind of humanist baptism in which the poet becomes a member "not of the *corpus mysticum Christi quod est ecclesia*, but the *corpus mysticum Adae quod est humanitas*." Dante is baptized, that is, "into the likeness of Adam, the purely human model of man's perfection and actualization" (492). In Kantorowicz's view, Dante's humanism transforms the dual nature of kingship into "the reflexiveness of 'man' and 'Man,' of *homo* and *humanitas*, of *Adam mortalis* and *Adam subtilis* . . . of body natural of man and body corporate of Man" (494). But there is some ambiguity here, for at the very end of the book, Kantorowicz seems to want to undo the quasi-developmental narrative—a story largely about secularization—that he seemed to be constructing all along. He now suggests that the trope of the King's Two Bodies is itself a kind of secondary development or projection into the domain of political theology of what is in reality a *dual nature proper to human beings as such*, that is, that Dante is simply reappropriating the human origins of the entire development and positing them as such: "It remained . . . to the poet *to visualize the very tension of the 'Two Bodies' in man himself*, to make *humanitas* . . . the sovereign of *homo*, and to find for all those intricate cross-relations and interrelations the most complex, terse, and simple, because most human formula: 'I crown and mitre you over yourself'" (495; my emphasis).[10]

---

10. One could argue that the passage from Christ-centered kingship to man-centered kingship (by way of law-centered and polity-centered kingship) is merely the unfolding of the meaning of the Christian logic of incarnation itself, the becoming-man of God.

In a sense, then, Kantorowicz's story already anticipates in certain ways what would appear to be a much later historical development, the passage of royal sovereignty into the body and life of the people, the "horizontal" or democratic dissemination of the dynamics of the King's Two Bodies into the domain of "popular sovereignty" and so into *everyman*. For Kantorowicz, this passage in some sense already occurs at the point where being human itself comes to appear as a kind of sacred *office* with which each member of the species is invested. But if Dante's "man-centered kingship" is given the last word, forming both a culmination and, as it turns out, an implicit point of departure and point of reference, the study as a whole—including its last, "humanist" chapter—is haunted by Kantorowicz's first use of a literary text in the book, one in which the "lower" element in the tension informing the dual nature of man is imagined not so much as *homo* mastered by a sovereign *humanitas*; to use Giorgio Agamben's favored term, it appears, rather, as a *homo sacer* left over by the dissolution of the pompous body of a king. This is not the natural human body left over once all of one's social vestments have been stripped away, but something more like the rotting flesh of the sublime body, what remains when its sublimity has wasted away.

This drama of (royal) destitution, the stages of which Kantorowicz traces in Shakespeare's *Richard II*, is all the more important given what Kantorowicz says about the playwright's responsibility for establishing the trope of the twinned nature of the king in the political imagination of the West. Here, too, Kantorowicz stresses the fundamentally human nature of the dynamics elaborated in the discourses of theology, law, and political theory. Shakespeare made manifest the complex semiotic and somatic complexity of the royal personage without the need of "the subtleties of legal speech . . . *since such a vision would arise very naturally from a purely human stratum*"; one is, in a word, freed from the historical, philological labor of establishing the bard's knowledge of and reception of legal debates, "since the image of the twinned nature of a king, *or even of man in general*, was most genuinely Shakespeare's own and proper vision" (25; my emphasis).[11] Finally, "if that curious image, which from modern constitutional thought has vanished all but completely, still has

11. In her *The Queen's Two Bodies: Drama and the Elizabethan Succession* (London: Royal Historical Society, 1977), Marie Axton argues that the doctrine of the monarch's two bodies was actually widely disseminated in the last part of the sixteenth century because of the intense preoccupation—above all, among lawyers—with the complex issues of royal succession to the "virgin Queen." The medium for this dissemination was, in part, theatrical entertainments performed by lawyers at the various inns of court.

a very real and human meaning today, this is largely due to Shakespeare. It is he who has eternalized that metaphor" (26).

As we follow Kantorowicz in his reading of *Richard II* as "the tragedy of the King's Two Bodies" (26), it is important to emphasize that the point here is not that Shakespeare allows us to see—and thus "see through"— the artifice of royalty and of political symbolism more generally, to recognize the pompous theatricality of all rites of symbolic investiture, to see in them the performative construction of social reality and so gain a safe and ironic distance from them; it seems rather that what grips us in the work is a function of the poet's capacity to show us that there is more reality in such theatrical appearances (of the court and the theater itself) than in our everyday reality, that our inner life is deeply informed by the logic of those appearances, by the circulation of some "real" in them qua theater of appearances. The point is thus not, as Kantorowicz himself at times seems tempted to conclude, the realization that the world of politics is, just like theater, organized by manmade fictions and so not real, not grounded in anything substantial, but rather that in such fictions we might discover some truth about our own inner lives, fantasies, moral commitments, political passions, might catch a glimpse of the substance that sustains their uncanny vitality.[12]

This is one of the areas where I differ with some of the recent critical literature on *The King's Two Bodies*. Victoria Kahn, in her compelling discussion of his work, suggests that Kantorowicz's treatment of both Shakespeare and the English Revolution—including the beheading of Charles—illustrates the ways in which the fundamental argument of the book links it to a tradition of liberal constitutionalism. As she puts it, "*The King's Two Bodies* shows how the idea of the two bodies could morph into the distinction between person and office, which in turn played a crucial role in the dethroning of Charles I in 1649. If charisma is one effect of the king's two bodies, the other is—at least in the long run—constitutionalism."[13] Although I think that Kahn's reading is much more sensitive to the complexities of Kantorowicz's argument than those that see in *The*

12. I will return to the question of the "real" of Shakespeare's theater in chapter 5, when I address Carl Schmitt's essay *Hamlet or Hecuba*.

13. Victoria Kahn, "Political Theology and Fiction in *The King's Two Bodies*," *Representations* 106 (Spring 2009): 79. Marie Axton had already noted that some of the figures involved in the legal elaboration and theatrical dissemination of the doctrine of the two bodies—including Edmund Plowden—were Catholics appointed by Mary Tudor who had a vested interest in minding the gap between Elizabeth and her crown. "It is understandable that these men should seek to minimize the personal impact of the new sovereign and should emphasize the continuity of the monarchy in their professional work. . . . The judges affirmed their allegiance by exalting the Queen's body politic while at the same time they frustrated the wishes of her body natural" (*Queen's Two Bodies*, 16).

King's Two Bodies some form or other of an unreconstructed *Führer*-cult, I have a quarrel with what she ultimately takes to be the saving grace of the work, namely its focus on the fictive dimension of the political theological institutions at issue.[14] As she summarizes her thesis, "Kantorowicz finds in literature an exemplary self-consciousness about the symbolic dimension of human experience, about the human capacity to make and unmake symbolic forms."[15] This leads Kahn to the vision of a progressive, liberal humanism, one ultimately grounded in aesthetic education, or *Bildung* (albeit one that has digested some of the lessons of deconstruction with regard to the reading of figural language): "In modern terms, we might say that, in Kantorowicz's reading of Shakespeare and Dante, literature reveals both its capacity for ideological critique and for enabling fictions of human community. It can serve as an antidote to political theology of the Schmittian sort, even as it authorizes a new vision—a new 'secular political theology,' to borrow Kantorowicz's phrase—of the human community."[16] As I have been arguing, political theology of every kind involves not only what Kahn refers to as enabling fictions but also, and perhaps more importantly, their more ambivalent and recalcitrant *underside of fantasy*. In a word, the point is not that Shakespeare helps us to see through the theatrical and rhetorical machinery at work in all political theology—that he leads us down the yellow-brick road toward the unmasking of the Master of Oz, toward the discovery that the emperor is naked. The point is rather to acknowledge that there is more political theology in everyday life than we might have ever thought, though it is surely much more difficult to identify in the absence of the body of a royal personage where it could be focused and dramaturgically

14. Kahn's approach is at least in part intended as a critique of those who see in *The King's Two Bodies* a direct link to Kantorowicz's earlier literary and political career in Germany, one in which he not only participated in the culturally conservative circle of writers and intellectuals around Stefan George but also took part in paramilitary actions against the left in the armed struggles following World War I. David Norbrook, for example, suggests that *The King's Two Bodies*, though written in the United States after Kantorowicz's forced emigration from Germany (he was a Jew whose own mother perished in a concentration camp), continues to be steeped in the poetry of power and the cult of the imperial body that informed the author's earlier study of Frederick II, a book that had a considerable following among the Nazi elite. Following Sander Gilman's lead, Norbrook even suggests that this "cult of the human-divine body offered a release from the waves of anti-Semitic propaganda against the deformities of the Jewish body." David Norbrook, "The Emperor's New Body? *Richard II*, Ernst Kantorowicz, and the Politics of Shakespeare Criticism," *Textual Practices* 10, no. 2 (1996): 334. Norbrook goes on to claim that Kantorowicz's reading of *Richard II* as a tragedy belongs to a tradition of counterrevolutionary interpretations of the play that link Richard's deposition to the "tragic" fate of Charles I.

15. Kahn, "Political Theology and Fiction," 81.

16. Ibid.

elaborated. And indeed, this truth seems to become most poignantly tangible in what Kantorowicz calls the "rite of degradation" (36) performed on Richard, a process "cascading," he says, "from kingship to kingship's 'Name,' and from the name to the naked misery of man" (27).[17]

What Shakespeare sets before us is a vision of what Walter Benjamin has argued was central to the conception of seventeenth-century theater more generally, namely the uncanny proximity of the *sovereign* and the *creature*, of the former's mode of, to use a Lacanian locution, *extimate-belonging* and the latter's mode of *intimate nonbelonging*.[18] Kantorowicz elsewhere refers to this transformation as a *metamorphosis* from "Realism" to "Nominalism" and finally to a state of wretchedness akin to what Schreber characterized as becoming-*Luder* (29). What appears at the end of such a metamorphosis—and one should also hear the Kafkan resonances of this word—is not the natural, animal body left over once the symbolic trappings that had been "encrusted" upon it have been fully removed, but rather a glimpse of what remains once one's entitlements to enjoyment have been reduced to the minimal one to *enjoy bare life*. What remains at the end of Richard's degradation is the appearance of the semio-somatic surplus that comes to amplify the human body when it is invested with a symbolic office, as minimally conceived as that office might be. What remains at the zero-level of investiture is, so to speak, just the fleshly substance of this surplus. This is, of course, hardly the humanism Dante had in mind, though Kantorowicz's pairing of the two writers in the organization of his book would seem to suggest that it is something that cannot fail to haunt every form of humanism.

In each stage of Richard's deposition, Shakespeare bears witness to a wretchedness—a *Ludertum*—that is both more and less, "higher" and "lower," than the naked misery of mere animal life, not because humans are unable to live as animals, but because this wretchedness is correlated with the dynamics of positing, posing, and deposing at work in the

17. Here one might recall Lacan's characterization of the process of foreclosure or refusal at work in Schreber's psychosis: "the lack of the Name-of-the-Father in that place which, by the hole that it opens up in the signified, sets off a cascade of reworkings of the signifier from which the growing disaster of the imaginary proceeds, until the level is reached at which signifier and signified stabilize in a delusional metaphor." Jacques Lacan, "On a Question Prior to Any Possible Treatment of Psychosis," in *Ecrits: A Selection*, trans. Bruce Fink (New York: Norton, 2002), 207. It is perhaps worth noting that Lacan was working on the Schreber material in the same years (the mid to late 1950s) when Kantorowicz was completing *The King's Two Bodies*.

18. Benjamin makes his case in his *The Origin of German Tragic Drama*, trans. John Osborne (London: NLB, 1977). I return to these peculiar topological figures below when I discuss Agamben's work in more detail.

institution of kingship. Apropos of Richard's speech invoking "sad stories of the death of kings," Kantorowicz suggests that this "long procession of tortured kings passing review before Richard's eyes" points to the possibility of an inversion at the very heart of kingship: "The king that 'never dies' here has been replaced by *the king that always dies* and suffers death more cruelly than other mortals" (30; my emphasis). The immortality of the King reveals itself to be a kind of death drive immanent to the very station of kingship. The frantic and comedic aspect of this uncanny reversal—never dying/ever dying—is brought to the fore in the scene at Flint Castle in which Shakespeare "conjures up the image of another human being, the Fool . . . whom the poet otherwise introduces so often as counter-type of lords and kings." Here the Fool's presence allows Richard himself to play "fool of his royal self and fool of kingship. Therewith, he becomes *somewhat less* than merely 'man' or . . . 'king body natural.'" As "a fool playing king, and a king playing fool . . . Richard . . . is capable of . . . playing to the end . . . *the comedy of his brittle and dubious kingship*" (33; my emphasis). In the end, this peculiar status that is "somewhat less than merely 'man' or . . . 'king body natural'" is correlated with namelessness: "I have no name. . . . /And know not now what name to call myself" (4.1.245 ff.; cited in Kantorowicz, 37). We have entered here into that uncanny domain that Hannah Arendt, some years earlier, had elaborated as the state of the *stateless* produced, according to her own analysis, by the paradoxes of sovereignty once its center of gravity had moved from the court into the life of the people and their respective nation-states. Her great insight in the context of twentieth-century political transformations was that being rendered "merely human" results in becoming something *less than human and yet not simply animal*. Much as in the case of those rendered stateless in the wake of the wars and revolutions of the early twentieth century—and I will return to Arendt's analysis below—Richard's deposition is correlated with his exposure to a dimension of lawlessness immanent to the dynamics of sovereignty and sovereign succession that we have come to know as the state of exception or emergency, one that becomes manifest in the (state of) emergence of the new sovereign, Bolingbroke.

Richard's "tragedy of dual personality" reaches its climax in the mirror scene in act 4 in which "dissolves both his bankrupt majesty and his nameless manhood" (Kantorowicz, 39). Richard shatters the mirror when he can no longer recognize himself in it, when he is no longer able to see in it "the pompous body politic of king, of the God-likeness of the Lord's deputy elect, of the follies of the fool, and even of the most human griefs residing in inner man" (40). What remains at the end of Richard's "catop-tromancy" is too horrible to bear, "the banal face and insignificant *physis* of a miserable man, a *physis* now void of any metaphysis whatsoever." It is, Kantorowicz continues, "both less and more than Death. It is the *demise* of Richard, and the rise of a new body natural" (40).

But might we not here agree with Bolingbroke that what ultimately horrifies Richard is not simply the reflection of a miserable human body deprived of its sublimity but rather a kind of shadow or stain in the mirror, the dark matter of a kind of negative or abyssal sublime, precisely what can *not* be fully reflected in the mirror and yet is there with a thing-like density and insistence?[19] Kantorowicz points in this direction when he notes that Richard's deposition is itself a kind of "inverted rite . . . a long agonizing ceremony in which the order of coronation is reversed" (36), a rite performed with "sacramental solemnity, since the ecclesiastical ritual of undoing the effects of consecration is no less solemn or of less weight than the ritual which has built up the sacramental dignity" (35). Richard's deposition is, in other words, a kind of radical consecration, one that initiates him into the *unheimlich* office of bare or "sacred" life.

The German word for "horror," *Entsetzen,* which literally means to de-pose or de-posit, did indeed at one time signify the act of removing someone from a position of authority, the undoing of their *Einsetzung* or investiture. Among the first definitions listed in the entry for *Entsetzen* in the Grimm Dictionary is one that refers to the king's capacity to install (*setzen*) and depose (*entsetzen*) bishops, thereby putting us in the very midst of the Investiture Struggle between Church and State.[20] Horror thus places us in a semantic field of violent actions pertaining to the constitution and de-constitution of political and social realities; it can be understood as the experience of being violently thrown, removed, torn from one's position or place, of an undoing—a *flaying*—of one's symbolic skin. The crucial point, however, is that this deprivation manifests an uncanny positivity: the production of a horrible surplus that exceeds the "wretchedness" of mere animal life. What is exposed/produced in the course of this deposition is not simply the natural body of the king deprived of his superbody but rather the leftover of sublime flesh previously figured by that representational corporeality. The rites of degradation

19. "Bolingbroke: The shadow of your sorrow hath destroyed/The shadow of your face." 4.1.282–83.

20. The entry reads: "dem herrn und gebieter steht es zu, diener zu setzen und entsetzen; der könig setzet und entsetzet etliche bischöfe." Cited in the online version of Grimm Dictionary, http://germazope.uni-trier.de/Projects/DWB.

metamorphose the body of the *sovereign* not into that of an animal but into that of a monstrous *creature*.[21]

V

Once more, the guiding hypothesis of this volume is that the fundamental dynamics and features of the "physiology" of the sovereign elaborated by Kantorowicz—including the intimate structural relations of sublimity and horror, of the pompous body of the king and the *entsetzlich* body of the creature—do not disappear from the world once the place of the royal personage has been emptied and the principle of sovereignty relocated in the will, life, and fate of the "People." As I have already noted, though working within a quite different theoretical framework and coming from the opposite end of the political spectrum, another German-Jewish refugee formed in the crucible of Weimar Germany, Hannah Arendt, reached conclusions about the political life of modernity that could be read as the elaboration of the fate of the sovereign's two bodies in the space of postmonarchical European politics, that is, in a world without kings but only "People" and their leaders.

Arendt presented the broad outlines of this analysis in her *Origins of Totalitarianism*, published only six years before *The King's Two Bodies*. As we might expect, she locates the crucial moment in this "politico-semiotic" history in the late eighteenth century. With the loss of authority—in France, with the decapitation—of the monarch, the existence of a common interest and focal point of social identity transcending class antagonisms could no longer be sustained by the figure of the sovereign, the really existing "general equivalent" for subjects of the realm. The flesh of the social bond found its new locus of representational corporeality in the national community. What emerges with the disappearance of

---

21. For compelling readings of German baroque dramas that stage their own versions of such rites of degradation, see Koschorke et al., *Der fiktive Staat*, especially 141–50. In their discussion of Andreas Gryphius's drama *Carolus Stuardus*, the authors characterize the bare or naked life that remains of the sovereign as an abject corporeality that condenses into its flesh the abyssal dynamics of force and violence at the heart of the operations of sovereignty: "Just as the figures charged with sustaining the legitimacy of early absolutism are unable to repress into invisibility the circle of violence and counter-violence on which all political power depends, so does the *figura* of the suffering Christ who was meant to guarantee the transcendental warrant of that power find itself haunted by the demonic presence of another body: the body that is unredeemably naked [*heillos nackt*] and whose demise can no longer be masked or clothed by way of figures of incorporation/embodiment [*korporative Figuren*]" (150). What becomes manifest in a human being rendered "*heillos nackt*" is, I am arguing, no longer simply a vulnerable body but rather the spectral materiality of the *flesh*.

what Kantorowicz refers to as "polity-centered Kingship" is, in a word, a *nation-centered Polity*—the modern nation-state.

The authority and legitimacy of the state, which at a formal-legal level represents each citizen for all other citizens, was itself now seen to be "rooted" in the soil of a particular territory and in the linguistic and cultural resources linked to it. To be *enjoyed* in the full and complex sense of that word, membership in the polity required a form of "naturalization" that could, however, no longer be secured by reference to the pompous body of the king and the dynamics of his representational corporeality; the passage from early modern *subject* to modern *citizen* was thus supplemented, from the beginning, by the qualification of *national* identity.

The relocation of the fundamental point of reference and general equivalence, of the "carnal" operator of the symbolic and imaginary unification of states (from monarch to national community or *People*), which now become *nation-states* proper, had its violent primal scene in the French Revolution. For Arendt, the contradiction thereby inscribed within the constitution of the nation-state—the Declaration of the Rights of Man serves here as her proof text—proved to be fateful: "The secret conflict between state and nation came to light at the very birth of the modern nation-state, when the French Revolution combined the declaration of the Rights of Man with the demand for national sovereignty. The same essential rights were at once claimed as the inalienable heritage of all human beings *and* as the specific heritage of specific nations, the same nation was at once declared to be subject to laws, which supposedly would flow from the Rights of Man, *and* sovereign, that is, bound by no universal law and acknowledging nothing superior to itself."[22] Among the fateful consequences of this contradiction was that "from then on human rights were protected and enforced only as national rights and that the very institution of a state, whose supreme task was to protect and guarantee man his rights as man, as citizen and as a national, lost its legal, rational appearance" (230–31). The path was now open to all species of political romanticism; the institution of the state could now "be interpreted . . . as the nebulous representative of a 'national soul' which through the very fact of its existence was supposed to be beyond or above the law. National sovereignty, accordingly, lost its original connotation of freedom of the people and was being surrounded by *a pseudomystical aura of lawless arbitrariness*" (231; my emphasis). The very entity that was

22. Hannah Arendt, *The Origins of Totalitarianism* (New York: Harcourt Brace, 1975), 230. Subsequent references are made in the text.

to guarantee the rule of law thus itself occupied a domain above or beyond the law; the seemingly *given* or natural *particular*—the nation or the People—was in some sense "higher" than or above the *universal*, the law as *constituted*.

To enjoy the protection of the laws of the state, one had, in other words, to be seen to be an authorized participant in, to be *authentically animated* by, the life of the nation, a sphere or dimension that thereby formed a kind of quasi-natural, quasi-mystical—and so extralegal—supplement to the formal-legal authority of the state. A charismatic dimension of extralegality that had formally been located (no doubt always precariously and problematically) in the body of the king qua *lex animata* and that served to underwrite and animate the effectivity of law, to schematize its points of contact with living subjects, and to secure its perpetuity thereby shifted, Arendt argues, to the life of the nation and the body of the *People*. This peculiar supplement, of course, eventually came to be located not only in the geographically rooted culture, language, and folkways of the group but also in the "germinative plasma" of the thereby racialized members of the community.[23] The early modern clergy and court officials who, as Kantorowicz relates, theatrically attended to the effigy representing the "second body" of the king after the burial of his mortal remains, found their modern avatars among those men of science and medicine—the ultimate biocrats—who worked to isolate and protect the charismatic "stuff" or "matter" of general equivalence enjoyed by members of the race. The halls of records containing the birth certificates and other documents authenticating a person as rightfully enjoying the title and claim of Aryan racial heritage thus became, in the Nazi period, the primary locus of the "archive fever" contracted in the search to be accredited or certified—in German: to be *beglaubigt*, made believable—as a proper and legitimate member of the relevant social group.[24]

Among the more compelling observations Arendt makes in the course of her analysis of this shift is that in the great multinational empires of nineteenth-century Europe (Austria-Hungary and Russia), empires in which the "life of the People" formed the ideological kernel of the Pan-Germanic and Pan-Slavic movements, the "pseudomystical aura

23. I refer here again to the French eugenic thinker Vacher de Lapouge, cited in Roberto Esposito, *Bios: Biopolitics and Philosophy*, trans. Timothy Campbell (Minneapolis: University of Minnesota Press, 2008), 142.

24. I am alluding here to Jacques Derrida's important reflections on the concept of the archive and its relation to the psychoanalytic understanding of subject formation and the transmission of historical experience: *Archive Fever: A Freudian Impression*, trans. Eric Prenowitz (Chicago: University of Chicago Press, 1996).

of lawless arbitrariness" associated with that life force became the distinguishing feature of the *bureaucracy*. That is, in these empires the quasinaturalness of the people and the anonymous, machinelike functioning of bureaucratic administration seemed, paradoxically, to converge. Arendt's remarks on the bureaucracy of these still pretotalitarian empires in many ways already capture the features that culminated, during the Nazi period, in that radicalization of biopolitical administration that transformed all state institutions into one form or other of *thanato-political biocracy*.

As Arendt notes, neither the life of the people nor the decrees of bureaucratic administration are in need of justification. Both appear "to flow from some over-all ruling power" (243). Moreover, what Arendt says about the bureaucrat would seem to apply equally well to members of one of the pan-movements caught up in the surge of collective energy: "The bureaucrat, who by merely administering decrees has the illusion of constant action, feels tremendously superior to these 'impractical' people who are forever entangled in 'legal niceties' and therefore stay outside the sphere of power which to him is the source of everything" (243–44).[25] In modern bureaucracy just as in the life of national peoples, we are confronted with a new and dynamic locus of the incarnation of power and authority; in both we are confronted with a political entity or "corporation" that lives in—or perhaps better, lives off of—a kind of *perpetual state of exception*:

It is true that decrees are used by all governments in times of emergency, but then the emergency itself is a clear justification and automatic limitation. In governments by bureaucracy decrees appear in their *naked purity* as though they were no longer issued by powerful men, but were *the incarnation of power itself* and the administrator only its accidental agent. There are no general principles which simple reason can understand behind the decree, but ever-changing circumstances which only an expert can know in detail. People ruled by decree never know what rules them because of the impossibility of understanding decrees in themselves. (244; my emphasis)[26]

25. These passages seem to challenge, *avant la lettre*, Arendt's later writings about the "banality of evil"; here Arendt seems more finely attuned to the ways in which bureaucracy itself serves as a locus of the most intense, not to say sublime, sorts of passions. In a word, bureaucracy can itself function as the key locus of a *radical movement*.

26. Some of what Arendt says about bureaucracy recalls Kantorowicz's discussion of the consolidation of policies of taxation in early modern Europe. By the fourteenth century, "taxation, formerly linked to an unrepeatable event, now was linked to the calendar, to the eternally rolling wheel of Time. The state had become permanent, and permanent were its emergencies and needs, its *necessitas*." In other words, "the notion of *necessitas* began to be focused . . . upon the ordinary and (so to speak) budgetary needs of administration; and to meet these administrative needs the governments

We are thereby returned to the "mystical" dimension that Arendt first associated with the political romanticism of the national community: "And it is this pseudomysticism that is the stamp of bureaucracy when it becomes a form of government. Since the people it dominates never really know why something is happening, and a rational interpretation of laws does not exist, there remains only one thing that counts, the brutal naked event itself. What happens to one then becomes subject to an interpretation whose possibilities are endless" (245). We are here, as Arendt very quickly notes, in the element we have come to associate with the work of Franz Kafka, a writer who "knew well enough the superstition of fate which possesses people who live under the perpetual rule of accidents, the inevitable tendency to read a special superhuman meaning into happenings whose rational significance is beyond the knowledge and understanding of the concerned" (245–46).

One registers here a peculiar split within the notion of the "people." "People" signifies first and foremost the privileged national community, the set of those who, by right of birth (or by way of the relevant procedures of "naturalization"), *enjoy the entitlements* of citizenship; they are thus those who are entitled—indeed, even enjoined—to enjoy, to partake in that "pseudomysticism of lawless arbitrariness" that Arendt addresses in her remarks on political romanticism. But "people" also very clearly points to those who are most radically and intimately *exposed* to this lawless arbitrariness, to the "brutal naked event" of bureaucratic administration (Kafka's protagonist Josef K. shows us what it means to become a "man of the people" in this second sense). Citing other writings by Arendt, Giorgio Agamben addresses this split within the concept of the "people" at the conclusion of his own study of sovereignty (and the lawlessness immanent to it in the figure of the state of emergency or exception), noting that in several European languages the term *people* signifies "the poor, the disinherited, and the excluded." "One term," Agamben continues, "thus names both the constitutive political subject and the class that is, de facto if not de jure, excluded from politics."[27] He goes on to make the more general claim that this semantic ambiguity belongs to the larger history of Western politics that over and over and in one way or another persists in producing a cleavage within the very concept—and body—of the "people":

---

arrived at the new fiction of a *perpetua necessitas,* implying (not unlike the modern tenets of 'perpetual revolution') the perpetuation of something that, by definition, indicated an exception, some singular condition or some momentary deviation from the rule" (Kantorowicz, 286).

27. Giorgio Agamben, *Homo Sacer. Sovereign Power and Bare Life,* trans. Daniel Heller-Roazen (Stanford, CA: Stanford University Press, 1998), 176. Subsequent references are made in the text.

It is as if what we call "people" were in reality not a unitary subject but a dialectical oscil-lation between two opposite poles: on the one hand, the set of the People as a whole political body, and on the other, the subset of the people as a fragmentary multiplicity of needy and excluded bodies; or again, on the one hand, an inclusion that claims to be total, and on the other, an exclusion that is clearly hopeless; at one extreme, the total state of integrated and sovereign citizens, and at the other, the preserve—court of miracles or camp—of the wretched, the oppressed, and the defeated. (177)

Agamben concludes by drawing this pattern of semantic self-division (an example of what Freud called the antithetical meanings of primal words [exemplified by the word "cleave" itself]) into the orbit of terms that frame his political thought more broadly:

But this also means that the constitution of the human species in a political body passes through a fundamental division and that in the concept of "people" we can easily recognize the categorical pairs that . . . define the original political structure: bare life (people) and political existence (People), exclusion and inclusion, zoē and bios. The "people" thus always already carries the fundamental biopolitical fracture within itself. It is what cannot be included in the whole of which it is a part and what cannot belong to the set in which it is always already included. (177–78)

VI

Here, as throughout *Homo Sacer*, Agamben is drawing on—and histori-cally and conceptually generalizing—one of Arendt's most important contributions in her own study of the history of the modern nation-state. Agamben's claim is, in a word, that what Arendt discovered with respect to some of the consequences of the "excarnation" of sovereign rule and the "national" redistribution of the substance previously localized in the "strange material and physical presence" of the king turns out to be pro-foundly significant for the space of politics more broadly conceived.[28] Put somewhat differently, Agamben is trying to situate Arendt's work more deeply in the political theological tradition traced out by Kantoro-wicz, though with somewhat different theoretical emphases. No doubt among the most striking passages in *Origins of Totalitarianism* are those pertaining to what Arendt perceives as the emergence of a new class of people, whose numbers began to grow in the wake of World War I and

28. Once more, this is Foucault's formulation from *Discipline and Punish: The Birth of the Prison*, trans. Alan Sheridan (New York: Vintage, 1977), 208.

"whose rights were as little safeguarded by the ordinary functioning of nation-states in the middle of Europe as they would have been in the heart of Africa" (291). The emergence of this new personage that seems to embody a convergence of the most modern and the most archaic—and to represent a point of contact between Kafka and Conrad—came to signify, for Arendt, the fundamental symptom of modern politics, the point at which the inner contradictions of the nation-state congealed into a figure of fascination and repulsion. This new figure is the *stateless person*, someone whose political status is reduced to the zero-level of being simply *human.*

Because of the emergence of new political boundaries and the mass migrations of peoples in the wake of World War I and the Russian Revolution, Europe found itself confronted with vast numbers of displaced populations that could find no country into which they could be assimilated and no territory where they could establish a new community and enjoy the legal benefit of fundamental rights. "This first loss," Arendt writes, "which the rightless suffered was the loss of their homes, and this meant the loss of the entire social texture into which they were born and in which they established for themselves a distinct place in the world" (293). But a second loss turns the screw on the fate of displacement:

The second loss . . . was the loss of government protection, and this did not imply just the loss of legal status in their own, but in all countries. Treaties of reciprocity and international agreements have woven a web around the earth that makes it possible for the citizen of every country to take his legal status with him no matter where he goes. . . . Yet whoever is no longer caught in it finds himself out of legality altogether (thus during the last war stateless people were invariably in a worse position than enemy aliens who were still indirectly protected by their governments through international agreements). (294)

For Arendt, the crucial test as to whether one truly finds oneself at such a frontier of law is whether one can in some sense improve one's condition by committing a crime, thereby acquiring a minimum level of visibility before—or rather, now within—the law.[29] As we have already noted, at this frontier where one seems to be outside the purview of all particular laws, one is, paradoxically, most radically exposed to—positioned *before—*

---

29. "Only as an offender against the law can he gain protection from it. As long as his trial and his sentence last, he will be safe from that arbitrary police rule against which there are no lawyers and no appeals. The same man who was in jail yesterday because of his mere presence in the world . . . may become almost a full-fledged citizen because of a little theft" (Arendt, 286).

the pure force of law as such. It is the *entsetzlich* "positivity" created by this negativity or deprivation that Agamben most often refers to as *bare life* and that I have called *creaturely life*—a dimension *created*, in a word, by a process of destitution. We might put it this way: what Kantorowicz presents as the *entsetzlich* state of Richard II at the culmination of his deposition becomes a defining feature of the "form of life" of entire populations.

The true calamity of the stateless, who until early in the twentieth century could still be absorbed here and there by way of exceptional grants of asylum, a practice that became impracticable with the growing numbers of such people produced by the crises of war and revolution—that is, once the exceptional situation of statelessness became chronic—is, Arendt writes, "not that they are deprived of life, liberty, and the pursuits of happiness, or of equality before the law and freedom of opinion—formulas which were designed to solve problems *within* given communities—but that they no longer belong to any community whatsoever. Their plight is not that they are not equal before the law, but that no law exists for them" (295–96). As Arendt notes, even the Nazis sought, by means of law, to isolate the Jews within this juridical no-man's-land before embarking on their project of extermination. "The point is that a condition of complete rightlessness was created before the right to live was challenged" (296). The object of extermination is then an *entsetzlich* creature and the process of elimination one of disposing of already abject flesh: *Judentum* becomes collapsed into *Ludertum*.

The logic of this argument confronts us with the disturbing thought that even humanitarian interventions into the plight of the stateless (and so rightless) in some sense confirm their paradoxical "political" status as being *merely human*, of enjoying only the "the abstract nakedness of being human and nothing but human" (297). Such interventions in some sense serve to consolidate the paradox "involved in the loss of human rights, [namely] that such loss coincides with the instant when a person becomes a human being in general . . . *and* different in general, representing nothing but his own absolutely unique individuality which, deprived of expression within and action upon a common world, loses all significance" (302). This deprivation of a space in the world in which opinions can be significant and actions effective—this radical *poverty in world*—brings to a head the paradox Arendt first noted in the very wording of the Declaration of the Rights of Man:

If a human being loses his political status, he should, according to the implications of the inborn and inalienable rights of man, come under exactly the situation for which the declarations of such general rights provided. Actually the opposite is the case. It seems that a man who is nothing but a man has lost the very qualities which make it possible for other people to treat him as a fellow-man. This is one of the reasons why it is far more difficult to destroy the legal personality of a criminal, that is, of a man who has taken upon himself the responsibility for an act whose consequences now determine his fate, than a man who has been disallowed all common human responsibilities. (300)

Arendt's former teacher, friend, and lover, Martin Heidegger, had, in his lecture course of 1929–30, characterized the being of animals by the notion of *poverty in world*. As he famously put it, stones are without world, animals are poor in world, and humans are world-forming.[30] What Arendt is addressing in these passages is a possibility of human life, one that seemed to become painfully real and actual for large masses of people in the wake of war and revolution in twentieth-century Europe, that brings human beings into an uncanny proximity to this condition of radical poverty in world, a proximity that Arendt indeed characterizes as a "peculiar state of nature" (300). Where Arendt goes wrong is where she loses site of precisely the *peculiarity* of this nature, that is, when she refers to it as "the dark background of mere givenness, the background formed by our unchangeable and unique nature" (301). This is also the problem with Agamben's at times confusing treatment of the notion of "bare life." Just as in the case of the degradation of the sovereign as displayed by Shakespeare in *Richard II* (this "tragedy of the King's Two Bodies," as Kantorowicz called it), what appears with the emergence of the stateless is not simply the wretchedness of the human animal stripped of his or her social insignia; what appears is rather a bit of the *flesh* of the social bond itself, the stuff that the body of the sovereign was formerly charged with figuratively—and often theatrically—incorporating. We are confronted here not with *zoē* separated out from *bios* but with the stuff of the enigmatic jointure of *zoē* and *bios*, the surplus secreted where biological existence is converted into the minimal office that entitles and enjoins one to "enjoy" life. That is what makes the figure of the sovereign at his zero-degree of *kingship* and that of the stateless at their point of becoming "merely human"—of their zero-degree of human *kinship*—so *entsetzlich*, so monstrously creaturely. I would even say that efforts to posit this zero-

30. Martin Heidegger, *The Fundamental Concepts of Metaphysics: World, Finitude, Solitude*, trans. William McNeill and Nicholas Walker (Bloomington: Indiana University Press, 1995). I discuss Heidegger's notion of poverty in world in my *On Creaturely Life: Rilke, Benjamin, Sebald* (Chicago: University of Chicago Press, 2006).

degree of human kinship as an opening or passage to our "animal nature" function as a kind of screen or defense against the anxiety provoked by the proximity of creaturely life.

VII

As I have suggested, Giorgio Agamben has seized upon some of Arendt's crucial insights and arguments concerning the breakdown products of the system of nation-states and transformed them into the basis of a general theory about the relations between sovereignty and the vital sphere, the bodies and lives of those caught up in the political sets articulated by the operations of sovereign power in its multiple forms and guises. The general theory, which rightly or wrongly takes as its own historical point of departure Roman antiquity, itself culminates in a recapitulation of Arendt's primary thesis about the shift in the locus of sovereignty in the eighteenth century.[31]

The key concept that allows for the generalization of a political symptom of modernity—the condition of the stateless as analyzed by Arendt—into a general theory of sovereignty is that of the *state of exception*, one touched on by Arendt in her discussion of the practice of rule by decree that comes to inform the bureaucracies of modern nation-states. Agamben repeats, at some level, Marx's fundamental gesture. On the basis of the condition of the proletariat, of man reduced to the vital energies of his labor power—the figure of the "stateless" in the sphere of politico-economic relations—Marx posits all of human history as a struggle over the domination of that power, a struggle that comes to the fore in its purity only under conditions of modernity. In the same way, Agamben posits the "biopolitical" substance of the figure of the stateless as the "stuff" that has always been at stake in the history of sovereignty in the West. What is ultimately at issue is the way in which political power (as opposed to capital, with Marx) is able to appropriate a *surplus of flesh* to shore up its legitimacy, to transform *mere* power into *sovereign* power. For Agamben, the state of exception functions as a kind of production site of the flesh, this fundamentally ambivalent materiality that is, in starkly contrasting ways, invested in the body of the sovereign as well as of the *homo sacer*.

---

31. Although Agamben begins his history of sovereignty and the state of exception in Rome, he argues that the philosophical origins of his story lie in the Greek distinction between *zoē* and *bios*.

Here I might recall my concerns regarding Esposito's analysis of bio-politics. I expressed the worry that his use of the paradigm of immuniza-tion had a tendency to lose sight of the difference between *the protection of life* and the *administration of the flesh*. I have a similar worry about Agamben's use of the notions of "bare life" and *homo sacer* as the dimen-sion at issue in the state of exception. What accounts for the intimacy of the sovereign and the *homo sacer*—or as I prefer to put it, the sovereign and the *creature*—is that they are both distinctive bearers of the flesh, those who serve to figure, in radically different ways, the jointure of bod-ies and various forms and levels of normativity. It was Freud's great dis-covery, elaborated in detail in the work of Lacan, that when bodies are joined to language, one always gets stuck with an uncanny remainder representing a third dimension, a surplus of flesh that belongs to nei-ther yet secures the jointure of the two domains. As the privileged bearer and, as it were, "master" of the flesh, the sovereign is in a fundamentally precarious position; the sovereign is subject, in a singular fashion, to a radical ontological vulnerability whereby a form of life can become hor-ribly *informe*. This is what is registered in the *entsetzlich* rhythm of the rites of degradation suffered by Shakespeare's Richard II and described in such poignant detail by Kantorowicz. Richard's sublime "second body" does not disappear into thin air or get passed on, without remainder, to Bolingbroke; it persists as the flesh of the creature he has become.[32]

It is in this context that one must read Agamben's recapitulation of Arendt's claims regarding the threshold of modernity:

Declarations of rights must . . . be viewed as the place in which the passage from divinely authorized royal sovereignty to national sovereignty is accomplished. This passage assures the *exceptio* of life in the new state order that will succeed the collapse of the *ancien régime*. The fact that in this process the "subject" is . . . transformed into a "citizen" means that birth—which is to say, bare natural life as such—here for the first time becomes (thanks to a transformation whose biopolitical consequences we are

---

32. It is against this background that one can fully appreciate one of Hans Jürgen Syberberg's dramaturgical innovations in his film version of Wagner's *Parsifal*. Syberberg displaces the wound from the side of the suffering Fisher King and externalizes it as a kind of organ without body, a bit of living flesh ritualistically displayed and carried about on a pillow. In a discussion of the opera and the film that has informed much of my own thinking, Slavoj Žižek has furthermore insisted that "the fundamental problem of *Parsifal* is eminently a *bureaucratic* one: the incapacity, the in-competence of Amfortas in performing his ritual-bureaucratic duty." Žižek, *The Sublime Object of Ideology* (London: Verso, 1989), 76. We might amplify this insight by noting that at this point the bureaucrats of the Grail Society become true *biocrats*. *Parsifal* thereby becomes legible as a text in which the political theology of sovereignty and the biopolitics of modernity begin to become nearly indistinguishable.

only beginning to discern today) the immediate bearer of sovereignty. The principle of nativity and the principle of sovereignty, which were separated in the *ancien régime* (where birth marked only the emergence of a *sujet*, a subject), are now irrevocably united in the body of the "sovereign subject" so that the foundation of the new nation-state may be constituted. It is not possible to understand the "national" and biopolitical development and vocation of the modern state in the nineteenth and twentieth centuries if one forgets that what lies at its basis is not man as a free and conscious political subject but, above all, man's bare life, the simple birth that as such is, in the passage from subject to citizen, *invested with the principle of sovereignty*. (128; my emphasis)

What needs to be kept in mind here is that the body of the citizen that is invested with the principle of sovereignty is no longer an instance of *zoē*, no longer bare life in the sense of animal existence, but rather life insofar as it is posited as *bearer of the flesh*, as giving—always precarious—corporeal locus and shape to the element that holds the place of the jointure of life and law. In order to fulfill their office, discharge their charge as the new bearer of the principle of sovereignty, the people must—just as the king of the ancien régime did—undergo the ordeal of gemination, acquire a second, sublime body, one that is, as we have seen, always haunted by the *entsetzlich* possibility of becoming so much *creaturely* flesh. Modern politics is always also biopolitics not simply because the wealth of nations—the commonwealth—is now seen to reside in the well-being of its population but rather because the procedures of *Setzen* and *Entsetzen*, of positing and deposing, that formerly focused on the figure of the sovereign now transpire within the life of every citizen. In a word, the privilege and horror, the sublimity and abjection, of the flesh now belong in some sense to the fate of every member of the polity.[33]

Because modern biopolitics is, in essence, a politics of pure immanence, it has no means to address the dimension of the flesh in its spectral yet visceral insistence, as the locus of what I have characterized as a *surplus of immanence*. It must always conflate the flesh with the organs and tissues of the biological body, an error committed at times by Agamben himself in his own efforts to analyze this very phenomenon. I have

---

33. The sudden intrusion of this fate into the everyday life of the people was staged in the frenzy of terror and sacrifice that came to mark the French Revolution, a frenzy that could be seen to begin with the execution of the king and queen. As Peter-André Alt has aptly said, "the murder of the king and queen implies a sacralization of the life of the republic insofar as it introduces into it the blood that must pulsate throughout its now sovereign body." New sources of blood would, so to speak, have to be drained from the flesh of those *people* deemed to be enemies of the *People*. Peter-André Alt, "Der zerstückte Herrscher: Zur Dekonstruktion der politischen Theologie im Drama des 18. Jahrhunderts," in *Deutsche Vierteljahrsschrift für Literaturwissenschaft und Geistesgeschichte* 84, no. 10 (2010).

suggested that psychoanalysis is the one "science" that has developed an "organon" for the study of the vicissitudes of the flesh—this strange organ without body—in modernity. But I am equally convinced that numerous modernist writers and artists have discovered their own ways to elaborate these vicissitudes, to track the ways of the flesh in the everyday life of denizens of modern societies who now, in some sense, permanently dwell at the threshold between sovereign and creature. In chapter 3 I begin to unfold more explicitly the heightened responsiveness to the flesh shared by psychoanalytic thought and modernist aesthetics.

THREE

Toward a Science of the Flesh

I

In what is perhaps his most dreamlike prose text, "A Country Doctor," Franz Kafka describes in graphic detail the wound on the side of a young boy, the patient a district physician has been called to attend to in the middle of a snowy night:

> On his right side, near the hip, there is an open wound the size of a palmprint. Many shades of pink, dark in its depths and growing lighter at the edges, tender and grainy, with unevenly pooling blood, open at the surface like a mine. Thus from a distance. Close up, further complications are apparent. Who can look at that without giving a low whistle? Worms, as thick and as long as my little finger, rose-pink themselves and also blood-spattered, firmly attached to the inside of the wound, with little white heads, with many little legs, writhe up toward the light.[1]

The text is unusual for Kafka in its proximity to the sort of expressionist prose he was known to dislike, but it still very much bears the distinctive signature of the author. Here, as in so many other texts, the main character, the provincial doctor named in the title, is faced by a call he cannot fully respond to, a mandate or summons to work—call it a "charge"

---

1. Franz Kafka, "A Country Doctor," in *Kafka's Selected Stories*, trans. Stanley Corngold (New York: Norton, 2007), 63.

or "ex-citation" (from *excitare,* to call out or summon)—that turns out to be impossible to discharge. Kafka indicates in the text that there might be large, historical reasons for this impossibility, among them the preponderance of a false conception of medical knowledge and capacities in a secular world. The problem seems to be that in such a world spiritual needs now register largely as bodily, somatic disturbances: "Always asking the doctor to do the impossible. They have lost their old faith; the pastor sits at home, plucking his vestments into shreds, one after the other; but the doctor is supposed to accomplish everything with his tender, surgical hands."[2] Here a sacerdotal investiture crisis—the priest literally shreds his vestments—resonates as a bodily symptom that induces, in its turn, an *excess of demand* with respect to the medical arts, one that generates its own investiture crisis: the doctor's inability to fulfill, to satisfy the normative pressures, of his office.[3] The immediate proximity of these remarks to the characterization of the boy as being "blinded by the *life in his wound* [my emphasis]" suggests that one can begin to grasp the meaning of this palpitating life-substance and the crisis it materializes only against the background of this collapse of the spiritual into the corporeal, of transcendence into an immanence that can no longer be mastered by the available "sciences of immanence."[4]

II

One will recall that the dream that Freud himself saw as the inaugural dream of psychoanalysis—the dream in which the paradoxical "stuff" of the symptom makes a dramatic appearance—is itself a kind of parable of a "country doctor" overwhelmed by the demands of his office. Much as in the case of Kafka's provincial physician, the famous dream of Irma's in-

---

2. Ibid.

3. This exposure to an excess of demand is figured at the end of the story as the doctor's nakedness and sense of irremediable loss, betrayal, and errancy: "Naked, exposed to the frost of this unhappiest of ages, with an earthly carriage, unearthly horses. I, an old man, wander aimlessly around. My fur coat is hanging at the back of the carriage, but I cannot reach it, and not one of this agile rabble of patients lifts a finger. Betrayed! Betrayed! A false ringing of the night bell once answered—it can never be made good again." Ibid., 65.

4. In his remarks on Wagner's *Parsifal,* Slavoj Žižek, who, as we have noted, underlines the bureaucratic dimension of the Grail Society, explicitly links Kafka's text to Wagner's: "Amfortas's problem is that as long as his wound bleeds *he cannot die,* he cannot find peace in death; his attendants insist that he must do his duty and perform the Grail's ritual, regardless of his suffering, while he desperately asks them to have mercy on him and put an end to his suffering by simply killing him—exactly like the child in 'A Country Doctor,' who addresses the narrator-doctor with the desperate request: 'Doctor, let me die.'" *Sublime Object of Ideology* (London: Verso, 1989), 76.

jection stages the insufficiency of the sciences of immanence (including, first and foremost, medicine) for the treatment of hysterical symptoms. It thus marks for Freud the very birth of psychoanalysis, its emergence precisely as the "science" that is called on the scene by the hysteric's body, one that manifests a strange excess of life that both belongs and does not belong to the body in question. At one point in this dream, which for the most part circulates around Freud's concern that he might have missed some sort of purely physiological cause of Irma's suffering—and so that he himself failed to be a proper man of science, failed to satisfy the normative pressures of his office—Freud looks into his patient's mouth; what he encounters there places Irma into a kind of kinship relation with the boy in Kafka's story: "She then opened her mouth properly and on the right I found a big white patch; at another place I saw extensive whitish grey scabs upon some remarkable curly structures which were evidently modeled on the turbinal bones of the nose."[5] In the dream Freud places himself in an impossible situation, one in which he can only lose. If Irma is physically sick, then he has failed as a physician; if it is, rather, her hysterical symptoms that persist in spite of Freud's treatment, then he has failed as the inventor of a new science and therapy of psychopathology. The key to the dream ultimately lies in Freud's discovery—indeed, we might call this the inaugural, self-reflexive "finding" of psychoanalysis—of the ways in which his own mind has gotten (dis)organized around the fantasy of being found to be wanting in the face of the normative pressures of an office or a symbolic mandate.[6]

In a somewhat apocalyptic commentary on this primal scene of psychoanalysis—and indeed, citing the dream visions and interpretations of the book of Daniel—Jacques Lacan writes:

There's a horrendous discovery here, that of the flesh one never sees, the foundation of things, the other side of the head, of the face, the secretory glands *par excellence*, the flesh from which everything exudes, at the very heart of the mystery, the flesh in as much as it is suffering, is formless, in as much as its form in itself is something which provokes anxiety. Spectre of anxiety, identification of anxiety, the final revelation of *you are this—You are this, which is so far from you, this which is the ultimate formlessness.* Freud

5. Sigmund Freud, *The Interpretation of Dreams*, trans. James Strachey (New York: Avon, 1965), 139–40.

6. Jonathan Lear has underlined the centrality of this dynamic in Freud's understanding of dreams and unconscious formations more generally. See his *Freud* (New York: Routledge, 2005). My greatest debt of gratitude goes to Marcia Adler, who helped me at so many levels to understand what this dynamic looks and feels like in a lived life.

comes upon a revelation of the type, *Mene, Tekel, Peres* at the height of his need to see, to know, which was until then expressed in the dialogue of the *ego* with the object.[7]

In his seminar on *The Four Fundamental Concepts of Psychoanalysis*, Lacan returns to this flesh that one never sees and identifies it as that which Freud famously baptized as the *libido*, the very substance of human desire, the element of psychosomatic life that, if things go well enough, gets "invested" in objects in the world. Here Lacan characterizes it as the ungraspable *organ of the drive* and gives it his own name, "lamella." He also produces his own scientific myth, one that, however, belongs not so much to the tragic lineage of sacrificial practices on which Freud draws but rather to the more comedic—and, to some extent, horror—tradition of the story of the birth of human Eros as related by Aristophanes in Plato's *Symposium* (one will recall that that story involves multiple cuts and divisions of the human animal):

If you want to stress its joky side, you can call it *l'hommelette*. This *hommelette*, as you will see, is easier to animate than primal man, in whose head one always had to place a homunculus to get it working.

Whenever the membranes of the egg in which the foetus emerges on its way to becoming a new-born are broken, imagine for a moment that something flies off, and that one can do it with an egg as easily as with a man, namely the *hommelette* or the lamella.

The lamella is something extra-flat, which moves like the amoeba. It is just a little more complicated. But it goes everywhere. And as it is something . . . that is related to what the sexed being loses in sexuality, it is like the amoeba in relation to sexed beings, immortal—because it survives any division, any scissiparous intervention. And it can run around.

7. Jacques Lacan, *The Seminar of Jacques Lacan: Book II, The Ego in Freud's Theory and in the Technique of Psychoanalysis, 1954–1955*, trans. Sylvana Tomaselli (New York: Norton, 1991), 154–55. The reference to the book of Daniel is relevant not only because it is itself a book of dreams, prophetic signs, and interpretations, but also because it links such matters to the fate of kings and questions of sovereignty. Before giving King Belshazzar his interpretation of the enigmatic writing on the wall, Daniel (the name means *God is my judge*) recalls the fate of Nebuchadnezzar in terms that prefigure Shakespeare's series of "sad stories of kings," perhaps most centrally that of King Lear: "But when his heart was lifted up and his spirit was hardened so that he dealt proudly, he was deposed from his kingly throne, and his glory was taken from him; he was driven from among men, and his mind was made like that of a beast, and his dwelling was with the wild asses; he was fed grass like an ox, and his body was wet with the dew of heaven until he knew that the Most High God rules the kingdom of men, and sets over it whom he will." Daniel 5:20–21, Revised Standard Version. Daniel then provides his prophetic interpretation of the enigmatic signifiers that appeared to Belshazzar: "This is the interpretation of the matter: MENE, God has numbered the days of your kingdom and brought it to an end; TEKEL, you have been weighed in the balances and found wanting; PERES, your kingdom is divided and given to the Medes and Persians." Daniel 5:26–28.

Well! This is not very reassuring. But suppose it comes and envelops your face while you are quietly asleep. . . .

I can't see how we would not join battle with a being capable of these properties. This lamella, this organ, whose characteristic is not to exist, but which is nevertheless an organ—I can give you more details as to its zoological place—is the libido.[8]

Lacan goes on to link this uncanny creature—one that embodies, as he puts it, "immortal life . . . irrepressible life, life that has need of no organ, simplified, indestructible life," to the concept of the *object* in psychoanalysis:

It is precisely what is subtracted from the living being by virtue of the fact that it is subject to the cycle of sexed reproduction. And it is of this that all the forms of the *objet a* that can be enumerated are the representatives, the equivalents. The *objets a* are merely its representatives, its figures. The breast—as equivocal, as an element characteristic of the mammiferous organization, the placenta for example—certainly represents that part of himself that the individual loses at birth, and which may serve to symbolize the most profound lost object. I could make the same kind of reference for all the other objects. (198)

Lacan insists that the division he has in mind is not one that can be captured by a polarity grounded in an immediately legible natural substrate, that is, in any simply "given" difference between the genders. It has to do rather with the fact that human beings are caught in the dimension of "the signifier" that represents them for other signifiers, that is, that human life transpires within a space of representation, a space in which we relate to one another through the medium of titles and entitlements in and through which we earn or fail to earn recognition. It is this medium that Lacan refers to as "the field of the Other": "The subject is born in so far as the signifier emerges in the field of the Other. But, by this very fact, this subject—which was previously nothing if not a subject coming into being—solidifies into a signifier" (199). It is only because human beings must be invested with symbolic traits, must undergo, in one fashion or another, fundamental ordeals and rites of investiture—a kind of death and rebirth in the field of the Other—that they "have libido" in the first place, the capacity to enjoy by means of the strange organ Lacan calls lamella.

8. Jacques Lacan, *The Four Fundamental Concepts of Psychoanalysis*, trans. Alan Sheridan (New York: Norton, 1981), 197–98. Subsequent references are made in the text.

Against this background, we can better understand Lacan's commentary on the conclusion of Freud's Irma dream. First Freud: "Not long before, when she was feeling unwell, my friend Otto had given her an injection of a preparation of propyl, propyls . . . propionic acid . . . trimethylamin (and I saw before me the formula for this printed in heavy type). . . . Injections of that sort ought not to be made so thoughtlessly. . . . And probably the syringe had not been clean."[9] In his own interpretation of the dream, Freud himself notes that trimethylamin was a substance with a possible link to the chemistry of sexual processes: "Thus this substance led me to sexuality, the factor to which I attributed the greatest importance in the origin of the nervous disorders which it was my aim to cure."[10] But as we know, this was a cure that intervened into the peculiar "chemistry" of the libido not by way of injections (or hypnotism, or the laying on of hands) but rather by way of speech. Lacan, for his part, returns to the discourse of religion to underline precisely this dimension, the one that, again, locates the symptom and the cure in the field of the Other:

The dream, which culminated a first time, when the *ego* was there, with the horrific image I mentioned, culminates a second time at the end with a formula, with its *Mene, Tekel, Upharsin* aspect, on the wall, beyond what we cannot but identify as speech, universal rumor. . . . Like my oracle, the formula gives no reply whatsoever to anything. But the very manner in which it is spelt out, its enigmatic, hermetic nature, is in fact the answer to the question of the meaning of the dream. One can model it closely on the Islamic formula—*There is no other God but God*. There is no other word, no other solution to your problem, than the word.[11]

We are libidinal beings, that is, we desire in a human rather than an animal sense, because our enjoyment is entwined with the signifier, with titles and entitlements, with the various "offices" with which we come to be invested in the world. The strange surplus flesh that Freud called libido and that constitutes the stuff of our erotic attachments in the world is "born" from the fact that our being is compelled to unfold within a matrix of signifying representations, a field never quite made to the measure of the animal that we also are. It is this very lack of measure, this lack of fit, that opens the wound correlative to our passions and that

9. Freud, *Interpretation of Dreams*, 140.
10. Ibid., 149.
11. Lacan, *Seminar II*, 158.

accounts for the peculiar stuff of which dreams are made. Indeed, on the basis of the dream of Irma's injection, Freud proposed, in essence, that the process he called the "dream work," the unconscious elaboration of latent thoughts into the manifest content of the dream, should be understood as *the fleshing out* of the desire to satisfy the normative pressure that circulates through the field of the Other. More precisely, the dream work—and unconscious mental activity more generally—would seem to be triggered by the anxiety linked to the prospect of being caught out, of finding oneself in an extraterritorial locus *outside* of this dialectic of desire, in that uncanny place we have linked to the Kafkan topology that locates the figure caught up in the state of exception *before the law*. This is, then, not so much an anxiety about being found wanting with respect to the demands of some normative authority as it is one about *not being found at all*, of being reduced to the paradoxical status outside of any status, to the radical indignity of creaturely life.

III

Another way of getting a handle on this notion of the flesh is to return to another primal scene in Freud's writings, the famous *fort/da* game he analyzed in what is no doubt his most speculative work of metapsychology, *Beyond the Pleasure Principle*. It was, of course, in this text that Freud first elaborated in detail what Lacan characterized as the two sides of the drive and what Freud himself presented as two distinct drives, the life-affirming, unity-forming erotic drive and its dark, polar opposite, the death drive. The text as a whole comprises a series of reflections on the notion of psychic trauma, the concept that had, of course, at one time served as the key term for all of Freud's thinking about the unconscious and the neuroses. Indeed, it is generally thought that with the advent of "libido theory," Freud had more or less put to rest the "trauma theory" of symptom formation. But as we have already seen, this view is highly misleading since libido is, at some level, the very substance of a wound correlative to the emergence of the human subject (as represented by a signifier). What makes *Beyond the Pleasure Principle* such a crucial text is that it is one of the places where Freud tries to think trauma and libido together; no doubt it was this effort that led him, for better or worse, to posit the existence of an autonomous death drive.

Jonathan Lear, as part of a larger effort to overcome what he takes to be Freud's misguided insistence in this matter, has presented one of the clearest accounts of the *fort/da* game in the literature.[12] For Lear, what Freud characterizes as an autonomous drive bent on destruction and aggression should be understood, rather, as an instance of the mind's capacity, even tendency, to disrupt its own functioning when it is under pressure, when it suffers an excess, a "too much," of psychic stress. The crucial matter for Lear is what occurs in the wake of such self-disruption; what Freud observes in the game invented by his young grandson is an example of things going well after an experience of such "too-muchness." The game, the invention of (or initiation into) which Lear describes as part of the prehistory of the development of the virtue of courage, is, in his words, "prompted by a rip in the fabric of life":

If we are trying to respect the child's point of view, we cannot even say that the game is prompted by loss. For it is only after the game is installed that the child will begin to have the concept of loss or absence. Only when the game is established will the loss be a loss *for him*. The outcome of the game is to convert what would otherwise be a nameless trauma into a loss. The child had been inhabiting a less differentiated field of "mother-and-child": it is this field that is disturbed by the mother's absence. (92)

As Lear narrates the story, what happens next is that the child experiences "*internal pressure* to enact the disturbance," a "buildup of pressure" that is simply too much for the child to contain. "And now there is an enactment of self-disruption: the child throws the spool and says 'o-o-o-o.' This is a moment of self-disruption in an already disrupted life. What this disruption is *for* really depends on what happens next" (92–93). What precisely does *not* happen in the case of Freud's grandson is the development of a traumatic neurosis, a state in which, as one might imagine, he would have gotten stuck repeating the initial outburst of sounds, something that would ultimately have kept him from gathering a thought around what had happened to him. Instead, Freud's grandson finds a way to discharge his overcharged state into the space of representations, to let the too much of pressure or stress he feels become, at least in a minimal fashion, a *signifying stress*, one enacted in the form of the cultural achievement of a game played with what is at hand: a spool and a couple of signifiers, heard by Freud as *fort/da*. It is worth quoting Lear at length on this:

---

12. Jonathan Lear, *Happiness, Death, and the Remainder of Life* (Cambridge, MA: Harvard University Press, 2000). Subsequent references are made in the text.

In being able to get to "da," the child is able to bring his experience together rather than blow it apart. The invention of the game converts this rip in the fabric of experience into an experience of loss. It creates a cultural space in which the child can play with loss: in this way he comes to be able to tolerate and name it. This is an instance in which a way of functioning according to the pleasure principle and way of functioning according to the reality principle get installed at the same time. On the one hand, all sorts of playfulness and loose associations are now possible: it is only now that the mind can wander around the idea of mother's absence. On the other hand, it is only in this play that the concept of mother's absence (and reappearance) emerges. One might say that the child has either invented or joined a form of life in which mother exists as a distinct "object." . . . Inventing the game, the child thereby creates the capacity *to think* about mother's absence. It is precisely in the creation of these sorts of playful activities that a child enters the space of reasons. (94)

But as Lear quickly underscores, the form of life the child now inhabits is haunted by *the trace of a missing link*, the lack of a signifier for the initial trauma, the namelessness of the rip in the fabric of life that called forth—ex-cited—the child's creative capacities in the first place. The form of life in which we have the capacity to lose (because we have the concept and name of loss) is, we might say, *not all*:

The name of loss requires the game of loss: it requires inventing ways of living with the loss that one has just named. Once the game is established, once the child can face his loss courageously, once the mind can function according to the pleasure principle, the question of what lies beyond (or before) gets covered over. What gets hidden is the nonteleological occasion for courage: the disruption of the fabric of life to which courage can only be a retrospective response. Once the child can experience loss as a loss—that is, once the child has established the game—he is no longer experiencing that which was the occasion for the development of the capacity to experience loss. If we think of a name as standing unproblematically for that which it names, then an *inaugural* act of naming like this always misses its mark. In this sense, "facing reality" always leaves something out. (95)

And it is precisely the insight into this remainder that Lear presents as Freud's crucial contribution: "What does get left out, to put it paradoxically, is not another 'thing,' but a disturbance of the fabric of life which occasioned this further development of the capacity to face reality. Freud's deepest insight, I suspect, is that, appearances to the contrary, *life can never be lived without remainder*" (96; my emphasis). It is this paradoxical residue of a tear that forms the very flesh of psychic life, the spectral "thing" that *drives* the form of life in which it never appears and yet allows what does appear to get a (libidinal) grip on us. This is, of course, the very thing that Freud, in his later topology, found himself compelled to refer to simply as *It*.[13]

The place where I slightly disagree with Lear's presentation concerns his *narrative articulation* of the crucial moments: (1) initial tear in the fabric of life; (2) act of inaugural naming. Indeed, much of the first part of Lear's book—a discussion of the meaning of the concepts of "the good" and "happiness" in Aristotle's ethics—argues that inaugural naming, the injection of an enigmatic or oracular signifier into a form of life, can itself induce something like a trauma or tear in the fabric of that life. In a word, naming can itself produce the flesh-wound—and remainder—it is retroactively seen as serving to cover over.[14] Indeed, the case in question functions for Lear as the exemplary instance of such a paradoxical convergence of (inaugural) naming and the wound such naming would, given the presentation of the *fort/da* game, seem to serve to stitch over and thereby "heal." As he puts it apropos of Aristotle's evaluation of aristocratic virtues and their place in the good life, "On the surface it looks like the expression of a teleological worldview that only the best should live in the best way. Yet this position also expresses, as it covers over, an anomaly in the system: namely, that the human race is the only species in nature almost all of whose members are failing to flourish. This disruption of the harmonious order is caused precisely by the introduction of 'happiness' as the purported concept by which we should evaluate our lives" (57).

My "dialectical" solution to this dilemma would be to say that we are no longer dealing here with a purely epistemological problem, one pertaining to the limits of our analytic or cognitive capacities; it is, rather, one that belongs to the phenomenon itself. The undecidability in question—Does the traumatic disruption in the fabric of being come first or does the very naming meant to heal this wound also participate in the opening of the wound and, so, the production of the surplus/remainder of flesh that drives/haunts the form of life opened by the inaugural naming?—is, in a word, ontological. "Having libido" is, I am arguing, correlated to the persistence of this very undecidability, to the fact that every answer or solution to it *remains fundamentally unsatisfying*. And

---

13. Freud's term, *Es*, has, of course, been translated as *Id*.

14. As Lear puts it apropos of Aristotle's discussion of happiness, "by injecting 'happiness' as the organizing goal of human teleology Aristotle manages to disrupt the teleological structure itself" (56).

that is to say that libido, this somatically sublime and sublimely somatic element in excess of our animal being, is the very thing that both *enables and troubles* human flourishing. Put somewhat differently, the facilitation of human vitality within a field of representations is driven by an excess that has no proper place within that field; in every such "matrix" there remains a surplus. Freud's fundamental insight was that without that surplus element we would never experience questions of meaning as being genuinely *meaningful*, as being truly *worth our while*.

IV

As these remarks suggest, the difficulties generated for human flourishing by the dimension of the flesh pertain to all forms of human life and never just to individuals. Libido theory is, in other words, from the start a special kind of *social theory*. In a certain sense, then, the problem for psychoanalysis has really never been how to generalize from the level of the individual to that of the collective (this has always been the charge brought against attempts to "apply" psychoanalysis to society) but rather to show how individuals get initiated, drawn into, "seduced" by, the ways in which historical forms of life have—always precariously and provisionally—come to terms with fundamental impasses plaguing human flourishing more generally. For both the individual and the collective, the central problem pertains to a "missing link" in the genesis of human subjectivity, one that becomes manifest in our various modes of engagement in the world. At some level, the notion of a missing link never loses its connection to the evolutionary concept of a gap in the chain of species formation; only here what is missing is *constitutive* of the species in question, that is, it is something that cannot be found by further scientific research in the development of biological capacities. It pertains to the fundamental gap between animal and human flourishing, a gap that has several aspects and consequences that can each be approached from different angles.

We have already encountered one aspect of the missing link in Lear's portrayal of the difference between a nameless trauma and a genuine experience of loss. Paradoxically, in order to experience loss *as* loss—and to enter the space of the "as" more generally—we must "lose" or "miss" something along the way. We might further note that what we "lose" or "miss" in order to enjoy the capacity to *experience* loss already points to two distinct dimensions of the "missing link": the original breach in the fabric of being; the gap between the (proto-)experience of this breach and what we come to experience *as* a loss within the "space of reasons" the opening of which has been pressured or driven by the original breach. But as we have also seen, this process leaves a remainder. When we acquire the capacity to experience loss as loss, we get stuck with a strange sort of surplus—this is what Lear calls a "remainder of life" and I refer to as the *flesh*—correlated to the missing link at the genesis of this capacity, of the process that makes it ours.

The gap or missing link between a breach in the fabric of being and its status as a loss, that is, something *thinkable* within a conceptual space, already implies a second aspect that could be thought more generally as one pertaining to the emergence of language, the space of the "as." As Žižek has put it in terms borrowed from the structuralist tradition of linguistics and cultural sciences,

The very idea of a synchronous circular order . . . implies a gap, a discontinuity in its genesis: the synchronous "structure" can never be deduced from a diachronous "process" without committing a *petitio principii*. All of a sudden, by means of a miraculous leap, we find ourselves within a closed synchronous order which does not allow of any external support because it turns in its own vicious circle. This lack of support because of which language ultimately refers only to itself—in other words: this void that language circles in its self-referring—*is* the subject as "missing link." *The "autonomy of the signifier" is strictly correlative to the "subjectivization" of the signifying chain*: "subjects" are not the "effective" presence of "flesh-and-blood" agents that make use of language as part of the their social life-practice, filling out the abstract language schemes with actual contents; "subject" is, on the contrary, the very abyss that forever *separates* language from the substantial life-process.[15]

To put it in the terms I have been using here, in order to become a human subject, the "flesh-and-blood" of our existence as animals—even social animals—must be supplemented by a surplus of "flesh" that is the very stuff of a missing link or gap. *Being subject* means, in this context, to be *libidinally implicated* in the symbolic network into which, to use Heidegger's formulation, one has been contingently "thrown." If we are to feel alive to the world in the human sense, we must "grow" an excessive organ that we "enjoy" without ever truly owning it.

Elsewhere in his work, Žižek addresses the missing link as the locus of passage across the "evolutionary" gap from animal to human existence.

15. Slavoj Žižek, *For They Know Not What They Do: Enjoyment as a Political Factor* (London: Verso, 1991), 201.

Wherever this transition is in question, Žižek returns to a remarkable passage from Hegel's Jena period:

The human being is this night, this empty nothing, that contains everything in its simplicity—an unending wealth of many representations, images, of which none belongs to him—or which are not present. This night, the inner of nature, that exists here—pure self—in phantasmagorical representations, is night all around it, in which here shoots a bloody head—there another white ghastly apparition, suddenly here before it, and just so disappears. One catches sight of this night when one looks human beings in the eye—into a night that becomes awful.[16]

For Žižek, this passage concerns an "ontological necessity of 'madness,'" one that "lies in the fact that it is not possible to pass directly from the purely 'animal soul' immersed in its natural life-world to 'normal' subjectivity dwelling in its symbolic universe." He goes on to suggest that "the entire psychoanalytic experience focuses on the traces of the traumatic passage from this 'night of the world' into our 'daily' universe of *logos*," concluding that the "tension between the narrative form and the 'death drive,' as the withdrawal-into-self constitutive of the subject, is thus the missing link that has to be presupposed if we are to account for the passage from 'natural' to 'symbolic' surroundings."[17] Here, too, we encounter the now-familiar ambiguities. Is the missing link the tear in the fabric of being that opens the "night of the world" or the gap between the "night of the world" and any name we could possibly give to it, any narrative we could tell of our "awakening" from it? Again, I would suggest that the solution is that we have to fold these ambiguities (and what remains unsatisfying in all attempts to resolve them) into the phenomenon of the missing link itself.

Giorgio Agamben, in his own study of the various ways in which the human and natural sciences have attempted to locate and conceptualize this missing link from animal to human life—attempts that he subsumes under the heading of the "anthropological machine"—has characterized this "night of the world" as a sort of *conceptual* state of exception, one in which only the violence of a decision can traverse the gap in question, a violence that, however, bears unwitting witness to the gap in question. The various versions of this "machine" are, he writes,

16. Cited in *The Metastases of Enjoyment: Six Essays on Woman and Causality*, by Slavoj Žižek (London: Verso, 1994), 145.
17. Slavoj Žižek, *The Ticklish Subject: The Absent Center of Political Ontology* (London: Verso, 1999), 35.

able to function only by establishing a zone of indifference at their centers, within which—like a "missing link" which is always lacking because it is already virtually present—the articulation between human and animal, man and non-man, speaking being and living being, must take place. Like every space of exception, this zone is, in truth, perfectly empty, and the truly human being who should occur there is only the place of a ceaselessly updated decision in which the caesurae and their rearticulations are always dislocated and displaced anew. What would thus be obtained, however, is neither an animal life nor a human life, but only a life that is separated and excluded from itself—only a *bare life*.[18]

As I have been arguing, what Agamben here calls "bare life," a term he borrows from Walter Benjamin's reflections on the violence at work in the constitution of political collectivities, needs to be understood as the spectral dimension of the flesh correlative to a gap—a missing link—that haunts any narrative of the emergence of human subjectivity. In the work for which he is far better known and which we have discussed in the previous chapters, Agamben focuses almost exclusively on this political dimension of states of exception and their relation to a missing link at the foundation of all human institutions. What Žižek says about the "closed synchronic order" of language "which does not allow of any external support because it turns in its own vicious circle," applies, in a word, to the order of political institutions as well, that is, to the "closed synchronic order" of states. States of exception are the sites where, so to speak, the viciousness of the vicious circle at the core of the life of such institutions comes to the fore.

V

I have referred to the notion of the flesh as an organ not cut to the measure of the human body. In Freud's view, of course, it is the *phallus* that functions as the representative organ of this kind—as the "general equivalent" of the flesh, as the excessive organ that represents the flesh for all other organs—and symbolic castration as the "operation" by which human beings become encumbered with the workings of this surplus appendage. In the theory of castration, the missing link we have been

18. Giorgio Agamben, *The Open: Man and Animal*, trans. Kevin Attell (Stanford, CA: Stanford University Press, 2004), 37–38. As I have indicated, Agamben at times equivocates on this last point and associates bare life with animal life, thus losing sight of what I take to be his most important insight.

76

exploring up to now is registered as a kind of *missing member* (the German language nicely captures the link between the relevant meanings of "link": what is at issue is *das fehlende Glied*, a formulation that can mean either missing link or missing limb of the body).

Of particular importance are the two dimensions of castration that correspond to two different meanings of the word "enjoyment" and the ways these meanings are entwined with the notion of entitlement. As we have already noted, enjoyment can signify the enjoyment of the rights and privileges—along with the normative pressure—that belong to a particular "office," to a symbolic role or status. When one is invested or charged with the responsibilities of an office, appointed as the rightful bearer of the title associated with that office, one enters into the enjoyment of the various appurtenances of that office. Such appurtenances do not, however, belong to one by nature; they are in some sense "prostheses" of the office itself. In a book the title of which, *Organs without Bodies*, signals the centrality of this topic for his thinking, Žižek links these matters to the notion of kingship and, indeed, to all rites of symbolic investiture:

So, what is symbolic castration, with the phallus as its signifier? One should begin by conceiving of the phallus as a signifier—which means what? From the traditional rituals of investiture, we know the objects that not only "symbolize" power but put the subject who acquires them into the position of effectively *exercising* power. If a king holds in his hands the scepter and wears the crown, his words will be taken as the words of a king. Such insignia are external, not part of my nature: I don't own them; I wear them to exert power. As such, they "castrate" me: they introduce a gap between what I immediately am and the function that I exercise (i.e., I am never fully at the level of my function). This is what the infamous "symbolic castration" means. Not "castration as symbolic, as just symbolically enacted" . . . but the castration that occurs by the very fact of me being caught in the symbolic order, assuming a symbolic mandate. Castration is the very gap between what I immediately am and the symbolic mandate that confers on me its "authority."[19]

To take our paradigmatic case, the dimension of castration that Žižek does not address here concerns not the level of the "fictive" dimension of the king's symbolic status but rather the phantasmatic carnality of his being: the formation of a kind of second, spectral body, one composed precisely of the *flesh of the gap* introduced into one's being by way of the

19. Slavoj Žižek, *Organs without Bodies: On Deleuze and Consequences* (New York: Routledge, 2004), 87.

"castrating" procedures of investiture. My claim is that this paradigmatic case, one elaborated with breathtaking erudition by Ernst Kantorowicz, has, with the emergence of popular sovereignty, become the stuff of every one of our own private "cases" of a life in the flesh. That also implies that the very topic of castration and the emergence of psychoanalysis as its master theory need to be understood against the background of the dissolution of the king's second, sublime body and its precarious migration into the life of the people. This means that we need to take Freud's metaphor apropos of the place of dreams in the theory and practice of psychoanalysis more literally: the "royal road" to the unconscious at some level serves to mark out the migration and circulation patterns of the "royal remains" in the life of the people.

But enjoyment also bears the connotation of sensual or sexual enjoyment, a notion much better conveyed in the French word that became the signature concept in Lacan's rereading of Freud's libido theory: *jouissance*. To convey the link between *jouissance* and castration, Alenka Zupančič has made productive use of Aristophanes' famous speech on Eros to which we have already referred.[20] As Zupančič has emphasized, the myth of the emergence of Eros related by the famous Greek comic playwright contains not one but two moments of cleavage or cutting. The first, more famous one involves the cutting of human beings into separate halves who then forever long for their missing complement (the gods had worried about human arrogance generated by their sense of self-sufficiency). But it turns out that such a division created its own problems. Because each half-being longed for her or his missing half, these new, partial creatures did little else than search for and try to perpetuate a state of completion. To remedy this problem, Zeus intervenes a second time: he cuts and relocates the genitals of each partial being to the front and introduces the practice of interior reproduction (in their prior state, the creatures would, like cicadas, produce their children in the ground). As the text makes clear, after this additional cut, sexual satisfaction takes on a kind of autonomy with respect to reproduction or any other productive purpose.[21] At the conclusion of this series of divine operations, human beings are left in the curious state where they not only lack some-

---

20. Alenka Zupančič, *The Odd One In: On Comedy* (Cambridge, MA: MIT Press, 2008). Subsequent references are made in the text.

21. Zupančič cites the passage in the *Symposium* (191 c–d) where Aristophanes underscores this aspect of supplementarity, which comes to light in homosexual intercourse: "So that when a man embraced a woman, he would cast his seed and they would have children; but when a male embraced a male, *they would at least have the satisfaction of intercourse*, after which they could stop embracing, return to their jobs, and look after their needs in life" (cited in Zupančič, 188; my emphasis).

thing for which they eternally yearn; they also get a supplementary kind of enjoyment that causes, that becomes the object of, its own series of complications. As Zupančič puts it, we get a strange sort of overlapping of a logic of complementarity and a logic of supplementarity, an overlapping in which the antithetical meanings of the word "fix" (as well as, we might add, "cleave") are active: "We could . . . say that the fixing of the genitals is not only that which enables some kind of relationship between the two, but also and at the same time that which '*comes between*' the two, and the logic of which is—most literally—at odds with the logic of unification and fusion" (190). The crucial cut that displaces the genitals—castration in its more familiar sense of introducing a separation between the body and the organ of *jouissance*—is, thus, a "separation or split that also adds or attaches to each 'half' something that (locally and indirectly) links them together, while at the same time making them (relatively) independent (so that they can go about their business and take care of themselves). The genital organ is fixed on top of the beloved object, so to speak, on top of the two halves, superimposed on them" (190).

Just as entitlements introduce a gap into our being and endow us with an enjoyment that does not naturally belong to us, so does the quasi-autonomous status of sexual enjoyment (whose foundation myth is narrated by Aristophanes) introduce a gap and a kind of exteriority at the very place where we imagine ourselves to experience the highest, most intense, and most intimate form of self-feeling and immediacy. In Zupančič's words, "the concept of castration is in fact precisely that which constitutes the relationship between man and his enjoyment as a relationship of a constitutive 'encrusting.' Castration is this very cut into the supposedly immediate link between the subject (or the body) and enjoyment, yet a cut that comes in the form of an additional 'appendix enjoyment'; it refers to a gap that separates the body, from within, from its enjoyment, and *at the same time* binds it to it" (191–92). In her summary of this largely Lacanian perspective on castration, Zupančič emphasizes the antithetical meaning of one of Lacan's key concepts:

Yet the Lacanian revolution in relation to this notion consists precisely in his positing castration at the point of structural coincidence of a lack and a surplus, a coincidence between "no more enjoyment" and "more enjoyment," a coincidence so elegantly expressed in the French term *plus-de-jouir*, which can have both meanings. In other words, the fact that the body is separated from its own enjoyment does not imply simply a painful loss or deprivation: the separation refers above all to the fact that enjoyment emerges as relatively autonomous, it emerges through an interval in relation to the one whose enjoyment it is. It is only because of this interval that enjoyment becomes enjoyment in the first place. . . . Castration is not simply an amputation of enjoyment, but precisely its emergence in the form of an appendix, that is, in the form of something that belongs to the subject in an essential, yet not immediate way; something that belongs to the subject via a necessary interval. (192)

For psychoanalysis, then, symbolic castration is the ordeal whereby the joint between the body and the order of language (and human institutions more generally) comes to be established as the very "site" at which we acquire a "too much" of psychic reality, one that Freud characterized as libido, the substance of human sexuality (one "formula" for which seemed to appear to him in his dream of Irma's injection). We might say, therefore, that the entwinement of entitlement and enjoyment takes place in the *ordeal* of symbolic castration and that the "phallus" functions as the signifier, the key reference point, of its traversal. As Zupančič puts it, "It is because this paradoxical joint between the biological body and the Symbolic is inherently sexual (in the sense that it constitutes the generative source of human sexuality) that its effect is called castration. The 'phallic signifier' as the signifier of castration (also referred to as the signifier of lack) is, one could say, the signifier of the *missing link* between the biological and the Symbolic (or between nature and culture) *as the generic point of sexuation*" (207).

Now the point of all of this is not, as critics of psychoanalysis often claim, to posit the phallus as the inevitable and eternal symbol or title of the human initiation into the complex entwinements of entitlement and enjoyment, but rather to understand its capacity to endure in its status, to sustain the charisma of being the true and only source of erotic charisma, the "gold standard" of objects endowed with erotic value. The point is to show how the ups and downs of a part of the male body come to acquire their aura and sublime mystery, how a biological endowment takes on a surplus value, how its tumescence is amplified by the *stuff of the flesh* that is, in turn, correlated with the multiple meanings of the "missing link" we have been reviewing. Citing Lacan's particular pride in presenting the theory of the castration precisely as a way of "*dethroning the phallus*" (205; my emphasis), Zupančič argues that psychoanalysis offers the most compelling strategy available for "the removal of the phallus from the mode of necessity to that of contingency" (205). As Lacan himself put it, "it is only as contingency that, thanks to psychoanalysis, the phallus, reserved in ancient times to the Mysteries, has stopped not being written. Nothing more" (cited in Zupančič, 205).

What I am trying to argue is that such a process of "dethroning" has been at work in the modernist sensibility—in its libidinal economy—all along. As we saw in Kafka's "Country Doctor" (and will see in a series of other examples in part 2 of this study), the dethroning of the "sovereign" phallus—and the "phallic" sovereign—must be grasped as the undoing of the ways in which certain fundamental figures, images, and tropes have managed to give contour and shape to what can otherwise appear under the more amorphous (or *informe*) aspect of surplus flesh. If, as Lacan puts it, the phallus has stopped not being written with the advent of the psychoanalytic theory of symbolic castration, then this was because Freud was able to register a tear in the fabric of patriarchally organized being, the social link established within the "discourse of the master." This allowed him to gather a new way of thinking around its central metaphor—the phallus—and to develop a theory of the "substance" at issue in its longstanding status as master signifier or general equivalent of erotic objects.[22] Put somewhat differently, if the phallus begins to lose its "transcendental" status, then what begins to make itself felt is the very substance of the missing link, the spectral yet visceral flesh veiled by this sublime (im)posture. When the sovereign thing, whether phallus, father, or king, can no longer discharge the duties of its office, it discharges the remains of the flesh it has heretofore pretended or appeared to embody. The *arcana imperii*, the secret of the master/sovereign, becomes a kind of chronic, spectral secretion of the social body at large, one registered as a surplus of immanence that oscillates between the sublime and the abject and calls forth the apparatuses of biopolitical administration. Against this background it thus makes perfect sense that Foucault's inquiries into biopolitics would culminate in a history of sexuality.

VI

We are, in this way, brought back to the issues first raised by Kafka's country doctor. There a physician, a figure dedicated to the healing of illness according to the protocols of the sciences of immanence, encounters a "flesh-wound" that itself seems to incarnate the becoming immanent of what had previously been charged with transcendence and had been the charge of men of the cloth to care for, men who now pull apart the meaningless remnants of their investiture as theologians, as "scientists

22. Much of my thinking on these matters is indebted to Jean-Joseph Goux's groundbreaking work on the concept of the general equivalent in economy, politics, sexuality, and family organization. See his *Symbolic Economies: After Marx and Freud*, trans. Jennifer Curtiss Gage (Ithaca, NY: Cornell University Press, 1990).

of divinity." This juncture, where the flesh becomes overly proximate as a surplus element immanent to everyday life that can no longer be fully addressed by religion and yet exceeds the capacities, "transcends" the horizon, of the natural sciences, is precisely where Freud's new mode of thinking emerges. What I have elsewhere referred to as the "psycho-theology of everyday life," as a heightened attentiveness to the vicissitudes of "creaturely life"—and that Franz Rosenzweig characterized as "the new thinking"—is, as we can now see, a mode of thinking "with" or "in" the flesh. We can also see that it becomes misleading to analyze the core crisis of modernity under the sign of loss, of losing our access to transcendence, of becoming, as Lukács famously put it in his *Theory of the Novel*, "transcendentally homeless"; the "death of God" would seem rather to concern a fateful process of becoming stuck with an excess, a *too-muchness*, within the space of immanence. It is not simply that we cannot come to terms with our lot as finite human subjects but rather that our finitude itself suffers from a kind of intrinsic dysfunction, a lack of measure and balance.

To return once more to Judge Schreber's secret history of modernity, readers of his memoir will recall that he repeatedly characterized the bizarre and invasive somatic manipulations and torments he claimed to have undergone (and eventually systematized into a cosmo-theological system) as *übersinnlich*. This word is usually translated as "supersensible" or "supernatural" and refers to phenomena that exceed the domain of sense experience. But it will have become clear that what Schreber was onto—or perhaps better, what was *onto him*—was precisely the sort of surplus of immanence we have been tracking. What Schreber was trying to capture with this word was what captured and captivated him: the flesh that forms at or, better, *as* the conjunction of a surplus-sense and a surplus-sensuousness. It is clearly along the same lines that one would have to understand Nietzsche's notion of the *Übermensch*: the human being who has taken on the task of living with this fleshly surplus of immanence, who affirms as *good* the creaturely excess that throws into question any notion of a balanced order of creation. What Nietzsche referred to as the "last man" attempts, by contrast, to construct a life of happiness defined precisely as a life of pure immanence *without surplus*. The "last man" is, we might say, not so much an ascetic as an anorexic—a kind of "hunger artist"—with respect to the flesh.

In another short prose text published together with "A Country Doctor," Kafka, a writer who knew a thing or two about the arts of hunger, offers us one of the proper names of the dimension we have been tracking and that Freud eventually referred to simply as "It." As the title of the text indicates—*Die Sorge des Hausvaters*, or "The Worry of the Father of the Family"—whatever *It* is, it appears to be correlated to a disturbance at the place of paternal agency and, I am suggesting, of figures of sovereignty more generally. Written around the same time as Freud's *Beyond the Pleasure Principle*, the text might indeed be read as one in which the remainder of the "flesh-wound" in the fabric of being that Freud's grandson tries to master by means of a small spool (along with the repetition of a few phonemes that Freud hears as *fort/da*) acquires an uncanny autonomy that challenges any sort of mastery and integration into a recognizable form of life, where the spool itself becomes uncannily alive and acquires the attributes of the libido-creature Lacan mythologized under the name "lamella."

The text also provides further evidence as to how, after the eighteenth century, the dilemmas of creaturely life become entwined with the constitution of the nation-state and the meanings of national identity, how matters of the flesh become democratized and, given the ways in which democratic states took shape, *nationalized* (the thing that was a king now becomes, to a very large extent, the *Nation-Thing*). Given Kafka's problematic connection to issues of national identity as a (primarily) German-speaking Jew in Prague at the very moment when the Austro-Hungarian Empire was undergoing a mad, scissiparous process of its own, it makes sense that Kafka's writings would bear witness to this crucial historical aspect of the dimension we have been tracking.

The occasion of the worry of the paterfamilias who narrates Kafka's short prose text is a strange creature called "Odradek," who, as I have indicated, manifests a family resemblance to the toy referred to in Freud's discussion of the *fort/da* game: "At first it looks like a flat, star-shaped spool for thread, and in fact, it does seem to be wound with thread; although these appear to be only old, torn-off pieces of thread of the most varied kinds and colors knotted together but also tangled up in one another. But it is not just a spool, for a little crossbar sticks out from the middle of the star, and another little strut is joined to it at a right angle. With the help of the second little strut on the one side and one of the points of the star on the other, the whole thing can stand upright, as if on two legs."[23] Odradek appears to represent an anomaly with respect to any known principles of coherence or purposefulness: "It is tempting to think that this figure once had some sort of functional shape and is now merely broken. But this does not seem to be the case; at least there is no evidence for such a speculation; nowhere can you see any other beginnings or

23. *Kafka's Selected Stories*, 72–73. Subsequent references are made in the text.

fractures that would point to anything of the kind; true, the whole thing seems meaningless yet in its own way complete" (72). Or further: "I ask myself in vain what will become of him. Can he die? Everything that dies has previously had some sort of goal, some kind of activity, and that activity is what has worn it down; this does not apply to Odradek" (73). In spite of—or perhaps because of—this peculiar overlapping of perfection and deficiency, animation and mute woodenness, the creature exhibits a remarkable mobility, as if its recalcitrance to classification were itself a form of motility: "In any case, it is impossible to say anything more definite about it, since Odradek is extraordinarily mobile and impossible to catch" (72). For the purposes of our discussion here, it is the opening paragraph of the text that is of central importance. There the narrator anticipates the uncertainties pertaining to the creature's ontological status by noting the linguistic controversy pertaining to its name: "Some say that the word *Odradek* has roots in the Slavic languages, and they attempt to demonstrate the formation of the word on that basis. Still others maintain that its roots are German and that it is merely influenced by the Slavic. The uncertainty of both interpretations, however, makes it reasonable to conclude that neither pertains, especially since neither of them enables you to find a meaning for the word" (72).

No doubt because of Kafka's well-known obsession with the semantic resonances of his own name, scholars have largely ignored the narrator's warnings and have struggled to identify specific meanings embedded in the name "Odradek." This work has, of course, involved considerable research about the possible roots of the name in different central European languages, above all German and Czech, the two languages in which Kafka was fluent. Max Brod has suggested, for example, that "an entire scale of Slavic words meaning 'deserter' or 'apostate' is evoked: deserter from the kind, *rod*; deserter from *Rat* [counsel], the divine decision about creation, *rada*."[24] To this the Kafka scholar Wilhelm Emrich adds the associations with the Czech verb *odraditi*, "meaning to dissuade or deter someone from something." Emrich then brings together Germanic and Slavic etymologies, writing that *odraditi* itself stems from the German word for counsel, *Rat*. "The subsequent Slavic 'influence' is embodied in the prefix *od*, meaning *ab*, 'off, away from,' and in the suffix *ek*, indicating a diminutive." He concludes by suggesting that "Odradek . . . would therefore mean a small creature that dissuades someone from something,

24. Cited in "The Gesture in the Name," by Werner Hamacher, in *Premises: Essays on Literature from Kant to Celan*, by Werner Hamacher, trans. Peter Fenves (Stanford, CA: Stanford University Press, 1999), 319.

or rather, a creature that always dissuades in general."[25] Werner Hamacher adds to this list a series of further connotations:

Rada means not only *Rat* (counsel) but also series, row, direction, rank, and line; *rád* means series, order, class, rule as well as advisable, prudent; *rádek* means small series, row, and line. Odradek would thus be the thing that carried on its mischief outside of the linguistic and literary order, outside of speech, not only severed from the order of discourse (*Rede*) but also outside of every genealogical and logical series: a *Verräter*, a "betrayer" of every party and every conceivable whole. . . . "Odradek" means apostate—from the continuum of generation, line, rights, discourse, *ratio*, logic. . . . "Odradek" means dissidence, dissense, and a defection from the order of meaning. "Odradek" thus "means" that it does not mean.[26]

Hamacher brings this vertiginous exploration of linguistic roots to a point of self-canceling self-reference: "Odradek is the 'od-radix': the one 'without roots'; in Czech, *odrodek*, the one without its own kind, the one who 'steps out of the lineage' (*odroditi*—to degenerate, to be uprooted). 'Odradek' is, in short, the one who belongs to no kind and is without counsel, the one with neither a discourse nor a name of his own. *Odradek* is a word from at least two languages, *between* at least two languages, and thus a 'word' belonging to neither—a hybrid word and a hybrid between a word and a non-word."[27] Finally, and most importantly in the present context, Hamacher returns us to the crucial point of linkage of *zoē* and *bios*, nature and culture, that has been at issue throughout this study. Noting that Odradek responds to the interrogations of the paterfamilias by claiming to have no fixed abode, Hamacher characterizes Odradek as "'Od-adresa,' without address, between body and language, laughter and rustling, living organism and dead writing on 'fallen leaves' or 'fallen pages' (*Blätter*). . . . Odradek, an anarchist before all laws, wanders everywhere, even on the border between life and death."[28]

Kafka published this text in 1919, just after World War I and the breakup of the Austro-Hungarian Empire, the period also when Freud was developing his new topology of the mind and revising his theory of the drives to encompass a dimension "beyond the pleasure principle," a somatic-sublime dimension that is, as I have been arguing, that of the flesh: the spectral yet visceral persistence of a tear in the fabric of being that

---

25. Cited in ibid., 319–20.
26. Ibid., 320–21.
27. Ibid., 321.
28. Ibid., 325.

perturbs—threatens to make *informe*—the life that forms around it. If we read Kafka together with Freud's work of the same period, we are enabled to appreciate more fully the historical index of Freud's theoretical reflections as well as the implications of the worry or care—the *Sorge*—at issue in *Die Sorge des Hausvaters* for the "philosophy of the flesh" elaborated by Freud. Both writers have homed in on a dimension of human existence that is, in some sense, constitutively homeless and yet somehow co-constitutes every experience of a passionate attachment to the various places and forms of life that we come to call home.

As we have seen, the restructuring of the map of Europe in the wake of World War I produced a kind of chronic state of emergency in which more and more people were confronted with a political and existential status not unlike that of Kafka's strange spool-like creature. More and more people came to acquire the uncanny status—or rather nonstatus—of precisely a remainder of life, a life dominated by the spectral aspect of the flesh. Hannah Arendt characterized these stateless people—people who were in a quite radical sense "Od-adresa," without symbolic standing of any kind—as the core symptom of modern politics. Giorgio Agamben, taking up Arendt's work, saw in them the modern avatars of the ancient figure of the *homo sacer*, or "sacred man," a figure of radical exposure and destitution. And it was, of course, the Jews, many of whom were speakers of Yiddish (that curious dialect between Germanic and Slavic languages) who became the exemplary *homo sacer* over the next decades, just as they were for Saint Paul, some two thousand years earlier, the exemplary bearers of a life in the flesh. It makes good sense, then, that Freud and Kafka, two German-Jewish survivors of the Austro-Hungarian Empire, provide crucial testimony as to the ways of the flesh at this moment in history.

PART TWO

FOUR

Was heisst Schauen?
On the Vital Signs of
Visual Modernism

I

The French Revolution is, of course, universally seen to mark the period of transition from kings to "people" as the bearer of the principle of sovereignty. It makes sense, then, to begin a discussion of the modern reorganization of the "physiology" of the body politic and its impact on the visual arts with a discussion of one of the most famous paintings to emerge out of the crucible of that historical turning point, indeed a painting that appears to be dedicated to this very project of a reconfiguration of the flesh in the wake of the king's—or better, the King's—demise. My guide in this discussion is T. J. Clark, who himself begins his critical history of visual modernism with a seemingly exorbitant claim about the status of the painting in question, Jacques-Louis David's *Death of Marat*, in the history of modern art. I hope it will become clear in the course of these reflections why and how this painting can serve as a kind of allegory for my project as a whole. In his *Farewell to an Idea: Episodes from a History of Modernism*, Clark writes: "My candidate for the beginning of modernism—which at least has the merit of being obviously far-fetched—is 25 Vendémiaire Year 2 (16 October 1793, as it came to be known). That was the day a hastily completed painting by Jacques-Louis David,

Jacques-Louis David, *Death of Marat* (1793). Oil on canvas, 165 × 128 cm. Musées Royaux des Beaux-Arts de Belgique, Brussels, Belgium. Photograph: Scala / Art Resource, New York.

of Marat, the martyred hero of the revolution—*Marat à son dernier soupir,* David called it early on—was released into the public realm."[1]

Rather than try to rehearse the full complexity of Clark's stunning argument, I focus on what for me provides the real key to his claim about the singular status of the *Death of Marat* in his broadly conceived history of modernism. Concerning David's own uncertain grasp of the stakes of his painting and the staging of its initial viewing, Clark writes that David at the very least "knew that picturing Marat was a political matter, part of a process of making [the Revolution] a Jacobin property. . . . He believed that a new world was under construction. No doubt he saw in the cult of Marat the first forms of a liturgy and ritual in which the truths of the revolution itself would be made flesh—People, Nation, Virtue, Reason, Liberty" (29).[2] The problem, however, was that such conversions, still possible within the context of the political theology of kingship (and the forms of picture-making it sponsored), did not and perhaps could not succeed under revolutionary and postrevolutionary conditions. "Marat could not be made to embody the revolution because no one agreed about what the revolution was, least of all about whether Marat was its Jesus or its Lucifer. David's picture—this is what makes it inaugural of modernism—tries to ingest this disagreement, and make it part of a new cult object" (38). But this answer too is insufficient. For it is not simply a matter of a provisional disagreement as to the meaning of events, but rather of an impasse affecting the possibility of converting events—and these events in particular—into representative images and bodies that would convincingly incarnate their truths. The problem is that the events in question put under pressure the entire apparatus of *representation* in all its complex and intersecting meanings. And it is this impasse that, as Clark puts it, forms the gate through which contingency comes to invade painting.[3]

What, as Clark puts it, "changed the circumstances of picturing for good" (46) was precisely the entrance of the People onto the stage of

1. T. J. Clark, *Farewell to an Idea: Episodes from a History of Modernism* (New Haven, CT: Yale University Press, 1999), 15. Subsequent references are made in the text.

2. In an earlier formulation, Clark refers to this process as that of making Marat a *totem* (26). Here one should no doubt recall Freud's hypothesis of the emergence of totemism out of the murder of the primal father and the incorporation of his powers by way of the ritual repetition of the totem meal—the symbolic enjoyment of his sublime flesh.

3. William Vaughan's more modest reading of the painting suggests that contingency, a word he does not himself use, is manifest above all in the generic tensions operative in the work, in David's struggle to yoke together the authority of academic history painting, the pathos of commemoration, and the urgency of propaganda in the midst of an unstable political situation. See Vaughan, "Terror and the Tabula Rasa: David's *Marat* in its Pictorial Context," in *David's "Death of Marat,"* ed. William Vaughan and Helen Weston (Cambridge: Cambridge University Press, 2000), 77–101.

power formerly occupied by the monarch: "That is to say, [the Revolution] tried to put one kind of sovereign body in place of another. And the body had somehow to be represented without its either congealing into a new monarch or splitting into an array of vital functions, with only instrumental reason to bind them together" (47). *Contingency*, Clark concludes, "is just a way of describing the fact that putting the People in place of the King cannot ultimately be done. The forms of the social outrun their various incarnations" (47). This means that there is a great deal more at stake here than a provisional disagreement as to the meaning of events. It is rather a question of a fundamental impasse affecting the concept and procedures of representation. The task was to put forth a body that would, as it were, incarnate the now empty place of the king, the figure that had traditionally been charged with corporeally representing the subject for all other subjects of the realm. The task would be, in a word, to *incarnate* in some ostensibly new way the *excarnated* principle of sovereignty: "Marat . . . had to be made to stand for the People. By now the enormity of the task should be clear: not just that Marat was such a disputed object, pulled to and fro by the play of factions (though this indeed is part of the problem), but that at a deeper level any body was inadequate to what had now to be done. Or any technique of representation. That representation was henceforth a technique was exactly the truth that had not to be recognized" (47).

The real tour de force of Clark's reading of the *Death of Marat* consists in his account of the ways in which David's painting ends up succeeding at bringing this fundamental impasse to a commanding painterly presence, one that evokes precisely what I have characterized as the spectral yet visceral dimension of the flesh no longer figured and contained by means of the royal physiology—by the King's Two Bodies. For Clark, the locus of the flesh is not exactly where we might assume it to be, that is, in Marat's wounded body, but rather in the large, empty upper half of David's canvas or, at the very least, where the one seems to extend or metamorphose into the other. As Clark puts it, David's treatment of the body "seems to make Marat much the same substance—*the same abstract material*—as the empty space above him. The wound is as abstract as the flesh" (36; my emphasis). The flesh that can no longer be figured by the body of the king becomes, in a word, the *abstract material* out of which the painting is largely made. The empty upper half of the painting stands in for a missing and, indeed, impossible representation of the People: "It embodies the concept's absence, so to speak. It happens upon representation as technique. It sets its seal on Marat's unsuitability for the work of incarnation" (47). The scumbled surface forming the upper half of the painting thus no longer functions as a simple absence but rather as a positive, even oppressive presence, "something abstract and unmotivated, which occupies a different conceptual space from the bodies below it. This produces, I think, a kind of representational deadlock, which is the true source of the *Marat*'s continuing hold on us." This is, Clark continues, the "endless, meaningless objectivity produced by paint not quite finding its object, symbolic or otherwise, and therefore making do with its own procedures" (48).

Clark goes on to link this apparent failure to a kind of shame that will forever haunt modernism; we might even say that the abstract material out of which the upper half of the painting is made just is the ectoplasmic substance of this haunting: "In a sense . . . I too am saying that the upper half is a display of technique. But display is too neutral a word: for the point I am making, ultimately, is that technique in modernism is a kind of shame: something that asserts itself as the truth of picturing, but always against picturing's best and most desperate efforts." In David, this shame emerges precisely at the point and in the space where "'People' ought to appear, as a kind of aura or halo" (48). What appears at the missing place of the new sovereign body is a kind of dream work made painterly flesh in the pure activity of painting; the empty upper half of the image forms not so much a vacancy as the site of an excess of pressure, a signifying stress that opens onto a vision of painting as pure drive:

And yet the single most extraordinary feature of the picture . . . is its whole upper half being empty. Or rather (here is what is unprecedented), not being empty, exactly, not being a satisfactory representation of nothing or nothing much—of an absence in which whatever the subject is has become present—but something more like a representation of painting, of painting as pure activity. Painting as material, therefore. Aimless. In the end detached from any one representational task. Bodily. Generating (monotonous) orders out of itself, or maybe out of ingrained habit. A kind of automatic writing. (45)

My own sense is that the shame at issue here pertains not simply or even foremost to painting's failure to reach its object, to what Clark here characterizes as a distinctively modernist stuckness in technique, artifice, mediation, self-reflexivity, and so forth—a shame, ultimately, of painting's "nominalism," its moving within a frictionless universe untethered from lived life and the things that make it matter; it pertains, rather, to an almost defiling contact with the flesh that one has torn free from the king's sublime physiology and claimed for the People. Among other things, David's painting shows us just how difficult it would be to redeem, to make good on this claim. To put it in the form of a paradox, we might also say that the history of European art from this point on was in some sense dedicated to the task of *figuring out abstraction*, this eventful opening onto the nonfigurative. Put somewhat differently, the normative pressures proper to painting—the pressures pushing toward what counts as excellence in painting—were mutating in response to a radical transformation of the political and social form of the normative pressures informing lives more generally.

II

In this context, I would like to recall the two moments of extreme intensity achieved in Freud's famous dream of Irma's injection, both of which Lacan characterized as a kind of prophetic (and, perhaps in some sense, *automatic*) writing on the wall. The first was reached in the image of the inflamed tissues of Irma's throat, the second in the letters of a formula that Freud sees in the dream, one he associates with the chemistry of human sexuality. These two elements are, in a way, also present in David's painting: the first in the form of Marat's wounds (and sickly, puffy skin more generally), the second in the pieces of paper filled with writing that stand in a kind of visual symmetry with respect to Marat's martyred, Christ-like body. Clark, for his part, places considerable emphasis on these bits of writing, seeing them as more than a means for the idealization of Marat as exemplary friend of the people.[4] For Clark, these bits of writing are the place where, to use a Lacanian locution, the signifier falls into the pictorial space whose meanings it is meant to authorize and becomes an object among other objects, one that juts forward beyond the picture plane and toward the spectator with a peculiar insistence. Rather than sealing the meaning of the image, these discursive bits function instead as a thinglike surplus of script that, as it were, "objects" to any claim as to the legibility of the historical situation. Apropos of the words just out of sight in Marat's letter and presumed to be "de la patrie," Clark asks, "But is there a final phrase at all? Of course there looks to be something; but it is so scrappy and vestigial, an extra few words where

4. See, for example, ibid., 84: "David presents Marat's death as if it were an *exemplum virtutis*. But it was difficult to make this portrayal fit with the facts of the assassination. Marat had to be shown dying not just as a victim, but also as a hero, making some kind of sacrifice. This is where the fiction of the letter comes in. According to the picture, Marat has just received a letter from Corday asking for help and has himself just finished a letter in which he is sending financial assistance. He is a victim, it is implied, of his own burning desire to help others. He died because he responded to Corday's plea for help."

there really is no room left for anything, that the reader continually double-takes, as if reluctant to accept that writing, of all things, can decline to this state of utter visual elusiveness. Surely if I look again—and look hard enough—the truth will out. For spatially, this is the picture's starting point. It is closeness incarnate" (40). Clark adds that these bits of painted writing become "the figure of the picture's whole imagining of the world and the new shape it is taking. . . . The boundaries between the discursive and the visual are giving way, under some pressure the painter cannot quite put his finger on, though he gets close" (42).[5]

But as Clark has so persuasively argued, it is in the swirling, vertiginous void that fills the picture's upper half that this pressure finds its "proper" place—its *nonresting place*—in the visual field. The spectral materiality of the flesh that forms at the impossible jointure of body and letter, soma and signifier, enjoyment and entitlement—a dimension that can neither be fully imagined nor, finally, be spelled out in a formula—finds its inaugural *modern* figuration in that dense, agitated, painterly writing on the wall. Clark is right, then, to see in the painting the opening onto a new aesthetic dimension, and one that has a very precise historical index. What makes modernism modernism is that its basic materials are compelled to engage with and, as it were, model the dimension of the flesh that is exacerbated to an unbearable degree by the representational deadlock situated at the transition from royal to popular sovereignty. What, in historical experience, can no longer be elevated, sublimated, by way of codified practices of picture-making to the dignity of moral allegory, introduced into a realm of institutionally—and, ultimately, transcendentally—authorized meanings, now achieves its "sublimity" in a purely immanent fashion, that is, in the various ways in which the vicissitudes of this abstract yet inflamed materiality itself becomes the subject matter of the arts.

I would like to emphasize, once more, the difference between the flesh qua *partial object*, on the one hand, and *parts of the body* functioning (or not functioning) in harmony within a discrete organism, on the other. To put it in rather oversimplified art-historical terms, what Clark describes apropos of the *Death of Marat* demonstrates that the dissolution of the image of Leviathan that forms the famous frontispiece of Hobbes's book on sovereignty (and of the form of sovereignty represented by that

---

5. The *assignat* visible in the image adds an additional twist to the "signifying stress" elaborated by Clark. It introduces the problem of the "backing" of paper money—by gold, land, some piece of the real—at this crucial historical juncture, the capacity, that is, of paper currency to float free of value (see Clark, 48–50).

image) does not simply yield a multitude, a swarming, unruly mass of "body parts"—in this case, individuals—adrift and uncoupled from any form or organization. The "mass" that is unleashed by way of the excarnation of sovereignty, the dissolution of the king's sublime body, is one that now, so to speak, metastasizes *within* each individual, one that can indeed "crowd" out the self from within. To put it another way, what Freud discovered was that individual psychology and the theory of the libido are always, at a profound level, a *theory of masses*.

III

There is one matter that Clark does not address with respect to the context of the painting, but it is one that does, I think, link up in significant ways with the subject of our investigation. I am thinking of Jean-Paul Marat's active participation in the quasi-scientific culture of the time, a culture that was preoccupied with identifying the materiality of invisible forces at work in nature and human life. Marat's work on the nature of light and heat was more or less contemporaneous with the arrival in Paris of Franz Anton Mesmer, whose "discovery" of animal magnetism and the healing practices developed in relation to it aroused considerable interest in prerevolutionary France. As Robert Darnton has expressed it in his study of the ways in which science, pseudoscience, and politics intermingled in this period, the intense preoccupation with animal magnetism and "mesmerism" in the decades prior to the Revolution served as a kind of "camouflaged political theory" that served to elaborate some of the same issues at the center of Rousseau's *Social Contract*, doing so in a manner that for a time attracted considerably more attention than Rousseau's own writings.[6]

Darnton tries to account for the appeal of mesmerism in prerevolutionary France in several ways. He argues that the superfine fluid that Mesmer had claimed to identify, which "penetrated and surrounded all bodies" (3), had its own intrinsic appeal by bringing down to earth, so to speak, the diverse and invisible forces of heat, light, electricity, and magnetism. In a way, Mesmer had condensed the invisible forces of nature within a single and universal *material* element, one that could, above all,

6. See Robert Darnton, *Mesmerism and the End of the Enlightenment in France* (Cambridge, MA: Harvard University Press, 1968), 3. Subsequent references are made in the text. Darnton notes that "French pamphleteers produced at least twice as many works on mesmerism as on the six-month political crisis accompanying the first Assembly of Notables" (41).

be harnessed for the alleviation of human pain and suffering. As Darnton concisely summarizes the principle of medical mesmerism, "Sickness . . . resulted from an 'obstacle' to the flow of the fluid throughout the body, which was analogous to a magnet. Individuals could control and reinforce the fluid's action by 'mesmerizing' or massaging the body's 'poles' and thereby overcoming the obstacle, inducing a 'crisis,' often in the form of convulsions, and restoring health or 'harmony' of man with nature" (4). Darnton goes on to emphasize the theatricality of mesmeric healing, describing in detail the sorts of medical performances Mesmer and his followers staged, spectacles that prefigure the theater of hysteria that Jean-Martin Charcot put on a century later at the Salpêtrière.

But it was not so much the "mesmerizing" theatricality of these healing sessions or the explanatory potential of the theory behind them that generated the particular appeal of mesmerism for those who soon participated in the political upheavals in Paris. As Darnton sees it, the key to the attraction was in the first instance that this one truly *universal* fluid appeared to represent a "discovery that would put an end to human suffering" (83). It was furthermore one that was aggressively persecuted by the scientific institutions of the ancien régime. The mesmerists "showed that privileged bodies, supported by the government, were attempting to suppress a movement to improve the lot of the common people" (85). What attracted political radicals to the movement "was Mesmer's stand against the academic bodies that often dispensed success or failure for obscure individuals like themselves, who were scrambling for recognition as men of letters and science. Mesmer's fight was their fight" (90). Among such radicals was Jean-Paul Marat, who had himself "fought for years to win his rightful seat in the Academy of Sciences." "That place belonged to him, he felt, because he had wrestled with hundreds of experiments and filled thousands of pages with irrefutable arguments in order to unseat the great Newton and reveal to the world the true nature of light, heat, fire, and electricity—which were produced by invisible fluids rather like Mesmer's" (93). Darnton goes so far as to suggest that "Marat's desire to avenge himself against the Academy of Sciences provided the main thrust behind his strange revolutionary career, which was principally a campaign against conspirators," in a word, against the forces of "academic despotism" (94).

Marat's devoted disciple Jacques-Pierre Brissot brought these various strands of radical mesmerism together in a pamphlet that already adumbrates the biopolitical trajectory marked by the shift from the authority of the sovereign to that of those charged with managing the health of the populace: "Don't you [academicians] see, for example, that mesmerism is a way to bring social classes together, to make the rich more humane, to make them into real fathers of the poor? Wouldn't you be edified at the sight of the most eminent men . . . supervising the health of their servants, spending hours at a time mesmerizing them?" (cited in Darnton, 97). This biopolitical shift was to a large extent already embedded in Mesmer's conception of the healing process, which, as another historian of mesmerism has noted, "placed *the physician and his body* at the center of the cure. The physician, like the healers of old, would lay hands on the ill and perform miraculous cures. He could use the magnetism of his own organism to restore the patient's harmony, lost through illness."[7]

I would suggest that in this context the real precursors to the physician's mesmeric body and hands were not some generic "healers of old" but rather the French and English monarchs, whose bodies were for centuries thought to be endowed with the "royal touch," the capacity to heal particular illnesses—above all the condition referred to as scrofula, the so-called *king's evil*—by the laying on of hands.[8] With mesmerism we find ourselves at that point of transition we have been exploring throughout this study at which a new set of theories, practices, and concepts are put to work to locate and manage *the vicissitudes of the flesh* at a crucial juncture in the political theology of sovereignty. That is, the mesmeric fluid represents not so much a pseudoscientific condensation of the multiple invisible forces of *nature*; it functions rather as one of the names of the flesh at the point at which the matter and charisma of the King's sublime body—his "strange material and physical presence," to use Foucault's formulation—becomes dispersed into the new locus of sovereignty, the people. Mesmerism represents, in other words, the adumbration of the "new physics" that Foucault would posit as the *dispositif* of modern governmentality.

I am arguing here not simply that a royal prerogative linked to the sacred dimension of kingship passes into the hands of physicians, that is, that prince-physicians become physicians *tout court*, scientists of a now-disenchanted immanence. I am suggesting something more radical, namely that the bodies of the citizens of modern nation-states take on a surplus element, one that actually challenges the entire ideology of disenchantment and secularization and that introduces into immanence an excess it cannot fully close in upon. One might recall that in

7. Adam Crabtree, *From Mesmer to Freud: Magnetic Sleep and the Roots of Psychological Healing* (New Haven, CT: Yale University Press, 1993), 7; my emphasis.

8. Marc Bloch's famous study of this phenomenon was written around the same time as Kantorowicz's *King's Two Bodies*. See Bloch, *The Royal Touch: Monarchy and Miracles in France and England*, trans. J. E. Anderson (New York: Dorset Press, 1989).

his *Farewell to an Idea*, T. J. Clark situates his reading of the *Death of Marat* within a larger story about the disenchantment of the world, a story that he claims "is still far from ended" (50). My argument has been that the charms, the stuff of enchantment, not only have never disappeared from the modern world but that they insinuate themselves even more powerfully into the fabric of everyday life, that they in some quasi-literal way *get under the skin* of the modern subject.[9] What now perturbs immanence—the space of our so-called disenchanted modernity—is the flesh that previously formed the stuff of the King's sublime physiology, the "sacred" materiality that endowed him with his miraculous healing capacities and belonged to him by virtue of what Marc Bloch called, in his study of the "royal touch," "the supernatural aura which surrounded those crowned heads."[10]

I am suggesting, then, that the "health" of the flesh in some sense never ceases to be a political theological matter, even after the king— whose exceptional *body* represented the *head* of the *body politic*—has lost his head and the principle of his rule has been excarnated. It is now every head that, so to speak, has a body of its own, one for which each citizen is now also uniquely answerable. It is the substance of this responsibility that now circulates in the social space, not as the supernatural aura surrounding a few crowned heads—the stuff of miraculous royalty—but rather under a series of new and in some sense more "democratic" names, among them "animal magnetism" and "mesmeric fluid." And it also informs, as I have suggested, the dense painterly agitation that fills the upper half of David's painting of the death of Marat, a figure who also claimed to have discovered, in the terms of the popular science of his day, the secrets of this universal fluid in which we all ostensibly bathe.

By displacing mesmerism from the history of natural philosophy and science to a history concerned with the afterlife of the political theology of sovereignty, we also gain a richer understanding of the genealogy of psychoanalysis qua "philosophy of the flesh." I do not mean to say that the usual stories of the formation of psychoanalysis in the crucible of Freud's education and apprenticeships in the various laboratories, clinics, and scientific paradigms of the end of the nineteenth century are wrong.

9. The German word for what is charming or enchanting is *reizvoll*, full of *Reize*. *Reiz* also signifies the stimulation or excitation of nerves. Freud defines trauma in *Beyond the Pleasure Principle* as a *Reizüberflutung*, an experience of being flooded over by nervous excitation that is able to breach the *Reizschutz*, or protective shield of the ego. The old seduction theory mutates, in a sense, into a theory of our capacity to become overly or excessively "charmed" or "enchanted" by someone, something, or some experience; when that occurs we might say that we are *partially mesmerized*.

10. Bloch, *Royal Touch*, 4.

Freud absorbed and mastered the reigning biophysical and psychophysical theories, the experimental practices of the period, the studies linking mental illness to heredity and degeneration, the studies of nerve tissue and reflex action.[11] What I am suggesting, rather, is that in coming up against the limits of those various paradigms, theories, and practices, Freud was also to some extent taking leave from the sciences of pure immanence and entering into proximity of the uncanny dimension that perturbs it, the flesh that forms at the jointure—the "X" of the chiasmic relays—of enjoyment and entitlement. And this is, as I have argued in these pages, the dimension that is fundamentally at stake in the political theology of sovereignty.[12]

IV

As Marina Warner has noted, the word *phantasmagoria* entered the lexicon with the popular Gothic horror shows that Etienne-Gaspard Robertson staged in Paris in the 1790s and called the Phantasmagoria.[13] Warner traces the history of the forms, media, and technologies that, like the fluid first posited by Franz Mesmer, serve to make visible a sublime materiality that now comes to represent not so much the invisible forces of nature as the spirit world and soul stuff—the *ectoplasm*—thought to stand in some sense apart from and above nature. What I am suggesting is that the history of modern biopolitics *and* the history of such "phantasmagoria" need to be grasped as two aspects of a single structural shift that marks the threshold of modernity: the relocation of the dimension of the flesh from the body of the king to that of the people.

It is not without interest, then, that in one of his most rhetorically charged evocations of the dimension of the flesh, Jacques Lacan takes as his point of reference a story about mesmerism, Edgar Allan Poe's "The Facts in the Case of M. Valdemar." (Against the background of our discussion of David's painting, one could easily imagine an alternative title to Poe's story: "Valdemar à son dernier soupir.") The first-person narrator tells of his recent preoccupation with mesmerism and his curiosity about

11. For a fine survey of this series of apprenticeships, see George Makari, *Revolution in Mind: The Creation of Psychoanalysis* (New York: HarperCollins, 2008).

12. To put it once more in terms I have suggested in previous work, I would say that what is at issue in the genealogy of psychoanalysis I am constructing is not so much "animal" as "creaturely magnetism," the attractions and repulsions that pass between human subjects insofar as they are not just animal bodies who also inhabit the space of reasons, but beings also made of *flesh*. *Creaturely life* is animal life amplified by the dimension of the flesh.

13. Marina Warner, *Phantasmagoria* (Oxford: Oxford University Press, 2006), 15.

the fact that apparently no one had ever investigated the boundary between life and death by means of this technique, that "no person had
yet been mesmerized *in articulo mortis*."[14] The narrator asks a terminally
ill acquaintance, a certain M. Ernest Valdemar, to allow him to attempt
the experiment with him. The prospects appeared good, for Valdemar
has already shown himself to be susceptible to mesmerism. His advanced
state of tubercular dissolution—it is referred to in the story as phthisis,
meaning literally to waste away—furthermore has made it possible to
predict the time of his demise. When the time of death finally arrives, the
narrator is called on the scene and puts Valdemar into a mesmeric trance
that miraculously preserves a kind of animation beyond the point of
death. The story reaches a climax at the moment when Valdemar answers
the narrator's question whether he is asleep with the following words:
"Yes;—no—I *have been* sleeping—and now—now—*I am dead*" (281). The
narrator's attempt to describe the voice uttering these words—he refers to
the utterance as a distinct "syllabification"—is worth quoting at length:

There was no longer the faintest sign of vitality in M. Valdemar; and concluding him
to be dead, we were consigning him to the charge of the nurses, when a strong vibra-
tory motion was observable in the tongue. This continued for perhaps a minute. At
the expiration of this period, there issued from the distended and motionless jaws a
voice—such as it would be madness in me to attempt describing. There are, indeed,
two or three epithets which might be considered as applicable to it in part; I might say,
for example, that the sound was harsh, and broken and hollow. But the hideous whole
is indescribable, for the simple reason that no similar sounds have ever jarred upon the
ear of humanity. There were two particulars, nevertheless, which I thought then, and
still think, might fairly be stated as characteristic of the intonation—as well adapted
to convey some idea of its unearthly peculiarity. In the first place, the voice seemed to
reach our ears—at least mine—from a vast distance, or from some deep cavern within
the earth. In the second place, it impressed me (I fear, indeed, that it will be impossible
to make myself comprehended) as gelatinous or glutinous matters impress the sense
of touch. (280–81)

The narrator then relates that Valdemar remained in this state of what
we might call *mesmeric undeadness* for a period of seven months. At
that point he and the attending physicians decide to attempt to break
the trance, to free Valdemar from his somatic purgatory, in a word, *to
awaken him to his own death*. For what follows, the narrator writes, "it is

14. Edgar Allan Poe, "The Facts in the Case of M. Valdemar," in *The Complete Stories of Edgar
Allan Poe* (New York: Doubleday, 1984), 276. Subsequent references are made in the text.

quite impossible that any human being could have been prepared": "As I rapidly made the mesmeric passes, amid ejaculations of 'dead! dead!' absolutely *bursting* from the tongue and not from the lips of the sufferer, his whole frame at once—within the space of a single minute, or even less, shrunk—crumbled—absolutely *rotted* away beneath my hands. Upon the bed, before that whole company, there lay a nearly liquid mass of loathsome—of detestable putridity" (283).

In the same seminar in which he analyzes Freud's dream of Irma's injection, Lacan cites this scene in conjunction with a discussion of *Oedipus at Colonus*, the tragedy of the *entsetzlich* dissolution of the once-great king who now finds himself reduced, as Lacan puts it, to "the scum of the earth, the refuse, the residue, a thing empty of any plausible appearance."[15] Lacan characterizes the conclusion of Poe's story with an evocation of liquefied flesh, "something for which no language has a name, the naked apparition, pure, simple, brutal, of this figure which it is impossible to gaze at face on, which hovers in the background of all the imaginings of human destiny, which is beyond qualification, and for which the word carrion is completely inadequate, the complete collapse of this species of swelling that is life—the bubble bursts and dissolves down into inanimate putrid liquid."[16] As I have been arguing, this "naked apparition" that hovers in the background of all the imaginings of human destiny is not the body in its utter vulnerability, not the precarious biological life we share with the animal and vegetable "kingdoms," but rather the enigmatic substance of sovereignty at the historical moment at which it is uncoupled from its primary locus, the body of the king. In Poe's story mesmerism serves as a technique to isolate and manipulate this substance, to separate it out from the biological life of its bearer. And here too this uncanny materiality of the flesh seems to form at the jointure of body and signifier, that is, in the utterance of the undead Valdemar whose voice touches the ear "as gelatinous or glutinous matters impress the sense of touch."

V

To pick up the main thread of my argument, I am putting forth what might at first glance appear to be a rather idiosyncratic genealogy of modernism.

15. Jacques Lacan, *The Seminar of Jacques Lacan: Book II, The Ego in Freud's Theory and in the Technique of Psychoanalysis, 1954–1955*, trans. Sylvana Tomaselli (New York: Norton, 1991), 232.
16. Ibid., 231–32.

As I see it, modernist artists stand under the compulsion to respond to the ever-ramifying biopolitical pressures generated by the displacement of the king—and the practices of picture-making sponsored, in some fashion, by the political theology of his representative corporeality—by "the people" in the wake of the French Revolution. This displacement introduced into "the people" a spectral yet visceral surplus immanence: the flesh that attaches to this new subject-bearer of sovereignty as an always ambivalent and uncanny "distinction," an element that would appear both to bind and threaten with dissolution the body politic of modern nation-states (and as we have seen, this threat can call forth efforts at a *final solution*). Modernist art is, I am suggesting, a significant relay point for the excitations—the *Reize*—of the flesh, a site where at least some artists resolved to "take on" the ways in which the modern subject has been compelled to "take on" flesh. This is the point of the main title of this chapter, which is modeled on that of Martin Heidegger's book *Was heisst Denken?* There, Heidegger suggests that the question is not so much about the essence of thinking—What is thinking? What sort of an activity is this thing we call thinking?—but rather about that which *addresses* thinking, calls thinking on the scene in the first place, summons it out, excites it, demands thinking as a response, and thereby makes it matter. What calls forth *looking* in modernist art is, I am suggesting, the ways in which it assumes the pressures of the surplus that perturbs the space of immanence.

A significant strand of the scholarship and criticism of modernism has already staked out the terrain in question—the specific sort of materiality that makes modernist art matter in the ways it does—in terms introduced into discussions of modernity by the French writer Georges Bataille. I am thinking, above all, of the work of Rosalind Krauss and Yve-Alain Bois. In their groundbreaking exhibition catalogue *Formless: A User's Guide*, the two critics propose their own idiosyncratic take on modernism, one that reads its history "against the grain" of those views that see in it above all a rich array of experimental practices opened by the discovery of the autonomous formal values of the components of the painted surface.[17] That discovery was made possible, as the story goes, by the liberation of art from the compulsion or need to represent or illustrate scenes, individuals, events of religious, historical, or cultural significance. Bataille's work and, above all, his (early) concept of the *informe* provide Krauss and Bois with the crucial point of reference for their revisionist reading of major strands of modernist aesthetic ambitions and practices.

---

17. Yve-Alain Bois and Rosalind Krauss, *Formless: A User's Guide* (New York: Zone Books, 1997), 24–25.

Before I turn to this important and compelling reading of visual modernism, I would like to say a few words about the larger resonances of Bataille's writings for my own project. Bataille, of course, wrote extensively not only on the topic of sovereignty but also on embodiment, partial objects, decomposition, the ambivalence of the sacred, the space of exception—a great many of the issues of concern in this study. Furthermore, he did so to a certain extent under the impact of his own psychoanalysis and significant contact with psychoanalytic circles.[18] In many ways, Bataille's preoccupations and experiments place him in rather close proximity to Daniel Paul Schreber, the figure I have invoked at various points in this study. Indeed, that key word of Schreber's *Grundsprache* or "basic language"—*Luder*—that, as I have indicated, brings together connotations of sexuality, death, and putrescent flesh, could be considered to be an eminently Bataillean locution. One might, moreover, venture the argument that the name of Bataille's "secret society" and journal, Acéphale, signals nothing short of the attempt to stage the next and final act in the great historical drama of sovereignty in the West: the decapitation not, as in the terror of the French Revolution, of the royals and all enemies of the *People* but rather of that newly sovereign entity itself. One might indeed wonder whether this was not part of Bataille's lifelong fascination with the photograph first given to him by his analyst, Adrien Borel, in 1925 of a Chinese victim of *ling'chi*, the torturous death by a thousand cuts. That is, might this fascination not be part of the paradoxical attempt to "identify" with the *rump* of being human, to inhabit or incarnate *directly* the fleshy remainder/surplus we have been tracking all along?[19] If these hunches are not off the mark, then Bataille's later reflections on sovereignty could be grasped as a set of reflections not on the "discourse of the master" but rather on what Lacan referred to as the "discourse of the analyst," a discourse distinguished by the paradoxical attempt to occupy the place of an excremental remainder that induces, in turn, the other's evacuation or emptying out, his separation precisely from the master or sovereign signifiers that heretofore dominated his libidinal life, subordinated his enjoyment to the servility and service of goods.

We might think of this shift from sovereign qua master to the peculiar and difficult mastery exhibited by the analyst as a revaluation of the

18. The friendship between Bataille and Lacan has been discussed by, among others, Elisabeth Roudinesco in her *Jacques Lacan*, trans. Barbara Bay (New York: Columbia University Press, 1997).

19. For a highly nuanced study of Bataille's relationship to this image, see Robert Buch, *The Pathos of the Real: On the Aesthetics of Violence in the Twentieth Century* (Baltimore: Johns Hopkins University Press, 2010). I am grateful to Robert Buch for sharing his manuscript with me.

prefix that generally signifies what stands above or higher than other things: in English "over" or "super"; in French "sur"; in German "über." In an early essay on the philosophical and cultural "work" performed by this prefix—ultimately the work of idealization and sublimation—Bataille takes aim above all at his enemies in Breton's surrealist camp as well as at Nietzsche's conception of the "superman" (at least the way Bataille understood the term at this time). What is at issue, he writes, is the "tendency . . . found in contemporary surrealism, which maintains . . . the predominance of higher ethereal values (clearly expressed by the addition of the prefix *sur*, the trap into which Nietzsche had already fallen with *superman*). More precisely, since surrealism is immediately distinguishable by the addition of low values (the unconscious, sexuality, filthy language, etc.), it invests these values with an elevated character by associating them with the most immaterial values."[20] Bataille concludes his essay with a call to suspend all such "Icarian subterfuge" and to cast the eyes downward: "By excavating the fetid ditch of bourgeois culture, perhaps we will see open up in the depths of the earth immense and even sinister caves where force and human liberty will establish themselves, sheltered from the call to order of a heaven that today demands the most imbecilic elevation of any man's spirit."[21]

In Bataille's later work, it is as if the prefix that formerly signified the posture of elevation, of standing above and over, has come to stand for the very *sur*plus or excess of immanence we have been tracking. The "superman" becomes, in this way, the one who has accepted responsibility for bearing a too-muchness, for being a placeholder of the flesh that exceeds any corporeal or corporate boundaries, who has "sovereignly" foreclosed the space and privilege of sovereign immunization. I understand this to be the achievement of what Bataille refers to as "the moment illuminated by a miraculous light, the light of the *sovereignty of life* delivered from its servitude."[22] This is what allows Bataille to write, "A king is the creature par excellence of the miracle; in his person he concentrates the virtues of a miraculous presence" (211). Pushing Hegel's master-slave dialectic to its limits, Bataille argues that only by, as it were, consecrating himself to the *gnosis* of the utter nullity of the project of self-preservation/ immunization does the sovereign subject become in some

---

20. Georges Bataille, "The 'Old Mole' and the Prefix *Sur*," in *Visions of Excess: Selected Writings, 1927–1939*, by Georges Bataille, trans. Allan Stoekl, Carl Lovitt, and Donald Leslie Jr. (Minneapolis: University of Minnesota Press, 1985), 39.

21. Ibid., 43.

22. Georges Bataille, *The Accursed Share: An Essay on General Economy*, trans. Robert Hurley (New York: Zone Books, 1993), 207; my emphasis. Subsequent references are made in the text.

sense *untouchable*. The operation Bataille ultimately aims at inducing in his reader is not unlike the process of *deposition* or *dethronement*—of *Ent-Setzen*—that Kantorowicz described apropos of Shakespeare's Richard II. This "rite of degradation," as Kantorowicz called it, follows the pattern of a "cascading: from divine kingship to kingship's 'Name,' and from the name to the naked misery of man."[23] For Bataille, this creaturely misery, if affirmed in the right way—that is, without the expectation of any sort of spiritual elevation, any *spiritual return on this divestment*—establishes a bit of the *kingdom*, enters into the "miraculous light . . . of the sovereignty of life delivered from its servitude." In a sense, the task is, paradoxically, to become "mired down" in a dimension that stands *below* that of the world of things and thereby to become "relieved of the heaviness that the world of utility imposes on us, of the tasks in which the world of objects mires us down" (243).

One will perhaps have noticed that Bataille has here more or less followed the messianic script of the Christian incarnation. It is, however, one that now—and this is the crux of this heterodox Christianity or Christian heterology—refuses the next series of acts, refuses, that is, to allow itself to be transfigured or uplifted, to become the support of any spiritual principle or value. If it is to become the basis of a new community, a new social link, this bit of kingdom will be one that gets disseminated horizontally in and through the base materialism of the flesh and without becoming incorporated into a church or any other *corpus mysticum*. This would be a community established by way of a *contagious untouchability*.

It is beyond my competence to determine or evaluate the coherence of Bataille's project across the many years and phases of his life as a writer and thinker. Indeed, I suspect that my brief sketch of this project has served to mask many tensions and contradictions in the writings. But what I find to be the ultimate limitation of the work is what I can only characterize as its extreme and violent *passion for the real*, a passion that seems never fully to escape from the syndrome that Elias Canetti identified as the ultimate disease of power: the syndrome of the *survivor*.[24] Indeed, it is the syndrome that Canetti posited as the real core of Schreber's psychosis, a view that allows him to read the judge's *Memoirs* as a kind of precursor to *Mein Kampf*. For Canetti the survivor is the figure driven

---

23. Kantorowicz, *The King's Two Bodies*, 27.

24. I borrow the phrase "the passion for the real" from Alain Badiou, who posits it as the key to his own secret history of modernity, or at least of the twentieth century. See Badiou, *The Century*, trans. Alberto Toscano (Cambridge: Polity Press, 2007). Elias Canetti develops his theory of the survivor in *Crowds and Power*, trans. Carol Stewart (New York: Seabury Press, 1978).

to sacrifice the world, to consecrate, consign, assimilate the rest of humankind to the entropic forces of base materiality, in a word, to reduce everything to shit, which as I see it thereby ceases to function as the operator of, to use Bataille's term, a radical heterology and instead comes to resemble a mad dream of a total, scatological homogenization.

A further reservation about Bataille's work has been proposed by Robert Buch, who suggests that what Bataille ultimately misses in the midst of his fascination with the images of the *ling'chi* is a dimension captured by another writer who likely knew the photographs in question: Franz Kafka. Among Buch's arguments is that in his famous story "In the Penal Colony," Kafka presents the tortured body not as a site that delivers on the promise of ecstatic passage beyond the symbolic order but rather as one that stages the violence of the subject's inscription into it.[25] As Buch furthermore suggests, one of the ways Kafka's work distinguishes itself from Bataille's is through its embrace of the dimension of the comedic. And indeed, comedy can help us to make a crucial distinction that often appears to be missing in Bataille's work and in that of writers who identify with his radical and, as I have suggested, fundamentally scatological conception of materialism.

VI

There is a strong tendency to assume that the comedic and the scatological essentially belong together, that, not to put too fine a point on it, "poop jokes" capture the very essence of what is at stake in the convulsive release of laughter, a topic of considerable interest to Bataille.[26] A recent film, *The Aristocrats*, might even be marshaled as evidence for the fundamentally Bataillean dimension of human comedy and laughter.[27] The film is a documentary of sorts, in which a series of comedians are invited to tell their version of a joke that is apparently quite well known in stand-up comedy circles in the United States; the punch line of the joke provides the film's title. It is a joke rarely told outside of circles of comedians, and yet the comedians interviewed in the film insist on its exemplary status for capturing the fundamental structure—and ultimately

---

25. See, once more, Robert Buch, *Pathos of the Real*.

26. For a fine discussion of the Bataillean conception of laughter, see Anca Parvaluscu, *Laughter: Notes on a Passion* (Cambridge, MA: MIT Press, 2010).

27. The film was directed by Paul Provenza and released in 2005.

anal character—of humor. The film gives the impression that a kind of secret society is divulging its dark side—stand-up comedy's *arcana imperii.*

The joke does have a clear and straightforward structure. It provides a
simple narrative that frames a space for virtuosic improvisation in which
the carnivalesque mixes with a kind of state of exception.[28] The frame
narrative goes something like this: A family walks into a talent agent's
office; the father says that he has a great family act he wants the agent
to represent. The agent is interested and asks to see what they do. At
that point, in a mixture of vaudeville and de Sade, the various members
of the family—father, mother, three or four kids—proceed, in a kind of
collective *passage à l'acte*, to engage in all manner of perverse sexual and
scatological acts with and on each other (in some versions animals are
involved as well). The gleefully sadistic description of the performance,
which typically culminates in acts of incest performed in pools of shit
and vomit, constitutes the improvisatory middle section of the joke. A
bit horrified, the talent agent finally asks the father what he calls the act
and receives the answer/punch line "the aristocrats!"

The film's argument about the irreducible and essential *lowness* of
comedy and laughter, what we might, in the spirit of the film's title, refer
to as their extravagant vulgarity, is a familiar one, indeed something of a
cliché. Tragedy is the genre appropriate to the noble and serious, comedy
to the low and unserious; tragedy lives off our capacities for sublimation, comedy off our need for desublimation. In more Bataillean terms,
laughter and comedy are always linked to a fundamental drive toward
debasement as the primary modality of pure expenditure available to
human beings, expenditure whose only product is the irredeemable gift
of *waste.* Indeed, the film seems to equate laughter with the process of
getting wasted as the path back into a "general economy" beyond the
servicing of goods. The film, which one could even imagine as a single,
long comedic "roast" of Georges Bataille, is no doubt onto something
true about laughter and comedy. But there is a crucial dimension of the
comedic that runs the risk of getting lost in the scatological orgy of such
a general economy.

Here I would like to return, once more, to Alenka Zupančič's dialectical theory of comedic materialism, one that locates the density of the
real not in the muck that drags human beings from their narcissistic self-

---

28. In this context it is interesting to note that one of the most celebrated versions of the joke
featured in the film was told by Gilbert Gottfried at a roast for Hugh Hefner very shortly after the
attacks of 9/11, when comedians were preoccupied with the dilemma of what sort of comedy might
be appropriate so soon after a national trauma.

idealizations and posturing back to the low, vulgar concreteness of their bodily being, but rather in the idiotic persistence of their "highness." As Zupančič puts it apropos of the familiar comic scenario of an aristocrat—say, a baron brimming with self-importance and confidence in his social standing—who stumbles over a banana peel or slips into the mud,

We have only to think about it a little in order to see that what we are dealing with here is in no way an abstract-universal idea (belief in the elevated nature of his own aristocratic personality) undermined, for our amusement, by intrusions of material reality. Or, to put it differently, we are not dealing with an abstract perfection, belied by human weaknesses and limitations to which this VIP is nonetheless subjected. On the contrary, is it not only too obvious that the capital human weakness here—what is most human, concrete, and realistic—is precisely the baron's unshakeable belief in himself and his own importance: that is to say, his presumptuousness? *This* is the feature that makes him "human," not the fact that he falls into a muddy puddle or slips on a banana peel.[29]

According to this view of comedy, the base materialism we associate with the genre turns out to be not merely the repressed animal support of our spiritual pretentions but rather a surplus element "secreted" by the abstract universality of spirit and agitating it from within. Zupančič is thereby able to point to the fundamentally conservative aspect of a great number of comedies that ultimately leave the "highness" of the symbolic statuses subjected to comedic debasement intact, "fundamentally untouched in their abstract purity, since the dirt is absorbed by the human side, which is then forgiven as belonging to the 'necessary evil.'" A comedy of this kind, she argues, remains "caught in an abstract dualism of the concrete and the universal and, much as it may emphasize the side of the concrete, this concrete remains but one element in the constellation of the universal versus the concrete, which is itself purely abstract" (31). The dialectical view of comedic materialism proposed by Zupančič is, I would suggest, among the strongest arguments against the Gnostic tendencies of Bataille's writings and comedies that share in its dualist worldview.[30] For Zupančič, comedy is not dualist at all but is rather the genre par excellence of a *troubled monism*, or, as I have been phrasing it, of a surplus or "too-muchness" of immanence. Zupančič thus concludes

---

29. Alenka Zupančič, *The Odd One In: On Comedy* (Cambridge, MA: MIT Press, 2007), 29. Subsequent references are made in the text.

30. Here, of course, *gnosis* lies on the side of the base. See Bataille, "Base Materialism and Gnosticism," in *Visions of Excess*, 45–52. There Bataille speaks of a *licentious* Gnosticism.

this part of her argument by suggesting that, for example, a true comedy about aristocracy must be structured in such a way

that the very universal aspect of this concept produces its own humanity, corporeality, subjectivity. Here, the body is not an indispensable basis of the soul; an inflexible belief in one's own baronage is precisely the point where the soul itself is as *corporeal* as possible. The concrete body of the baron, which repeatedly falls into the puddle of human weaknesses, is not simply the empirical body that lies flat in the mud, but much more the belief in his baronage, his "baronness." This "baronness" is the real comic object, produced by comedy as the quintessence of the universal itself. To put it in psychoanalytic terms: here, the ego-ideal itself turns out to be the partial (comic) object. (32)

Recalling Kantorowicz's characterization of Shakespeare's *Richard II* as "the tragedy of the King's Two Bodies," we might say that comedy is the means of transposing what Kantorowicz describes as Richard's experience of cascading "from kingship to kingship's 'Name,' and from the name to the naked misery of man," into the autonomous movement of an *object* agitating the bodies and spaces of a community, not unlike that peculiar creature named *Odradek* who occasioned the worries of the father of the family in Kafka's story.[31]

VII

My hope is that this digression will help us to evaluate the uses to which the Bataillean notion of the *informe* is put by Bois and Krauss in their efforts to brush modernism against the grain. Most importantly, the two critics propose to deploy the concept of the formless or *informe*, first defined by Bataille in a "critical dictionary" of terms published in an issue of the journal *Documents*, as an *operational* concept. Here they are more or less following Bataille's own definition of the term as a *procedure* of debasement:

A dictionary begins when it no longer gives the meaning of words, but their tasks. Thus *formless* is not only an adjective having a given meaning, but a term that serves

---

31. At this point in her argument, Zupančič recalls Lacan's remark "that a lunatic is not some poor chap who believes that he really is a king; a lunatic is a king who believes that he really is a king" (32). My argument has been that this lunacy has been democratized: it is now the people who believe they are the People.

to bring things down in the world, generally requiring that each thing have its form. What it designates has no rights in any sense and gets itself squashed everywhere, like a spider or an earthworm. In fact, for academic men to be happy, the universe would have to take shape. All of philosophy has no other goal: it is a matter of giving a frock coat to what is, a mathematical frock coat. On the other hand, affirming that the universe resembles nothing and is only *formless* amounts to saying that the universe is something like a spider or spit.[32]

As Bois summarizes in his introductory essay to *The User's Guide*, the *informe* "is not so much a stable motif to which we can refer, a symbolizable theme, a given quality, as it is a term allowing one to operate a declassification, in the double sense of lowering and of taxonomic disorder. Nothing in and of itself, the formless has only an operational existence: it is a performative, like obscene words, the violence of which derives less from semantics than from the very *act* of their delivery."[33]

The operational aspect of the term becomes especially significant in the context of the authors' efforts to distance themselves from the turn to "abjection" in a great deal of art of the past decades. As Krauss suggests in the concluding essay of the volume, the theory and practice of abject art, which take their cue above all from the work of Julia Kristeva, remain ultimately committed to the semantic field of the wound and fixated on the image of woman *as* wound even while endeavoring to deflate the fetish quality of the female body: "The wound on which much of 'abject art' is founded is . . . produced in advance as semantic, as it thematizes the marginalized, the traumatized, the wounded, as an essence that is feminine by nature and deliquescent by substance" (244).

Bois and Krauss divide the operations of the formless into a series of basic procedures that in different ways seek to undo and disperse what has been *in-formed*. In Bois's words, "these operations split off from modernism, insulting the very opposition of form and content—which is itself formal, arising as it does from a binary logic—declaring it null and void" (16). Among the operations in and through which modernism, so to speak, learns to curse, to attack or disrupt its own tendencies, however playful, toward form-giving and world-making, Bois and Krauss emphasize four distinct clusters: the push toward horizontality, the practices of a base materialism, the introduction of pulse into the visual field, and the submission of form to the effects of entropy, pure expenditure, wasting

32. Bataille, "Formless," in *Visions of Excess*, 31.
33. Bois and Krauss, *Formless*, 18. Subsequent references are made in the text.

away. I mention *play* because it might be helpful to try to grasp what is at issue in these procedures against the backdrop of our earlier discussion of the *fort/da* game. What Bois and Krauss mean by the *informe* are not procedures of *Trauerarbeit*, of working through loss by means of the sort of play that Freud observed in the behavior of his grandson, but rather ways in which precisely the *Trauerarbeit/Trauerspiel* of mourning *disrupts itself*, keeps returning, so to speak, to the initial tear in the fabric of being that occasioned the efforts at mastery through play. Notwithstanding Krauss's objections to the abject, we might say that they are procedures for sustaining the *jouissance* of this "flesh-wound" of being—something that cannot be fully captured by the semantics of *loss* or *lack*—beyond the pleasure principle that guides the activity of play.

Even though I think that this is precisely where they go wrong, it thus makes a certain sense that much of what Bois and Krauss focus on in their catalogue has, as they see it, an aspect not so much of the childish but rather of the *infantile*, a state imagined to stand closer to a not-yet-human animality, to what still creeps and crawls on the ground and in the dirt. The attack on verticality, for example, is seen to involve a freeing up of a repressed and, as it were, still *uninformed*, infantile-animal being: "Man is proud of being erect (and of having thus emerged from the animal state, the biological mouth-anus axis of which is horizontal), but this pride is founded on a repression" (26). Part and parcel of this attack on what is perceived to be the repressive aspect of verticality is—and here, think again about the *fort/da* game—the attack on sign systems. Bois thus praises Marcel Duchamp as "a pitiless sleuth" who was able to "put his finger on . . . semiological repression" (28). He claims of Duchamp's *Three Standard Stoppages* that it "knocks one of the most arbitrary systems of the sign there is (the metric system) off its pedestal to show that once submitted to gravity, once lowered into the contingent world of things and bodies, the sign does not hold water: it dissolves as an (iterable) sign and regresses toward singularity" (28).

How the emphasis on horizontality might function in the larger project of "brushing modernism against the grain" can be seen in Krauss's account of Pollock's drip paintings and their canonical reception: "The power of Pollock's mark as index meant it continued to bear witness to the horizontal's resistance to the vertical and that it was the *material* condition of this testimony—the oily, scabby, shiny, ropey qualities of the self-evidently horizontal mark—that would pit itself against the visual formation of the Gestalt, thus securing the condition of the work as *formless*." "It makes no difference," she continues, "that the most prestigious reception of Pollock's work . . . would read past this mark, repressing its implications by a series of complicated recodings that turned the metallic paint into transcendental fields and the ropey networks into hovering, luminous clouds, thereby attempting to resublimate the mark, to lift it into the field of form" (97).

Very similar sorts of aesthetic insults generated by the procedures of the *informe* are grouped under the heading of "base materialism." Again, it is a matter of *cursing out* any sort of "highness," any sort of idealism still harbored by the form-content opposition (or dialectic). One hears in Bois's characterization of Bataille's notion of base materialism something akin to the voice of the sovereign, only it seems to be one who still shits in his pants: his majesty the infant, the true master of "the science of what is wholly other," namely, scatology: "Bataille's 'matter' is shit or laughter or an obscene word or madness: whatever cuts all discussion short, whatever reason cannot drape with a 'mathematical frock coat,' whatever does not lend itself to any metaphorical displacement, whatever does not allow itself to be in-formed. According to Bataille, matter is seductive waste, appealing to what is most infantile in us, since the blow it strikes is devolutionary, regressive, low" (29–31). Again, the distinctive feature of such devolutionary "sovereignty" (not to say *tyranny*) is that it works, above all, to behead and disperse or, to use the name of the other two procedures listed by Bois and Krauss among the operations of the *informe*, it works to introduce "pulse" and "entropy" into what might otherwise stand and persist as a self-identical *work*: "Each time that the homogeneous raises its head and reconstitutes itself . . . the job of the *informe* . . . is *to decapitate it*" (71; my emphasis).

In the same issue of the journal in which Bois and Krauss published excerpts from their *User's Guide*, another member of the *October* collective, Hal Foster, registered a certain amount of frustration with the limits of the critical vocabulary both of the "formless" and the "abject" for thinking about the kinds of pressures under which modern and contemporary artists have labored and for imagining the possibilities of new kinds of aesthetic responses to those pressures. Foster suggests that both Breton and Bataille represent a certain failure of the imagination and ultimately offer as options for aesthetic practice little more than an oscillation between "oedipal naughtiness or infantile perversion": "To act dirty with the secret wish to be spanked, or to wallow in shit with the secret faith that the most defiled might reverse into the most sacred, the most perverse into the most potent."[34] It is, of course, gratifying that Foster cites

---

34. Hal Foster, "Obscene, Abject, Traumatic," *October* 78 (Fall 1996): 118. Foster unpacks these intuitions in great detail in *The Return of the Real* (Cambridge, MA: MIT Press, 1996).

my work on Schreber as a resource for thinking beyond this impasse, "to rethink transgression not as a rupture produced by a heroic avant-garde posited outside the symbolic order, but as a fracture traced by a strategic avant-garde positioned ambivalently within this order."[35] But as I have been arguing in this volume, Schreber's delusional intuitions about this "new thinking" need, in turn, to be placed in the context of the history of biopolitics (as a chapter in the political theology of the West) and the ways in which that history permeates our most basic sense of what it means to be alive and expressive as a human being.

VIII

In another highly ambitious attempt to reconstruct the history of visual modernism—to brush it against the grain of formalist readings—the philosopher J. M. Bernstein places the question of the vital sphere and what it means to be alive at the very center of his story.[36] For Bernstein, too, what is at stake in modernist art is the production of a kind of surplus animation that lays claim to our attention with a unique sort of authority. For Bernstein, however (and here he would seem to be as far from Bataille as one could possibly be), one will only adequately understand what it is that claims our attention, what summons, excites, calls out—rather than *cursing* out—our attentive looking, if one grasps this demand as one pertaining to the conditions under which human beings can flourish, can be good at being the mortal, embodied subjects they are. On this view, aesthetic authority ultimately derives from the ways in which a work of art remains somehow in touch with and responsive to what Bernstein characterizes as the *normative authority of nature*. For Bernstein, the surplus we have been tracking throughout this study is, in the end, the symptom of lives lived under conditions that have imposed insurmountable structural obstacles to human flourishing, to the capacity for meaningful sensory experience within a vibrant form of life made to the measure of embodied subjects. Modernism represents for Bernstein the effort to track the fate of such experience once it has been hounded out of the built space of human community. The aesthetic pleasure afforded by modernist art represents, for Bernstein, the displaced and distorted

35. Foster, "Obscene, Abject, Traumatic," 115.
36. J. M. Bernstein, *Against Voluptuous Bodies: Late Modernism and the Meaning of Painting* (Stanford, CA: Stanford University Press, 2006). Subsequent references are made in the text.

form—both meanings are nicely captured in the German word *entstellt*—in which such "goodness" remains available to modern subjects.

Bernstein situates his readings of modernist art—his primary objects are works by Chaim Soutine, Anthony Caro, Frank Stella, Jackson Pollock, Marcel Duchamp, Robert Ryman, and Cindy Sherman—within a relatively familiar narrative of modernity. It is a story of the disenchantment of nature induced by the increasing dominance of technical rationality in human life, the ever-ramifying "administration" of the world that captures sensuous particularity within a grid of disembodied forms of general equivalence (scientific formalization, commodity exchange, bureaucratic organization). It is a process that in the same stroke anesthetizes and overstimulates, virtualizes and reifies, isolates and aggregates. Though he does not specifically cite Walter Benjamin, his argument largely parallels the latter's claims about the degradation of experience in modernity, the transformation, as Benjamin famously put it, of *Erfahrung* into *Erlebnis* and beyond that into the stuff of pure traumatic shock—call it "experience" beyond the pleasure principle. In his essay *The Storyteller*, Benjamin characterizes this transformation as one that abandons "the tiny, fragile human body" to a force field of destructive torrents and explosions that are as much structural as they are martial or material.[37]

For Bernstein, too, the fate of this fragile body and its apparent lack of fit with a world it must nonetheless inhabit are at the core of the story. "Disenchantment" signifies here a process that delegitimates our experience of ourselves and our being-in-the-world as vulnerable and dependent beings, disqualifies the dimension of emphatic experience in which sentient embodiment, the felt fact of aliveness, still bears a normative significance in relation to the object world and other human subjects. "What has been excised from the everyday," Bernstein writes, "is the *orientational significance of sensory encounter, sensory experience as constitutive of conviction and connection to the world of things*. The emptying of sensory encounter of orientational significance is our mortification" (3). The warrant of all such significance is, as Bernstein emphatically puts it (paraphrasing T. J. Clark), "the thing of all things, the body" (261). It is ultimately the fundamental continuity of human and animal life, along with the mimetic capacities—capacities for felt affinity with what is alive—with which such life is endowed, that is mortified by the processes of modernization, processes that include "the subsuming of

---

37. Walter Benjamin, "The Storyteller," trans. Harry Zohn, in Walter Benjamin, *Selected Writings*, vol. 3, *1935–1936*, ed. Howard Eiland and Michael Jennings (Cambridge, MA: Harvard University Press, 2002), 144.

the use values of particular goods beneath the exchange value of monetary worth, or the domination of intersubjective practices by norms of instrumental reason that yield the rationalization or bureaucratization of our dominant institutions" (23). At this point, the only naturalism that appears as intelligible is one that posits nature as a realm of purely mechanical causation. Our links to animality—what Bernstein refers to as our "circumambient nature"—are not simply eliminated; rather, they are delegitimated, at best relegated to a zone of ostensibly primitive, animistic beliefs, beliefs that now readily circulate in the domain of New Age practices and wisdom.[38] Bernstein's project is to reclaim this zone of "animism" for a more robust conception of the space of reasons—one that can encompass "the normative authority of natural form" (297)—a project that requires the aid not of New Age techniques for the recuperation of embodied orientation but of *modernist painting*, the set of practices that would seem, more than any other, precisely to have left nature and any thought of natural form behind.[39]

IX

It is, thus, not so much that the arts must always remain grounded in the representation of the human form. Rather, if they are to get a grip on us

38. In an essay on the work of John McDowell, Bernstein nicely summarizes his view of "circumambient nature": "The moment of nature that underwent petrification by being turned into a law-governed totality, what Kant calls 'empirical reality,' cannot be equivalent to the nature that is revealed through mathematical physics since that nature just is a law-governed totality. Rather, the nature that has been discounted by rationalized reason is the nature whose operations are not strictly reducible to the natural-scientific paradigm, the nature intrinsic in and the counterpart of our embodiment (and the embodiment of creatures biologically like us). For such animals, like ourselves, objects appear relative to embodied needs and desires: things to be eaten, places for hiding or making a home, objects to be attacked and defended against, things to be protected and nurtured. Because the way in which objects appear in this scenario is relativized to our embodiment, and the embodiment of creatures like us, and hence is proto-meaningful, it does not follow that this relativization or qualification in their appearing is a work of *projecting* (proto-)meaning on to them. On the contrary, much of the point of claiming that we are *parts* of a wider natural world (shared with the higher mammals), and that our forms of activity are a natural outgrowth from more primitive forms of animal behavior, is to deny that meaningful behavior is *sui generis* or an unconditioned imposition of meaning onto an otherwise meaningless flux. We could not ethically (conceptually) care about preventing unnecessary suffering unless suffering pain was 'already' something which beings constituted like ourselves naturally sought to avoid." J. M. Bernstein, "Re-enchanting Nature," in *Reading McDowell: On "Mind and World,"* ed. Nicholas H. Smith (London: Routledge, 2002), 224.

39. It should be noted that there are some historical and cultural intersections between New Age movements and modernism in the arts, particularly in the area of dance. One thinks, for example, of the confluence of these currents in places like Ascona in the early decades of the twentieth century. See, for example, Martin Green, *Mountain of Truth: The Counterculture Begins: Ascona, 1900–1920* (Hanover, NH: University Press of New England, 1986.

in any real way, they must, Bernstein argues, persist as the site of significant sensory experience—and its grounding in that "thing of all things,
the body"—at a historical moment when the natural and social sciences
have all but transformed the body into a site of calculation, discipline,
and functional optimization: "The conceit upon which my argument
turns is that *the arts have become the bearers of our now delegitimated capacity
for significant sensory encounter: emphatic experience*" (7). Key to Bernstein's
argument—and we might see this as a Cavellian supplement to the story
of disenchantment—is that it is only because of the persistence of something like aesthetic "aura" or "charisma" that we can resist the deep pull
of the *skepticism* endemic to the reigning forms of rationality. It is only
by virtue of the insistence, if only as a breakdown product, of emphatic
experience in the practices of modernist art—experience that always remains grounded in the sentience we share with the animal kingdom—
that human subjects can assure themselves that they are not Fichtean
idealists whose conceptual schemes spin freely in a frictionless universe
positing but never *touching* the "not I":

Only through emphatic experience could we be "in touch" with what is other to the
products of the spontaneity of the mind, hence *others* in themselves rather than their
being mere mirrors reflecting what has been imposed upon them by the mind's spontaneous, general forms, hence truly sensible others. The arts provide, so to speak, the
sensory experience of particulars writ large. . . . The task of the arts is to rescue from
cognitive and rational oblivion our embodied experience and the standing of unique,
particular things as the proper objects of such experience, albeit only in the form of a
reminder or a promise. (7)

To put it another way, Bernstein argues that without such a reminder,
one that, in modernist art, often appears in the form of a hypercathected
remainder or indigent *leftover* of the "thing of all things," we would float
freely in a nominalist universe of arbitrary signs where language would
never be pinned to, be beholden to, the world of things. There would
never be what Bernstein characterizes as "the jointure of orders of fact
with orders of feeling, call it *an expressive empirical order*" (99; my emphasis). In a word, without some form of naturalism, there would be cul-
turalism all the way down and therewith a kind of utter deadness. This,
Bernstein argues, is what modernist art, albeit in modes that may appear
to be *entstellt*, itself "argues."

A modernist work of art worthy of its name—one that does not, to use
Michael Fried's formulation, sink to the level of mere "objecthood"—
manages to transfigure the *becoming abstract* of such an expressive

empirical order into a new locus of significant sensory encounter. If our capacity for pleasure is linked to a sense of fit with the world (this is what Bernstein ultimately means by "expressive empirical order") and if that sense of jointure or fitness is what is under assault in modernity, what is thrown out of joint, modernism, Bernstein suggests, paradoxically *saves pleasure* by pushing it—think again of the word *Entstellung*— *beyond the pleasure principle*. The trauma of abstraction, the extirpation of significant sensory encounter from the (thereby) disenchanted world, is itself posited as the sublime representative of *the real* that is lost in this very process. Modernist art places at the heart of its procedures what for Bernstein figures as the fate of the sensuous particular more generally; it posits "*the continuation of the slaughter of its authority* as the plenipotentiary of the authority of living nature" (10). And again, the claim here is that only as such does a work of art possess *aesthetic authority* for us. We might think here, once more, about the upper half of David's painting *Death of Marat*. What, on this view, we are seeing, what makes a normative claim on our attention—that is, what others ought also to be responsive to if they are to be alive to what is happening to their very aliveness—is the passing of the "authority of living nature" out of the embodied subject and into its last (non)resting place: the abstract materiality of modernist art.

X

Bernstein's study culminates in an exploration of the genre that he sees as registering the vengeful persistence of life's tautological impulse—*life wants to live*—in the midst of a disenchanted universe: *horror*. Horror functions here as a significant chapter in the history of the aesthetics of the sublime, as the place where contact can be made with the limits of culture, where lives caught in rigidifying social orders connect once more with an unmasterable nature that might shatter and so animate them. Only now the source of animation is the very fact of mortification itself: "If nature is what is wholly repressed and repudiated as a condition for rational society, then the limit is no longer an external or exterior other, but the suffering of our mortified lives with respect to what might animate them" (295). The disastrous event has already happened: "What needs to be made visible now, brought to expression, is the violence that has already been done to the subject, that has already murdered the autonomous subject and left in her place the walking dead, the zombie, the monster. The monstrous here has a narrow and precise signification: it represents the dead *in* the apparently living, the living in what is deathly, the gross vitality of what is apparently dead, the boundary between the living and the dead as becoming indeterminate" (295). For Bernstein, the living dead return because they act as the last available plenipotentiary of the impulse of life for mortified, deadened subjects. Horror, a word that brings together the signification of the two German words we have been using here, *Entsetzen* and *Entstellung*, provides what looks to be the "natural" (non)resting place of our mortified nature: "*In horror, all that is left of nature is the inversion of natural form: the continuous dismemberment of the—normative—unity of the animate organism*. But if this inversion is all that is left, then the normative authority of natural form is transferred into its opposite: what ought never to be seen, the endless work of dismemberment, is what must be seen if nature is to be seen at all" (297). As Bernstein concludes this peculiar dialectic, one can discern the polemic against the Bataillean affirmation of dismemberment, decomposition, entropic dissolution; if modernism actively affirms such processes, it does so in a rather more ambivalent key than the one championed by Bataille:

Our desire and fascinated repulsion at the horrible thus replays in the mode of disgust the duplicity of the original sublime [*desire* for nature beyond rigid social forms; *threat* of unmasterable nature] only now the moment of pleasure is dispatched into awareness of our mortification: the too much animation of active dismemberment . . . has become the unique point of access to the limit of rational form. Horror, then, addresses an anxiety that life does not live, in relation to an inarticulate and unfelt belief concerning the normative authority of life, of memberment as the impulse of the living. . . . the authority of memberment, the claim of the animated, unified living body, continues, survives, in the compelling disgust at dismemberment. (297)

The prominence of horror as a crucial locus of the claims of aliveness is prefigured for Bernstein in the "fatty carnality" of Chaim Soutine's canvases, their demonstration of "an affinity between . . . paint-on-canvas . . . and inner body parts" (298). This affinity, in which "each nexus of brush strokes is a paint image, like *a twitch, cringe, or writhing*" (70; my emphasis), functions in this work as a "transcendental induction . . . for the sake of reinstating the claim of 'is living' as a material a priori necessary for the possibility of meaningfulness generally" (67). But it is the work of Cindy Sherman, an artist generally associated with postmodern art practices and attitudes, that serves as Bernstein's key witness for the "too much animation" that paradoxically testifies to the mortification of embodied subjectivity in modernity.

XI

Among Bernstein's most compelling claims in his discussion of Sherman's work is his suggestion of the links between her deservedly famous series *Untitled Film Stills* and the later images that feature grotesquely distorted faces and bodies, bizarre arrangements of human and prosthetic limbs and organs, and images of decomposing flesh. The stills, which feature Sherman in a series of photographs evoking clichés of femininity proper to various film genres, would seem at first glance to argue for the capture, without remainder, of female subjectivity by the image repertoire of feminine being made available by the culture industry, a capture that can be suspended, if at all, only by a canny practice of ironic citation or parodic performance. Bernstein argues, however, that "the camera's disinterested gaze pierces the artifice of the setup, the elaborate paraphernalia of scene, pose, and construction, and by the very reiteration of images imposes a wholly indeterminate singularity as the anxious object of each picture: this is Cindy Sherman. . . . *The story they tell is, finally, of the unbearable tension between anxious singularity and clichéd identity*" (276). As Bernstein narrates Sherman's career as an artist, this anxious singularity will come to be increasingly materialized, made carnal as the stuff that will ultimately figure the limits of the culture industry's capacity to captivate, "figuring a significant materiality of meaning that will animistically exceed the image and imply a material or somatic reality that the clichéd image cannot capture" (279).

Bernstein reads Sherman's later photographs as a kind of salvage work, as so many efforts to rescue a remnant of aliveness out of this vertiginous confusion of inside and outside, rigidity and ooze. In his reading of Sherman's *Untitled #244*, an image showing a magnified section of a bruised and dirtied limb leaking blood (we cannot tell what part of the body is being shown), the glistening red trickle that Bernstein insists "is still our lifeblood" holds the place of the anxious singularity he earlier identified with the artist's proper name:

This disquieting, queasy-making image in which outside and inside fluidly exchange positions should key us to Sherman's insistent depictions of orifices—mouths, anuses, vaginas—as operating similarly, that is, as revealing the extent to which skin is not, cannot be, a container, that the sense of containment, and hence the sense of a reassuring distinction between inside and outside, is illusory. This exposure of the inside, turning it out (by turning the flesh in), is not for the sake of destroying the integrity of the skin, but rather of reanimating it by folding it back into the viscous fluid life inside, against the pretense the skin has become. If normally for visible bodies the skin separates what is visible from what *ought* to be hidden, Sherman's practice interrogates the functioning of that ought, and hence the dualism of inside and outside it generates as a force of repression and self-repudiation, as deathly. The categorical imperative making the skin the container is as repressive of life as Kant's moral sublimation of it. Again, what leaks and seeps in *Untitled #244* is our *life*. (301)

And with regard to this cluster of works more generally, Bernstein argues that "in their gross, hallucinatory moment of sensuous excess they conjure an auratic animism, but one quite remote from the human face or the human figure: it is misplaced life, boil, livid pimples, leaking flesh, and fleshy tongue that now bear the full burden of the claim that life lives, lives on in its organic animation, its pulsating decomposition, its disgusting remnants" (302).

What concerns me here is the way in which, in the midst of the semantic vertigo generated by Sherman's work and his own efforts to conceptualize it, Bernstein keeps landing on the side of organic, animal life as the dark background and true locus of our singularity. It is thus wonderfully refreshing to find the following admission of a profound uncertainty that is, I think, much more in touch with what is at stake in the works he surveys:

The uncanniness of aesthetic perception is thus not only the experience of meaning in what otherwise lacks meaning—brute sounds, paint-on-canvas; in order for something to be meaningful it must equally be the bearer of life. Artistic materialism, in theory and practice, is a form of (illusory) animism. The production of auratic works is the production of a semblance of a living thing, the animation of the undead. Or perhaps, more precisely, the wedding of materiality and meaning in modernist works is sublinguistic, recalling or invoking the kind of proto-meaning, meaning before meaning, the anticipation of meaning borne by bare life. *I am unsure exactly how to phrase this without it spinning utterly out of control.* (262; my emphasis)

My modest proposal is to suggest that this spinning, this semantic vertigo, *belongs to the object itself,* that it is not something that hinders our access to, or our capacity to conceptualize, the animation in question, but rather something that co-constitutes it. But that, of course, means that the object can no longer be equated with "bare life" if what is understood thereby is *zoē,* the life we share with other animals, or as Bernstein tends to put it, the normative authority of natural form. All the while holding to that view, Bernstein keeps reaching toward the zone of indistinction between the voice of nature and the voice of culture, the locus of a "proto-meaning" he himself, at least at one symptomatic moment, characterizes as *aporetic*.[40] To stick to the metaphor of the voice, we might say that the voice Bernstein hears but misidentifies (as the voice of nature) is the sonority that arises within this zone. This, I would submit, is precisely the insight that Bernstein keeps stumbling on but is never able to recognize and so mobilize for an understanding of aesthetics, ethics, or politics. To put it somewhat differently, if beneath the skin there is more "life" than we bargained for—think again of the country doctor's discovery in Kafka's story—this is because what we find there is not only tissue, blood, bones, nerves (as what "ought" not be seen) but also the fleshly surplus we take on when we are taken in by the historical, cultural modes by which our bare lives come to be "naturalized."[41] What modernist art registers and elaborates is not the loss of the normative authority of nature but rather a radical historical shift affecting our capacity to figure an excess of normative pressure that gets under the skin of embodied subjects as beings of language, as animals compelled to live their lives in the field of the Other, the space where enjoyment and entitlement are inexorably intertwined.

What is at issue in the so-called disenchantment of nature cannot, finally, be captured by the notion of a "fitness" of embodied subjectivity and world, which is ultimately a secularized version of what the religions of revelation call *providence*; what is at stake is rather the possibility of feeling *libidinally implicated* in the world, of being in the world in a fundamentally erotic sense, in a word, of being in love with the world—*of finding the world to be enchanting*.[42] What Bernstein suggests is that mo-

40. Bernstein writes, "The repudiation of the *authority* of nature is a necessary condition for the possibility of rational society. My argument is not meant to dispute this necessity, but only to reveal why it must remain aporetic. There is aporia here because, although we cannot forgo the cultural effort of self-authorization without self-defeat, without making our commitments in principle unintelligible and things for which we are not accountable and responsible, that effort of pure self-authorization cannot be completed. To be sure, it will always be logically incomplete because it is subject to historical contingency; but, or so I am claiming, it will always be ontologically and so rationally incomplete because there is a *claim of nature*—say, the authority of suffering—that cannot be *exhausted* by its social acknowledgment. . . . One way of stating this might be to say that nature is a *forever lost source of authority*" (382–83).

41. The semantic vertigo at issue here should already be apparent in the word used to certify someone as properly belonging to the symbolic order of the nation-state: *naturalization*.

42. One might recall here the ambiguities of one of the German words for expressing what is enchanting: *reizvoll*, full of charms. As we have noted, what is *reizvoll* might also be characterized as what induces a surfeit of *excitations*, a state that is in danger of becoming a *Reizüberflutung*, an overstimulation that breaches the *Reizschutz*, the protective shield of the ego. One might say that

dernity induces a fundamental disruption in this love relation, literally and metaphorically a kind of breakup *with* and so *of* the world (and self). At some level, human subjects are no longer able to fully throw in their lot with the world in a libidinal sense. Their inscription into the space of meaning has become depleted of erotic charge, fails to secure a powerful libidinal bond with social reality. We are there, in the midst of the social space, but this space feels dead and we, too, no longer feel alive. Our *jouissance* is no longer dependably dispersed amid our doings in the world but congeals into dense, symptomatic blockages that, as Bernstein argues, can be elaborated only in the realm of (modernist) art, and even there only with great difficulty and never fully successfully.

As I have indicated, Bernstein's project bears certain resemblances to Heidegger's efforts to make manifest the ways in which human beings always already find themselves in the midst of an understanding of Being. This allows for encounters with entities understood *as such and such*, opens the space for relevant judgments and responses to the sorts of claims such entities make on our attention and practical engagements in the world. Heidegger refers to this space as that of a prediscursive disclosedness or *Erschlossenheit*, as the horizon of intelligibility—Heidegger often speaks of a clearing or *Lichtung*—in which something can appear to us as the sort of being it is. Bernstein is above all interested in our pre- or nondiscursive grasp of the predicate "is living," our capacity to orient ourselves within the space of relevant responses and modes of acknowledgment with respect to living things. At one point in his efforts to unpack this thought, he turns not to Heidegger but rather to a passage in Wittgenstein's *Philosophical Investigations*. The passage is especially interesting given Heidegger's famous distinction between the kinds of "worldliness" manifest in different kinds of entities. As I have already noted, Heidegger had, in a 1929–30 lecture course, distinguished between the stone, which he called *weltlos*, the animal, which he called *weltarm*, and the human, which he called *weltbildend*.[43] Here is Wittgenstein's rather more intuitive take on the same—or at least, a related—set of distinctions:

Look at a stone and imagine it having sensations.—One says to oneself: How could one so much as get the idea of ascribing a *sensation* to a *thing*. One might as well ascribe it to a number!—And now look at a wriggling fly [*eine zappelnde Fliege*] and at once these

---

what Bernstein discovers in modernist art is the way in which a *lack of enchantment* converges with an uncanny *excess of enchantment*, or what I have characterized as a sort of enchantment beyond the pleasure principle.

43. We might add to the triad the Bataillean gesture of *world-shitting*.

difficulties vanish and pain seems able to get a foothold here, where before everything was, so to speak, too smooth for it.

And so, too, a corpse seems inaccessible to pain.—Our attitude to what is alive and to what is dead, is not the same. All our reactions are different.[44]

Again, by saying that *all* our reactions are different, Wittgenstein is pointing to that disclosedness or nondiscursive space in which our encounter with things is *always already oriented* in fundamental ways with respect to the being of the entity before us. Bernstein's project has been to demonstrate the ways in which our fundamental orientation with respect to the predicate "is living" has become radically attenuated under conditions of modernity, has been forced to hibernate, so to speak, into the media of modernist aesthetic practices. My "slight adjustment" to Bernstein's work has been to argue that human beings have a capacity—and indeed live under the compulsion—to wriggle or twitch in a way that is quite different from the way of flies or any other animals (even when in pain), that their wriggling bears witness to a different kind of animation, one born in the semantic vertigo that infects the conceptual field of "the animate" and that enters human life by way of the procedures by which such life comes to be "naturalized." The pathos and limits of Bernstein's project derive from what I see as his profound attunement to but ultimate failure to grasp the distinctiveness of human "twitching" or "wriggling." I have, of course, been arguing that it may not be possible to remain responsive to this dimension without the resources made available by Freud, who, one will recall, first grasped the *Urphänomen* of human wriggling in the uncanny body of his central European neurotics, a body whose flesh—and the biopolitical pressures it incarnated—he very much shared.

XII

Given Bernstein's attraction to the "fatty carnality" of paint-on-canvas in the work of Soutine or to images of "leaking flesh" in Sherman's later photographs as negative placeholders of the possibility of genuine sensory encounter, his insistence that "the too much animation of active dismemberment" serves, in modernist visual culture, as the final (non)resting place of "memberment as the impulse of the living," it comes as something of a surprise that he finds no place for the work of Francis Bacon in his story. Bernstein himself registers this surprise, noting

---

44. Ludwig Wittgenstein, *Philosophical Investigations*, section 284, cited in Bernstein, 55.

that he has no easy answer as to why he finds Bacon's work unpersuasive. He speculates "that the drama of skin, the drama of its failures of containment, becomes histrionic rather than compelling in Bacon's distortions," that they offer "the wrong sort of objective correlative of the phenomenon he is seeking to express" (381). He does, however, suggest that Gilles Deleuze's unabashedly affirmative study of Bacon shares some of the central concerns of his own project. My sense is that Bernstein's intuition is at least in part correct here, but only because Deleuze, too, in spite of his radically different philosophical ambitions and trajectory, gets caught up in some of the same sorts of confusion I have noted with respect to Bernstein's "vitalism." Paradoxically, Bernstein's commitment to "memberment" and Deleuze's commitment to life *beyond organicity*, to what he calls, following Artaud, the "body without organs," converge in what I see as serious misreadings of the dimension I am calling the flesh.

A good deal of what almost every critic has written about Bacon takes as its point of departure statements the painter made about his work in a set of interviews he gave over the course of some twenty years with the critic David Sylvester. There Bacon insists, for example, that one of his central ambitions as an artist is to induce a kind of neuroaesthetic experience on the part of the spectator. He tries, that is, to produce images that capture and record the reality at issue—and this is, for the most part, one related to the sheer fact of embodiment—such that the painting acts directly on the *nervous system* of the viewer, transmitting to it the vital forces at work in the appearance in question. This can only succeed, Bacon argues, to the extent that these forces can be seen to break through and with the narrative or illustrative aspect of the image, to introduce into the figurative dimension of the painting a sufficiently convulsive shudder, one that can no longer be interpreted as a recognizable form of emotional expressivity, but only registered as the impact of quanta of sensation on the nervous system.[45] Deleuze, as we shall see, places just such remarks at the center of the "logic of sensation" he elaborates with respect to Bacon's work.

---

45. At the end of this chapter I will return to my discussion of David's painting *The Death of Marat*. In this context, one might recall part of the speech David gave in the Convention the day after presenting his painting to the assembly: "It is not only by charming the eyes that artistic monuments have attained their goal, but in penetrating the soul, in making a deep impression on the mind akin to that made by reality itself—it is then that deeds of heroism and civic virtue, presented to the people's view, will *electrify their souls* and breed a passion for glory and devotion to the welfare of the fatherland." Cited in Tony Halliday, "David's *Marat* as Posthumous Portrait" in *David's "The Death of Marat,"* ed. William Vaughan and Helen Weston (Cambridge: Cambridge University Press, 2000), 68; my emphasis. Bacon, apparently, simply wants to *electrify the nervous system* of the viewer.

Bacon posits this neuroaesthetic position as the key to his lifelong effort to do "a kind of tightrope walk between what is called figurative painting and abstraction. It will go right out from abstraction but will really have nothing to do with it. It's an attempt to bring the figurative thing up onto the nervous system more violently and more poignantly."[46] In a later interview, after again insisting on the anti-illustrational thrust of his work, he distances himself from abstract painting even more aggressively: "One of the reasons why I don't like abstract painting, or why it doesn't interest me, is . . . that abstract painting is an entirely aesthetic thing. . . . It is only really interested in the beauty of its patterns or its shapes," while what remains central to his own project is, as he puts it, "returning fact onto the nervous system in a more violent way" (59).

A great deal of time is spent in the interviews trying to clarify the correlations between what Bacon calls "the mystery of the appearance" and "the mystery of the making" (105), correlations, that is, between what I have characterized as Bacon's neuroaesthetic objectives and his painterly procedures, his mode of working with materials. The primary focus of these reflections is the painter's experimentation with accident and contingency, with the various methods of self-disruption Bacon employs that serve to keep the canvas in a state of agitation, from settling too easily with what he calls "the illustrational facts of the image" (105). "Half my painting activity," Bacon asserts, "is disrupting what I can do with ease" (91). Or as he puts it elsewhere, "one knows that by some accidental brushmarks suddenly appearance comes in with a vividness that no accepted way of doing it would have brought about." For that reason, he continues, "I'm always trying through chance or accident to find a way by which appearance can be there but remade out of other shapes" (105). Indeed, when Sylvester suggests that such accidents serve to generate "the otherness of those shapes," Bacon responds by hyperbolically proposing that his ideal would be "just to pick up a handful of paint and throw it at the canvas and hope that the portrait was there" (107).

At various points in the interviews, the conversation turns to Bacon's well-known preoccupation with photography and his use of photographs for his portrait work. On a first approach, one might say that the convulsive *shudder* that Bacon tries to introduce into his images, at least in part through experiments with various ways of disrupting or attacking the forms taking shape on the canvas, is related to what he refers to as

---

46. David Sylvester, *The Brutality of Fact: Interviews with Francis Bacon* (New York: Thames and Hudson, 2008), 12. Subsequent references are made in the text.

the "assault" already suffered by appearances under the impact of the *shutter* speed of photography and film. "I think," Bacon says, "one's sense of appearances is assaulted all the time by photography and by film. So that, when one looks at something, one's not only looking at it directly but one's looking at it through the assault that has already been made on one by photography and film" (30). Admitting to having always felt "haunted" by photographs, Bacon suggests that the spectrality at issue there emerges by way of a self-difference introduced into the object by the sheer fact of being photographed: "I think it's the slight remove from fact, which returns me onto the fact more violently." This gap or remove becomes a kind of point of access: "Through the photographic image I find myself beginning to wander into the image and unlock what I think of as its reality more than I can by looking at it" (30).[47] This gap of self-difference—the "slight remove from fact"—is even more extreme in the photographic motion studies made by Eadweard Muybridge, whose se-ries of images of wrestlers were especially important for Bacon's paintings of male coupling.[48] But perhaps above all, photography provided Bacon with a stronger sense of his task as a *recorder of fact*, indeed of what he characterized as the *"brutality of fact"* (182; my emphasis).

In response to Sylvester's request to clarify the difference between an illustrational and a nonillustrational form, Bacon brings together sev-eral aspects of his process and ambition as an artist and suggests that it is precisely by means of the solicitation of contingency into the image that a "fact" comes to be recorded in a way that is related to but distinct from photography. "I think," he responds, "that the difference is that an illustrational form tells you through the intelligence immediately what the form is about, whereas a non-illustrational form works first upon sensation and then slowly leaks back into the fact. . . . This may have to do with how facts themselves are ambiguous, how appearances are ambiguous, and therefore this way of recording form is nearer to the

47. Bacon also notes that the photographs he typically uses as the basis of his paintings them-selves often show signs of wear and tear, have themselves already undergone a process of distortion under the impact of time and human handling. They have, we might say, been absorbed into the rhythms of *natural history*. About a relatively late painting of a landscape, Bacon explains to Sylvester that it, too, was based on a photograph, but one that "had got torn up and it formed to some extent the shape that the grass has. It kept on being trampled on so much in all the chaos of where I work, and, when I pulled it out, it had practically all fallen away, but there was just this sort of fragment of grass left" (162).

48. "Actually," Bacon says, "Michelangelo and Muybridge are mixed up in my mind together, and so I perhaps could learn about positions from Muybridge and learn about the ampleness, the grandeur of form from Michelangelo, and it would be very difficult for me to disentangle the influ-ence of Muybridge and the influence of Michelangelo" (114).

fact by its ambiguity of recording" (57). When Sylvester presses Bacon to distinguish further this ambiguity from one achieved by high-speed photography that, as Sylvester puts it, "produces an entirely unexpected effect which is highly ambiguous and exciting, because the image is the thing and it isn't," Bacon introduces the motif of *aliveness*: "I think the difference from direct recording through the camera is that as an artist you have to, in a sense, set a trap *by which you hope to trap this living fact alive*. How well can you set the trap? Where and at what moment will it click?" Bacon goes on to emphasize the distinction between the texture of photographs, which "seems to go through an illustrational process onto the nervous system," and that of painting, which "seems to come immediately onto the nervous system" (57–58; my emphasis).

With these metaphors of "trapping" and "capturing," we have touched on what might be the most significant feature of Bacon's work and no doubt the one that has come to function as his signature as an artist. For as I have noted, the "living fact" at issue for most of Bacon's work pertains to the condition of embodiment, to the fact of aliveness, to the human condition of being, so to speak, horribly stuck with or riveted to that fact. Given the recurring motif of crucifixions in Bacon's work, we might even say: *crucified on the fact of one's aliveness*. This set of relations is elaborated further in a telling exchange between Bacon and Sylvester. It touches on the peculiar convergence in Bacon's paintings of the artificial and the visceral, something that often lends his images the aspect of a surreal medical or scientific experiment. Here, however, the dominant metaphor is that of hunting and trapping:

FB Well, it's in the artificial structure that the reality of the subject will be caught, and the trap will close over the subject-matter and leave only the reality. One always starts work with the subject, no matter how tenuous it is, and one constructs an artificial structure by which one can trap the reality of the subject-matter that one has started from.

DS The subject's a sort of bait?

FB The subject is the bait.

DS And what is that reality that remains, that residue? How does it relate to what you began with?

FB It doesn't necessarily relate to it, but you will have created a realism equivalent to the subject-matter which will be what is left in its place. You have to start from somewhere, and you start from the subject which gradually, if the thing works well at all, withers away and leaves this residue which we call reality and which perhaps has something tenuously to do with what one started with but very often has very little to do with it. (180–82)

It is at the end of this exchange that Bacon coins the phrase the "brutality of fact."

XIII

As I have indicated, it is this set of relations—let's call it the brutality of the living fact of aliveness and its modes of aesthetic capture—that provides Gilles Deleuze with his key point of access to Bacon's oeuvre, one he sees as organized around a "logic of sensation."[49] I want to examine the way Deleuze "fleshes out" this logic apropos of Bacon, because the philosopher's work has so often been seen as among the most significant philosophical challenges to the psychoanalytic approach to the "vital sphere" of embodied subjectivity.

In the preface to his study, Deleuze lays out the general and, in some sense, ordinary ways in which he sees this logic at work in Bacon's paintings, paintings that have for the most part been viewed as images of bodies turned inside out and faces frozen in eternal screams under the impact of some unnamed and perhaps unnamable horror (this is no doubt what Bernstein means when he characterizes Bacon's work as "histrionic"). Citing Bacon's own claim that he was more interested in the scream than in any particular horror, Deleuze attempts to de-dramatize—and, above all, de-psychologize—Bacon's spare though often theatrical stagings of bodies under various kinds and degrees of pressure, pressure that becomes manifest in the medium of paint made flesh and flesh made paint:

In the long run Bacon's Figures aren't wracked bodies at all, but ordinary bodies in ordinary situations of constraint and discomfort. A man ordered to sit still for hours on a narrow stool is bound to assume contorted postures. The violence of a hiccup, of a need to vomit, but also of a hysterical, involuntary smile. . . . Bacon's bodies, heads, Figures are of flesh, and what fascinates him are the invisible forces that model flesh or shake it. This is not the relationship of form and matter, but of materials and forces; to make these forces visible through their effects on flesh. . . . What fascinates Bacon is not movement, but its effect on an immobile body: heads whipped by wind, deformed by an aspiration—but also all the interior forces that climb through flesh. To make spasm visible. The entire body becomes plexus. (xxix)

---

49. Gilles Deleuze, *Francis Bacon: The Logic of Sensation*, trans. Daniel Smith (Minneapolis: University of Minnesota Press, 2003). Subsequent references are made in the text.

At this point Deleuze adds a remark that reiterates a cliché in the reception of Bacon (the irony here is that Deleuze otherwise stresses the considerable work Bacon does to clear the canvas of all cliché): "If there is feeling in Bacon, it is not a taste for horror, it is pity: pity for flesh, including the flesh of dead animals" (xxix). As we shall see, one of the sources of error in Deleuze is, in the terms I have proposed in part 1 of this study, to conflate becoming-*creature* with becoming-*animal*, a figure that recurs in numerous writings by Deleuze.

The confusion in question tends to gather around some of the key terms of Deleuze's analysis: body, flesh, spirit, and meat. In the chapter that most directly addresses the images in Bacon's work of flayed flesh, of faces that no longer seem to cover their interiors, of carcasses of animals, of distended, contorted bodies wrapped around themselves, other bodies, or some sort of object or armature, of bodies that seem to leak their substance into shadowy pools of ooze, Deleuze returns to the imperative of pity that he registers as the content of the address emanating from such images (in the following he refers specifically to the famous *Painting* of 1946):

Pity the meat! Meat is undoubtedly the chief object of Bacon's pity, his only object of pity, his Anglo-Irish pity. On this point he is like Soutine, with his immense pity for the Jew. Meat is not dead flesh; it retains all the sufferings and assumes all the colors of living flesh. It manifests such convulsive pain and vulnerability, but also such delightful invention, color, and acrobatics. Bacon does not say, "Pity the beasts," but rather that every man who suffers is a piece of meat. Meat is the common zone of man and the beast, their zone of indiscernability; it is a "fact," a state where the painter identifies with the objects of his horror and his compassion. The painter is certainly a butcher, but he goes to the butcher shop as if it were a church, with the meat as the crucified victim. . . . Bacon is a religious painter only in butcher shops. (21–22)[50]

For Deleuze, the term *meat* best characterizes the fundamentally non-human dimension of the "fact" that ultimately preoccupies Bacon—the one he wants to transmit directly to the viewer's nervous system—and serves to "animalize," if I might put it that way, the spirit at issue in this peculiar "church," the butcher shop. For Deleuze this point is linked to

50. In this context, Deleuze cites a well-known remark the painter made to Sylvester: "I've always been very moved by pictures about slaughterhouses and meat, and to me they belong very much to the whole thing of the Crucifixion. . . . Of course, we are meat, we are potential carcasses. If I go into a butcher shop I always think it's surprising that I wasn't there instead of the animal" (cited in Deleuze, 22).

the further claim that Bacon is, as a portraitist, a painter not of faces but rather of *heads*:

For the face is a structured, spatial organization that conceals the head, whereas the head is dependent on the body, even it if is the point of the body, its culmination. It is not that the head lacks spirit; but it is a spirit in bodily form, a corporeal and vital breath, an animal spirit. It is the animal spirit of man: a pig-spirit, a dog-spirit, a bat-spirit. . . . Bacon thus pursues a very peculiar project as a portrait painter: *to dismantle the face*, to rediscover the head or make it emerge from beneath the face. (19)[51]

Deleuze finally subsumes under the heading of meat that visual feature that figures so prominently in Bacon's work: the mouth forming into a scream. "It is important," he writes, "to understand the affinity of the mouth, and the interior of the mouth, with meat, and to reach the point where the open mouth becomes nothing more than the section of a severed artery" (23). This allows him to posit the mouth as simply another opening or line of flight through which the corporeal pressures that for Deleuze constitute the "body without organs" attempt to escape: "The mouth then acquires this power of nonlocalization that turns all meat into a head without a face. It is no longer a particular organ, but the hole through which the entire body escapes, and from which the flesh descends. . . . This is what Bacon calls the Scream, in the immense pity that the meat evokes" (23–24). Or as he puts it rather succinctly at the very beginning of the chapter from which these passages come, the pressures at issue in Bacon—the pressures of flight, of escape, of emergence into the open—are figured in such a way that "meat" represents only a transitory phase in a larger process of dissipation whereby the figure finally merges with the material structure supporting it: "The head-meat is a becoming animal of man. In this becoming, the entire body tends to escape from itself, and the Figure tends to return to the material structure" (25). Deleuze concludes this thought with a vision of what he takes to be

---

51. Deleuze links the two features he associates with the figure of *meat*—the dismantling of the face; man's becoming-animal—with the procedures of self-disruption that Bacon described to Sylvester: "The deformations the body undergoes are also the *animal traits* of the head. This has nothing to with a correspondence between animal forms and facial forms. In fact, the face lost its form by being subjected to the techniques of rubbing and brushing that disorganize it and make a head emerge in its place. The marks or traits of animality are not animal forms but rather the spirits that haunt the wiped-off parts, that pull at the head, individualizing and qualifying the head without a face" (Deleuze, 19). It is as if Deleuze were trying to turn on its head Freud's claim that totem animals originally served as ambivalent substitutes for the murdered primal father; for Deleuze, Freud's myth of the primal father seems, rather, to occult the more fundamental fact of man's animal spirit, one that only truly becomes manifest at the point at which he is reduced to being *meat*.

ultimately at issue in Bacon's work: a kind of death drive that would return human life to the fully impersonal "vitality" and "justice" of nonorganic matter wandering nomadically in—or rather, *as*—the desert: "It is this extreme point that will have to be reached, in order to allow a justice to prevail that will no longer be anything but Color or Light, a space that will no longer be anything but the Sahara. Which means that, whatever its importance, becoming-animal is only one stage in a more profound becoming-imperceptible in which the Figure disappears" (25).[52]

In a chapter called "Hysteria," Deleuze articulates in even more dramatic tones what he takes to be the ultimate thrust of Bacon's project, the facilitation of the body's escape from the confines of its organic composition, from what renders it all too visible and recognizable within a space of representation. I will quote from this section at length because I think it clarifies what Deleuze sees as the task of all great art: to undo or render inoperative the subject's libidinal implication in the space of signifying representations, to separate out something like a purely vital pressure from the pressures that enter life by way of subjection to normative authority. In a sense, the ultimate thrust of Bacon's work, as Deleuze sees it, is the visual invocation of *entropy* posited as the supreme mode of *vitality*: "It is a whole nonorganic life, for the organism is not life, it is what imprisons life. The body is completely living, and yet nonorganic. Likewise sensation, when it acquires a body through the organism, takes on an excessive and spasmodic appearance, exceeding the bounds of organic activity. It is immediately conveyed in the flesh through the nervous wave or vital emotion" (40). Again, this "logic of sensation" is aimed, above all, at the order of representation, at rendering that order inoperative: "When sensation is linked to the body in this way, it ceases to be representative and becomes real; and *cruelty* will be linked less and less to the representation of something horrible, and will become nothing other than the action of forces upon the body, or sensation (the opposite of the sensational). As opposed to a *misérabiliste* painter who paints parts of organs, Bacon has not ceased to paint bodies without organs, the intensive fact of the body" (40).

---

52. Deleuze is alluding here to a remark Bacon made to Sylvester in the context of a larger discussion of the painter's experiments with accident and contingency: "And in a way you would love to be able in a portrait to make a Sahara of the appearance—to make it so like, yet seeming to have the distances of the Sahara." Sylvester, 56.

XIV

At this point in his presentation, Deleuze refers to Wilhelm Worringer's influential dissertation *Abstraktion und Einfühlung* (*Abstraction and Empathy*). This short treatise, first published in 1908, argued that European art history had for the most part failed to grasp a great deal of nonclassical art because it had failed to appreciate the specific *Kunstwollen*, or *will to art*—Worringer borrows the term from Alois Riegl—operative in different epochs and forms of life. Worringer's work played a significant role in a larger cultural movement aimed at reevaluating art and architecture that favored abstract, nonorganic forms over against more classical styles that took as their primary point of reference the form and sensory-motor mobility of the human body in lived space. The classical orientation reflected, for Worringer, a more general sense of being at home in the world and, above all, a sense of embodiment that was perceived as enjoying a just fit with the relevant spaces of practical engagement in the world.[53] Works of art and architecture grounded in empathy reflect, on this view, an instinctive commitment to the space of immanence as a fitting locus of human habitation; their style manifests a fundamental trust in the world of appearance as ultimately made to the measure of man, one that Worringer characterizes as a "happy, pantheistic relation of trust between man and the appearances of the external world."[54] Abstraction, by contrast, asserts itself in the arts on the basis of a profound sense of *lack of fit*, a sense precisely of not being at home in the world. It is, as Worringer sees it, thus always accompanied by distinctly spiritual values and the longing for transcendence, features that Worringer associates with the suppression of vitality—its displacement toward a beyond—and what he characterizes as a kind of claustrophobia (he speaks of *Raumscheu* as well as *Platzangst*).[55]

---

53. This sense of "fitness" is, as we have seen, the foil for Bernstein's understanding of modernism. According to Bernstein, postclassical art achieved the ideal of this just fitness between embodied subjectivity and world only in some rare cases of seventeenth-century Dutch realism, above all in some canvases of Pieter de Hooch: "De Hooch . . . gave us for the first and perhaps only time a wholly sensible world of touch and sight that was sufficient in itself, a world of things that was fit for sensory encounter and that thus affirmed us in our sensuous nature. This discovered self-sufficiency of the world is, at the same time, the sufficiency of the practice of painting to the world" (43).

54. Wilhelm Worringer, *Abstraktion und Einfühlung: Ein Beitrag zur Stilpsychologie* (Munich: Piper, 1981), 49.

55. Ibid., 49.

Of particular interest for Deleuze is Worringer's view of Gothic art and architecture that forms something of a compromise formation between abstraction and empathy, one in which, as Worringer puts it, "man has extended his capacity for empathy to mechanical values. They are for him no longer dead abstractions but rather vital movements of force."[56] It is above all in the Gothic cathedral that the "uncanniness of this living mechanism [*das Unheimliche dieser lebendigen Mechanik*]" becomes most tangible: "Here constructive relations are not clarified by a feeling for the organic as with the construction of Greek temples; rather purely mechanical relations of forces are brought into view for themselves. Moreover these relations of forces are, in their content and trajectory, intensified to a maximum degree by means of a capacity for empathy that has extended itself to what is abstract. What we encounter is not the life of an organism but rather that of a mechanism."[57]

Deleuze adapts Worringer's historical typology of artistic styles by elevating what the latter sees as a Gothic sort of abstract expressionism to a *general theory of immanence* characterized as a zone of intensities made precisely not to the measure of the human organism. For Deleuze, this zone opens, or, perhaps better, is constituted by, the escape or flight of bodies out of the constraints of organic form, their metamorphosis and ultimate dissipation into the virtual realities of color, form, line, vibration, rhythm.[58] These are, paradoxically, the realities that for Deleuze constitute the true materiality of the body; there, where the body escapes from itself, it "discovers the materiality of which it is composed, *the pure presence of which it is made*" (47; my emphasis). This means that organicity, the very feature that for Worringer allowed for a sense of "empathy" or feeling at home in the world—what I have characterized as the feeling of being libidinally implicated in the space of representation—becomes, for Deleuze, the very mark or stigma of a defensive enclosure, of a withdrawal from the space of immanence. The space of immanence is in this view precisely *not* a space of representation but rather of pure sensation, a space not of human bodies enjoying a sense of being at home in the world, endowed with a capacity for speech and action in the "field of the Other," but rather of flesh and nerve that directly relay the rhythmic mobility of an "almost unlivable Power" (39). Deleuze can, thus, in some sense agree with Worringer that art produced according to this "logic of

56. Ibid., 155.
57. Ibid., 157–58.
58. As Deleuze puts it in one of many such formulations, "The entire series of spasms in Bacon is of this type: scenes of love, of vomiting and excreting, in which the body attempts to escape from itself *through* one of its organs in order to rejoin the field or material structure" (16).

sensation" manifests a high spirituality. "But this spirituality is a spirituality of the body; *the spirit is the body itself, the body without organs*" (41; my emphasis). Recalling that Worringer characterized the classical worldview of empathy as *pantheistic*, one marked by a sense of harmony, even consubstantiality with worldly being, we might characterize Deleuze's position as a *pantheism of flesh and nerve*, one whose congregation meets in a sort of virtual butcher shop.

I have spent so much time with Deleuze's reception of Bacon because, to put it in the form of a terrible pun, my beef with him so clearly concerns the status of the flesh that has been the theme of this study. My concern is that Deleuze's approach, in its rejection of the dimension of representation—what Lacan calls *the logic of the signifier*—as constitutive of the space of immanence and, indeed, as the dimension that introduces into it that surplus of immanence I have been calling the flesh, is compelled to construe the field of operation of *the logic of sensation* as the virtual, and pantheistic, animality of meat. Paradoxically, Deleuze's approach turns out to be both *too virtual* and *too material*. He wants to take Bacon at his word when he claims, for example, that his crucifixion paintings render man's "status" as so much meat deprived of all spiritual elevation above his bare, animal life. But he also wants this meat and animality to be grasped as a kind of purely virtual reality, one that concerns not the lives of living creatures but rather the vitality of the process of creation itself as the preontological, nonorganic life that is precisely *not of this world*. By, as it were, absolutizing what I have characterized as a surplus of immanence, by transforming it into the very *substance of immanence*—this is the pantheistic gesture Deleuze inherits from Spinoza—Deleuze virtualizes the space of immanence, the space of lived life, in its entirety.[59]

59. A very similar line of critique has been articulated with respect to Deleuze's work as a whole by Peter Hallward in his study *Out of This World: Deleuze and the Philosophy of Creation* (London: Verso, 2006). As Hallward very succinctly puts it apropos of Deleuze's writings on cinema, what interests the philosopher is "the perception of creative time *as such*, 'cut off from the world' and purged of any actual creature" (114–15). This point, Hallward continues, is linked to the ways in which Deleuze has taken up Worringer's distinction between the abstract or "crystalline" and the "organic: "The time-image is . . . precisely not an image in the usual (or actual) sense of the term. It is not a relation between perceiver and perceived, so much as 'a perception as it was before men (or after),' the perception of a time and space 'released from their human coordinates'. . . . Crystalline perception proceeds, in other words, at the scale of cosmic creation itself" (116). Finally, Hallward nicely captures the paradoxical status of Deleuzian vitalism as one situated precisely "out of this world" (the citations are, again, from Deleuze's writings on cinema): "It involves the intuition of a 'pure, immanent or spiritual light, beyond white, black and grey,' and 'as soon as this light is reached it restores everything to us.' Such intuition restores 'faith in the world' precisely by tapping into the intensity that creates it. By giving up our creatural coherence we attain that non-organic life which pulses through the universe as a whole and maintains the immediate identity of 'brain and

To return to my claim concerning the convergence of Bernstein's position and that of Deleuze, we can see that both philosophers remain committed to a kind of *vitalist naturalism*, though posited under exactly opposite signs. For Bernstein, vitality is always linked to organicity, to "memberment as the impulse of the living." Only when thwarted does this impulse manifest itself as horror, as "the too much animation of active dismemberment" (297). Deleuze's vitalism runs in exactly the opposite direction. For Deleuze organic form is the very sign of the mortification of life, of life that, paradoxically, comes truly alive only in the process of the dissipation of organic form, in the return to the pulsations of the nonorganic life of creative forces. One might view these positions as two takes on the true nature of the *drive* in Freud. Bernstein clearly bets on the "life drive," one that manifests itself in the capacity of living things to develop ever-greater organizational unity, while Deleuze's wager rests on the "death drive," understood here as the vital impulse of organic life to dissipate, to (repeatedly) return to the state of inorganic matter, whether in motion or not.[60]

XV

I would now like to return to Bacon himself and try to make the case that what ultimately commands authority in his work does indeed pertain to what both Deleuze and Bernstein detect as *drive impulses* operative in these (and related) images. But I will try to show that these impulses have a precise historical index, that they acquire their conjoined urgency and specificity as traces of what remains of the King's Two Bodies in the wake of the transfer of royal sovereignty to the body and life of the People. I would like to make the transition to this set of reflections by first noting

---

cosmos'" (116–17). For a related series of objections to Deleuze's approach, see Slavoj Žižek, *Organs without Bodies: On Deleuze and Consequences* (New York: Routledge, 2004).

60. Deleuze discerns three kinds of forces in Bacon's work: those of isolation that "become visible when they wrap themselves around the contour and wrap the fields around the Figure"; those of deformation, "which seize the Figure's body and head, and become visible whenever the head shakes off its face, or the body its organism"; and finally those of dissipation, "when the Figure fades away and returns to the field" (53). The forces of cosmic dissipation are at work above all in Bacon's last works, where Deleuze appears to see the telos of the painter's development: "The scrambled or wiped-off zone, which used to make the Figure emerge, will now stand on its own, independent of every definite form, appearing as pure Force without an object: the wind of the tempest, the jet of water or vapor, the eye of the hurricane. . . . The fact that we are familiar with only a few instances of this new organization in Bacon's work . . . must not make us rule out the possibility that this is a nascent period, which would be characterized by an 'abstraction' that no longer has any need of the Figure. The Figure is dissipated by realizing the prophecy: you will no longer be anything but sand, grass, dust, or a drop of water" (28).

very briefly the ways in which the conversion Deleuze undertakes—in this instance, by way of an engagement with Bacon—of a surplus of immanence made urgent under conditions of modernity into something like the pulse of cosmic life itself, converges with Roberto Esposito's attempt to convert the thanato-political catastrophe that opened at the boundaries between sovereignty and biopolitics into a purely affirmative biopolitics. These attempts to perform a (post-)Nietzschean affirmation of life amount to what I would characterize as a *biopolitical pantheism.*

At the conclusion of his discussion of the concept of flesh in the history of biopolitics, Esposito turns to the work of Francis Bacon—and to Deleuze's study of the painter—as testimony to the prospect of this new kind of biopolitics, one that would be not *over* life but *of* life. This turn is itself framed by Esposito's invocation of Saint Paul and the need to reimagine what the resurrection of the flesh might mean in the wake of the thanato-political turn of biopolitics: "To 'rise again,' today, cannot be the body inhabited by the spirit, but the flesh as such: a being that is both singular and communal, generic and specific, and undifferentiated and different, not only devoid of spirit, but a flesh that doesn't even have a body."[61] After suggesting that biotechnology, the "biopolitical possibility of the ontological and technological transmutation of the human body," offers the hope of a new thinking of the flesh "outside of Christian language," that innovations in prosthetic devices and transplant technology represent "a non-Christian form of incarnation," Esposito locates Bacon at the threshold of this brave new world of biopolitical pantheism: "But that this new biopolitical feature (which inevitably is technopolitical) doesn't lose every point of contact with its own Christian archetype is witnessed in the artist who, perhaps more than any other, has placed the theme of the flesh outside of the body . . . at the center of his own work." By pushing to its limit the "biopolitical practice of the animalization of man," by reducing human life to "the disfigured figure of butchered flesh" (168)—the "butchered, deformed, and chapped flesh [that is] the flesh of the world"—Bacon opens up the possibility of what for both Deleuze and Esposito constitutes a sort of "other *jouissance*" distinct from any sort of sovereign *jouissance,* namely that of enjoying nothing more and nothing less than the "common fact: the common fact of man and animal" (169).[62]

---

61. Roberto Esposito, *Bios: Biopolitics and Philosophy,* trans. Timothy Campbell (Minneapolis: University of Minnesota Press, 2008), 167. Subsequent references are made in the text.
62. Esposito cites here Deleuze's study of Bacon.

But once again, what gets lost in this "common fact"—this conflation of creatureliness and animality—is precisely the specific nature of the "brutality of fact" that is at issue in Bacon's images and that provides them with the historical index that continues to command our attention. In their rush to get beyond the last traces of the political theological tradition in the space of modernity, both thinkers lose contact with what I take to be the animating force of Bacon's work, one that, as Esposito duly notes but fails to integrate, remains tied to the semantic universe of that tradition for important reasons. They lose contact, that is, with the nature of the excess or surplus of immanence that perturbs the space of modernity, precisely by flattening it to the "common fact of man and animal" and the biopolitical pantheism that ostensibly flows from it. By wagering on what is clearly taken to be a utopian vision beyond any reference to the political theological tradition, a vision seemingly grounded in something like a perpetual *state of emergence*—a state of *pure natality*, to use Arendt's term—this work can never give rise to a renewed and reconfigured engagement with the forms and locations of normative pressure that define the symbolic order of modern societies.[63]

XVI

Bacon himself has been partly responsible for these sorts of readings of his work. I have already noted the neuroaesthetic language he uses to characterize his artistic ambitions—his goal to transmit the "fact" of appearances directly onto the nervous system of the viewer—which is, in turn, linked to his vigilance with regard to the seductions of narrative or illustration in his work. He has furthermore tried to distance himself from the religious connotations of the multiple crucifixion paintings he has done, insisting that the cross is, above all, "a magnificent armature on which you can hang all types of feeling and sensation," sensations he quite specifically links to those evoked by pictures of slaughterhouses and meat (cited in Sylvester, 44, 23). And when Sylvester pushes him to say more about his series of images of (often screaming) popes, he insists

---

63. I am tempted to say that this new version of the "pantheism debate," a debate that seems to return at the end of each century under a different guise, might fruitfully be put as a debate between an affirmative biopolitics—what I am calling a *biopolitical pantheism*—on the one hand, and the *creaturely messianism* of the modern German-Jewish tradition of thought represented by figures like Franz Rosenzweig and Walter Benjamin, on the other. The debate would, of course, need to be further complicated by taking into account the ways in which this messianism itself ramifies into Christian and Islamic versions.

that they all derive primarily from an obsession with the painterly qualities of Velázquez's famous painting of Pope Innocent X (24–25).[64] Upon
further questioning, however, Bacon acknowledges the singular status
of the pope: "It is true, of course, that the Pope is unique. He's put in a
unique position by being Pope, and thereby like in certain great tragedies,
he's as though raised onto a dais on which the grandeur of this image
can be displayed to the world" (26). He furthermore concedes to Sylvester
that the uniqueness of both Pope and Christ relates to, as Sylvester puts
it, "the special situation of the tragic hero" (26).

The theme of the tragic hero gets taken up in a later conversation,
when Bacon indicates that the distortions to which he submits an image
(distortions meant, as he puts it, "to bring it back to a recording of the
appearance" [40]) are in some sense indices of what remains for modernity of what was, for the great tragedians of antiquity and the early modern period, the representative arc of the life of a mythic—and typically,
royal—personage: "Of course, I think that, if one could find a valid myth
today where there was the distance between grandeur and its fall of the
tragedies of Aeschylus and Shakespeare, it would be tremendously helpful. But when you're outside a tradition, as every artist is today, one can
only want to record one's feelings about certain situations as closely to
one's own nervous system as one possibly can" (43). To bring my argument to a point, it is as if, in Bacon's work, that tragic arc had contracted
into a kind of twitch or violent facial tic, a convulsive movement of nerve
that now afflicts the flesh of every subject.

This view is, I think, further supported by Bacon's remarks concerning
the singular greatness of Velázquez: "In Velázquez it's a very, very extraordinary thing that he has been able to keep so near to what we call illustration and at the same time so deeply unlock the greatest and deepest
things a man can feel. Which makes him such an amazingly mysterious
painter. Because one really does believe that Velázquez *recorded the court
at that time* and, when one looks at his pictures, one is possibly looking
at something which is very, very near to how things looked" (28; my emphasis). Bacon, as we have seen, also sees himself as engaged in an act of
"recording." He must do so, however, at a time when the center of gravity
of the political and libidinal economy of society has shifted away from
the court or, for that matter, from any stable center, and when the tragic
arc of the royal personage has mutated into the biopolitical pressure that
now pulsates in—or better, *as*—the flesh of everyday life. Bacon, one

---

64. Interestingly, Bacon insists that he actively avoided seeing the original painting and worked
instead strictly with photographs of it.

will recall, turned regularly to Muybridge's photographic studies of motion to help him in his efforts to capture the traces of bodily movement, indeed of extreme restlessness, in paintings of bodies "at rest." I am, in essence, suggesting that the convulsive, spasmodic motion at issue in much of Bacon's work pertains to something like the rhythm Kantorowicz described apropos of Shakespeare's portrayal of royal deposition. One has to imagine a Muybridge motion study of Richard II's deposition, its cascading movement, as Kantorowicz put it, "from kingship to kingship's 'Name,' and from the name to the naked misery of man."

This perspective allows us, I think, to make sense of several features of Bacon's work. Critics have often noted the theatrical setup of Bacon's portraits, the way he uses various sorts of armature, pedestals, and platforms to isolate and display his object "as though raised on a dais." One thinks of his use of railings, tables, chairs, beds, colored discs—these often call to mind a circus ring—and, of course, those strange cubicles that enclose the central figure as if in a glass booth. These various structures mark, I would suggest, the transition from court and church to various political and biopolitical spaces of modernity: the hysterical theater (think of Charcot's clinic), the surgical theater, the glass box in which Eichmann eventually sat at his trial in Jerusalem. Together they create a kind of experimental space in which bodies are subject to mostly invisible torments and the viewer is variously interpellated as scientist, tormentor, complicit bystander, voyeur. This theatrical setup becomes especially poignant—Bernstein would say "histrionic"—when the forces moving through the figure's body seem to push their way out by way of a scream. I would agree with Deleuze that such images create the impression of a body under impossible duress, a body that seems to want to escape from itself. What I am suggesting is that the pressure at issue here needs to be grasped as testimony to the fact that, as I have said earlier, every head now has a "body" of its own, one in which the symbolic, imaginary, and real elements of sovereignty push against the skin of its bearer. The complex stresses that once took on the shape and corporeal density of the thing we call a king—stresses that include, above all, the paradoxical "charge" of the sovereign exception—now press directly on or, perhaps better, as the flesh of every subject.

I would like to return, once more, to T. J. Clark's compelling analysis of David's *Death of Marat*. Clark, one will recall, argued that the scumbled surface forming the upper half of David's painting no longer functions as a simple absence but rather as a positive, even oppressive presence, "something abstract and unmotivated, which occupies a different conceptual space from the bodies below it," one that produces "a kind of representational deadlock" that provides, in turn, "the true source of the *Marat's* continuing hold on us." This is, as Clark put it, the "endless, meaningless objectivity produced by paint not quite finding its object, symbolic or otherwise, and therefore making do with its own procedures" (48). I am arguing that what Bacon shows us—*what he records*, just as Velázquez once "recorded the court"—is the further, modernist destiny of what Clark intuited in the upper half of the *Death of Marat*: the surplus of immanence that spreads out from the missing place of the figure of the king and now gets under the skin of the People along with all the complexities and complexes that once made up the King's Two Bodies.

FIVE

The Stages of the Flesh: Shakespeare, Schmitt, Hofmannsthal

I

Marie Axton, in her study of the role of theater and popular entertainments in the dissemination of the doctrine of the "King's Two Bodies" in the second half of the sixteenth century, emphasizes that this period was one of high anxiety with respect not only to the problem of royal succession but more generally to "the very principles by which government and authority are perpetuated." The legal and political problem of succession was, of course, especially acute because of Elizabeth's status as "virgin queen." The lawyers who participated in the debates about succession—in large measure by way of propagandistic theatrical performances—were, by dint of training and professional concerns, particularly sensitive to the historical pressures gathering around the very institution of kingship: "The circumstances of the Reformation, the antecedent body of ecclesiastical law, the shifts in land ownership relating to the crown, the peculiar circumstances of the Tudor succession were all factors which helped to shape their theories of kingship and to popularize them."[1] Axton's fundamental thesis is that the theory of the King's Two Bodies that Kantorowicz transformed into

---

1. Marie Axton, *The Queen's Two Bodies: Drama and the Elizabethan Succession* (London: Royal Historical Society, 1977), ix.

an indispensable concept for the analysis of the politics, aesthetics, and culture of early modernity acquired its true urgency in the context of the uncertainties and anxieties of the Elizabethan succession, a context that, as she shows in some detail, was saturated by theatrical efforts to elaborate the theory and its implications.[2] As she and others, including Kantorowicz, have noted, among the lawyers who were most deeply involved at all levels of this political, social, and religious turbulence was the figure who was to become best known for his contributions to the cultural foundations of modern science, Francis Bacon.[3]

In 1902, the young Hugo von Hofmannsthal published a short prose piece set a few short months after the queen's death in 1603 (as we shall see, either the author or the narrator seems to forget this little fact) and ostensibly written by one Philip Lord Chandos to his patron and mentor Francis Bacon. The text, called in German simply *Ein Brief* (in English often referred to as the *Chandos Letter*) has become one of the most influential texts of the modernist canon and is generally thought to be the single most concise and compelling account of the so-called crisis of language, or *Sprachkrise*. 'In the first part of the twentieth century, this crisis also incited, among others, Karl Kraus and Ludwig Wittgenstein to their own epoch-making reflections on language.'[4] I hope to shed new light on this crucial literary artifact (and what it stands in for with respect to central features of European modernity and modernism) by taking seriously the fact that it was addressed to Bacon, a detail that is often acknowledged in the scholarship but typically plays a relatively minor role in the hermeneutic engagement with the details of Hofmannsthal's text. I will try to do so by way of an admittedly peculiar detour through a text that, on the face of it, would seem to have little to do with the *Chandos Letter*, Carl Schmitt's essay on Shakespeare, *Hamlet or Hecuba*, itself written more than fifty years after the publication of Hofmannsthal's text.[5]

As an initial justification for this strange route, I would note that the years of interest in Schmitt's essay, roughly 1600–1603 (these are the

2. For this reason, she suggests that Kantorowicz's speculations concerning the question of Shakespeare's familiarity with the doctrine of royal gemination become largely irrelevant.

3. The painter Francis Bacon claimed to be related to the Renaissance lawyer, statesman, and scholar.

4. The canonical study of the centrality of the *Sprachkrise* for an understanding of at least Viennese modernity is Allan Janik and Stephen Toulmin, *Wittgenstein's Vienna* (New York: Touchstone, 1973).

5. Carl Schmitt, *Hamlet or Hecuba: The Intrusion of the Time into the Play*, trans. David Pan and Jennifer Rust (New York: Telos, 2009). Subsequent references are made in the text. The German original was first published in 1956 and has been reprinted several times. See Carl Schmitt, *Hamlet oder Hekuba: Der Einbruch der Zeit in das Spiel* (Stuttgart: Klett-Cotta, 2008). My own reading of the essay is deeply indebted to the brilliant introduction to the translation by Julia Lupton and Jennifer Rust.

years in which Shakespeare wrote and first staged *Hamlet* against the backdrop of a profound crisis of royal succession and investiture), more or less overlap with the period of existential turmoil that, for Chandos, culminated in the emergence of a new and more "creaturely" mode of thinking and writing. Schmitt's essay may also, in the end, provide relevant criteria for evaluating the ways in which Hofmannsthal makes use of the Elizabethan period in the *Chandos Letter*, that is, what it would mean to give serious interpretive weight to the historical setting in one's engagement with the text. Schmitt's essay is, namely, itself a meditation on the relation between history and art, on what it means to take seriously, in one's engagement with works of art, the explicit or implicit presence of historical figures and, above all, the impact of historical events and forces—and by that Schmitt means political events and forces.

II

In the course of his essay, Schmitt explicitly distinguishes three ways in which history asserts itself in art in general and in theater in particular—he speaks of "several degrees and kinds of historical influences" (22)—only one of which demands serious consideration. It does so because it touches on what he refers to as an *Ernstfall*, a serious or critical situation demanding decisive action without, however, providing the coordinates for such action. We might indeed say that it is just such an accumulation of the pressures of "demand" without clear normative direction regarding a course of action that itself proves to be decisive for Schmitt's understanding of the aesthetic realm, an understanding he exemplifies in his reading of *Hamlet* (and the multiple meanings of acting in Shakespeare's most famous work). Schmitt thinks that only by addressing the nature of such pressures can one account for the lasting vitality of this play, its status as what he refers to as a *living myth*.

The first level at which historical figures and events assert themselves in the realm of aesthetic representation is what Schmitt calls *Anspielung*, or allusion. In the context of *Hamlet*, Schmitt notes several examples marked by retaining only a certain scholarly or literary historical interest. He points to the allusion in the fourth act (4.4.18–20) to the sand dunes of the Ostende that the English defended against Spain in 1601; the allusion in the first act of the second quarto (1.2.54) to the coronation of James I.; and the absence in the second quarto of one of the reasons for suicide listed in Hamlet's most famous soliloquy ("to be or not to be") that was still present in the first quarto, that is, before James took the throne: "a tirants raigne" (23).

The second way history asserts itself in the ostensibly autonomous realm of aesthetic invention and play (as we shall see, this is the version of the "aesthetic ideology" that Schmitt's essay ultimately aims at challenging) is what he calls *Spiegelungen*, genuine reflections or mirrorings. "Here," Schmitt writes, "a contemporary event or figure appears in the drama as in a mirror and determines a picture there in its lines and colors" (23). His prime example for such mirroring is the way in which the life and death of the Earl of Essex—a crucial figure not only for Shakespeare but also for Bacon—have left traces in the play, including the use of Essex's last words on the scaffold in Horatio's speech on the death of Hamlet. Although Schmitt also allows that Essex may have to some extent also served as a model for Hamlet's melancholic character (a claim made by John Dover Wilson, an author on whom Schmitt otherwise much depends), he remains ultimately committed to the view that the crucial historical connection in the work is between Hamlet and James I, a link or mode of influence that, like a kind of black hole, twists or bends the space and action of the play. It is this more radical mode of influence that Schmitt refers to as a genuine *Einbruch*: an irruption or intrusion (literally, a break-in) of historical time into the space of theatrical play. As he puts it, "next to the fleeting allusions and the true mirrorings, there is yet a third, highest kind of influence from the historical present. These are the structurally determining, genuine *intrusions*. They cannot be common or ordinary, but their consequences are that much deeper and stronger" (25).

Here it should be noted that part of Schmitt's argument about the ways in which the looming figure of James ultimately absorbs and supersedes the presence of Essex in the play rests on a reference to the logic of dreams. Given the support of the Essex circle for James in the struggle around the succession to Elizabeth and the close ties between Shakespeare's troupe and this circle, it should not be surprising that in the wake of Essex's imprisonment and execution in 1601, "features of the character and fate of the Earl of Essex wove themselves into the image otherwise determined by James. This is not unnatural," Schmitt continues, "because such stage plays form a kind of 'dream-frame.' . . . Just as people and realities merge with each other in a dream, images and figures, events and situations are interwoven in a dream-like way on the stage" (24). Schmitt's crucial point here, though he does not say it this way, is that only on the basis of the third kind of influence—the so-called intrusion of time into the play—does the true "dream work" of the aesthetic realm get mobilized. It is, Schmitt insists, only James and what James stands in for in the historical context in question that can generate the strange dream—the "living myth"—we call *Hamlet*. The other details that enter into the play in the form of allusions and mirrorings would seem to have more the status of so many *Tagesreste*, or "day's residues," that Shakespeare's "dream work" used in the composition of *Hamlet*. Against this background it makes sense that Schmitt, like a good interpreter of dreams, is able to detect the presence of the central figure of the play—James I—by way of symptomatic distortions he discerns in the "manifest content" of the aesthetic object. What makes *Hamlet Hamlet* (and for Schmitt that also means what makes *Hamlet* a genuine *tragedy* rather than a baroque *Trauerspiel*) turns out to be something in *Hamlet* that is more than *Hamlet*, some unnamed cause, some scandal or trauma that can only be reconstructed on the basis not of allusions or mirrorings but of what appear as peculiar swerves or torsions in the work. Schmitt's interpretation thereby becomes an analysis not so much of dramatic form as of a series of curious *deformations* that register what remains "alive"—or perhaps better, *undead*—in Shakespeare's play.[6]

The emphasis on deformation, on a dimension at work in the aesthetic object that is in some way "extimate" to it—inside it yet only partially incorporated—is aimed, to a very large extent, at a notion of aesthetic creation and reception that emerged in the context of German aesthetic theory over the course of the eighteenth and nineteenth centuries. The tradition became associated with a certain "aesthetic ideology," which emphasized the sovereign autonomy of the artist-genius in his free, creative play with his materials and the ways in which the reception of works of art calls forth parallel experiences or states of freedom in the "consumer" of the work. In Johannes Türk's terms in a fine essay on *Hamlet or Hecuba*, this is a tradition that posits the aesthetic sphere as "the location of a *pleasure beyond individual existential interests*, in which all faculties of man engage in the free play of the imagination." It was, of course, Friedrich Schiller who famously attempted to translate the lessons of this understanding of aesthetic experience into a pedagogical

---

6. In *The King's Two Bodies*, Kantorowicz focuses not on *Hamlet* but rather on *Richard II*, a play he explicitly characterizes as a "tragedy of the King's Two Bodies." In his discussion, however, Kantorowicz underlines the crucial role that *Richard II*—and, above all, the deposition scene—played in the struggle around the succession to Elizabeth, pointing out, for example, that the Earl of Essex ordered a special performance of *Richard* to be played in 1601 before supporters at the Globe Theater. These are precisely the sorts of events—in the case of the staging of *Richard II*, the intrusion of a *play* into historical time—that are central in Schmitt's reading of *Hamlet*.

project that, as Türk emphasizes, formed the basis of a social utopia: "The beautiful leads man to the development of political rationality and form, and from there it leads back into the now formed concrete life." As Türk concludes, "Aesthetic theory promised to solve the tensions and struggles inherent in life by translating it into the program of an aesthetic education capable of circumventing the political."[7]

Schmitt, for his part, takes aim at this tradition and posits, instead, a notion of disturbed or disrupted play.[8] Rather than securing a locus of pleasure beyond individual existential interests, the "aesthetic experience" at issue for Schmitt opens onto *existential interests beyond the pleasure principle*. This, for Schmitt, is what is ultimately signified by the choice "Hamlet or Hecuba." In the famous soliloquy delivered upon hearing the player's speech about Hecuba's grief over Priam, Hamlet compares the tears the player is able to summon for a mythic figure of antiquity with his own paralysis in the midst of the personal and political pressures—"the motive and the cue for passion"—that would seem to demand not only grief but decisive action. As Schmitt puts it, Hamlet is "astonished to learn that there are people who, in the performance of their duties, weep over something that does not concern them in the least and has no impact upon their actual existence and situation" (42–43). For Schmitt this ultimately means that the audience is being solicited precisely *not* to weep for Hamlet the way the player weeps for Hecuba. "We would, however, in point of fact weep for Hamlet as for Hecuba if we wished to divorce the reality of our present existence from the play on the stage. Our tears would then become the tears of actors. We would no longer have any purpose or cause and *would have sacrificed both to the aesthetic enjoyment of the play*" (43; my emphasis). What keeps the audience from succumbing to the lure of the aesthetic ideology invoked by the player's theatrical virtuosity is, according to Schmitt, a kernel of historical reality that breaks or steals its way into the play and addresses us, as it were, from beyond the pleasure principle. This "realistic core of the most intense contemporary significance and timeliness [*ein Wirklichkeitskern von stärkster Gegenwart und Aktualität*]" (45) pertains to the status

---

7. Johannes Türk, "The Intrusion: Carl Schmitt's Non-Mimetic Logic of Art," *Telos* 142 (Spring 2008): 77; my emphasis. As Türk nicely puts it, "the free play of the faculties in the aesthetic experience affirms the harmony between man and the world, pity opens the audience's mind to others' suffering and thereby to ethics, and in the sublime the individual is made aware of its freedom and morality" (77).

8. Two different meanings of *play* are involved here. It is not only the particular *theater play* that is disrupted but also the entire realm and dynamic of *aesthetic play*. Through this disruption, Schmitt argues, the generic character of the theater play is transformed from baroque *Trauerspiel* to modern *tragedy*.

of James and the epochal turbulence he and the Stuarts more generally represented for the audience of *Hamlet*.

Before proceeding to the details of Schmitt's elaboration of this *Wirklichkeitskern*, I would like to suggest that one way to grasp what is at issue for Schmitt is to compare his "meta-aesthetical" understanding of *Hamlet*—his conceptualization of the dimension that, so to speak, tragically deforms the genre of *Trauerspiel*—to Franz Rosenzweig's remarks about the tragic hero in his *Star of Redemption*. Rosenzweig presents the tragic hero as the mythic shape of what he calls the *metaethical self*.[9] The term is meant to address the singularity of the human being that *intrudes* into the generic predicates that otherwise identify and locate the person in a network of social relations. To use Arendt's suggestive term, Rosenzweig insists that there are two kinds or levels of *natality* in human existence. The first marks a human being's natural entrance into the world, his or her birth to a space of possibilities, to the genres of living (well or badly) available within a form of life. The second level of natality marks the emergence of an indivisible kernel of self-sameness, a dimension of pure self-reference that persists in all "possible worlds" and yet remains recalcitrant to any generic identification or community standard of goodness (this is what Rosenzweig means by "*meta*ethical"). Rosenzweig abbreviates one's birth into the multiple genres of living as $B = A$: what is particular (*das Besondere*) enters into the general or generic (*das Allgemeine*). The equation stands for the "personality" or what we might call the *man with qualities*. The birth of singular selfhood is abbreviated by the tautology $B = B$, which stands for the pulse of a defiant yet mute insistence that bears witness to—that is the "birth-mark" of—one's self-sameness: "*Whatever* changes about me *I am still me!*" The language Rosenzweig uses to characterize the birth of the metaethical self resonates powerfully with Schmitt's notion of the genre-shattering *Einbruch* of time into the space of play:

9. Franz Rosenzweig, *The Star of Redemption*, trans. William W. Hallo (Notre Dame, IN: University of Notre Dame Press, 1985). Subsequent references are made in the text. I have discussed this concept at length in my *On the Psychotheology of Everyday Life: Reflections on Freud and Rosenzweig* (Chicago: University of Chicago Press, 2001). I will not address in any detail the connections between Schmitt's work and that of Walter Benjamin, a topic that Schmitt specifically addresses in the second appendix to *Hamlet or Hecuba* and that has occupied the scholarship for years (Schmitt essentially tries to oppose what we might call his own *Origin of English Baroque "Tragedy"* to Benjamin's *Origin of German Baroque "Trauerspiel"*). One might recall, however, that Benjamin's own study of baroque *Trauerspiel* was itself indebted to his engagement with the very passages in Rosenzweig's *Star* that address the nature of the tragic self. The most important treatment of the Schmitt-Benjamin relation with respect to the material of concern here remains Samuel Weber, "Taking Exception to Decision: Walter Benjamin and Carl Schmitt," *Diacritics* 22, nos. 3–4 (Autumn–Winter 1992): 5–18.

Character, and therefore the self which bases itself on it, is not the talent which the celestials placed in the crib of the young citizen of the earth "already at birth" as his share of the commonweal of mankind [*am gemeinsamen Menschheitsgut*]. Quite the contrary: the day of the natural birth is the great day of destiny for individuality, because on it the fate of the distinctive [*das Schicksal des Besonderen*] is determined by the share in the universal [*den Anteil am Allgemeinen*]; for the self, this day is covered in darkness. The birthday of the self is not the same as the birthday of the personality. For the self, the character, too, has its birthday: one day it is there. It is not true that character "becomes," that it "forms." One day it assaults man like an armed man and takes possession of all the wealth of his property. . . . Until that day, man is a piece of the world even before his own consciousness. . . . The self breaks in and at one blow robs him of all the goods and chattel which he presumed to possess [*Der Einbruch des Selbst beraubt ihn mit einem Schlage all der Sachen und Güter, die er zu besitzen sich vermaß*]. He becomes quite poor, has only himself, knows only himself, is known to no one, for no one exists but he. (71)

It is this dimension that marks the self as constitutionally unfit for politics, that renders him un- or "impolitical": "The self is solitary man in the hardest sense of the word: the personality is the 'political animal'" (71).

For Rosenzweig, understanding the nature of this second order of natality—a sort of birth to *Unheimlichkeit*—will lay the groundwork for developing a modern philosophical conception of the biblical categories of creation, revelation, and redemption. As I have elsewhere argued, these categories provide Rosenzweig with the resources to launch a powerful critique of the violence he associates with the operations of sovereignty.[10] Yet Schmitt, the thinker most associated with an affirmative stance with respect to such violence, has, in *Hamlet or Hecuba*, also homed in on a dimension that in some sense lacks a proper place, a part that remains excessive or *unheimlich* in relation to the whole—the political and economic home—to which it in some sense continues to belong. Schmitt locates this dimension in what he characterizes as two "shadows" or "dark areas" of the play. These peculiar zones, where either something is expressed by failing to be directly addressed or something happens by failing to happen, are, as Schmitt puts it, "in no sense mere historical-political connections, neither simple allusions nor true mirrorings"; they instead mark off "two given circumstances that are received and respected by the play and around which the play timidly maneuvers. They disturb the

---

10. I have tried to develop this line of thought in "Miracles Happen: Benjamin, Rosenzweig, Freud, and the Matter of the Neighbor," in Slavoj Žižek, Eric Santner, and Kenneth Reinhard, *The Neighbor: Three Inquiries in Political Theology* (Chicago: University of Chicago Press, 2005).

unintentional character of pure play and, in this respect, are a *minus*. Nevertheless, they made it possible for the figure of Hamlet to become a true myth. In this respect they are a *plus*, because they succeeded in elevating *Trauerspiel* to tragedy" (44).[11]

III

For Schmitt the fundamental scandal or impasse at work in these "dark areas" concerns the fact that James's mother, Mary Stuart, who had been executed by Elizabeth in 1587, was thought to be involved in the murder of her second husband, Lord Darnley, the father of James. Because of Shakespeare's close ties to the Essex circle, key supporters of James in the struggle over the succession to Elizabeth, the playwright was severely constrained in his efforts to elaborate—to draw into the realm of aesthetic play—the personal, political, and larger historical issues surrounding the succession. He was, above all, constrained by what Schmitt refers to as "the taboo of the queen," the need, that is, to hold open the question of Gertrude's guilt in the murder of King Hamlet (one will recall that the first quarto was completed before James took the throne and the second quarto after the coronation; Schmitt largely relies on the earlier quarto):

Out of consideration for James, the son of Mary Stuart, the expected successor to the throne, it was impossible to insinuate the *guilt* of the mother in the murder of the father. On the other hand, the audience for *Hamlet*, as well as all of Protestant England and particularly of course London, was convinced of Mary Stuart's guilt. Out of consideration for this English audience, it was absolutely impossible to insinuate the *innocence* of the mother. Thus the question of guilt had to be carefully avoided. The plot of the

---

11. This generic shift might well have implications for the way in which, to use the famous title of Stanislavski's book, *an actor prepares* for a play such as this one. In act 3, scene 2, when Hamlet gives the players his tips for their crucial play within the play, he seems to recommend a certain naturalism, that is, that the actors not "o'erstep the modesty of nature," noting that the purpose of playing "was and is, to hold as 'twere the mirror up to nature; to show virtue her own feature, scorn her own image, and *the very age and body of the time his form and pressure*" (my emphasis). Given the rot in the body politic—a rot correlated with the out-of-jointness of time—it is safe to say that any attempt to hold a mirror up to the body of this particular time will show a body distended by pressures that render it horribly deformed. Hamlet uses the words "form" and "pressure" in act 1, scene 5, when he promises to the ghost of his father that he will banish from his thoughts "all forms, all pressures past" in order, we might say, to sustain his fidelity to the excess of pressure injected into his life by the mandate transmitted by the spectral voice of these royal remains. I am grateful to Freddie Rokem for pointing out these two passages, in a paper he gave on May 22, 2010, at the University of Chicago, entitled "Inscriptions of Speech: Socrates, Ion, Hamlet, and the Players."

drama became unclear and inhibited as a result. A terrible historical reality shimmers through the masks and costumes of the stage play, a reality which remains untouched by any philological, philosophical, or aesthetic interpretation, however subtle it might be. (18)

Because of this taboo, Shakespeare was, in other words, unable to follow the generic paths laid out either by the Nordic legend of *Amleth* that Shakespeare used in the composition of his play—here the son allies himself with his mother against the usurper—or by Greek tragedy, notably the path followed by Aeschylus's Orestes, where the son kills the murderer as well as his mother: "These are the two simple answers from Greek tragedy and Nordic legend. Even today, one would have to say that there is no third way and the mother cannot remain neutral, provided that one takes seriously the son's commitment to revenge and fully accepts the mother as a human person. The strangeness and opaqueness of Shakespeare's *Hamlet* is that the hero of the revenge drama takes neither one route nor the other" (12).

Because the "curse" on the House of the Stuarts was historically so complex (one that produces, namely, a modern rather than an ancient kind of tragedy), this first "dark area" is accompanied by a second one attesting to what Schmitt characterizes as a still more powerful intrusion of historical time into the realm of play: "the transformation of the figure of the avenger into a reflective, self-conscious melancholic" (19), or what he nicely abbreviates as the "*Hamletization of the avenger*" (21). And so again, what makes *Hamlet Hamlet* is the intrusion of a dimension into the hero and the play bearing his name that endows both with a kind of excess or surplus that Schmitt ultimately characterizes as a *Mehrwert* or *surplus value* (45), the very thing that opens *Trauerspiel* onto genuine tragedy. In the passage where he introduces this Marxist concept to characterize the excessive element in *Hamlet*, Schmitt's language itself produces a kind of rhetorical excess marked by a proliferation of the prefix "*un*," the marker of an impasse or blockage with respect to the meaning of the word to which it is attached (English uses both the prefixes "un" and "in"). I will cite both the English and the German texts:

This surplus value lies in the objective reality of the tragic action itself, in the enigmatic concatenation and entanglement of indisputably real people in the unpredictable course of indisputably real events. This is the basis of the seriousness of tragic action, which, being impossible to fictionalize or relativize, is also impossible to play. All participants are conscious of an ineluctable reality that no human mind has conceived—a reality externally given, imposed and unavoidable. This unalterable reality is the mute rock upon which the play founders, sending the foam of genuine tragedy rushing to the surface. (45)

Dieser Mehrwert liegt in der objektiven Wirklichkeit des tragischen Geschehens selbst, in der rätselhaften Verkettung und Verstrickung *un*bestreitbar wirklicher Menschen in den *un*berechenbaren Verlauf *un*bestreitbar wirklicher Ereignisse. Darauf beruht der *un*konstruierbare, nicht relativierbare Ernst des tragischen Geschehens, der infolgedessen auch nicht verspielbar ist. Alle Beteiligten wissen um eine *un*umstößliche Wirklichkeit, die kein menschliches Gehirn erdacht hat, die vielmehr von außen gegeben, zugestoßen und vorhanden ist. Die *un*umstößliche Wirklichkeit ist der stumme Felsen, an dem das Spiel sich bricht und die Brandung der echten Tragik aufschäumt.[12]

What becomes clear in such formulations is that what I have characterized as Schmitt's meta-aesthetical approach is by no means meant as an antitheatrical polemic; it rather aims at discovering the "extimate" dimension in theater that generates the manic proliferation of theatricality that culminates in the triplication of levels of play-acting in the third act of *Hamlet*, something that Schmitt characterizes as a magnification or intensification—a *Sich-Potenzieren*—of play rather than the production of mere ironic self-reflexivity.[13] For Schmitt, this extimate surplus is lodged in the historical figure of James, who finds himself at the center of a series of radical, epochal transformations tearing at the social fabric of England. James paradoxically embodies the two meanings of the title of this study: "the royal remains." He persists in his status as consecrated sovereign, insisting in his own writings on the divine right of kings secured in royal bloodlines; but he also represents a radical shift in the very logic of representation, one that locates this royal as a remainder of a medieval conception of kingship that has, however, not yet been reorganized into the political entity Hobbes later theorized as the theologically neutralized administrative state and that was at some level already in existence on the Continent. He embodies, in a word, the very tear in the fabric of being that he also strives to disavow. To use Freud's locution, James functions for Schmitt as a kind of ideational representative, or *Vorstellungsrepräsentanz*, of the complex historical forces driving England

12. Schmitt, *Hamlet oder Hekuba*, 46–47; my emphasis.
13. "The play on stage could magnify itself as play without detaching itself from the immediate reality of life. Even a double magnification was possible: the play within the play, whose possibility found its astonishing realization in Act Three of *Hamlet*. Here one can speak even of a triple magnification, because the preceding pantomime, the 'dumb show,' once again mirrors the core of the tragic action" (Schmitt, 41–42).

out of the Middle Ages but also, as Schmitt will also insist, into a future that in some sense swerves from the course taken by the sovereign states of the Continent.

Regarding the agonistic pressures pushing toward a new kind of political theology of sovereignty, one in which, to borrow from Benjamin's famous allegory, theology will be forced to hide under the table of the centralized state and animate the machinery of sovereignty from below— from off-stage—Schmitt emphasizes above all the unfortunate destiny of James and the Stuarts more generally as the unwitting and ultimately fragile vessels of such pressure. As Schmitt puts it, "the philosophizing and theologizing King James embodied . . . the entire conflict of his age, a century of divided belief and religious civil war" (25). Or, "The unhappy Stuart lineage from which James descended was more deeply involved than others in the fate of the European schism of belief." Or more succinctly still: "He [James] was thus literally from the womb immersed in the schisms of his era" (27). One might say that in the case of James I, his "second birth," the emergence of the peculiar torsion that (birth-)marked him as a potentially tragic figure, transpired before his natural birth.

The twists and turns at issue become poignantly manifest in a no doubt unintentional irony embedded in the verb Schmitt uses to characterize James's impossible self-assertion in the midst of the de facto religious and political state of emergency that defined the epoch. The verb is *sich behaupten*, which literally means to give oneself a "Haupt," to crown oneself, so to speak, as head or leader. Schmitt describes James as the "unhappy son of an unfortunate lineage, who asserted himself [*dieser unglückliche . . . sich behauptende Sohn eines unglücklichen Geschlechts*] painstakingly between his Catholic mother and her Protestant enemies, between intriguing courts and unruly noble factions, between fanatically disputing priests and preachers" (28). The unfortunate son of this unfortunate king was, of course, himself *ent-hauptet*, separated from his head.

IV

The intrusion of time into the play is, in the case of *Hamlet*, more complex still, in Schmitt's view. On the one hand, Schmitt repeatedly emphasizes what he characterizes as the still "barbaric" conditions of political and cultural life in England, conditions that testify to a kind of *underdevelopment* in comparison with the conditions on the Continent, an underdevelopment that, however, accounts for the elemental vitality of the theater in the Elizabethan world. Schmitt explicitly distinguishes this vitality from the theatricalization of the world associated with the baroque *Lebensgefühl* that permeated life at the courts of continental Europe: "In Shakespeare's Elizabethan England the baroque theatricalization of life was *still ungrounded and elementary—not yet* incorporated into the strict framework of the sovereign state and its establishment of public peace, security, and order, as was the theater of Corneille and Racine in the France of Louis XIV. In comparison with this classical theater, Shakespeare's play in its comic as well as melancholic aspects was coarse and elementary, *barbaric and not yet 'political'* in the sense of the state-centered politics of the time" (41; my emphasis).

In the second appendix to *Hamlet or Hecuba*, in which Schmitt explicitly attempts to distinguish his perspective from that of Walter Benjamin with respect to Shakespeare and the concepts of *Trauerspiel* and tragedy, Schmitt provides a fuller account of the nature of England's underdevelopment in comparison to the Continental states, states that conformed much more closely to the notion of the state as developed in political thought from Bodin and Hobbes to Hegel. For such thinkers the state represented an *imperium rationis*, a realm of objective reason that would put an end to the confessional wars that had torn Europe apart for at least a century: "The century of civil wars between Catholics and Protestants could only be overcome by deposing the theologians [*Enthronung der Theologen*]. . . . In place of the medieval order of feudal castes and estates arose a public order of peace and security created and maintained by the legitimizing achievement of a new entity: the *state*." And it is in this new institutional context, Schmitt continues, that "the word *political* acquires a polemical meaning and consequently the thoroughly concrete sense of an antithesis to the word *barbaric*" (63). The new political entity that takes the place of an order still defined by notions of sacred kingship—a notion that, as we have seen, James still to some degree held on to—"transforms men-at-arms, the existing good order, alimentation, and lawfulness into organizations characteristic of the *state*: army, police, finance, and justice. Through these organizations, the state establishes what it calls a 'civilized existence' [*polizierten Daseins*]. In this way, politics, police, and *politesse* become a remarkable troika of modern progress opposed to religious fanaticism and feudal anarchy—in short, to medieval barbarity" (63).

These are transformations we have to some extent already tracked in our discussion of Esposito's thought concerning the immunological dimension of modern biopolitics. For Esposito, as we have seen, the new Continental order of centralized, territorial states marks the development of an understanding of political life that places the self-preservation of life—and thus questions of risk—at the heart of the new administrative calculus of sovereignty.[14] One will recall Esposito's formulation of the passage from an in some sense more robust (in Schmitt's terms, *barbaric*) medieval order to the *poliziertes Dasein* secured by sovereign immunization: "This occurred when natural defenses were diminished; when defenses that had up to a certain point constituted the symbolic, protective shell of human experience were lessened, none more important than the transcendental order that was linked to the theological matrix. It is the tear that suddenly opens in the middle of the last millennium in that earlier immunitarian wrapping that determines the need for a different defensive apparatus of the artificial sort that can protect a world that is constitutively exposed to risk."[15] Schmitt's argument is, essentially, that Shakespeare's *Hamlet* registers more fully than any other work of art of the early modern period this *tear* in the fabric of the medieval order of being. We might say that it occupies the place of a kind of *structural interregnum* in the history of governmentality in Europe. As Schmitt puts it, "Shakespearean drama in general and *Hamlet* in particular is *no longer* religious in the medieval sense, but *neither* is it state-centered or political in the concrete sense that the state and politics acquired on the European continent through the development of state sovereignty during the sixteenth and seventeenth centuries" (59).

But at this very point in his argument, Schmitt transforms this "no longer but not yet" into something rather different. England, according to Schmitt, was not simply underdeveloped with respect to the sovereign states of the Continent; it was, in another sense, *prematurely developed*, historically more advanced, already moving *beyond* the order of territorial states that defined the politics of the Continental powers. To use Deleuzian terms, an initial and traumatic *deterritorialization* of the system of medieval attachments culminated, in continental Europe, in that process of reterritorialization that marks the emergence of the new order of sovereign states. England, for its part, followed a different developmental path, one that, Schmitt argues, progressed from one order of deterritorialization to another, even more radical one that shifted the

---

14. Schmitt's problem with this new form of sovereign rule was that it was in danger of becoming a purely administrative machinery without the "stuff" that could mobilize the sort of passionate attachment that constitutes a vibrant polity. That is to say, Schmitt was worried that the new apparatus of sovereign administration lacked the dimension of *flesh* that was, as it were, still kept alive in the Roman Catholic understanding of representation. See Carl Schmitt, *Römischer Katholizismus und politische Form* (Stuttgart: Klett-Cotta, 2008). Because Schmitt lacked an understanding of the place of biopolitics in the "history of the flesh," he could not see just how centrally this "stuff" figured in the new political order.

15. Roberto Esposito, *Bios: Biopolitics and Philosophy*, trans. Timothy Campbell (Minneapolis: University of Minnesota Press, 2008), 55.

center of gravity of political power *from land to sea*. Schmitt continues from the passage I just quoted that locates Shakespeare in a sort of structural interregnum: "In spite of the many contacts and ties with the continent, and some commonalities in the transition from the Renaissance and Baroque, English drama cannot be defined by such labels. It belongs to the thoroughly peculiar historical evolution of the island of England, which had then begun its elemental appropriation of the sea [*dem elementaren Aufbruch zu der großen Seenahme*]" (59). If, in other words, there is a genuine *Einbruch* of time into Shakespeare's *Hamlet*, it is because the play is, by way of symptomatic distortions and deformations, able to register in some fashion not simply the dissolution of the medieval world before its reconstitution according to a new and modern political theology of sovereignty—one that, as we have seen, keeps theology hidden below the table—but also another historical dynamic: the elemental *Aufbruch* into a maritime and ultimately entrepreneurial and commercially based organization of life and politics. For Schmitt this radical "sea change" is already signaled by what we might characterize as the *adventure capital* of an emerging entrepreneurial class. This was "a life at the first stage of an elemental departure [*eines elementaren Aufbruches*] from land to the sea, the transition from a terrestrial to a maritime existence. Such seafarers and adventurers as the Earl of Essex and Walter Raleigh belonged to the elite" (47–48).[16] The concluding remarks of *Hamlet or Hecuba* place maximum emphasis on the revolutionary dynamic at work in this new chapter in the *nomos of the earth* even if, as Schmitt also asserts, its full force did not become clear until later centuries:

Measured in terms of the progress toward civilization that the ideal of continental statehood . . . signifies, Shakespeare's England still appears to be barbaric, that is, in a pre-state condition. However, measured in terms of the progress toward civilization that the Industrial Revolution . . . signifies, Elizabethan England appears to be involved in a phenomenal departure from a terrestrial to a maritime existence—a departure, which, in its outcome, the Industrial Revolution, caused a much deeper and more fundamental revolution than those on the European continent and which far exceeded the overcoming of the "barbaric Middle Ages" that the continental state achieved. (65)

Paradoxically, then, the "barbarism" of Shakespeare's theater results from its involvement in a historical dynamic that pushes beyond the "bar-

---

16. One might compare this with Hannah Arendt's treatment of rather different classes of "adventurers" in the development and maintenance of colonial empires in the nineteenth century. See her *The Origins of Totalitarianism* (New York: Harcourt Brace, 1975), 147–57.

baric Middle Ages" more powerfully—more "barbarically"—than does the civilizing process associated with classical state sovereignty, that is, with the politics, police, and *politesse* of courtly life. What Shakespeare was able to convey by way of the deformations—the dark areas or shadows—he introduced into his material was a sense of the disjunction between the consciousness of James, and of the Stuarts more generally, and the historical forces they were nonetheless in some fashion fated to embody. It is just such a disjunction that produces what Schmitt refers to as the *surplus value* that circulates through Shakespeare's *Hamlet*, a surplus that was, in some sense, only *latently manifest* in the play until Schmitt's interpretation.

V

To get a better grasp of what I take to be the real stakes of Schmitt's reading, I would like to return, very briefly, to Jonathan Lear's discussion of the *fort/da* game, this attempt, on the part of Freud's grandson, to stage a kind of *Trauerspiel* around his mother's absence, one that would precisely *not* result in tragedy. In his account of the developmental achievement marked by the emergence of the child's capacity to play with the wooden spool and the signifying dyad *fort/da*, Lear emphasized the persistence of a remainder that in some way haunts the play in and through which the child is enabled to experience what happened to him *as* a loss. Schmitt's argument in *Hamlet or Hecuba* is that Shakespeare found a way to *stage* the remainder—what remains precisely *unverspielbar*—in his play. In this case, it is a remainder pertaining to a tear in the fabric of a prior form of life, in the "immunological wrapping" provided by the medieval ideology of sacred kingship.[17] It is this inclusion of the remainder—*the flesh*

17. Franco Moretti, who engages with both Schmitt and Benjamin in his reading of Shakespeare, makes a somewhat similar argument, emphasizing, above all, the dynamic at work in the deconsecration of the king, a process that prepared the way for his final departure from the scene and the entrance of the people onto the stage of history: "Tragedy disentitled the absolute monarch to all ethical and rational legitimation. Having deconsecrated the king, tragedy made it possible to decapitate him." Franco Moretti, *Signs Taken for Wonders: On the Sociology of Literary Forms* (London: Verso, 2005), 42. For Moretti, too, the vitality of this theatrical form depends on a disjunction between a historical fate and its intelligibility: "Fully realized tragedy is the parable of the degeneration of the sovereign inserted in a context that *can no longer understand it*" (55). For Moretti, this process of degeneration serves to release the poetic dimension of language from its rhetorical use-value, a process of decoupling—and here we find a certain echo of Schmitt's analysis—not yet achieved on the Continent: "Instead of the lucid Cornelian continuity between word and action, a radical discrepancy, or category difference, makes words impotent and actions mute. This mistrust in the practical force of language—so different from what his culture envisioned—makes Shakespeare's soliloquies the first manifestations of 'poetry' in the modern sense of being emancipated from a rhetoric conceived

of royal remains—that, in Schmitt's view, disrupts or deforms *Hamlet* and *thereby keeps it hauntingly alive* as a defining myth of modernity.[18]

The "too-muchness" of Shakespeare's play thus functions, in the terms I have been proposing, as a sort of archive—or better, *archive fever*—that registers a fundamental mutation in the "physiology" of the body politic and, above all, of *the body of its head.*[19] It is thus for very good reason that, as Marie Axton has argued, the time of the composition of *Hamlet* was a period when the doctrine of the King's Two Bodies had reached a sort of crisis point, which became decisive for the future of the institution of kingship over the next centuries. It is these mutations that allowed for the execution of Charles I some fifty years after the composition of *Hamlet* and of Louis XVI at the end of the following century, when this history entered a new phase, in which the "People" asserted themselves—*sich behaupteten*—and came to embody the head of their own body politic. Before I return to the phase of the story that is of primary interest in this study, the one that, as I have been arguing, comes to be feverishly archived in modernist works of art, I would like to say one more thing about the nature of dreams and how I think one should understand Schmitt's appeal to dream logic in the construction of his argument.

In his discussion of the "barbarism" of Shakespeare's play and the context of its performance and reception, Schmitt pays special attention to the institution of theater and the modes of address (to the audience) he attributes to the form. Schmitt underlines the importance of a shared public sphere "that encompasses the author, the director, the actors, and the audience itself and incorporates them all" (35). The need for the audience to grasp the stakes and issues of the play involves, as Schmitt suggests, a capacity not only to follow what is manifest in the action of the play. It also implies that the audience must be able to be gripped by what is only *latently manifest* in the play (in the form of its "latent dream thoughts") as well as by the pressures that sustain the gap between the latent and the manifest. This is what Schmitt is after when he says, "Even the dreams that the dramatist weaves into his play must be able to become the dreams of the spectators, with all the condensations and displacements of recent events" (36). But as we have seen, the "recent events" include the opening of a *structural interregnum* that did not fully

---

as the art of convincing" (70). As we have seen, T. J. Clark makes a similar argument regarding the "emancipation" of *paint* at the moment of the king's decapitation.

18. We might further note that the most famous words of the play, "to be or not to be," themselves constitute a kind of *fort/da* dyad.

19. Again, my point of reference is Jacques Derrida, *Archive Fever: A Freudian Impression*, trans. Eric Prenowitz (Chicago: University of Chicago Press, 1996).

take shape in the lifetime of the London audience of Shakespeare's play. What does it mean to weave such events into the fabric of a play, that is to say, to include them as the *remains* of a form of life *that is not yet at its end*? Here I would like to turn, again, to Jonathan Lear's notion of ontological vulnerability, a concept that pertains directly to the question of the dream work involved in the process of working through the *time of the demise* of a form of life.[20]

Lear's account of the ways in which the Crow Indians negotiated the transition from life as a nomadic hunting society to life on a reservation pays particular attention to the resources provided to the community by the dream visions of select members of the tribe, along with their communal interpretations. As Lear notes, "the Crow had an established practice for pushing at the limits of their understanding: they encouraged the younger members of the tribe (typically boys) to go off into nature and dream. For the Crow, the visions one had in a dream could provide access to the order of the world beyond anything available to ordinary conscious understanding" (66). But under certain historical conditions, these dream visions could provide something even more important: the resources for a kind of orientation and what Lear calls "radical hope" in the face of a collapse of the very order of the world. The man who became the Crow chief during the critical period of transition to life on the reservation, Plenty Coups, had, at the age of nine, a dream vision that was registered by the tribe as just this sort of cultural resource. Lear explains that "young Plenty Coups's dream was of a different order. It did not predict any particular event, but the change of the world order. It was prophetic in the sense that the tribe used it to face up to a radically different future" (68).

It is sufficient to emphasize, without going into the details of the dream and its tribal interpretation, that "Plenty Coups's dream was a manifestation of anxiety," an affect that "would . . . have been an appropriate response of people who were sensitive to the idea that they were living at the horizons of their world" (76). Plenty Coups's dream registered the sort of *Einbruch* of time into the pleasure principle that otherwise informs the primary processes of the dream work, generating, instead, a different kind of dream-play, one whose "deformities" allowed the community to engage, in some fashion, with the very edge of the intelligibility of their world and so with the ontological vulnerability that ultimately informs every form of life. As Lear puts it, "Plenty Coups's

20. Jonathan Lear, *Radical Hope: Ethics in the Face of Cultural Devastation* (Cambridge, MA: Harvard University Press, 2006). Subsequent references are made in the text.

dream seems to have been an integral part of a process by which the tribe metabolized its shared anxiety" (77). But here it is crucial to understand the locus of this anxiety:

It helps . . . to conceptualize the anxiety not as specifically located in this or that person but as diffused throughout the tribe. It is the tribe that is anxious. Or, perhaps even more accurately, a way of life is anxious—though it cannot yet say what it is anxious about. Young Plenty Coups picked up these inchoate anxieties and turned them into dreamlike form. He dreamt *on behalf of* the tribe. . . . This was the beginning of a process by which Plenty Coups became entangled in the tribe's history—and in which he took on the burden of an anxious way of life. (78)

My argument has been that Shakespeare functions in much the same way for Schmitt.

One will recall that at the end of *Hamlet* the hero gives his dying voice to Fortinbras, a transmission of royal legitimacy that also finally took place in 1603, when Elizabeth gave her dying voice to the election of James. In the most famous of last words of world literature, Hamlet says to Horatio:

O, I die, Horatio!
The potent poison quite o'er-crows my spirit.
I cannot live to hear the news from England,
But I do prophesy th'election lights
On Fortinbras. He has my dying voice:
So tell him, with th'occurents, more and less,
Which have solicited—the rest is silence. (5.2.332–37)

What Schmitt's *Hamlet or Hecuba* suggests is that these words and the play more generally prophesy *the dying of the dying voice,* the end of the form of life in which such voices could still have anything but poetic authority. But Schmitt's argument has also been that in certain rare cases, poetic speech attains the status of what he calls "living myth," by which I understand something on the order of the visions Plenty Coups dreamed on behalf of his tribe. Shakespeare's theater has, in other words, been an indispensable resource in allowing its audiences to work through the structural interregnum, the turbulent void at the heart of their (early) modernity. But as I have been arguing, some of the most radical implications of that interregnum did not become fully clear—remained latent— until it passed from the court and into the very heart of the People, those who were called upon to incorporate the surplus value of what remains of the King's Two Bodies. The People become those in whose voice the death of the dying voice silently resonates, leaving here and there, as another dream vision circa 1900 would have it, strange, fleshy formations on the throat.

VI

Now I would like to pursue this link between early modernity, modernity, and modernism by (as promised) taking seriously the historical context in which Hugo von Hofmannsthal chose to situate the figures and circumstances of his famous *Chandos Letter*, published a few short years after Freud's dream book.[21] The historical background of the text, invoked above all by the name of the letter's addressee, along with its dating, coincides exactly with the period and the events that Schmitt addresses in his treatment of *Hamlet*.

This short prose text has firmly established itself as one of the foundational texts of modernity, and of the "linguistic turn" that came to be associated with it, by compellingly conveying the sense of what it means for a *world* to break down at the very site at which its intelligibility comes to be articulated, if not constituted: in *language*. Put somewhat differently, the text helped to inaugurate the "linguistic turn" in twentieth-century thought by evoking so powerfully the limits and fragility of human language qua "house of being," to use Heidegger's famous formulation. Certainly among the most peculiar and gripping features of the text is that it manages to convey this nexus of ontological and linguistic vulnerability in sentences of striking formal beauty and precision, sentences the author infused with the tone of high Elizabethan prose modeled in part on that of Francis Bacon's essays, which, as we know, he had been reading at the time.

The "plot" of the little text can be summarized quite quickly. A young English nobleman, "Philipp, Lord Chandos, the younger son of the Earl of Bath," writes to Francis Bacon, his former patron and mentor at the court, to apologize and give a kind of accounting "for his complete abandonment of literary activity" (117). In the letter, dated "August 22, AD 1603," the now twenty-six-year-old Chandos explains his retreat to his

21. The text was first published in the German newspaper *Der Tag* in October 1902. I cite the translation in Hugo von Hofmannsthal, *The Lord Chandos Letter and Other Writings*, trans. Joel Rotenberg (New York: New York Review Books, 2005). Subsequent references are made in the text. References from the German are from Hugo von Hofmannsthal, *Gesammelte Werke*, ed. Bernd Schoeller (Frankfurt am Main: Fischer, 1978), 7:461–72.

country estate and now two-year silence as the result of a mental breakdown that made it impossible for him to continue along the trajectory
of the literary accomplishments that had clearly made him a darling of
the court and London society. After summarizing some of those accomplishments and the plans he had made for ever-more-ambitious literary
projects—projects that manifest a vast literary erudition and encyclopedic quality of mind—Chandos explains to Bacon the nature of the crisis
that put a sudden end to his literary activities and participation in court
society. He had, he explains, lost the capacity to experience language as
a vital locus of absorption in the world, in history, in ideas, in the passions, indeed in anything that could count as genuine experience. Instead, language itself had uncannily begun to assert and insert itself as his
singular "object" of experience precisely by breaking apart into so many
linguistic bits, which now seemed to clutter the space *between* him and
the world as the detritus of the very culture and *Bildung* that had been the
very substance of his existence. He goes on, however, to describe a series
of quasi-miraculous moments that now and again punctuate the otherwise mechanical, inwardly deadened way of living he has adopted at his
country manor amid his family and servants. These are moments when
he feels graced by the sudden infusion of a kind of pure and utterly affirmative life force occasioned by contingent encounters with the lowliest
and most insignificant elements of the everyday life of his environment.
He concludes the letter by lamenting his incapacity to express the essence
of these epiphanies that thereby remain, to use Scholem's formulation
apropos of Kafka's universe, a sort of *Nichts der Offenbarung*: revelations
at the zero-degree of any meaningful content.[22]

The *Chandos Letter* has long been viewed not only as a major work
of literary modernism but also as a significant autobiographical docu-
ment that allows us to grasp the rationale behind Hofmannsthal's own
move away from the lyric poetry and refined aestheticism that made
him a young star in Viennese literary society in the 1890s and toward
the more public and socially "relevant" genres of theater and opera, a
shift that led him to lifelong partnerships with Richard Strauss and Max
Reinhardt, among others, and his long association with the Salzburg Fes-
tival. The move away from the refined, erudite aestheticism of the early
writings to the more socially demanding engagement on a broader public

22. I am referring to Scholem's letter to Walter Benjamin, September 20, 1934. See *The Correspondence of Walter Benjamin and Gershom Scholem, 1932–1940*, trans. Gary Smith and Andre Lefevre
(Cambridge, MA: Harvard University Press, 1992), 142.

stage—"stage" meant both literally and figuratively—was accompanied by essayistic work on the arts, politics, and culture that culminated, in some sense, in one of his most famous and controversial essays, "Literature as the Spiritual Space of the Nation," in which he coined the infamous phrase "conservative revolution."[23] The name stuck as the favored term to capture the kind of modernist antimodernism associated with the writings of Carl Schmitt and others. For Hofmannsthal, this revolutionary fervor represented the restless search for new forms of community and communal passion, for affectively binding affiliations that demanded, in turn, new sources of spiritual and cultural authority that could, as it were, call such affiliations into being and sustain their vitality. The essence of this "revolution" functioned as a countermovement to the kind of vertigo first registered in the *Chandos Letter*. Hofmannsthal characterized that vertigo a few years later as the very essence of his age: "The essence of our epoch is multiplicity and indeterminacy [*Vieldeutigkeit und Unbestimmtheit*]. It can rest only on what glides and shifts underfoot [*Sie kann nur auf Gleitendem ausruhen*], and is conscious of the fact that what other generations believed to be solid is only *Gleitendes*. A quiet, chronic vertigo [*Schwindel*] vibrates in it."[24] Hofmannsthal is not, in my view, simply asserting that a certain *Unbehagen* or "discontent" shadows the lives of modern subjects living under the normative pressures of civilization; he is rather suggesting that not all is well with this *Unbehagen*, that, in a

---

23. The essay was first delivered as a lecture at the University of Munich in 1927.

24. Hugo von Hofmannsthal, "Der Dichter und diese Zeit," in *Gesammelte Werke*, vol. 8, 60. Typically, literary historians link this assessment to Hofmannsthal's affinities with the monism of Ernst Mach, who famously declared the ego to be unsalvageable as a firm locus of personal identity and to be made up of various and ever-shifting configurations of "sensations" (as we saw, Deleuze takes up such a "logic of sensation" in his commentary on Francis Bacon). But these words also clearly recall Marx's famous characterization of capitalism in *The Communist Manifesto*, sentences that in turn resonate with much of Georg Simmel's *Philosophy of Money*, a book Hofmannsthal knew well: "The bourgeoisie cannot exist without constantly revolutionizing the instruments of production, and thereby the relations of production, and with them the whole relations of society. Conservation of the old modes of production in unaltered form, was, on the contrary, the first condition of existence for all earlier industrial classes. Constant revolutionizing of production, uninterrupted disturbance of all social conditions, everlasting uncertainty and agitation distinguish the bourgeois epoch from all earlier ones. All fixed, fast-frozen relations, with their train of ancient and venerable prejudices and opinions, are swept away, all new-formed ones become antiquated before they can ossify. All that is solid melts into air, all that is holy is profaned." *Karl Marx: Selected Writings*, ed. David McLellan (Oxford: Oxford University Press, 1977), 224. For Hofmannsthal, the "conservative revolution" aims at bringing this uncertainty and agitation into a new state of equipoise, at drawing it into a new, binding constellation of social relations, something that could truly be achieved only through rhetorically and poetically compelling speech and performance. Such views manifest complex and disturbing affinities with the sort of aestheticization of politics that helped to mobilize the German masses into that thanato-political formation referred to as the *Volksgemeinschaft*.

word, the normal dis-ease that Freud famously linked to civilization had itself somehow taken ill.

VII

Before I begin to discuss the historical setting of the *Letter*, I would like to cite a few passages to give a more vivid sense of the various stages of Chandos's "decline" from a position of full literary and cultural sovereignty to one that bears a certain family resemblance to that of Richard II at the end of his deposition, as well as to Judge Schreber, whose cultivation of his own *Ludertum*—the fleshly "remains" of his juridical investiture at the Sachsen Supreme Court—afforded him isolated experiences of intense *jouissance*.

As I have noted, Chandos begins his letter by summoning up memories of past literary accomplishments and projects. These projects from which the narrator now feels utterly estranged were conceived and executed on the basis of what might be thought of as the exact opposite of estrangement: a sense of being fully at home in every aspect and dimension of the world, nature, history, and culture (one might think here of an extreme form of the capacity for immersion in what is other to oneself that Worringer characterized as *Einfühlung*). The narrator can, in a word, no longer comprehend his earlier sense of seemingly absolute nonestrangement, a condition readers have for the most part "diagnosed" as the narcissistic aspect of extreme aestheticism, the tendency to find oneself beautifully reflected in everything one encounters. Curiously, in his first attempt to characterize the chasm that now separates him from his earlier intellectual, aesthetic, and spiritual expansiveness, he commits what we might characterize as a parapraxis, or *Fehlleistung* (the more colloquial translation, "Freudian slip," retains a link to the meaning of *gleiten*): "Am I the same person," Chandos writes, "as the nineteen-year-old who wrote *The New Paris, The Dream of Daphne, Epithalamium*—those pastorals, tottering under the weight of their grand words, which a great queen and a number of overindulgent lords and gentry are gracious enough to still remember?" (117). Queen Elizabeth had, of course, died on March 24, 1603, some five months before the date of Chandos's letter. Although the coronation ceremony did not take place until July, James I was proclaimed king that same March day. This slip represents, I think, one of the ways in which, to use Schmitt's formulation, the time of a shifting, mutating political theology and *nomos* of the earth breaks into this particular space of aesthetic play. It may also, for that matter, be a marker of

Bacon's own highly precarious position under the new monarch. But I am getting ahead of myself.

The erotic (and, some might argue, perverse or masochistic) aspect of Chandos's literary ambitions comes through in his recollection of a project dealing with the myths and tales of antiquity that had provided seemingly inexhaustible resources for the plastic arts of the Renaissance: "I longed to enter into those naked, glistening bodies, those sirens and dryads, Narcissus and Proteus, Perseus and Actaeon, the same way a hunted deer longs to wade into the water. I wanted to disappear into them and speak out of them with their tongues" (119). Perhaps the most telling example of Chandos's earlier literary ambitions is provided by his description of a project he was considering at the point of his greatest confidence in his capacity to find himself in all he encountered (we might simply say, in *the All*). Indeed, he admits that the title of the project was to be *Nosce te ipsum*:

I planned to put together a collection of maxims like Julius Caesar's—you remember that Cicero mentions it in one of his letters. My plan here was to assemble the most remarkable utterances which I had collected during my travels in my dealings with the learned men and clever women of our time, with exceptional individuals from among the general public, and with the cultivated and distinguished. In this way I wished to combine beautiful classical and Italian aphorisms and reflections with whatever else I had run across in the way of intellectual baubles in books, manuscripts, and conversation, and also to include particularly beautiful festivals and pageants, strange crimes and cases of dementia, descriptions of the greatest and oddest buildings in the Netherlands, France, Italy, and much more. (119–20)

Chandos summarizes the state of mind that stood behind such ambitions as one of "continuous inebriation," in which he "saw all of existence as one great unity" (120). His next set of associations indicates that in this state he related to the world as if it were, in its entirety, a bountiful and providential matrix more or less comparable to what a Kleinian analyst would refer to as "the good breast": "And in all of nature I felt myself. To me there was no difference between drinking warm foaming milk which a tousled rustic at my hunting lodge had squeezed into a wooden bucket from the udder of a fine, mild-eyed cow, and drinking in sweet and frothy spiritual nourishment from an old book as I sat in the window seat of my study. The one was like the other" (120).

On the basis of such passages, Dominique Tassel has characterized the libidinal economy of Chandos's literary ambitions and activities as something even more primitive than narcissism. It seems, instead, to be

organized along the lines of a still autoerotic—and primarily *oral*—orientation, a relation to text and to language more generally as if it were
an inexhaustible supply of mother's milk. She captures this ultimately
nonrelational relation by means of a wonderful neologism, *laicture*.[25]
Chandos's breakdown occurs, we might say, when the shelf life of all this
lactic bounty begins to expire, when, according to Paul Celan's unforget-
table image, *the milk goes black*.[26] As Tassel and others who have taken up
her insight emphasize, the descriptions of language that Chandos uses
to characterize his crisis move within the semantic field of spoilage and
decay, thus marking the conversion of the delectable into the disgusting,
intoxicating goodness into toxic badness. Chandos famously begins the
account of his *Sprachkrise* by registering a profound disgust with abstract
concepts, as if the *soma* were itself performing a critique of what would
appear to be the metaphysical underpinnings of his prior relation to
language:

First I gradually lost the ability, when discussing relatively elevated or general topics, to
utter words normally used by everyone with unhesitating fluency. I felt an inexplicable
uneasiness in even pronouncing the words "spirit," "soul," or "body." I found myself
profoundly unable to produce an opinion on affairs of court, events in Parliament,
what have you. And not out of any kind of scruples—you know my candor, which
borders on thoughtlessness. Rather, the abstract words which the tongue must enlist
as a matter of course in order to bring out an opinion disintegrated in my mouth like
rotten mushrooms. (121)

The process of decay soon contaminates the entire field of language and
linguistic practices, producing states of mind that border on psychosis
and paranoia: "Everything came to pieces, the pieces broke into more
pieces, and nothing could be encompassed by one idea. Isolated words
swam about me; they turned into eyes that stared at me and into which
I had to stare back, dizzying whirlpools which spun around and around
and led into the void" (122).[27]

---

25. Dominique Tassel, "En lisant 'Une lettre,'" *Poétique* 66 (1987): 147.

26. Paul Celan's most famous poem, "Deathfugue," begins: "Black milk of daybreak we drink it
at evening/we drink it at midday and morning we drink it at night/we drink and we drink." *Selected
Poems and Prose of Paul Celan*, trans. John Felstiner (New York: Norton, 2001), 31. The question of
the originality of the locution "black milk" became the occasion of a legal and personal nightmare
for Celan when the widow of the poet Ivan Goll accused Celan of plagiarism.

27. Again, much of this language matches up with the ways in which Melanie Klein has characterized the "schizoid position" of the infant who converts anxiety into positive bits of badness and
projects them into the (m)other. See, for example, her 1946 paper "Notes on Some Schizoid Mechanisms," in *The Selected Melanie Klein*, ed. Juliet Mitchell (New York: Free Press, 1986), 175–200.

First attempts to see in his breakdown the workings of divine justice for the arrogance of his former stance, to embrace it as part of "the well-conceived plan of a divine providence" (120), come to nothing because the breakdown takes down with it those very religious concepts. But as two fine readers of Hofmannsthal have emphasized, Chandos does manage to retain a quasi-mythic understanding of the logic of his fate, namely as one comparable to that suffered by Tantalus, a figure whose crime also involved what could be called radical acts of oral transgression.[28] The passages that open this line of interpretation first note that the religious concepts to which he initially turned began to appear as "a grand allegory which stands over the fields of my life like a shining rainbow, at a constant remove, always ready to recede in case I think of running up and wrapping myself in the hem of its cloak" (121). The echoes of the Tantalus myth—above all, of his famous punishment—quickly become much more explicit: "How shall I describe these strange spiritual torments, the boughs of fruit snatched from my outstretched hands, the murmuring water shrinking from my parched lips?" (121).

Jacques Le Rider sees in this allusion to the punishment of Tantalus Hofmannsthal's own attempt to violently "wean" himself from the fantasy of a beautiful encyclopedic order of the universe accessible to the right sort of *gnosis*, indeed to the sort of classical *Bildung* that Chandos embodies and Hofmannsthal to a very large extent still enjoyed. In a jarring shift of metaphors, Le Rider compares the traumatic loss of (the fantasy of) the nourishing breast of *Bildung*—and the sense of the omnipotence of thoughts that goes with it—to the crash of a computer's operating system: "The book was the nourishing breast. But now the text has decayed. The cultural and scientific memory secured by writing [*Schrift*] has collapsed—not unlike the way one now speaks of the crash of a computer in which the 'data' of knowledge it had stored . . . transforms into chaos because of an irreversible 'system error.' "[29] The so-called "good moments" that Chandos goes on to experience in the midst of the otherwise devitalized existence he comes to lead might then be thought of as sites of emergence of new life, singular and spontaneous forms of

28. See Jacques Le Rider, *Hugo von Hofmannsthal: Historismus and Moderne in der Literatur der Jahrhundertwende*, trans. Leopold Federmair (Vienna: Böhlau, 1997); David Wellbery, "Die Opfer-Vorstellung als Quelle der Faszination: Anmerkungen zum Chandos-Brief und zur frühen Poetik Hofmannsthals," *Hofmannsthal-Jahrbuch zur Europäischen Moderne* 11 (2003): 282–308. Both versions of Tantalus's crime fit the description of oral transgression. One version has it that Tantalus shared the divine ambrosia he enjoyed at the table of the gods with mortals; according to a second version, he served up his own dismembered son, Pelops, to the gods. Later in the text, Chandos directly refers to the daughter of Tantalus, Niobe.

29. Le Rider, *Hofmannsthal*, 123.

self-organization out of the chaos. Be that as it may, the paradox Le Rider locates at the heart of the *Letter* is that Hofmannsthal made full use of all the resources of his learning and erudition to express the collapse of the cultural ideals embodied in such *Bildung*.[30]

In another recent interpretation of the *Letter*, David Wellbery has similarly argued that it is only by way of what he calls, taking up Tassel's insight, the "lactopoetic" model of reading that informed Chandos's pre-crisis existence that we can understand the reference to Tantalus at all. The transgression that calls for such punishment is located not in this or that deed—one looks in vain for it in the text—but rather in the oral *jouissance* at the heart of the poetological model that informed all of Chandos's previous relations to the world. The positing of the world as text, as ultimately legible and thus edible or consumable writing, allows it to be experienced in the mode of infantile, oral gratification. Chandos's earlier literary ambitions thereby register as efforts at a "post-infantile re-cuperation of the phantasm of orally mediated unity with the mother."[31] What interests Wellbery most is the nature of the new "poetology" that allows for the so-called good moments that Chandos manages to experi-ence—now and again and always contingently—once he has retreated from court society to his country residence.

In the *Letter*, Chandos tries to explain such moments to Bacon in the following terms:

30. Le Rider points to a wealth of cultural, historical, and literary references in the *Chandos Letter*. They include not only the borrowings from Bacon's own *Essays*, which Hofmannsthal was reading at the time, but also references to the second epistle in book 2 of Horace's *Epistles*, in which the author apologizes to his addressee for not having written sooner and explains the greater value of a well-ordered life over the writing of poetry. Le Rider also divines allusions to Herder, Novalis, and Baudelaire, along with important contemporaries such as Fritz Mauthner, who indeed felt "rec-ognized" in Hofmannsthal's text. He goes on to cite recent work claiming that Chandos ultimately functions as a kind of stand-in for Shakespeare—around 1900 the debates as to Shakespeare's true identity were quite vibrant (among the candidates for the "real" Shakespeare was Francis Bacon)—on the basis of the discovery in the National Portrait Gallery in London of the so-called Chandos Shakespeare, a portrait of the playwright that had belonged to a certain Count Chandos. Le Rider also cites a letter the author wrote on December 14, 1902, to Stefan George, in which Hofmannsthal uses some of the same terms as Chandos to explain his long silence and current inability to compose even short poems. Le Rider concludes that this complex network of references and allusions—we might say, with Schmitt, allusions and mirrorings—defeats all efforts to find the right "key" to the text; there are, he argues, simply *too many keys*: "Hofmannsthal's historicism is undermined by the play of montage which transforms the *Chandos Letter* into a text of multiple codes. The 'English style' of Shakespeare's epoch no doubt remains dominant, but the multiple points of contact with other epochs encoded in the text make it 'undatable'" (*Hofmannsthal*, 111). I would suggest that this undatability is itself the historical index in the text, that it marks the site where historical time traumatically intrudes into the text. As I shall further argue, the Elizabethan background is crucial in our effort to grasp what is at is at stake in this irruption.

31. Wellbery, "Opfer-Vorstellung," 291. Subsequent references are made in the text.

It will not be easy for me to convey the substance of these good moments to you; words fail me once again. For what makes its presence felt to me at such times, filling any mundane object around me with a swelling tide of higher life as if it were a vessel, in fact has no name and is no doubt hardly nameable. I cannot expect you to understand me without an illustration, and I must ask you to forgive the silliness of my examples. A watering can, a harrow left in a field, a dog in the sun, a shabby churchyard, a cripple, a small farmhouse—any of these things can become the vessel of my revelation [Offenbarung]. Any of these things and the thousand similar ones past which the eye ordinarily glides with natural indifference can at any moment—which I am completely unable to elicit—suddenly take on for me a sublime and moving aura which words seem too weak to describe. (123)

Further descriptions emphasize the status of "the overlooked" shared by the occasions of Chandos's "revelations," which are at some level revelations not of a "what" but rather of a "that": *that* the thing in question is there, that it is something, whatever it might be. The kind of empathy, or *Einfühlung*, to use Worringer's phrase once more, that Chandos experienced with respect to the *All* has undergone a radical "phenomenological reduction" and is now held in reserve for the somehow miraculous presence, the bare "that it is" of the *singular*:

At those moments an insignificant creature, a dog, a rat, a beetle, a stunted apple tree, a cart path winding over the hill, a moss-covered stone mean more to me than the most beautiful, most fervent [hingebendste] lover ever did on the happiest night. These mute and sometimes inanimate beings rise before me with such a plenitude, such a presence of love that my joyful eye finds nothing dead anywhere [auf keinen toten Fleck zu fallen vermag]. Everything that exists, everything I can remember, everything in the most muddled thoughts in my brain, appears to be something. (125; translation modified)

The most powerful evocation of the creaturely urgency Chandos now registers without being able to capture in words the essence of such urgency, of the pure insistence of the singular being-there of things, whatever they may be, concerns not a contingent encounter with the object in question but rather a kind of hallucinatory vision of profound, creaturely suffering, itself occasioned by a seemingly indifferent accident:

Recently, for example, I had a generous amount of rat poison spread in the milk cellars of one of my dairy farms. I went out riding toward evening, thinking no more about the matter, as you might imagine. As I rode . . . over deep, tilled farmland—nothing more significant in the vicinity than a startled covey of quail, the great setting sun off in the distance above the convex fields—suddenly this cellar unrolled inside me, filled with the death throes of the pack of rats. It was all there. The cool and musty cellar air, full of the sharp, sweetish smell of the poison, and the shrilling of the death cries echoing against mildewed walls. Those convulsed clumps of powerlessness, those desperations colliding with one another in confusion. The frantic search for ways out. The cold glares of fury when two meet at a blocked crevice. (123–24)

At this point, Chandos draws upon the resources of his *Bildung* in his effort to convey the force of this unfolding scene of mass death: "But why am I searching again for words, which I have sworn off! My friend, do you remember Livy's wonderful description of the hours before the destruction of Alba Longa? The people wandering through the streets that they will never see again . . . saying good-bye to the rocks on the ground. I tell you, my friend, this was in me, and Carthage in flames too; but it was more than that, it was more divine, more bestial—and it was the present, the fullest, most sublime present" (124).[32] Finally, Chandos returns to the motif of the maternal now marked by an utter helplessness amplified by its link to the house of Tantalus: "A mother was there, whose dying young thrashed about her. But she was not looking at those in their death agonies, or at the unyielding stone walls, but off into space, or through space into the infinite, and gnashing her teeth as she looked! If there was a slave standing near Niobe in helpless fright as she turned to stone, he must have gone through what I went through when the soul of this beast I saw within me bared its teeth to its dreadful fate" (124).[33]

32. The passage in Livy to which Chandos refers is that of a massive population transfer in which the victims are rendered mute by overwhelming despair: "Meanwhile mounted troops had been sent to Alba to deal with the transference of the population, and a force of infantry followed charged with the task of pulling down the buildings of the town. There was no panic when the soldiers marched in; none of the wild confusion of a captured town when a victorious army, forcing its way through smashed gates and over the rubble of battered walls, spreads with yells of triumph through every street and alley dealing universal destruction with fire and sword; none of the horror of a citadel falling to the final assault. On the contrary, there was silence—the silence of despair and the grief which could not speak. All hearts were numbed, all minds bewildered; looking at their possessions, the unhappy people could not decide what to take or what to leave; again and again they asked each other's advice, now standing distraught before their doors, now wandering aimlessly through the familiar rooms which they would never see again." Livy, *The Early History of Rome*, trans. Aubrey de Sélincourt (London: Penguin, 2002), 65–66.

33. I have already noted the disturbing resonances between the "blackening" of the lactic bounty invoked in the *Chandos Letter* and the image of "black milk" from Celan's "Deathfugue." I am tempted to say that what Hofmannsthal has achieved with his description of the rats dying in the milk cellars is the first representation in literature of the inside of a gas chamber, before the fact, of course. That Chandos links the image to Livy's description of the destruction of Alba Longa and the deportation of its population only amplifies the resonances. It is also well known that one of the more potent metaphors used by the Nazis to characterize the Jews was that of rats and other vermin.

In his reading of the *Letter*, Wellbery emphasizes this element of the maternal, noting the chain of associations between the startled brood of quail, the dying mother rat, and, finally, the very locus of this dramaturgy of death: the milk cellars of the dairy farm. The scene thereby becomes charged with a quasi-ritualistic dimension, becomes the enactment of the sacrificial cutting of the link to the maternal and the "lactopoetic" mode of being, a cut that allows Chandos to open to the possibility of a new existential stance in the world. As Wellbery puts it, it makes Being accessible to feeling "in its purest presence as naked life delivered over to the fate of unavoidable death" (296). The purging of the lactopoetic mode of desire functions as a ritual of purification and rebirth: "With the death of the mother rat in the milk cellar, Chandos experiences the definitive destruction of the lactopoetic phantasm. Not only does the rat suffer her demise but so does, above all, the Imaginary of the flow of milk [*das Imaginäre des Milchstroms*] as the foundation of the early poetics. And only out of this destruction does an authentic experience of Being arise" (296).

Wellbery goes on to trace a rich and complex network of links between the *Chandos Letter* and other of Hofmannsthal's writings in which we find the motifs of sacrificial violence, the cut of a knife into twitching flesh, and the peculiar *jouissance* associated with the ritualized approach to the boundary of life and death. In all of this, Wellbery underlines Hofmannsthal's nearly obsessive use of the verb *zucken* (and its multiple variations), a word that can signify the quick thrust of a knife, the twitching, convulsive movement of wounded flesh, and the *frisson* generated by the performance of the sacrificial act or witnessing it. For Wellbery, it is only insofar as the *Letter* registers, in the realm of aesthetic experience, the reverberations or aftershocks—the "after-twitchings"—of this archaic network of real, imaginary, and symbolic relations that Chandos's invocation of a poetics of the singular being in its bare, creaturely life can get a grip on the reader.[34]

As Wellbery sees it, the *Chandos Letter* belongs to the canon of modernism precisely because at a fundamental level it lives off of the fascination with sacrifice and the ambivalent affects it is able to mobilize. In his search for the sources of new passionate attachments in the midst of what he experienced as *das Gleitende*, the groundless relativity of values that permeates modern life, Hofmannsthal repeatedly turns to the

---

34. As Wellbery notes, Hofmannsthal himself claims that every poet must in some fashion register "in the tissue of his body the after-twitchings [*das Nachzucken*] of an archaic excitation that can hardly be measured anymore" (cited in Wellbery, 303). Wellbery insists that the archaic excitation or *Regung* at issue emerges out of primal scenes of sacrifice.

vitality seemingly promised by the *primal passion*, that of sacrifice, in which, as Wellbery puts it, the "suggestion of transcendence" is (aesthetically) produced in a transfer of affects emanating, ultimately, from the convulsive twitching of flesh (309).[35] Here Wellbery's argument about Hofmannsthal's early poetics more or less repeats, at the level of aesthetic experience, Elaine Scarry's claims apropos of the practices of torture and war. I would like to cite, once more, a crucial passage from her *Body in Pain*: "At particular moments when there is within society a crisis of belief—that is, when some central idea or ideology or cultural construct has ceased to elicit a population's belief either because it is manifestly fictitious or because it has for some reason been divested of ordinary forms of substantiation—the sheer material factualness of the human body will be borrowed to lend that cultural construct the aura of 'realness' and 'certainty.' "[36] From this perspective, it makes good sense that a society that had come to experience its very foundations as *gleitend* would be ready, in 1914, to make contact with the real not only by way of aesthetic experience and various vitalist philosophical movements, but also through a veritable mania for the ultimate sacrifice.

VIII

What can, however, be misleading in this otherwise compelling reading of Hofmannsthal's poetics of sacrifice is, I think, that it neglects the other side of what is registered as a need for transcendence, if only one produced by way of the "special effects" of poetic discourse, namely the need *to get clear* of the pressure of what I have been calling a surplus of immanence pushing against the boundaries of individual and collective bodies. The *lack* of orientation that Hofmannsthal tries to capture with the evocative phrase *das Gleitende* and, in some sense, to redress by means of a poetics nourished by the semantics of sacrifice must, I am arguing, also be grasped as an *excess of pressure* that fails to find a viable form of discharge. What is missing, we might say, is not energy, not affect, but rather the means to put into play psychic energy across viable networks

35. In this respect, Wellbery's reading locates Hofmannsthal within the lineage of twentieth-century writers and thinkers caught up in what Alain Badiou referred to as the *passion of the real* and Robert Buch as the *pathos of the real*. See once more Badiou, *The Century*, trans. Alberto Toscano (Cambridge: Polity Press, 2007); and Buch, *The Pathos of the Real* (Baltimore: Johns Hopkins University Press, 2010).

36. Elaine Scarry, *The Body in Pain: The Making and Unmaking of the World* (New York: Oxford University Press, 1985), 14.

of representations, to facilitate a distribution and dispersion of such energy. What causes anxiety is, in other words, not simply a loss of access to transcendence, to a transcendental source of normative authority, but rather the fact that such sovereign authority has in some sense *moved into the soma*, into the life of the people. There it takes on the aspect of a biopolitical "mass" intruding into and, as it were, *already twitching* within every sphere of human endeavor. The fundamental impasse that Hofmannsthal has homed in on—one that indeed seems to push toward the semantics of sacrifice and its dramaturgy of a *passage à l'acte*—is that the symbolic resources of the world he inhabits are uniquely unable to discharge the pressures they unceasingly generate in the life of every subject. And it was, as I have suggested, Hofmannsthal's Viennese neighbor Freud who elaborated a new thinking of and mode of engagement with this impasse and the twitching and shuddering "mass" that forms there.

We are thereby led to a second set of concerns regarding the meaning of sacrifice in the *Chandos Letter* in particular and in Hofmannsthal's oeuvre more generally. One will recall that Wellbery introduces the motif of sacrifice apropos of Chandos's hallucinatory vision of the rats dying in the milk cellar. But the empathy, the overwhelming *Einfühlung*, that Chandos experiences in the context of this vision is precisely with the sort of animal—vermin—generally seen to be unfit for sacrifice.[37] Chandos's immediate association with the deportees of Alba Longa from Livy's histories of the foundation of Rome (as well as with the destruction of Carthage) gives the scene of the dying rats—along with other instances of "the overlooked" in the text—a distinctly *political* coloring. That is to say, my hunch is that the rats offer us, rather than sacrificial victims in any straightforward sense, the figure of what Agamben has characterized—to some extent based on readings of Livy—as the *homo sacer*, the being *excluded* from the orbit of either human or divine law and by that very exclusion fully *included* in the sovereign exception. This shift of perspective from the mythico-religious order of sacrifice to the political or political theological order of sovereignty and bare, creaturely life is, I believe, supported by the context in which Hofmannsthal chose to situate the *Chandos Letter*.

Hofmannsthal was well acquainted with Francis Bacon's essays as well as his status as one of the founders of the modern methods and culture

---

37. Stanley Corngold has underlined this aspect of the insect or *Ungeziefer* that Gregor Samsa becomes in Kafka's *Metamorphosis*. See Stanley Corngold, introduction to Franz Kafka, *The Metamorphosis*, trans. and ed. Stanley Corngold (New York: Bantam, 1986), xix.

of science.[38] My hunch, however, is that the significance of the historical setting is to be sought not by way of tracing this or that passage, sentence, or turn of phrase to Bacon's writings, finished or unfinished—*both* Bacon and Lord Chandos failed to complete a biography of Henry VIII—or to piece together the various members of the Chandos line that made up the composite figure created by Hofmannsthal.[39] All such efforts would, I think, ultimately remain at the level that Schmitt characterized as lacking in seriousness insofar as they fail to touch on the *Ernstfall*, the critical situation at issue in the text. The difference here, of course, is that we are talking about historical material that breaks into the text across a gap of some three hundred years, which is something closer to what Walter Benjamin characterized as the actualization of historical forces as they become legible in the "now-time" of reading.[40] But both for Schmitt and for Benjamin—and, I think, for Hofmannsthal as well—the notion of the critical situation remained linked to that of *revolutionary time*, even if

38. Among the sources of citations he discovers in the *Letter*, H. Stefan Schultz focuses above all on Bacon's *Advancement of Learning*. See H. Stefan Schultz, "Hofmannsthal and Bacon: The Sources of the *Chandos Letter*," *Comparative Literature* 13, no. 1 (Winter 1961): 1–15. In his essay, Schultz refers to Hofmannsthal's letter to his friend Leopold von Andrian, written after the publication of the *Chandos Letter*. There Hofmannsthal insists that his primary stylistic concern in the text was to capture the *tone* of Elizabethan prose but that the content would be of contemporary significance. Among his reasons for using the mask of an invented figure writing to a known historical one was, he says, his desire to make the reader experience what seems distant and foreign as proximate, familiar, *nah verwandt*. Schultz ultimately argues that Hofmannsthal so freely mixed allusions to Elizabethan England, Roman letters, and texts by Goethe and Novalis, among others, that the significance of the historical setting cannot be seen as hermeneutically crucial. This is the same position taken by Le Rider, who, as we have seen, claims that the *Letter* is ultimately undatable.

39. Schultz lists the various Chandos figures that ostensibly went into the final composite: "No Lord Chandos is known by the name of Philip, there never was a connection between the Earls of Bath and the Chandos family, and the last Duke of Exeter had died in 1475. We do not know how Hofmannsthal became familiar with the name Chandos. He may have found it in Bacon. A Lord Chandos (or Chandoys) was among the 'three hundred gentlemen of prime note' present at Essex House on February 8, 1601. Apparently, he was a friend of the Earl of Essex, but not one of the conspirators, for he was one of the twenty-five peers who passed upon the Earls of Essex and Southampton on February 19, 1601. This was William, the fourth Lord Chandos, who died November 18, 1602 and cannot have written our letter, dated August 22, 1603. Yet the writer of our letter speaks of the Queen as though she were still living. Giles, third Lord Chandos, who died February 21, 1593/94, had entertained Queen Elizabeth on her progress at Sudeley Castle in September 1592, where on the second day of her stay the short but sorrowful tale of Daphne was performed. Is it accidental that among those 'pastorals . . . which a divine Queen and a few all too indulgent lords and gentlemen are gracious enough still to remember' and which Philip Chandos mentions among his youthful productions there is also a 'Dream of Daphne'? But only Grey Brydges, fifth Lord Chandos, who succeeded his father on November 18, 1602, would approximate in age the writer of our letter, who claims to be twenty-six. The fifth lord was known as a noble housekeeper of ample fortune, which he expended in the most generous manner." Schultz, "Hofmannsthal and Bacon," 12–13.

40. Benjamin's most famous formulation of this principle is to be found in his theses "On the Concept of History," trans. Harry Zohn, in Walter Benjamin, *Selected Writings*, vol. 4, *1938–40*, ed. Howard Eiland and Michael W. Jennings (Cambridge, MA: Harvard University Press, 2003), 389–400.

one understands the revolution to be "conservative." In the terms I have been developing here, this means that what is crucial in the text and the short-circuit it establishes with the years of the Elizabethan succession is a fundamental shift in the organization of the body politic and the status of the sovereign power that occupies the place of the *head* of that body.

Here I think it is sufficient to note the highly insecure and constantly shifting—*gleitend*—status Bacon enjoyed in the years leading up to and immediately following the queen's death. Bacon had been a member of the intimate circle around the Earl of Essex in much of the last decade of the sixteenth century, but he distanced himself from his patron once the latter had begun to fall out of favor with the queen and even became state prosecutor in the trial against Essex in 1601. Although this proved advantageous in the wake of the execution of Essex and his close advisers—the year, we assume, Chandos withdrew from the court—it proved to be a disadvantage once James had assumed the crown (James had developed a close relationship with Essex in the late 1590s). Bacon's position as "Learned Counsel" under Elizabeth had been secured solely through a verbal order of the queen and was nowhere officially registered. After the coronation, Bacon used all possible contacts, influence, and political strategies to repair the damage done by his involvement with the prosecution of Essex, to gain favor with the new monarch, and to secure a position in the new order. As Bacon's biographers put it, "When the Scottish King became James I of England in 1603, he remembered and rewarded those who had stayed true to his old friend the Earl of Essex. What little favor he did show to Francis Bacon in those early years of his reign was a consequence not of Francis' detachment from Essex but of his brother Anthony's steady attachment to his patron."[41] Though knighted in July 1603—along with three hundred others—Bacon's position in the new court at first remained precarious, requiring constant vigilance and effort to keep himself within view and in the favor of the new king. He did this at least in part through writings on politics aimed at influencing James. In the following years he enjoyed greater successes as a lawyer, statesman, and author and was eventually appointed lord chancellor and elevated to the titles "Baron Verulam" and "Viscount St. Albans." In 1621 he was prosecuted for the taking of bribes, dismissed from his office as lord chancellor, temporarily imprisoned, fined, and forced to retire to his country residence, where, ironically, he finally enjoyed the leisure that allowed for complete dedication to learning and writing.

41. Lisa Jardine and Alan Stewart, *Hostage to Fortune: The Troubled Life of Francis Bacon* (New York: Hill and Wang, 1999), 17.

   The political vagaries of life at the court created a view of Bacon—one he himself actively cultivated—that in certain ways would seem to correspond to the narrative of Chandos's life. As Jardine and Stewart put it, "In later years, Bacon was careful to separate his life into a 'before' period of political intrigue, treacherous behavior of friends and social climbing, and an 'after' of austere scientific inquiry in a country retreat. As a way of glossing over his perpetual struggles with the competing demands of his two possible careers to create a plausible 'life,' this worked. But it has left posterity with two clearly incompatible versions of Francis Bacon. All subsequent biography has struggled to resolve them."[42] What I am suggesting with respect to Chandos is that both the "before" and "after" of the narrator's still young life need to be grasped against the background of the turmoil that marked his addressee's career at the court in precisely the period in question in the *Letter*, that the dating and address of the *Letter* compels us to read the events and experiences related in it, at least in part, as the *Nachzucken* of an *Ernstfall* the revolutionary and "barbaric" character of which was the subject of Schmitt's study of *Hamlet*. What the fictional Lord Chandos relates in Hofmannsthal's *Letter* is, I am arguing, part of a history of political and aesthetic representation that in some sense culminated in the twitching flesh filling the canvases of that other Francis Bacon, who, for his part, claimed to be a distant relative of Baron Verulam and Viscount St. Albans.

   As I have already noted with respect to Freud, when Hofmannsthal wrote the *Letter* in the very early years of the twentieth century, this history was beginning to open upon a thinking of the flesh that seemed to offer the possibility of new possibilities of engaging with this creaturely materiality. Toward the end of the *Letter*, Chandos recalls the story about the orator Crassus (a story related in Bacon's *Apophthegms*), who claimed to have developed a profound attachment to a tame eel in his ornamental pond. Chandos apologizes to Bacon for the foolishness of this further example of what appears to be a kind of revelation of higher life in the midst of the low and overlooked and goes on to characterize the distinctly somatic aspect of his "new thinking" of what it means to be in the midst of life, a thinking in which putrescence and peace, *Ludertum* and a kind of love, belong together: "The image of Crassus is sometimes in my brain at night, like a splinter with everything around it a throbbing, boiling infection. Then it is as if I myself were beginning to ferment, to foam, seethe, and give off sparks. And the whole thing is a kind of feverish thinking, but thinking in a medium more direct, fluid, and passionate

42. Ibid., 19.

than words. It has whirlpools too, but ones which seem to lead not into the abyss as whirlpools of language do but into myself in some way, and into the lap of the most profound peace" (127).

IX

Hofmannsthal's preoccupation with the political theology of modernity—and the vicissitudes of creaturely life that belong to it—which I have attempted to bring into view in my reading of the *Chandos Letter*, stand fully in the foreground in the poet's nearly lifelong engagement with the most famous play of the Spanish Baroque, Calderón's *Life Is a Dream*. Hofmannsthal began to work on a free trochaic transcription of the play in 1901. Over the next years, his progress on the work remained fragmentary but provided him with the beginnings of the material that became, after World War I and the breakup of the Austro-Hungarian Empire, the kernel of his own radical revision of the play, *The Tower*, which itself underwent several significant mutations and appeared in print in no fewer than three different versions.[43] When he published the first scene for the Christmas supplement to the *Leipziger Tagesblatt* in 1924, Hofmannsthal provided a brief sketch of the play as a whole:

The play is a *Trauerspiel* in five acts; it takes place in a Polish Kingdom that is closer to timeless legend than to history and in a past century whose atmosphere is most closely related to that of the seventeenth. The scene presented here, the first of the play, shows the protagonist (Sigismund) at his lowest point from which, over the course of the following acts, he is elevated to the steps of the throne, then thrust back again into the night of prison, pulled out once more through a frightful revolution, and is finally, as King and Ruler in both the legitimate and revolutionary sense, taken down by an early death.[44]

It is beyond the scope of this discussion to attempt a comprehensive reading of the play, a project that would require close comparison of the published versions along with consideration of unpublished drafts, notes,

43. The two "canonical" versions—I will refer to them as the "first" and "second" versions—remain the one that appeared in book form in 1925 and the one published in 1927 that served as the stage version for its first theatrical productions in 1928. Hofmannsthal made the revisions to a large extent in light of criticisms by Max Reinhardt and Martin Buber, among others, and under the influence of his reading of a typescript of Benjamin's *Trauerspiel* book, sent to him by the author. The first version was not performed until 1948.

44. Cited in the afterword to Hugo von Hofmannsthal, *Der Turm*, ed. Werner Bellmann (Stuttgart: Reclam, 2000), 220. This volume is a reprint of the 1925 version.

and correspondence pertaining to the play's long process of evolution, not to mention the wealth of literary and scholarly sources from which Hofmannsthal drew in the composition of the work.[45] What I hope to achieve here is something far more modest; I would simply like to underline the elements in the play that allow us to deepen our appreciation for the political theological dimension of what, in the *Chandos Letter*, was presented as a new, yet still inarticulate, mode of *Einfühlung*, as a thinking responsive to the "twitchings" of creaturely life, a thinking that attempts to inhabit the "neighborhood" of its always singular appearances.

The family resemblance between Chandos and the figure of Prince Sigismund in Hofmannsthal's *Tower* is above all manifest at the level of the relation to language. Sigismund seems to embody more directly, more physically, not only the struggle with language Chandos experiences at the apex of his crisis but also the creaturely status of the various contingent occasions of the "revelations" that punctuate Chandos's postcrisis existence. In the first version of the play, Sigismund, who at this point lives in a kind of caged enclosure, is brought before the doctor who has been charged by the prince's guardian, Julian, to evaluate his health and competence. Julian, for his part, hopes to use the prince to mobilize and organize the already unruly masses in an uprising against the king, who has, just as in Calderón's play, condemned his son to this political *banlieu* on the basis of a prophecy that the royal succession would proceed by way of violent usurpation of father by son. One might say that the entire play takes place against a backdrop of a state of emergency that various kinds of leader-figures—Julian, the King, Olivier (a sort of proto-fascist soldier)—attempt to master by trying to instrumentalize what remains of personal, royal representation still embodied by Sigismund. This quasi-anarchic political situation—call it the *Ernstfall* at the heart of the play—is signaled early on by Olivier's apocalyptic declaration "All are against all [*Alle gehen gegen alle*]. Not a house will remain standing. They'll sweep

---

45. Indeed, as Jacques Le Rider has argued, one might be tempted to see *The Tower* as a kind of "Mourning-Play" for the very sort of audience (and literary culture more generally) that would have had the capacity to engage with the densely woven intertextual fabric of the work. From this point on, Le Rider suggests, writers of Hofmannsthal's literary ambition would, at least in the German-speaking world, have to depend upon the support and mediation of university scholars—of the guild of academic *Germanisten*—to maintain any sort of link to a broader audience. Against this background, Le Rider even suggests that "the prince locked up in the tower whose language only a small, select few are still able to understand could, in a certain sense, be seen as a self-portrait on Hofmannsthal's part." Le Rider, *Hofmannsthal*, 282. My own sense is that the play's intense engagement with issues of sovereignty and creaturely life retains its force even for contemporary readers and audiences, who might well miss the wealth of *allusions* and *mirrorings*, to use Schmitt's terms, that Hofmannsthal wove into the texture of the play.

up what's left of the churches like so much dirt."[46] When we first meet him, Sigismund is presented as a kind of wolf-man—he is actually dressed in a wolf skin—who, though fully capable of reading Latin texts, thanks to his guardian's humanitarian (and strategic) solicitude, dwells, not unlike the ape in Kafka's "Report before an Academy," in a zone of indistinction between human and animal. Anton, Julian's assistant, who provides bits of comic relief throughout the play, introduces the prince to the doctor, who is initially seized by horror in the face of the creature's state of utter destitution. As I have indicated, what is first emphasized is Sigismund's troubled relation to language:

Doctor: Can't you call him? Coax him? Has he no sense? [*Ist er denn ohne Vernunft?*]
Anton: That one? Why he knows Latin and can get through a fat book as though it
   were a side of bacon.—But sometimes a word sticks in his mouth and he can't get
   it out [*Aber manchmal krampft sich ihm's Wort im Mund und er bringts nicht heraus*].
   (191; *GW*, 264)

His first utterances are mechanical repetitions of those of Anton:

Anton (*beckons to him*): There, sit down beside me.
Sigismund (*parrotlike*): Sit down beside me. (191)

The prince's entrance on the stage as a sort of half-man, half-beast, along with his initial, parrotlike utterances, have led to comparisons with Kaspar Hauser as well as other figures—some produced experimentally by, among others, the Scottish king James IV—who seemed to offer to educated Europeans the prospect of witnessing the emergence of a kind of pure, natural language, the language of Adam.[47] Sigismund himself

---

46. Hugo von Hofmannsthal, *The Tower*, 1925 version, trans. Michael Hamburger, in *Selected Plays and Libretti*, ed. Michael Hamburger (New York: Pantheon, 1963), 182 (translation modified). Subsequent references are made in the text. German citations are taken from Hofmannsthal, *Gesammelte Werke*, vol. 3, subsequently referred to as *GW*. The figures around Olivier see the hand of the Jews in this apocalyptic turmoil, a refrain heard more than once in the play. The one Jewish figure in the play, Simon, attributes the current conditions to the fact that the king, in order to finance a disastrous war, has generated a hyperinflation by printing an excess of ultimately worthless currency. He laments that the figure of the king engraved on the face of all the newly minted currency has effectively lost both its symbolic and its economic value. One might also note that another figure in the play, a young monk, uses Chandos-like language to characterize the current state of the world, language the monk ostensibly reads from a tractate by Antonio de Guevera, a priest in the court of Charles V: "Depart World, for thou art not to be trusted; in thy house the past lingers on as a mere phantom, the present crumbles under our hands like a rotten and venomous fungus [*das Gegenwärtige zergeht uns als ein morscher und giftiger Pilz unter den Händen* (*GW*, 290)]" (234).
47. See, for example, W. G. Sebald's beautiful essay on the play, "Das Wort unter der Zunge: Zu Hugo von Hofmannsthal's Trauerspiel 'Der Turm,'" *Literatur und Kritik* 13 (1978): 294–303.

raises the question of his own seemingly liminal ontological status when, upon feeling the doctor's hand on his forehead, he asks, "Am I in the world? Where is the world?" (194) When he later encounters the peasant woman who looked after him in his early years, she encourages him to regard himself in Christ's image, pointing to a crucifix on the wall. His response once again underlines the zone of indistinction he feels himself to occupy. Recalling the image of a slaughtered pig he witnessed as a child, he answers in terms that bring to mind Francis Bacon's crucifix paintings (and the artist's comments about the meatlike aspect of Christ's tormented body): "I cannot keep them separate, me and him [Christ on the cross], and then again me and the animal that was hung from a cross-beam and drawn, full of bloody darkness inside. Mother, where is my end and where is the animal's end?" (256) The prince's creaturely status seemingly suspended between human and animal is itself produced by the extreme mode of his exposure to the force of law manifest in the sovereign decree that first banished him to the outer threshold—the *ban-lieu*—of the court and city. And as I have argued, such decrees themselves point to the liminal status of the sovereign himself, his peculiar capacity to suspend the law by virtue of his identification with the animating force of the law.

In the first scene of act 3, we witness the ultimately failed encounter between the prince and the king, a meeting arranged by Julian, who has his own designs on Sigismund. The king, for his part, needs the prince's popular support to master the turmoil raging in his kingdom and tries to turn him against Julian, whom he suspects of having his own political agenda. Early in the scene, which takes place in the queen's death chamber in the royal palace, the king's confessor declares to his ruler, "The law and sovereign are one" (271), and affirms the doctrine of the divine right of kings. When the prince is brought before his father, the king affirms the ultimately sanctioned lawlessness of his initial decree to banish his son: "Understand this, once and for all, Crown Prince of Poland: we can do no wrong as King to our subjects, as father to son. And though we had laid your head upon the block without trial, divine authority was bestowed upon us, and there is no one who could plead against us. For we were before you were—and so you were placed in our hands by God Himself" (286). Upon seeing his son recoil mutely in fear, the king continues to elaborate upon the political theology of his sovereignty: "These hands? Afraid of these royal hands? They are merciful, bountiful, they heal the sick man upon whom I place them. But reverence is due to them: you are right, my clever son. A king's hand is more eloquent than the sage's tongue. Their motion is a command, and that command comprehends the whole world: for it anticipates obedience. In commanding, the King resembles the Creator" (286–87). At the end of the king's speech, Sigismund can only ask: "Whence does it come—so much power?" The king's response—interrupted only by the prince's repetition of the question—reiterates the two dimensions at issue in the doctrine of the King's Two Bodies: the perpetuation of kingship across the gaps of succession and the status of royal power as the fount and foundation of all other secular powers.

Only the fullness of power avails: that in which we sit here, as the only one, solitary. Such is the power of kings. All other power is lent by him and mere semblance. . . . On the day it pleased God we entered into our right as an heir. A herald's cry bore it to every corner of the earth. The crown touched this anointed head. This mantle was laid on our shoulders. Thus there was a king again in Poland. For Basilius or Sigismund dies, but the King does not die. Do you begin to see who it is that confronts you? (287)

At a certain point in the dialogue, Sigismund can no longer contain himself. He strikes his father in the face, tears his sword from its scabbard, chases him until he collapses, strips the king of his mantle, and places it upon his own shoulders. Julian, seeing his moment, bows before Sigismund and proclaims "Long live the King!" But a further struggle ensues, the king's men overwhelm Sigismund and Julian, and the king is revived. It is quickly decided that the prince is to be banished once more. It is, however, the courtier's pronouncement of Julian's sentence that expresses most explicitly the nature of the ban as a kind of brutal pardon in which the victim is mercifully consecrated to a living death in a perpetual state of exception:

As for you, expect an immediate sentence for high treason and satanic conspiracy: only its execution is suspended, the sword of justice hangs by one hair over your head each day and each night. In spite of it all, your deeds, and whatever may have driven you to them in the depth of your dark mind, shall be covered with a merciful veil by the indulgence of our exalted monarch. . . . The place where you will end your days is that tower, isolated high up in the mountains. Whoever meets you even a musket-shot away from its walls, whether he be a freeman or serf, shall deal with you as with one twice outlawed and condemned [*der vollzieht an dir die Acht und Aberacht*]—shall give your blood and your bones to the earth, your eyes to the birds, your tongue to the dogs. (297–98; *GW*, 333)

As the courtier emphasizes, anyone declared to be "twice outlawed and condemned" may be killed with impunity. It is, of course, this peculiar status of being included in the law—exposed to the pure force of law—by being excluded from its specific protections that Giorgio Agamben has subjected to so much historical, philological, and philosophical scrutiny. And as Agamben has also emphasized, to be caught up in the paradoxical topology of the state of exception also means to enter into a further zone of indistinction, that between human and animal, the zone of what I have been calling creaturely life. We might say that two orders meet in the state of exception: the *political* order of sovereignty and the scientific-experimental order of *knowledge* in which the boundary between the human and the animal is at issue.[48] As Agamben has put it with respect to the ancient Germanic tradition alluded to in *The Tower*, "the monstrous hybrid of human and animal, divided between the forest and the city—the werewolf—is . . . in its origins the figure of the man who has been banned from the city." The mythical hybridity of the wolf-man's nature exactly corresponds to the set-theoretical paradox of the person caught in the state of exception, namely to be fully included in the law by being abandoned by it: "That such a man is defined as a wolf-man and not simply as a wolf . . . is decisive here. The life of the bandit, like that of the sacred man, is not a piece of animal nature without any relation to law and the city. It is, rather a threshold of indistinction and passage between animal and man, *physis* and *nomos*, exclusion and inclusion: the life of the bandit is the life of the *loup garou*, the werewolf, who is precisely *neither man nor beast*, and who dwells paradoxically within both while belonging to neither."[49]

Of equal importance in the present context is the relation Agamben posits between the status of the wolf-man and the state of nature that, in Hobbes's *Leviathan*, gives rise to the social contract that installs the sovereign in his rightful place, thereby immunizing the community (only now fully established as one) against harm. The state of nature in which *homo hominis lupus* figures for Hobbes not so much as a genuine historical or prehistorical epoch prior to genuine human community, but rather as the presupposed operation of an *epoché*, is a state of exception in which the city and its laws are viewed as if dissolved, thereby allowing the emergence of order to be experienced as meaningful and binding: "And this lupization of man and humanization of the wolf is at every moment possible in the *dissolutio civitatis* inaugurated by the state of exception. This

---

48. And as we have seen, the modern order of biopolitics represents a peculiar hybridization of these two orders, in which the will to govern and the will to know enter into new kinds of combinations and alliances.

49. Giorgio Agamben, *Homo Sacer: Sovereign Power and Bare Life*, trans. Daniel Heller-Roazen (Stanford, CA: Stanford University Press, 1998), 105. Subsequent references are made in the text.

threshold alone, which is neither simple natural life nor social life but rather bare life or sacred life, is the always present and always operative presupposition of sovereignty" (106). It thereby constitutes, as Agamben puts it, the "*Urphänomen* of politics"; it functions less as a form of life than as a fundamental and primordial *deformation*, "a zone of indistinction and continuous transition between man and beast, nature and culture" (109). It is, as I have argued, in just such motion and commotion at the jointure between nature and culture that human life takes on the surplus of flesh that, at least in the context of the early modern period, was still capable of attaching itself to royalty, of being shaped into the king's "second" body. What Hofmannsthal's *The Tower* explores is precisely what happens when this creaturely excess can no longer be contained and deployed by the figure of a sovereign master.

X

The two versions of the play offer two radically divergent outcomes of this crisis in which no single figure is able to fully execute the sort of decisive action that could muster and master the presuppositions of sovereign rule. In the first version, Sigismund is poisoned by a mysterious gypsy woman sent by Olivier, the cynical leader of the insurgent masses.[50] Before he dies, he declares the revolutionary advent of a new age: "What I bear within me is the spirit of foundation, not the spirit of possession; and the order I seek to establish is based on self-denial, self-dedication. For I do not seek to change this or that, but to change the whole, all at once; and then we shall all be citizens of the new age" (368). In a speech to the counts of his realm, he promises to join together with the Ottoman Empire and form an alliance in which the borders between rival groups will be erased (what is meant here is clearly not only feudal but also national, ethnic, and religious borders): "But as for your little realms, your houses, which you build in rivalry, and your creeds, which you hold in rivalry, I will not respect them, but confound your frontiers: I will mix all you little peoples anew in a great melting-pot" (368). Immediately upon his death, we witness the entrance of the figure of "the children's king"—*der Kinderkönig*—the messianic leader of a mass of orphaned children who already in some fashion embody in their daily lives the form

50. In a letter fragment, Hofmannsthal characterizes Olivier as "the embodiment of the rebelliousness of the lowliest, the eternal ochlocratic element." Cited in Bellmann's notes to Hofmannsthal, *Der Turm*, 196.

of life invoked in Sigismund's dying words. At the end of the play, a small choir of boys intone the Pentecostal chant *mitte spiritum tuum, et creabuntur, et renovabis faciem terrae*, while the children's king, *"clasping the sword of state in its scabbard,"* leads them offstage carrying the body of the prince.

Walter Benjamin, in his enthusiastic review of this version of the play, compares the children's king with Fortinbras in the context of a more general evaluation of the work as a genuine *Trauerspiel*. He furthermore claims—rather strangely, I think—that Calderón's Christian optimism is fully overcome, that "the demonic forces of the tower overwhelm" the prince, and that "dreams arise from the earth and the Christian heaven has long retreated from them."[51] By contrast, in a letter to Hofmannsthal, Martin Buber argued that "this children's king lacks Fortinbras's dramatic-legitimate function to lead out of the tragedy back into history; he signifies, rather, what is at the same time beyond tragedy and beyond history—the messianic—but for that, as beautiful as he is, he is just not true enough."[52] Whether it was under the impact of Buber's criticism, the reading of the manuscript of Benjamin's *Trauerspiel* book (Benjamin sent it to him in 1925), the need to make the play more dramatically viable for the stage, or pressures arising from the material itself, Hofmannsthal decided to eliminate the figure of the children's king from the final version. Olivier, the proto-fascist leader who sees himself as an instrument of fateful and impersonal historical forces, has Sigismund shot by snipers and emerges as the likely victor in the struggle for power. Sigismund's dying words—these are now the final words of the play—are delivered not to a successor but to the doctor and Anton: "Bear witness, I was here, though no one has known me."[53] So here, too, the dying voice of the sovereign dies, but as the author makes clear, the figure of the totalitarian leader is waiting in the wings.

But there is, I think, yet another "version" of the play haunting the two extant versions, one that hinges more precisely on the nature of dreams, the role of which is greatly diminished in comparison with Calderón's *Life Is a Dream*. Indeed, one of the few references to dreams left in the play is made by the courtier who pronounces Julian's sentence, which could itself be seen as the banishment to a state in which

51. Benjamin's review in Walter Benjamin, *Gesammelte Schriften*, ed. Hella Tiedemann-Bartels (Frankfurt am Main: Suhrkamp, 1972), 3:33.

52. Cited in Bellmann's notes to Hofmannsthal, *Der Turm*, 195.

53. The second version of *The Tower* is reprinted in Alfred Schwarz's translation in J. D. McClatchy, *The Whole Difference: Selected Writings of Hugo von Hofmannsthal* (Princeton, NJ: Princeton University Press, 2008), 491.

waking life and dream life lose their contours. Here, in contrast to *Life Is a Dream*, it is not the king but the king's guardian, Julian, who arranges for the fateful test of the prince's character as a potential successor to the throne. When the courtier pronounces Julian's sentence to dwell with Sigismund in a perpetual state of exception, he thus adds these words: "In your arrogance you recklessly uttered this word in His Majesty's presence: if, you said, your ward did not pass the test, these hours spent here were to be regarded as a brief dream in the midst of a heavy sleep. Now live up to those words, and drag out your life in this duty [to watch over Sigismund], which has been conferred upon you for an indefinite time" (298). At this point in the final moments of the third act, Julian is left alone with his assistant, Anton, and the doctor, a figure characterized by Benjamin as "a Paracelsian appearance who recognizes his own kind . . . in the mute creature."[54] In the ensuing dialogue, it is the doctor who tries to encourage Julian to fight on in the name of the prince, who, precisely as an extreme embodiment of creaturely life, appears to be *chosen* to lead his age toward genuine renewal, to "break chains like straw, blow away towers like dust" (300). When Julian questions him about the source of this faith, the doctor replies by alluding to the crucial part of the passage in Virgil that another physician—and indeed one named *Sigismund*—used as the motto of his *Interpretation of Dreams*: "*Acheronta movebo*. I shall unlock the gates of hell and turn the lowest into my tools—these words have been inscribed from birth on the tablets of your soul" (300). At the conclusion of the scene, the doctor responds to Julian's expression of awe by declaring, somewhat enigmatically, "I doubt that you will see me again. To liberate the powers is our office [*unser Amt*]; as for their end, it is governed by one who is higher than us" (302; translation modified).

I have referred to the fragment of a letter in which Hofmannsthal characterizes the major types of figures in the play. He mentions five: the legitimate king; the king's spiritual adviser, who has, when the play begins, already turned against him; Olivier, the representative of the "eternally ochlocratic element"; Julian, whom Hofmannsthal describes as the most difficult to define, and who embodies both worldly wisdom and the desire for power of the talented individual who, however, never finds his moment in history; and the children's king, whom the author refers to as "a born-again Sigismund."[55] The physician, perhaps because he is the

---

54. Benjamin's review of *The Tower*, in Benjamin, *Gesammelte Schriften*, 3:32.

55. Bellmann, in Hofmannsthal, *Der Turm*, 196–97. A major influence on Hofmannsthal's thinking about cultural, spiritual, and political rebirth was Konrad Burdach's study *Sinn und Ursprung der Worte Renaissance und Reformation*, first published in 1918 and reprinted in *Renaissance, Humanismus: Zwei Abhandlungen über die Grundlage moderner Bildung und Sprachkunst* (LaVergne, TN:

type of figure who, to use Weberian terms, is supposed to remain mindful of the vocation of science rather than of politics, is not even mentioned in this brief cast of character types. What Hofmannsthal seems never to have contemplated was the convergence of the will to govern and the will to know (life) in the paradoxical figure of the *biopolitical master*. Perhaps this was because Hofmannsthal saw in the physician the resources of another way out. For the "meta-political" figure of the physician is the one who appears to stand in closest, most *einfühlsam* proximity to creaturely life as the underside of sovereign power; he recognizes the princely aspect of the creature and the creaturely aspect of the prince. The allusion to Freud's dream book (in the context of an adaptation of *Life Is a Dream*) suggests as well that this physician knows a thing or two about the *royal road* to what in *The Tower* presents itself as the locus of the *royal remains* that have contracted into the flesh of the creature-prince. Although this doctor is neither a political master—traditional, rational, or totalitarian—nor a messianic savior, it would nonetheless seem that his realm of activity, his *office*, overlaps in important ways with both the political and the messianic. As the doctor's own final words at the conclusion of act 3 indicate, his task is to hold open the possibility of new possibilities in the realm of political life by, so to speak, insisting on the insistence of what remains of political theology in the flesh of the destitute creature.[56] This requires that he bring into play, put to use, those dreamlike remains as a kind of *pure means*, without trying to determine in advance the ends that might result. In this way, I think, he shows himself to be a kind of *phi-*

Bibliolife, 2009). There Burdach places special emphasis on the mythic image of the phoenix rising out of the ashes as a crucial source of medieval and early modern conceptions of rebirth and renewal. Kantorowicz also underlines the importance of this figure in the development of the concept of the King's Two Bodies.

56. This reading offers, I hope, a significant challenge to Carl Schorske's claim that Freud's use of the Virgil citation (and the project of psychoanalysis more generally) needs to be grasped as part of a larger effort to leave politics behind, as part of what he calls "a counterpolitical triumph of the first magnitude." Carl Schorske, *Fin-de-Siècle Vienna: Politics and Culture* (New York: Vintage, 1981), 203. More specifically, Schorske suggests that one needs to see Freud's use of the Virgil quote as a recantation of the explicitly political use of it by Ferdinand Lassalle on the title page of his 1859 pamphlet *The Italian War and the Task of Prussia*. As Schorske writes, "Lassalle, too, played with repressed forces, in his case the revolutionary forces of the people. That is why he chose the Virgil motto for his pamphlet. In it, Lassalle tried, *à la Juno*, to persuade the 'higher powers' of Prussia to lead the German people, in alliance with the Italians, in a war of national unification against the Habsburg state. But behind his persuasion lay a threat: Should Prussia fail to act, her rulers would learn to their sorrow 'in what strata of opinion power [actually] resides.' Lassalle thus threatened 'those above' with the latent forces of national revolution, with stirring up a political Acheron. Freud would have found it easy to appropriate Lassalle's legend, transferring the hint of subversion through the return of the repressed from the realm of politics to that of the psyche" (201). I have been arguing, of course, that this reading misses the ways in which Freud's work engages with the dimension in and through which the *people* come to identify themselves as the *People*.

losopher of the flesh. It is, I would suggest, just such a physician who would also have been able to grasp the nature of the destitution that allowed the Lord Philipp Chandos to open, in the wake of his breakdown, to the murmurings of the flesh of creaturely life. It makes good sense, then, that in the darker, second version of the play, Sigismund's final vision before exposing himself—perhaps knowingly—to the bullets of Olivier's henchmen, recalls an earlier memory that brings together, as in a Bacon painting, the less-than-human animal and the more-than-human Christ. Left alone with the physician and Anton, Sigismund recalls the vision once more: "The peasant had slaughtered a pig which was hung next to the door of my room, and the morning sun struck its inside which was dark, for its soul had been called away and had flown elsewhere. They are all joyful signs, but in what way I cannot explain to you."[57]

---

57. Hofmannsthal, *The Tower* (second version), as in McClatchy, *Whole Difference*, 489.

SIX

The Poet's Two Bodies: Rainer Maria Rilke's *The Notebooks of Malte Laurids Brigge*

I

When Rilke moved to Paris in 1902 to begin work on a monograph on Auguste Rodin, he was entering into what scholars typically refer to as the "middle period" of his career as a writer. The new period, extending from his arrival in Paris (a city he returned to again and again) to the beginning of his work on the *Duino Elegies* in 1912, is seen as one in which Rilke's writing became increasingly grounded in the study, contemplation, and exercise of *Einfühlung* with respect to the singularity and "objectivity" of his subject matter. This new *Sachlichkeit* in Rilke's stance toward the singular "object" in its specific mode of being present was in large measure inspired by the poet's growing appreciation for—and envy of—the craftsmanship, the artisanal mode of production, that he associated above all with painting and sculpture. He came to understand that only by clarifying and deepening his relationship with his own materials would it be possible to grasp the relevant materiality of the object world and what it is in that world that calls for poetic elaboration. One might indeed say that Rilke's career as a poet was dedicated to sounding out ever more precisely the specific ways in which, under the conditions of modernity, objects and people manifest this needfulness for poetic elaboration.

By the time he went to Paris, Rilke had already fallen under the spell of the plastic arts, in large part through his relationship to the members of the Worpswede artist colony, most importantly with the painter Paula Becker and the sculptor Clara Westhoff, whom he married in 1901. But it was under the impact of the encounter with Rodin (the poet's relationship with Rodin went through several different and often difficult phases, including a stint as the sculptor's private secretary) that Rilke's awareness of the problem of materiality and craftsmanship became acute. In a series of letters to Lou Andreas-Salomé, whose intellectual, emotional, and erotic tutelage had been the guiding force in the poet's life from 1897 to 1901, Rilke struggled to clarify what he understood to be his central task as a writer, namely to adapt in some fashion what he had observed about Rodin's way of being and working as an artist, one grounded in a profound relationship to *things*. That was, Rilke observed, the one place where the sculptor's apparent solitude was thoroughly transformed: "But to what is important he throws himself open, and he is wholly open when he is among things or where animals and people touch him quietly and like things. There he is a learner and beginner and spectator and imitator of beauties that otherwise have always passed away among the sleeping, among the absent-minded and unsympathetic. There he is the attentive one whom nothing escapes, the lover who continually receives, the patient one who does not count his time and does not think of wanting the next thing."[1] But as Rilke immediately notes, this mode of attention and concentration is itself anchored in the artist's artisanal mode of production:

And this way of looking and of living is so fixed in him because he acquired it as a handworker: at that time he attained the element of his art which is so infinitely simple and unrelated to subject matter, he attained that great justice, that equilibrium in the face of the world which wavers before no name. Since it was granted him to see things in everything [*Dinge zu sehen in allem*], he made his own the opportunity to build things; for that is his great art. Now no movement can confuse him anymore, since he knows that even in the rise and fall of a quiet surface there is movement, and since he sees only surfaces and systems of surfaces which define forms accurately and clearly. For there

1. Rilke to Lou Andreas-Salomé, August 8, 1903, in *Letters of Rainer Maria Rilke, 1892–1910*, trans. Jane Bannard Greene and M. D. Herter Norton (New York: Norton, 1972), 118. Subsequent references are made in the text.

is nothing uncertain for him in an object that serves him as a model: there a thousand little surface elements are fitted into the space, and it is his task, when he creates a work of art after it, to fit the thing still more intimately, more firmly, a thousand times better into the breadth of space, so that, as it were, it will not move if it is jolted. The object is definite, the art object [*das Kunst-Ding*] must be even more definite; withdrawn from all chance, removed from all obscurity, lifted out of time and given to space, it has become lasting, capable of eternity. The model *seems*, the art object *is*. (118–19)

Later in the same letter he laments his own deficiencies and shortcomings as an attentive and disciplined craftsman in the manner of Rodin. In a letter written just two days later (August 10, 1903), he attempts to convert his lament into an opportunity and path of development as a writer:

Somehow I too must manage to make things; written, not plastic things,—realities that proceed from handwork. Somehow I too must discover the smallest basic element, the cell of *my* art, the tangible medium of presentation for everything, irrespective of subject matter: then the clear strong consciousness of the tremendous work that lay before me would coerce and bend me to it: then I would have so infinitely much to do that one workday would resemble another, and I would have work that would always be successful because it would begin with the attainable and small and yet from the beginning would be in the great [*im Großen*]. (124–25)

In his next set of reflections concerning the nature of this element or "cell" of aesthetic labor and material, Rilke considers a series of possibilities, including one he explicitly associates with Hofmannsthal: "Does the handwork lie perhaps in the language itself, in a better recognition of its inner life and will, its development and past? (The big Grimm dictionary, which I once saw in Paris, put me on to this possibility.) Does it lie in some specific study, in the more exact knowledge of a matter [*einer Sache*]? . . . Or does it lie in a certain well-inherited culture? (Hofmannsthal would speak for that. . . .)" (125). The letter then returns to a tone of self-recrimination:

But with me it is different; toward everything inherited I have to be hostile, and what I have acquired is so slight; I am almost without culture. My continually renewed attempts to begin a definite course of study broke down pitifully; for exterior reasons, and because of the strange feeling that always surprised me during it: as if I were having to come back from an inborn knowledge by a wearisome road that again led to it by many windings. Perhaps the sciences at which I tried my hand were too abstract, and perhaps new things will come out of others? . . . But I lack books for all that and guides for the books.—But my *knowing* so little often distresses me. (125)

At this point Rilke leaves open the possibility that he could still discipline his attention to the life of things, above all to those things that even he has so often overlooked, passed by with indifference; he hopes, in a word, that he might still be able *to learn how to see.* This is, of course, what the aspiring poet Malte Laurids Brigge declares to be his primary project when he arrives in Paris as an impoverished twenty-eight-year-old Danish aristocrat with no literary accomplishments of any substance to his name.

II

In an earlier letter from that same summer (July 18, 1903), Rilke addressed the question of the fundamental element of his art in a rather different way, one that brings us fully, even violently, into the world of the *Notebooks.* The letter includes some of the most powerful and disturbing impressions that Rilke recorded during his first year in Paris, many of which he integrated, at times verbatim, into his novel. The letter focuses above all on what he refers to as "a new kind of animal" he had come across on the streets of the French capital. These animals had, he writes, "developed special organs, organs of hunger and death" and "were wearing the comfortless, discolored mimicry of the too great cities [*das trostlose, mißfarbene Mimicry der übergroßen Städte*]." They were, he continues,

holding out under the foot of each day that trod on them, like tough beetles, were enduring as if they still had to wait for something, twitching [*zuckten*] like bits of a big chopped-up fish that is already rotting but still alive. They were living, living on nothing, on dust, on soot, and on the filth on their surfaces, on what falls from the teeth of dogs, on any senselessly broken thing that anyone might still buy for some inexplicable purpose. . . . Pieces, pieces of people, parts of animals, leftovers of things that have been, and everything still agitated, as though driven about helter-skelter in an eerie wind, carried and carrying, falling and overtaking each other as they fall [*fallend und sich überholend im Fall*]. (109)

In this first extended description of the figures he later referred to, in *Malte,* as *die Fortgeworfenen,* or "outcasts," Rilke initially writes, "At most one took them in as an impression and looked at them with calm, detached [*sachlicher*] curiosity" (109). But soon after he admits his own profound susceptibility to them, indicating not so much empathy as one normally understands it but rather endangerment, a collapse of boundaries: "For I understood all those people, and although I went around them in a wide arc, they had no secret from me. I was torn out of myself into their lives, right through all their lives, through all their burdened lives" (111).

In the letter as in the novel that, over the next seven years, emerged in large measure out of the Paris experiences, Rilke's susceptibility to the outcasts focuses on their paradoxical corporeality and mode of animation.[2] They are described as broken marionettes—something wooden and lifeless—that nonetheless bear open wounds; as fragments of caryatids that carry "the entire structure of a pain" (109); as dead or rotting animals—or animal parts—still twitching with life. The limbs of these displaced and distorted creatures strike Rilke more as uncanny prosthetic extensions than as organic members of integrated, self-identical bodies: "There were old women who set down a heavy basket on the ledge of some wall (very little women whose eyes were drying up like puddles), and when they wanted to grasp it again, out of their sleeves shoved forth slowly and ceremoniously a long, rusty hook instead of a hand" (109–10). Lack of organic unity with respect to limbs and members is, for Rilke, redoubled at the level of the inner life of the body. "Nothing," he writes, "was so little laughter as the laughter of those estranged creatures: when they laughed, it sounded as though something were falling in them, falling and being dashed to pieces and filling them up with broken bits" (112).

This surreal physiology in which, by way of a series of chiasmic reversals, body parts become "partial objects" manifesting an uncanny,

2. The novel, which was published in 1910, was composed in multiple stages and in various cities of the European continent. It is made up of seventy-one discrete sections of prose linked to one another more by a pattern of theme and variation than by any sort of narrative logic. Indeed, one of the novel's central themes is what is presented as a distinctly modern inability to tell stories, a view that links the novel very closely to Walter Benjamin's conception of modernity. Rilke's publisher divided the novel into two parts, and that convention has remained in force. The first half of the novel is dominated by Malte's attempt to put on paper and organize, in basic ways, his overwhelming impressions of Paris. Most overwhelming is no doubt the impact—one might even say, *Einbruch*—of the "outcasts," against which he defends himself, at least in part, by way of identification with for the most part great, yet also deeply vulnerable, artists. The Paris experiences call forth, in turn, detailed memories from his childhood, which focus largely on figures and events in the manor houses of his paternal and maternal grandparents (these include multiple encounters with ghosts). The second half of the novel comes to be dominated more and more by Malte's reflections on literary and historical figures recalled from his life as a passionate yet ambivalent reader. Of particular importance among these recollections are two clusters of figures: women in love and various kinds of sovereigns in distress, mostly taken from fourteenth- and fifteenth-century French history. The novel concludes with a retelling of the parable of the prodigal son in which the story's central theme is transformed into the problem of "intransitive love," a kind of love that remains in excess of any object and that refuses, in turn, to contract into the recognizable form of a "love object."

semiautonomous vitality of their own, or in which bodily expressions of human aliveness—say, laughter—mutate into semimechanical objects that break into so many lifeless parts, is elaborated in detail in a passage of the letter that formed one of the longer Parisian "set pieces" of the novel. Rilke writes of a particular morning when, on his way to the Bibliothèque Nationale, the very place Malte describes as his one safe refuge from contact with the outcasts, he notices that various people on the street have focused their gaze in a particular direction. Only by following this collective gaze—the initial "object" of the encounter—does Rilke see what all the fuss is about: a slender male pedestrian in a black overcoat, whose inner agitation, beginning with a series of minor tics and twitches, expands into a kind of grand epileptic dance. It is almost as if this "object-gaze" is itself the disturbing entity that then passes into and takes possession of the unfortunate fellow in the overcoat and indeed first seems to take possession *of* the overcoat. In the letter, Rilke begins the scene like this: "Then I was suddenly struck by the peculiar behavior of the people coming toward me; most of them walked for a while with heads turned to look back, so that I had to be careful not to collide with them; there were also some who had stopped, and by following their gaze I arrived, among the people walking ahead of me, at a slender man in black, who, as he went along, was using both hands to turn down his overcoat collar which apparently kept standing up in an annoying way" (113). The entire scene then oscillates between pathos and comedy as the narrator's own gaze—in the letter as well as in the novel—becomes linked in an almost physical way to the agitation passing through the pedestrian's clothes and body. An occasion of considerable concern and anxiety features at its center the restless choreography—or better, the choreography of restlessness—of a kind of Chaplinesque slapstick. Although the narrator-witness would at first like to deny that there is anything laughable about the man in question, the initial description in both the letter and the novel clearly emphasizes the comedic dimension of a body seemingly possessed by a quantum of some sort of surplus energy that has nowhere to go. Here is the passage in the novel:

I was sure there was nothing laughable about this man's clothing or behavior, and was already trying to look past him down the boulevard, when he tripped over something. Since I was walking close behind him I was on my guard, but when I came to the place, there was nothing there, absolutely nothing. We both kept walking, he and I, with the same distance between us. Now there was an intersection; the man in front of me hopped down from the sidewalk on one leg, the way children, when they are happy, will now and then hop or skip as they walk. On the other side of the street, he simply took one long step onto the sidewalk. But almost immediately he raised one leg slightly and hopped on the other, once, quite high, and then again and again. This time too you might easily have thought the man had tripped over some small object on the corner, a peach pit, a banana peel, anything; and the strange thing was that he himself seemed to believe in the presence of an obstacle: he turned around every time and looked at the offending spot with that half-annoyed, half-reproachful expression people have at such moments.[3]

At this point the tic that has possessed the man's lower extremities seems to migrate into his clothing (as I have noted, in the 1903 letter the movement *begins* in the coat collar): "I noticed that something else had begun to annoy the man. His coat collar had somehow popped up; and as hard as he tried to fold it back in place, first with one hand, then with both at once, it refused to budge" (67). But then it becomes unclear where exactly to locate the source of recalcitrance: "Then I saw, with boundless astonishment, that in his busy hands there were two distinct movements: one a quick, secret movement that flipped up the collar, while the other one, elaborate, prolonged, exaggeratedly spelled out, was meant to fold it back down" (67–68). At this point, Malte's own terms of description collapse the distinction between physiology and signification, suggesting that the tic in question is a kind of "signifying stress" moving through the body, an observation that attaches Malte, a struggling writer, all the more passionately to the man (indeed, it is as if he had come upon a clear manifestation of what would become the "cell" of his art): "I recognized in the man's neck, behind his hunched-up coat and his nervously scrambling hands . . . the same horrible, *bi-syllabic hopping* that had just left his legs. From this moment I was bound to him. I saw that the hopping was wandering through his body, trying to break out here or there" (68). Recalling that Rilke had characterized the movement of the outcasts as a kind of "mimicry of the too great cities," Malte engages his own mimetic capacities to form a sort of comedy team with the epileptic, a joint choreography under the patronage of Saint Vitus: "A cold twinge shot down my spine when his legs suddenly made a small, convulsive leap; but no one had seen it, and I decided that I would also trip slightly if anyone began to look" (68).

3. Rainer Maria Rilke, *The Notebooks of Malte Laurids Brigge*, trans. Stephen Mitchell (New York: Vintage, 1990), 66–67. Subsequent references are made in the text. Citations from the German are taken from Rainer Maria Rilke, *Die Aufzeichnungen des Malte Laurids Brigge*, ed. Manfred Engel (Stuttgart: Reclam, 1997).

The description goes on for quite some time, even introducing new props, notably a cane the man uses to gain control over the agitation running down his back. But this strange urban *pas de deux* quickly passes from the register of the comic into that of a kind of horror in which panic and anxiety take over: "But I couldn't keep my anxiety from growing. I knew that as he walked and with infinite effort tried to appear calm and detached, the terrible spasms [*das furchtbare Zucken*] were accumulating inside his body; I could feel the anxiety *he* felt as the spasms grew and grew, and I saw how he clutched the cane when the shaking began inside him" (69). In the end, it is as if the thing that had entered into the man by way of the gaze of the crowd explodes out of him and, so to speak, returns to its place of origin:

As we stepped onto the bridge, it was all right. It was still all right. But now his walk became noticeably uncertain; first he ran two steps, then he stopped. Stopped. His left hand gently let go of the cane, and rose so slowly that I could see it tremble in the air. He pushed his hat back slightly and drew his hand across his brow. He turned his head slightly, and his gaze wobbled over sky, houses, and water, without grasping a thing. And he gave in. The cane was gone, he stretched out his arms as if he were trying to fly, and some kind of elemental force exploded from him and bent him forward and dragged him back and made him keep nodding and bowing and flung a horrible dance out of him into the midst of the crowd. For he was already surrounded by people, and I could no longer see him. (70–71)[4]

It is, of course, significant that Malte frames the entire sequence, which fills some six or seven pages of his notebooks, with sentences that compare

4. This urban scene, in which a crowd forms around an individual undergoing some sort of distress, is repeated many times in the novel. The very first sentences of the novel present such a scene: "So this is where people come to live; I would have thought it is a city to die in. I have been out. I saw: hospitals. I saw a man who staggered and fell. A crowd formed around him and I was spared the rest" (3). In a later passage, in which Malte wonders about the everyday life of the outcasts—"where they creep off to . . . and what they do with the rest of the long day and whether they sleep at night" (78)—as if contemplating the life-form of a strange species, he focuses on the figure of a man holding out crumbs of bread for birds: "And the more people gather around him—at a suitable distance, of course—the less he has in common with them. He stands there like a candle that is almost consumed and burns with the smallest remnant of its wick" (79). Such scenes are given an exemplary value in the long, lyrical passage early in the novel in which Malte wonders whether all that is essential in human life has in some way been squandered by a kind of fundamental inattentiveness. Among the series of "Is it possible?" questions, we find the familiar scene: "Is it possible that the whole history of the world has been misunderstood? Is it possible that the past is false, because we have always spoken about its masses, just as if we were talking about a gathering of many people, instead of talking about the one person they were standing around because he was a stranger and was dying?" (23).

his inner state in the wake of this strangely intimate nonencounter—one sustained more by a kind of corporeal attunement, a kind of *Nachzucken*, to use Hofmannsthal's formulation—with a crumpled and blank sheet of paper. This suggests that everything we have just read is meant to convey the basic contours of a trauma, an event that in some sense short-circuits the capacities of the subject to metabolize what was nonetheless—again, not so much passively as mimetically—experienced.[5] Against this background it makes sense that the letter of July 18 offers a rather different perspective on the nature of the "element" or "cell" of his "handwork" from the one Rilke offered in the context of his reflections on Rodin:

And many mornings were like that one—and evenings were like that. Had I been able to *make* the anxieties I experienced thus, had I been able to shape things out of them, real, still things that it is serenity and freedom to create and from which, when they exist, reassurance emanates, then nothing would have happened to me. But these anxieties that fell to my lot out of every day stirred a hundred other anxieties, and they stood up in me against me and agreed among themselves, and I couldn't get beyond them. In striving to form them, I came to work creatively on *them*; instead of making them into things of my will, I only gave them a life of their own which they turned against me and with which they pursued me far into the night. Had things been better with me, more quiet and friendly, had my room stood by me, and had I remained well, perhaps I would have been able to do it even so: to make things out of anxiety [*Dinge machen aus Angst*]. (115; translation modified)

III

I will be trying to show that in his *Notebooks of Malte Laurids Brigge*, Rilke succeeded in working the peculiar "stuff" or "object" of anxiety into an art object, a *Kunst-Ding*. Indeed, we have already seen this work in action in the description, in both the letter and the novel, of the twitch that seizes the body of the man on the streets of Paris. What is crucial to keep in mind, I think, is that this work demanded of Rilke that he take on the fundamental tension at the heart of his reflections on the nature

---

5. The two passages that frame the sequence read as follows: "And yet something happened that again took me up and crumpled me like a piece of paper and threw me away" (65); "I was empty. Like a blank piece of paper, I drifted along past the houses, up the boulevard again" (71). This image is prefigured in Rilke's poem "Autumn Day" ("Herbsttag"), which he composed in Paris in 1902: "Who has no house now, will never build one./Who is alone now, will long remain so,/will stay awake, read, write long letters/and will wander restlessly up and down/the tree-lined streets, when the leaves are drifting [*wenn die Blätter treiben*]." Rainer Maria Rilke, *The Book of Images*, trans. Edgar Snow (New York: North Point Press, 1994), 79.

of the "labor and materials" of his art. The anxiety Rilke set out to shape by way of an artisanal mode of production like the one he observed during his "apprenticeship" with Rodin was itself, as we shall see, in large measure the by-product of the radical transformation that this mode of production (and the form of life in which it had a place, in which it still made sense) was undergoing. To return to Jonathan Lear's crucial insight about anxiety, not only individuals but also collectivities, and not only collectivities but also forms of life, can be the locus of a diffuse anxiety, one that can, in turn, assume "plastic" shape through the dream work of this or that "designated dreamer." As we saw in the case of the apparent epileptic, the twitch that seizes this Parisian pedestrian—and that also so clearly seized Rilke's attention as something needful of poetic elaboration (one that begins with the registration of its "meter," its bisyllabic beat)—seems to move, like a kind of hot potato, from the crowd to the man and back out into the crowd.

The very first pages of the *Notebooks* quite explicitly underline the impersonal nature of the free-floating anxiety that Malte's own "freely hovering attention," to use Freud's term for the nature of analytic listening, was in the midst of tracking.[6] Wandering, map in hand, in the neighborhood of the military hospital Val-de-grâce, Malte momentarily shifts his focus from the visual to the olfactory field: "The street began to give off smells from all sides. It smelled, as far as I could distinguish, of iodoform, the grease of pommes frites, anxiety" (4; translation modified). Clearly trying to test and discipline this capacity to sense—*with* and *in* all senses—what is there, he takes a kind of protocol or inventory: "And what else? A child in a baby-carriage standing on the sidewalk: it was fat, greenish, and had a clearly visible rash on its forehead. This was apparently healing and didn't hurt. The child was sleeping with its mouth open, breathing iodoform, pommes frites, anxiety" (4; translation modified). At the end of this little chronicle, which concludes the first section of the novel, Malte seems to endow these minimal expressions of bare life amid a diffuse field of anxiety with an equally minimal dignity, that of pure facticity: "That is simply what happened [*Das war nun mal so*]. The main thing was, being alive [*daß man lebte*]. That was the main thing" (4).[7]

---

6. Freud first uses the term *gleichschwebende Aufmerksamkeit* in his 1912 paper "Ratschläge für den Arzt bei der psychoanalytischen Behandlung."

7. This emphasis on facticity, on the naked fact *that* something is there, *whatever* it might be, is clearly related to Heidegger's conception of thrownness or *Geworfenheit* as a crucial dimension of the being of human beings, a dimension registered, according to Heidegger, above all in the mood of anxiety. It thus makes a certain sense that Rilke's name for human beings whose life seems to have

The "atmospheric" nature of the anxiety that floats through the world of the novel is made even further explicit in a later passage in which it seems to absorb into its composition not only the distress of contemporary Paris (Malte later uses the word *Notzeit*, a term that could signify time of necessity, need, even emergency) but also that of past centuries:

The existence of the horrible [*des Entsetzlichen*] in every atom of air. You breathe it in as something transparent; but inside you it condenses, hardens, takes on pointed, geometric shapes between your organs; for all the torments and agonies suffered on scaffolds, in torture-chambers, madhouses, operating rooms, under bridges in late autumn: all this has a stubborn permanence, all this endures in itself and, jealous of everything that is, clings to its own dreadful reality. People would like to forget much of it; sleep gently files down these grooves in the brain, but dreams drive it away and trace the designs again. (73)

Here it is, once more, the "agency" of the dream work that responds to the insistence of *das Entsetzliche* across time, that repeatedly *insists on its insistence*. If there is a wish here, it is, I would suggest, for the possibility to mobilize the anxiety that might finally allow these (prato) memory traces that seem to cut into the very tissue of the brain's flesh to achieve vibrant legibility. That is precisely how Freud understood what it means to work through the effects of a trauma: the recuperation of the readiness to feel anxiety (*Nachholen der Angstbereitschaft*). The thought here is that what makes an event traumatic is that the victim was unable to feel the relevant sort of affect at the moment of its "impact," or *Einbruch*, and that the task of the therapy is to produce the experimental conditions under which that missed opportunity can in some sense be redeemed, thereby in some sense allowing the event *to take (its) place* for the first time.

Freud developed the notion of the recuperation of anxiety as a belated response to a trauma—an event that itself only begins to "arrive" after a period of latency—in the book we have already cited several times, *Beyond the Pleasure Principle*. As is well known, Freud's speculative discussion of trauma, written some ten years after the publication of *Malte*, provided some of the crucial concepts for Walter Benjamin's influential readings

---

contracted around this pure facticity of being there is *die Fortgeworfenen*, the outcasts. Heidegger cites a long passage from *Malte* in a lecture course in the summer of 1927, the year of the publication of *Being and Time*. See Martin Heidegger, *The Basic Problems of Phenomenology*, trans. Albert Hofstadter (Bloomington: Indiana University Press, 1988), 171–73.

of Baudelaire, a poet who plays a not-insignificant role in Rilke's novel. Benjamin's analysis of Baudelaire argues for the centrality of shock and trauma for understanding the conditions under which the French poet became the exemplary "hero of modern life," a status Malte clearly acknowledges but cannot and perhaps does not even hope to achieve. Benjamin refers to Freud's view that the ego functions, in part, as a kind of *Reizschutz*, or protective shield, filter, or buffer, against shock. When this membrane is breached by an invasive excess of stimulation, the ground is laid for the development of a traumatic neurosis, for a psychosomatic fixation that is not so much a memory trace as a placeholder of the breach in the protective shield, a blank memorial to a failure to prepare for the danger posed by, as Freud puts it, *"the excessive energies at work in the external world."*[8] As Benjamin glosses Freud's text, "the threat posed by these energies is the threat of shocks. The more readily consciousness registers these shocks, the less likely they are to have a traumatic effect. Psychoanalytic theory strives to understand the nature of these traumatic shocks 'in terms of how they break through the shield that protects against stimuli.' According to this theory, fright gains 'significance' in proportion to the 'absence of any preparedness for anxiety.' "[9]

Benjamin's language here has been seen to argue for a sort of psychophysical understanding of shock and trauma, that is, as names for the sort of overstimulation and sensory overload that characterizes the city, that emblematic space of modernity. In Rilke's novel, too, there are, in the sections dealing with Paris, passages that would seem to support such a view, to show how it functions in practice. Malte is presented as someone who seems always to be just on the verge of being overwhelmed by the sheer sensory excess of the urban environment, as someone who can survive its impact only by a kind of vigilance that is not so much a mode of attention as one of defensive neutralization. Indeed, this exercise of vigilance—always precarious in Malte's case—is precisely what Freud meant by *Reizschutz*. In the second section of the *Notebooks*, for example, Malte describes how he is unable, even in Paris, to give up his old habit of sleeping with the windows open, even though what comes through this frame is of an entirely different order from anything he experienced in the Danish countryside of his childhood. Here the extreme

---

8. Cited in Walter Benjamin, "On Some Motifs in Baudelaire," trans. Harry Zohn, in Walter Benjamin, *Selected Writings*, vol. 4, *1938–1940*, ed. Howard Eiland and Michael W. Jennings (Cambridge, MA: Harvard University Press, 2003), 317; my emphasis.

9. Ibid.

vulnerability of Malte's *Reizschutz* is registered in and through its very exercise:

Electric trolleys speed clattering through my room. Cars drive over me. A door slams. Somewhere a windowpane shatters on the pavement; I can hear its large fragments laugh and its small ones giggle. Then suddenly a dull, muffled noise from the other direction, inside the house. Someone is walking up the stairs: is approaching, cease-lessly approaching: is there, is there for a long time, then passes on. And again the street. A girl screams, Ah tais-toi, je ne veux plus. The trolley races up excitedly, passes on over it, over everything. Someone calls out. People are running, catch up with each other. (4–5)

Malte is finally able to sleep only when the sounds of a dog barking and a rooster crowing seem to restore for him, if only very provisionally, the aural landscape of his childhood.[10]

Here we might return, for a moment, to Benjamin's reflections on Baudelaire. Those reflections form part of a larger project that seeks to define modernity as the space and time in which one form of experience comes to be displaced by another. As Benjamin sees it, experience qua *Erfahrung* (this is surely the source of J. Bernstein's notions of *emphatic experience* and an *expressive empirical order*), in which the events of a hu-man life register only insofar as they are taken up into a dense weave of individual and collective memories and memory traces by way of various cultural practices—most importantly that of *storytelling*—is displaced by *Erlebnis*, a somehow more punctually intense yet "thinner" mode of ex-perience, in which individual sensory events are not so much taken up by the mind as neutralized by it: "The greater the shock factor in particu-lar impressions, the more vigilant consciousness has to be in screening stimuli; the more efficiently it does so, the less these impressions enter emphatic experience [*Erfahrung*] and the more they correspond to the concept of isolated experience [*Erlebnis*]. Perhaps the special achievement of shock defense is the way it assigns an incident a precise point in time in consciousness, at the cost of the integrity of the incident's contents. This would be a peak achievement of the intellect [*eine Spitzenleistung der Reflexion*]; it would turn the incident into an isolated experience."[11]

On this view, a traumatic neurosis falls outside of experience alto-gether. It neither enters into the *fabric* of an emphatic experience (*Erfah-*

---

10. As every reader of *Malte* knows, that aural landscape was itself already quite full of all sorts of disturbing and disorienting clatter. We will consider the nature of such "noise" in the following.

11. Benjamin, "Baudelaire," 319; translation modified.

rung) nor gets neutralized by way of insertion into a *series* of isolated bits of experience (*Erlebnis*). Trauma could thus at some level be understood as what escapes both *narrative elaboration* and *reflexive serialization*. If *Erfahrung* can be understood as experience that has been taken up, elaborated, and stored (*aufgehoben*) by way of narrative and *Erlebnis* understood more along the lines of pure images registered or "taken" (*aufgenommen*) in rough homology with a photographic apparatus, then what produces a trauma might be thought of as what leaves a purely indexical trace, something like a photograph lacking in the iconic dimension that would allow it to enter into a network, a "family" of resemblances, similarities, and associations; in a trauma one's sense of *what* has happened is always overwhelmed, even wiped out, by the pure "facticity" *that* it happened.[12] One might, against this background, view Malte's efforts at what he repeatedly refers to as *learning to see* as a kind of training or self-discipline in the art of parrying shocks, of converting potential traumas at the very least into a series of *Erlebnisse* (the division of the book into seventy-one notebook entries points in this direction), and perhaps ultimately, by way of long detours of associations with childhood, works of art, and various historical figures, into new sorts of *Erfahrungen*. (These would, as Rilke suggests, include among their "materials" the anxiety generated by the crisis of experience in the first place.) The choice to sleep with open windows might thus be viewed less as an old habit he is unwilling to abandon than as a technique of hardening, of *mortifying* that membrane that Freud called the *Reizschutz*. But as we have seen, his success is precarious at best. I want to argue, however, that what I am calling the psychophysical view of shock and trauma, a view that focuses above all on the overstimulation and sensory overload that mark the urban environment, fails to capture what is really at issue in what Freud refers to as the "excessive energies at work in the external world." There is indeed a "too-muchness" in the external world, but it is one that cannot be accounted for in strictly perceptual or psychophysical terms.[13] *The Notebooks of Malte Laurids Brigge* is surely one of the richest

12. To put it in terms proposed by Roland Barthes in his now-canonical meditation on photography, we might say that what Barthes refers to as the *punctum* of a photograph (in contrast with its *studium*, the legibility of all aspects of *what* has happened or is portrayed) points to the way in which a detail of a photograph can come to stand for this excess of the "that it happened" over the "what has happened." See Barthes, *Camera Lucida: Reflections on Photography*, trans. Richard Howard (New York: Hill and Wang, 1981).

13. As should be clear even from the few passages I have cited, Benjamin's own analysis of the "excessive energies," the too-muchness intruding into the lives of modern urban dwellers, did not limit itself to the level of perceptual or psychophysical mechanisms. This is equally true of Georg Simmel's writings on the city, even though the discourse of *nervous excitation* at times dominates the

and most "feverish" archives we possess with respect to the complexity of this excess, and it will ultimately return us to the political theological dimension of the flesh.

IV

One of the ways Malte tries to thicken his description of the *Notzeit* intruding into the world around him is through his attempts to register its impact on what we might call *the life of things*. In a long passage on the death of his paternal grandfather early in the novel, Malte writes,

Yes, it was a terrible time for these drowsy, absent-minded Things. Down out of books which some careless hand had clumsily opened, rose leaves fluttered to the floor and were trampled underfoot; small, fragile objects were seized and, instantly broken, were quickly put back in place; others, dented or bent out of shape, were thrust beneath curtains or even thrown behind the golden net of the fire-screen. And from time to time something fell, fell with a muffled sound onto the rug, fell with a clear sound onto the hard parquet floor, but breaking here and there, with a sharp crack or almost soundlessly; for these Things, pampered as they were, could not endure a fall. (12)

In another series that extends across the two parts of the novel, Malte addresses the famous tapestries in the Cluny Museum, "The Lady and the Unicorn." As compelling as Malte's description of the tapestries is (he imagines himself describing them to his mother's younger sister, Abelone), what is perhaps more significant is his reflections on their passage from objects that had a place in the fabric of an aristocratic life to objects displayed in a museum. These reflections directly address what Benjamin so famously characterized as the *loss of aura*: "Now even the tapestries of the Dame à Licorne are no longer in the old château of Boussac. The time has come when everything is leaving the houses; they can no longer keep anything. . . . No one from the family of the Delle Viste walks beside us with these Things in his blood. No one speaks your name, Pierre D'Aubusson, grandest Grand-master from an ancient house, by whose

---

analysis. His deservedly famous essay "The Metropolis and Mental Life," from 1903, for example, where Simmel develops a notion very similar to Freud's conception of *Reizschutz*, establishes right away the connection between "the intensification of mental life" [*die Steigerung des Nervenlebens*]—literally, the life of the nerves—that emerges out of "the rapid and continuous exchange between external and internal stimuli," on the one hand, and a series of other, more structural transformations that go hand in hand with urbanization, on the other. See "The Metropolis and Mental Life," trans. Edward A. Shils, in *Georg Simmel: On Individuality and Social Forms*, ed. Donald N. Levine (Chicago: University of Chicago Press, 1971), 325.

command perhaps these pictures were woven. . . . Now we come in front of them by chance among chance spectators" (131). Malte, of course, has himself directly experienced this tear in the fabric of experience that comes when houses "can no longer keep anything."

Yet another telling passage concerning the life of things focuses on the fate of a small tin can, or more precisely, on the *disturbance in the fit* between the can and its lid, an "event" first registered by the sound of the lid falling in the apartment of a next-door neighbor. Its resonances recall the way Malte speaks about neighbors more generally, the way sounds emanating from the invisible proximity of an adjoining room or apartment can, so to speak, get under the skin. Malte introduces a long series of recollections about neighbors with these words: "There exists a creature that is perfectly harmless; when it passes before your eyes, you hardly notice it and immediately forget it again. But as soon as it somehow, invisibly, gets into your ears, it begins to develop, it hatches, and cases have been known where it has penetrated into the brain and flourished there devastatingly, like the pneumococci in dogs which gain entrance through the nose" (168). In the case of the tin can, what ulti-mately enters Malte's ears is an intimation concerning the larger fate of objects, one that seems to transform the things that populate every-day life into so many "relatives" of Kafka's most famous object, *Odradek*. The clattering of the lid of the can on the floor is a sign for Malte that things have lost "their taste for their natural, silent functions. . . . They make attempts to evade their duties; they grow listless and negligent" (183). It is as if a more radical kind of desire or even drive has thrown off its rails the "normal" satisfactions associated with function and use value, with the goodness of being good at being just this thing and not another:

Let us agree on one point: the lid of a can . . . should have no other wish than to find itself on top of its can; this would be the utmost that it could imagine for itself; an unsurpassable satisfaction, the fulfillment of all its desires. Indeed, there is something almost ideal about being patiently and gently turned and coming to rest evenly on the small projecting rim, and feeling its interlocking edge inside you, elastic and just as sharp as your own edge is when you are lying alone. Ah, but there are hardly any lids now that can still appreciate this. (182–83)

In the following section, Malte compares the contemporary corrup-tion of things with images that recall the work of both Bosch and Bruegel. Indeed, it would seem to be only on the basis of his contemporary ex-periences in Paris—what Benjamin characterized as the *Jetztzeit*, or "now-time," of a critical situation—that various figures and events of the late medieval and early modern period become legible for Malte: "How well I now understand those strange pictures in which Things meant for limited and ordinary uses stretch out and stroke one another, lewd and curious, quivering [*zuckend*] in the random lechery of distraction. Those kettles that walk around steaming, those pistons that start to think, and the indolent funnel that squeezes into a hole for its pleasure. And already, tossed up by the jealous void, and among them, there are arms and legs, and faces that warmly vomit onto them, and windy buttocks that offer them satisfaction" (184). The episode of the tin can is given a certain Chandos-like quality by introducing the passage on the corruption of Things caused "by their association with humans" (183) with a reference to the *concept* in question, as if lid and can fit together only as long as the relevant concept remains intelligible: "And now both of them together form the concept 'can,' or more accurately, 'round can,' a simple, very familiar concept" (182).[14]

V

Against this background, it might be helpful to recall J. Bernstein's account of modernism as precisely the name for the set of historical forces that ultimately destroy any sense of "fitness" in the life of people and things, that "abstract" both from their shared life-world and, therewith, from themselves. For Bernstein, the great witness to the beauty and, so, goodness of such a belonging together of the life of people and the life of things is provided by sixteenth-century Dutch realist painting and,

14. There are other interesting parallels—and telling contrasts—between Chandos, the twenty-six-year-old aristocrat who withdraws to the country and stops writing, and Malte, the twenty-eight-year-old aristocrat who leaves the country for the city in order to become a better writer. In one section of the long "Is it possible?" sequence early in the novel, Malte raises a very Chandos-like question regarding the capacity of general concepts to "hold" together the sets they name: "Is it possible that we know nothing about young girls, who are nevertheless living? Is it possible that we say 'women,' 'children,' 'boys,' not suspecting (despite all our culture, not suspecting) that these words have long since had no plural, but only countless singulars?" (24). With respect to titles, Malte notes a further development that clearly resonates with Chandos's *Sprachkrise*. Recalling the various titles used to address his maternal grandfather during his childhood ("Your Excellency"; "General"), Malte writes, "And, to be sure, he had a right to be addressed that way; but it had been so long since he had held any position that such titles were now barely intelligible. It seemed to me, at any rate, as if no definite name could adhere to his personality, which was at certain moments so sharp, and yet, again and again, without any precise outline" (29). And as we shall see, Malte's goal is, in the end, not unlike that of Chandos, namely to master the capacity to respond to the urgent proximity of creaturely life.

above all, the work of Pieter de Hooch. In de Hooch's art, the pleasurable purposefulness of ordinary life in the midst of objects—its order of *Zweckmäßigkeit*—and the "purposefulness without purpose" that for Kant formed the essence of aesthetic beauty stood in a kind of preordained harmony, as if blessed by a sort of secular providence. One might think, here, once more of Worringer's concept of *Einfühlung* and his understanding, more generally, of the kind of art produced in cultures in which embodied subjectivity enjoyed a sense of natural fitness with the world.

Thinking above all of de Hooch's paintings of brickwork, Bernstein writes, "*De Hooch can paint the world because the world depicted is the constant crossing of nature as matter and order, and culture as matter and order. De Hooch's painterly materialism continually works to dissolve any permanent boundary between nature and culture, between subjective lives and the material conditions of those lives, without every denying the difference between them.*"[15] The brickwork that figures so largely in de Hooch's paintings and that gives to each scene "its materiality, its earthiness, its firmness of place" (35), thus figures, for Bernstein, as exemplary instantiations of the *fitness* or *jointure* between embodied subjectivity and world that Kant was after in his understanding of the (in principle shareable) pleasure at the heart of aesthetic judgment.[16] As Bernstein sees it, what distinguishes Dutch realism at its best is that transcendence does not so much *collapse* into immanence as find its way into a kind of ordinary domesticity that signals a fullness of absorption in the tasks of everyday life; here the absorption in the ordinary that is depicted is one that is deepened and enriched (rather than distanced, broken, ironically redoubled) by the reflective activity manifest in the practice of painting. Regarding this "convergence between a certain practice of painting and the form of life painted" that distinguishes the achievement of this realism, Bernstein writes:

15. J. M. Bernstein, *Against Voluptuous Bodies: Late Modernism and the Meaning of Painting* (Stanford, CA: Stanford University Press, 2006), 35–36. Subsequent references are made in the text.

16. Elaine Scarry, in her book-length essay *On Beauty and Being Just* (Princeton, NJ: Princeton University Press, 1999), takes up and amplifies this Kantian view to think through the sorts of address that natural and human-made beauty seem to direct to the beholder: "At the moment one comes into the presence of something beautiful, it greets you. It lifts away the neutral background as though coming forward to welcome you—as though the object were designed to 'fit' your perception. In its etymology, 'welcome' means that one comes with the well-wishes or consent of the person or thing standing on that ground. It is as though the welcoming thing has entered into, and consented to, your being in its midst. Your arrival seems contractual, not just something you want, but something the world you are now joining wants" (26).

And for this convergence to be possible . . . the kind of immanent transcendence that we think belongs to painting, its embrace of its medium as a way of celebrating the world, requires a comprehension of the world as immanently transcendent, as a satisfying, wholly secular place. *Realism, materialist realism, is thus not a question of likeness, achieved or failed, but of a fitness between the powers that are painting's own and the world represented.* In making this argument turn on a question of *fitness* or amenability between the powers of painting and the world painted, the structure of my claim is formally akin to how Kant demonstrates the possibility of aesthetic reflective judgments of taste in general—that is, as a matter of the fitness between our subjective powers of judging and nature. (37)

Bernstein's claim with respect to de Hooch's scenes of ordinary life in Delft, a life evoked, in part, by the textures of lime-leached brickwork, is even more radical—and more elegiac—than Benjamin's famous evocation of storytelling as a cultural practice that served to sustain the vitality of *Erfahrung*, of emphatic experience. These scenes provide us, he writes, "for the first and perhaps only time a wholly sensible world of touch and sight that was sufficient in itself, a world of things that was fit for sensory encounter and that thus affirmed in us our sensuous nature. This discovered self-sufficiency of the world is, at the same time, the sufficiency of the practice of painting to the world. In 'at the same time' is located the possibility of realism, art's secular autonomy" (43).

Bernstein posits the small miracle of this realism (in his story, this epiphany of art's secular autonomy took place around 1658 in the Low Countries) as the essential background for grasping and evaluating the achievements of modernism: "With the brick wall before our eyes, the immediacies of a Pollock or de Kooning can be felt as the wounded abstractions they are, perhaps as encapsulations of the moment when the material object has been 'liquified' by the fire of modernity before disappearing into the vacuum of mathematics or the indifference of exchange value" (45).[17] Against the background of de Hooch's brick walls, "ordi-

17. The *Duino Elegies*, the cycle of poems Rilke began to compose some two years after the publication of *Malte*, strongly resonate with Bernstein's characterization of the status of the ordinary in modernity. The verses in the Ninth Elegy concerning the poet's task with respect to things, to the object world of everyday life—or rather, to an object world that has already been touched by the forces of "liquifaction"—are especially poignant in this context: "Perhaps we are *here* in order to say: house,/Bridge, fountain, gate, pitcher, fruit-tree, window—/at most: column, tower." And in the next verse: "*Here* is the time for the *sayable, here* is its homeland./Speak and bear witness. More than ever/the Things that we might experience are vanishing, for/what crowds them out and replaces them is an imageless act./An act under a shell, which easily cracks open as soon as/the business inside outgrows it and seeks new limits." The Seventh Elegy is in some ways even more specific about the forces of "liquifaction": "And the external/shrinks into less and less. Where once an enduring house was/now a cerebral structure crosses our path, completely/belonging to the realm of

nary life" becomes for moderns something of a utopian ideal, an object of intense longing rather than the given space of everyday-ness. Not surprisingly, then, Bernstein presents his notion of the "secular everyday" in erotic terms, as a kind of coupling or wedding, a place where the "concreteness" of all that brickwork is understood as a growing together ("concrete" comes from *con-crescere*, to grow together) of nature and culture understood as complementary domains. It is, Bernstein writes, "the wedding of meaning and matter, social sign and natural order," one performed by de Hooch "without a sense of the abstractions that are already beginning to make that marriage appear as only ideal, a thing of painting alone," and this, apparently, because de Hooch in 1658 "does not feel the stress of the abstractions that are already occurring" (44).

There is a surprising paradox at work in this view. What becomes, in modernity (or as Bernstein seems to suggest, at just about any time other than around 1658 in northern Europe), the real object of longing and desire is precisely not transcendence but rather a *livable immanence*. But that implies that immanence—let's call it our finite life as embodied subjects in a material world—is fundamentally and internally out-of-joint, that it cannot quite close in on itself, that it is plagued by a peculiar dimension of "too-muchness." Our fundamental problem is, in a word, not that we lack access to a transcendent order of significance but that the order of immanence is in some sense *at odds with itself*. As Alenka Zupančič has put it in her study of comedy from which I have already drawn, the problem apparently resolved (at least according to Bernstein) at one singular, miraculous moment in seventeenth-century Dutch painting is not so much that we cannot accept our finitude and thus always long for the infinite, but rather that there is "a fundamental *contradiction in this finitude itself.*"[18] And as many good comedies know, this is the problem that every marriage, starting perhaps from the one between meaning and matter, social sign and natural order, has to deal with over and over again.

Zupančič's argument returns us to the comedic dimension of the scene from *Malte* in which the narrator pursues and, by way of a kind of corporeal mimicry, attaches himself to a man plagued by a twitch moving through his body, a twitch that Rilke suggests we view, in turn,

---

concepts, as though it still stood in the brain." *The Selected Poems of Rainer Maria Rilke*, trans. Stephen Mitchell (New York: Vintage, 1984), 200–201. What is, of course, distinctive about Rilke's take on these matters is that the poetic saying of these endangered species of objects serves to entrust them to the strange angels of the *Elegies* who appear to belong neither to the space of immanence nor to that of transcendence.

18. Alenka Zupančič, *The Odd One In: On Comedy* (Cambridge, MA: MIT Press, 2007), 52. Subsequent references are made in the text.

as a kind of mimicry—really an *involuntarily tracking*—of an excess "out there," an excess moving, vibrating, twitching through the social space of the "too vast cities." In her study, Zupančič takes aim at the "metaphysics of finitude" often associated with comedy, the view, namely, that the genre offers us a way to embrace with humor our human finitude, to acknowledge through laughter the absence of a transcendent order, to accept with comedic dignity the limitations and imperfections of our human, all-too-human lives in all their vulgar and undignified carnality. Instead, she argues that comedy is above all a genre dedicated to a "physics of the infinite," one that implies a fundamental *lack of fit* not only between man and the world but also internal to man. On this view, the human exists at the point where a lack of fit between nature and culture is redoubled into a lack of fit between culture and culture, between man and himself. In comedy, this *disproportion* quite regularly manifests itself through the presence of a sort of indestructible organ without body, "something that persists, keeps reasserting itself and won't go away, like a tic that goes on even though its 'owner' is already dead" (49). In this respect, she continues, "one could say that the flaws, extravagances, excesses, and so-called human weaknesses of comic characters are precisely what account for their *not* being 'only human.' More precisely, they show us that what is 'human' exists only in this kind of excess over itself. . . . A human being . . . interests comedy at the very point where the human coincides with the inhuman; where the inhuman 'falls' into the human (into man), where the infinite falls into the finite, where the Essence falls into appearance and the Necessary into the contingent" (49–50). Zupančič's view thus differs considerably from the metaphysics of finitude that informs the conceptual horizon and pathos of Bernstein's conception of "the world as immanently transcendent, as a satisfying, wholly secular place":

And if it is true that the comic universe—much more than the tragic universe—builds within the horizon of immanence, that it abandons the reference to the Beyond and always situates the Essence in a concretely existing situation, it does not do so simply by closing off the finite self in relation to the (infinite) Beyond, by excluding it from its field of reference. On the contrary, it does so by *including* it in the immanence, in the given situation. The Beyond is included in the world and in the human as the heterogeneous element on account of which a man is never simply and only a man. "Man is only man" is ultimately an axiom of abstract idealism; basically it states nothing but "man is not God." Whereas the true materialistic axiom, promoted by comedy, is, rather, "a man is not a man." (Zupančič, 50)

In contrast to the metaphysics of finitude, which encourages us to re-
nounce all reference to the infinite Beyond, comedy's "physics of the
infinite" deploys the "infinite Other as the very material Real of human
life as such" (50).[19] But this means, as I have noted, that immanence is
itself an internally disordered space, one "curved" by the presence in it
of an element that belongs neither to nature nor to culture. Comedy,
one could say, is always, at some level, *physical comedy*, but only because
comedic physicality includes this dimension of immanent excess on account of which "a man is never simply only a man."[20]

19. There is a certain Levinasian ring—or whistle—to these remarks. Indeed, they bring to mind
Emmanuel Levinas's reference to a scene from Chaplin's *City Lights* as a key to grasping the dimension at issue in the ethical relation to the other. In a 1935 essay recently published under the title *On
Escape*, Levinas refers to the scene in which Chaplin's tramp swallows a whistle at a party given by
his benefactor; every time he hiccups, a whistling sound emanates from his body, as if the infinite
Other that forms "the very Real of human life" had a voice, constituted a peculiar kind of vocal
object. One might think of this scene as "Chaplin meets Odradek."

20. In this context one might recall the famous characterization of beauty from Friedrich
Hölderlin's epistolary novel *Hyperion*. In the final letter of book 1, Hyperion, a modern Greek inspired by new love and the promise of the political and cultural renewal of his homeland, recalls
in extravagant and elegiac tones the glory of ancient Athens. At the core of the Athenian conception of freedom, religion, and philosophy lies, according to Hyperion, a certain conception and
experience of beauty, one he tries to capture in the formula attributed to Heraclitus, *Hen Diapheron
Heauto*, which Hölderlin translates as *das Eine in sich selber unterschiedne*, the One differentiated in
itself. *Friedrich Hölderlin: Hyperion and Selected Poems*, ed. Eric L. Santner (New York: Continuum,
1990), 67. What Hyperion is generally thought to mean with the formula is the harmonization of
tensions and forces within a unified whole, which can be correlated to the notion of a work of art
qua organic totality that is internally articulated in such a manner that all parts/members, in their
very distinctiveness, uniquely contribute to and fully participate in the whole grasped as a kind of
nature elevated to a higher power. "The moment of beauty was now well known to men," Hyperion
writes; "it was there in life and thought, the infinitely singular existed [*das Unendlicheinige war*]" (67;
translation modified). The connotations of the formula are in part taken from the context in which
Hölderlin encountered it in Plato's *Symposium*. There Eryximachus, the physician at the gathering,
proposes Heraclitus's formula to capture the sort of love and sympathy that must obtain among the
parts of the body if they are to harmonize in optimal fashion, to join together for the sake of the
health of the whole. When this harmony degenerates, it is the physician's task "to reconcile the jarring elements of the body, and force them, as it were, to fall in love with one another." Eryximachus
continues, "And so, gentlemen, I maintain that medicine is under the sole direction of the god of
love. . . . And it must be obvious to the most casual observer that the same holds good of music—
which is, perhaps, what Heraclitus meant us to understand by that rather cryptic pronouncement,
'The one in conflict with itself is held together, like the harmony of the bow and of the lyre.'" *Plato:
The Collected Dialogues*, ed. Edith Hamilton and Huntington Cairns (Princeton, NJ: Princeton University Press, 1973), 540. What I am proposing here is that one ought to understand the Heraclitian
formula—in Plato as well as in Hölderlin—in connection with the figure who was meant to speak
at this point in the dialogue but who yielded his place to Eryximachus because of a bout of that
most banal registration of an inner excess, the *hiccups*: Aristophanes. As we have seen, the comedic
author's own mythic story of the origin of the "curved space" of erotic longing challenges the very
idea that the human body could be grasped as an organic whole at all. This entire sequence in the
Symposium figures, for Zupančič, as a good substitute for the lost part of Aristotle's *Poetics* dealing
with comedy and thus offers the founding text on comedy one has always felt to be missing in the
ancient sources. See Zupančič, 185–89.

Zupančič follows Lacan's lead in locating the "leak" in human finitude, that which causes human finitude to be always a failed finitude, in the incidence of the signifier:

The nature of this incidence is always problematic; the link between the body and the signifier produces and includes a point that is not reducible to either one of them. To put it very simply: in order for this link to be established, something needs to be subtracted (from the body). This produces a third element, a blueprint of a third dimension of human existence, which is not simply the body, and does not have symbolic standing: Lacan calls it the "partial object," the object *a*. Object *a* is the Lacanian name for the materiality of the leak in human finitude. It is the very thing that runs against and belies the doxa that "there are only bodies and languages." (52)[21]

Finally, Zupančič offers a Hegelian contrast between what she characterizes as still-deluded religious approaches to "failed finitude" and the task of a genuine atheism (one that, as her book argues, can perhaps best be grasped and sustained by way of rigorous engagement with comedy): "Human finitude has a hole in it, and it is precisely this 'hole' (and its consequences) that different religious discourses both mobilize as their driving force and respond to by their narratives, which provide specific frames of reference for this failed finitude. In this respect, if atheism means anything, it means that the one thing 'modern' man needs to accept or take upon himself is not (simply) finitude, but precisely this 'hole in finitude,' instead of hopelessly and always unsuccessfully 'filling it in' with more or less pathetic assertions about human finitude" (53).[22]

VI

Rilke's *Notebooks of Malte Laurids Brigge* is, I think, among the more compelling literary efforts we possess that try to show us what this labor might look like, what it means to take on not simply one's finitude but

---

21. Zupančič is referring here to Alain Badiou's characterization of what he considers to be the hegemonic ideology of contemporary global capitalism.

22. In my previous work I have tried to argue that the religions of revelation—and here I follow the lead of Franz Rosenzweig—can be understood precisely as efforts to orient our responsiveness to our neighbor as a being plagued by a hole in his finitude. Indeed, my notion of a "psychotheology of everyday life" is meant to capture this very dimension that cannot be grasped by the sciences and discourses of pure immanence. One of the distinguishing features of the Jewish tradition is, we might say, the bringing together of ethical mindfulness and comedy, of love and absurdity, with respect to God and neighbor.

the "hole in finitude," including, as we have already seen in the poignant comedy of a sort of epileptic *pas de deux*, the paradoxical surplus "object" that would seem to be correlated to it. I would suggest that the numerous passages in the novel announcing the task of new beginnings, of *Anfängerschaft*, need to be read as references to various aspects and dimensions of this labor, the ultimate goal of which would be, as we have seen, to make things out of such uncanny objects. This would include the long passage early in the novel that begins with a confession of a kind of subjective destitution or nullity, one that allows for a *new thinking*: "I sit here in my little room, I, Brigge, who am twenty-eight years old and completely unknown. I sit here and am nothing. And yet this nothing begins to think and thinks, five flights up, on a gray Paris afternoon, these thoughts" (22). What follows is the inventory of questions we have already noted, pointing to all the ways in which this labor has been neglected. The passage begins with a question that sets the pattern for all the others: "Is it possible, it thinks, that we have not yet seen, known, or said anything real and important? Is it possible that we have had thousands of years to look, meditate, and record, and that we have let these thousands of years slip away like a recess at school, where there is just enough time to eat your sandwich and an apple?" (22).

References to the problem of new beginnings occur throughout the novel. Regarding the difficulty of grasping the inner changes he feels under the impact of Paris, Malte writes, "I am a beginner in my own life" (72). Later, reflecting on what he perceives as Ibsen's obstinacy toward the end of his life, Malte pictures the author at his window observing the passersby: "You wanted to see the people passing by; for the thought had occurred to you that someday you might make something out of them, if you decided to begin" (83–84). The recollection of a childhood conversation in which Malte's mother struggles to understand her sister Ingeborg's apparent resignation at the end of her life picks up the rhythm of the earlier "Is it possible?" passage: "But to think that no one is tempted to understand! If I were a man . . . I would meditate on it in the proper order and sequence, and right from the beginning. For there has to be a beginning, and if one could only grasp it, that would already be something" (86). And reflecting on the ways in which men have neglected the complexities and difficulties of love, Malte wonders: "But now that so much is changing, isn't it time for us to change? Couldn't we try to gradually develop and slowly take upon ourselves, little by little, our part in the great task of love? . . . What if we started from the very outset to learn the task of love, which has always been done for us? What if we went ahead and became beginners, now that much is changing?" (135).

One will also recall the remarkable scene where Malte finally accepts that the Brigge clan is at its end. It is the moment when the heart of his father's corpse is perforated so that he may be officially declared to be dead in accordance with his last will and testament: "I wasn't thinking of my own heart. But when it occurred to me later, I knew for the first time with total certainty that it didn't come into consideration for this purpose. It was an individual heart. It was already at its work of beginning from the beginning" (159). And, of course, the retelling of the parable of the prodigal son that forms the novel's conclusion itself concludes with an invocation of a possible new beginning by way of a certain kind of memory work and repetition: "Above all, he thought of his childhood, and the more calmly he recalled it, the more unfinished it seemed; all its memories had the vagueness of premonitions, and the fact that they were past made them almost arise as future. To take all this past upon himself once more, and this time really, was the reason why, from the midst of his estrangement, he returned home" (259). And as is the case with so many modernist novels, one has the feeling that it is only after having finished the book that one is really prepared to begin it (again), to take on the specific sorts of hermeneutic—and ethical—challenges it presents.

There is much more to say about the various topics and dimensions implicated in the labor of taking on our failed finitude, its "hole" or "leak": love, childhood, the enigma of another's subjectivity, the work of memory, the ambiguous role of repetition, the death of a form of life. With respect to love, for example, it becomes clear in the course of the novel that the love at issue for the author is one that does not try to fill in the hole in finitude—in oneself or the beloved—but one that, rather, cultivates it, works to let it come forth as the shared basis of erotic encounter (this suggests that the pathos and metaphysics of finitude may indeed be one way of *avoiding* this encounter). For the moment, however, I would like to think about what is specifically *modern* about this labor as it is presented in the novel. Not surprisingly, Rilke suggests that the place where in modernity our finitude seems to fail most strikingly—where the "hole in finitude" becomes most difficult to assume—is precisely in our dying.

VII

The changing status of death in modernity is, of course, a central motif in Benjamin's work. In his famous essay "The Storyteller," he writes, for example, that over the course of the nineteenth century, bourgeois soci-

ety achieved, "by means of medical and social, private and public institutions," something remarkable "which may have been its subconscious
[*unterbewußt*] main purpose: to enable people to avoid the sight of the
dying." What distinguishes modernity, he suggests, is the displacement
of the dying from the spaces of everyday life: "In the course of modern
times, dying has been pushed further and further out of the perceptual
world of the living. It used to be that there was not a single house, hardly
a single room, in which someone had not once died. . . . Today people live
in rooms that have never been touched by death."[23] Very early in *Malte*,
a book that begins by characterizing Paris as a city to which people come
to die, Rilke announces this mutation as one of the central motifs of the
novel. Reflecting on the Hôtel-Dieu, Malte writes, "Already in the time
of King Clovis people were dying here, in a few beds. Now there are 559
beds to die in. Like a factory of course. With production so enormous,
each individual death is not made very carefully; but that isn't important.
It's the quantity that counts. Who is there today who still cares about a
well-finished death? No one. Even the rich, who could after all afford this
luxury, are beginning to grow lazy and indifferent; the desire to have a
death of one's own is becoming more and more rare" (8–9).

It is against this background that the description of the death of Malte's
paternal grandfather, Chamberlain Brigge, assumes its specific density
and gravity. It is portrayed as the last truly individual death of the Brigge
line, indeed as one that has in some sense already lost its proper setting,
the form of life in which such a death would still have a place. Perhaps
more accurately, what dies with Brigge just *is* the form of life in which dying had its proper place. It makes a certain sense, then, that in his dying
Chamberlain Brigge demands to be carried from room to room of his vast
manor-house, as if he were trying to find the domestic space that could
still shelter his dying, where his dying could *take place* (one will recall its
effects on the life of Things in those rooms): "The long, ancient manor-
house [*Herrenhaus*] was too small for this death; it seemed as if new wings
would have to be added on, for the Chamberlain's body grew larger and
larger, and he kept wanting to be carried from one room to another, bursting into a terrible rage if, before the day had ended, there were no more
rooms that he hadn't already been brought to" (10). Or as Malte puts it,
it is not so much his grandfather that made these and other demands but
his death, which thereby assumes the quality of a demonic vocal object:

23. Walter Benjamin, "The Storyteller," trans. Harry Zohn, in Walter Benjamin, *Selected Writings*,
vol. 3, *1935–1936*, ed. Howard Eiland and Michael Jennings (Cambridge, MA: Harvard University
Press, 2002), 151.

"But there was something more. There was a voice, the voice that, seven weeks before, no one had known: for it wasn't the Chamberlain's voice. This voice didn't belong to Christoph Detlev, but to Christoph Detlev's death" (13). It was this death that, as Malte puts it, "was alive now," that made demands: "Demanded to be carried, demanded the blue room, demanded the small salon, demanded the great banquet-hall. Demanded the dogs, demanded that people laugh, talk, play, stop talking, and all at the same time. Demanded to see friends, women, and people who had died, and demanded to die itself: demanded. Demanded and screamed" (13). Indeed, it is as if what persists with a kind of tyrannical vitality for the ten weeks it takes Brigge to die is a personification—or, at the very least, a vocalization—of what Freud called the *death drive*, one that gathers into itself the obstinate force of Brigge's character and endows it with a sort of awful majesty:

It had come for ten weeks, and for ten weeks it stayed. And during that time it was master, more than Christoph Detlev Brigge had ever been; it was like a king who is called the Terrible, afterward and for all time. . . . This was not the death of just any old man with dropsy; this was the sinister, princely death which the Chamberlain had, all his life, carried inside him and nourished with his own experiences. Every excess of pride, will, and authority that he himself had not been able to use up during his peaceful days, had passed into his death, into the death that now sat squandering these things at Ulsgaard. (15)[24]

· In the "Storyteller" essay, Benjamin links the status of death in the narrative tradition at issue in his discussion with another significant concept that runs through his writings: *natural history*: "Death is the sanction

24. This passage anticipates Franz Rosenzweig's characterization of the "metaethical self," which, as we have seen, is a kind of demonic kernel of self-sameness that persists throughout one's life and in all possible worlds. Noting that the contours of this self become palpable in old age, i.e., at the point at which one is "barely" alive and so has, at some level, already left nature (including one's social "second nature") behind, Rosenzweig writes: "Thus the self is born on a definite day. . . . It is the day on which the personality, the individual, dies the death of entering the genus [i.e., in progeniture]. . . . This speechless, sightless, introverted *daimon* assaults man first in the guise of *Eros*, and thence accompanies him through life until the moment when he removes his disguise and reveals himself as *Thanatos*. This is the second, and, if you will, the more secret birthday of the self, just as it is the second, and, if you will, the first patent day of death for individuality. . . . Whatever of the self becomes visible to us lies between these two births of the *daimon*." Franz Rosenzweig, *The Star of Redemption*, trans. William W. Hallo (Notre Dame, IN: University of Notre Dame Press, 1985), 71–72. It is against the background of Rosenzweig's notion of the birth of the metaethical self in contrast to the birth of the personality that one would have to analyze Malte's numerous recollections of birthday parties in which he feels fundamentally misrecognized, as if everyone had brought presents for the *personality*, where for Malte what was truly at issue was the *self*.

for everything the storyteller can tell. He has borrowed his authority from death. In other words, his stories refer back to natural history."[25] As I see it, "natural history" or the "natural-historical" is Benjamin's general term for what we have characterized as the "third dimension" of human existence, which exceeds both the natural and the cultural-historical while figuring the zone of their jointure—where they cleave together at the point where they cleave apart.[26] The term signifies not so much that nature, too, has a history or that the human agents of history are also part of the natural order, but rather that *forms of life* are also "mortal," also return to dust—the indifference of matter—and thus are themselves, in some sense, *susceptible to death anxiety*. Or perhaps more accurately (and paradoxically): what we think of as our "own" death anxiety, this affect that would seem to isolate and individuate us more radically than anything else, *does not simply belong to us* as discrete individuals but is, rather, "out there." To exist in a form of life means to exceed mere life (*zoē*) precisely by becoming subject to another dimension of death: the death of the form or framework—the *life-world*—of one's "second nature."

There is another aspect of the notion of the "second death," namely the *symbolic* death one "suffers" by way of mortuary ritual, by being registered *as dead* in the "big Other" of the symbolic community/tradition.[27] What I want to emphasize here is that if the form of life or tradition in which one lives becomes attenuated or "dies," there is no longer the possibility of undergoing a symbolic death. We can, in a word, suffer a symbolic death only if we live in a form of life with viable forms of putting the dead to rest, letting the dead be dead. Chamberlain Brigge dies, as I have suggested, at the very point where the possibility of a "proper" second death—one that could be claimed or "owned" by a community—becomes radically attenuated. A key aspect of our "failed finitude" pertains to this redoubling of our dying, to the structural possibility of *failing to die* a second death because the form of life in which such a death could

25. Benjamin, "The Storyteller," 151.
26. How different Benjamin's understanding of the natural historical is from Bernstein's notion of a *fit* between natural order and social sign can be heard in the former's emphasis on the link between natural history and allegory, a symbolic mode that thrives at the inflamed gap between matter and meaning: "The greater the significance, the greater the subjection to death, because death digs most deeply the jagged line of demarcation between physical nature and significance." And for this reason "allegory . . . declares itself to be beyond beauty." Benjamin, *The Origin of German Tragic Drama*, trans. John Osborne (London: NLB, 1977), 166, 178.
27. In this context, one might recall the status of Malte's father before the piercing of his heart, the point at which he came to be "officially" counted as dead in accordance with the stipulations of his own last will and testament, a demand that, in turn, outlasted his physical death.

be accomplished is itself moribund. In Benjamin's parlance it is this "natural-historical" constitution of human life that accounts for the leak or hole in our finitude.

To put it somewhat differently, the "third dimension" called into being by the binding of biological life to a form of life, of nature to culture, of the body to the signifier, is reanimated—we might say it comes alive with a vengeance—at the time of death, and this all the more so, the less we are able to elaborate the passage from life to death by means of the cultural practices of mourning and mortuary ritual (instead of merely "administering" death with the aid of medical or social scientific "experts"). The "metaphysics of finitude" that has become such a dominant strand of modern and postmodern thinking might thus be thought of not so much as a therapy directed at our inability to let go, that is, to suffer and accept the loss of transcendence, to fully embrace the quiet dignity of our finite lives in a realm of pure immanence—to be fully secular, as it were—but rather as a symptom of an intensification of the "third dimension" materializing the leak in our finitude. It would be a symptom, then, not so much of a "transcendental homelessness" as of an ontological vulnerability that marks creatures whose biological being passes through the signifier, a vulnerability that takes on a particular acuteness under conditions of modernity.

VIII

Rilke registers the condition of ontological vulnerability in numerous ways throughout his novel. As we have seen, Malte becomes obsessed with the so-called outcasts, people who appear not to be simply homeless, but, as their designation suggests, to have been violently excluded from the existential shelter of a form of life. They seem to be the ordinary versions of what Arendt described in her discussion of the exceptional political condition of statelessness, a condition that did indeed become chronic in the decades after the publication of Rilke's novel. As Malte puts it, emphasizing the distinctive creatureliness of the *Fortgeworfenen*, "For it is obvious that they are outcasts, not just beggars; no, they are really not beggars, there is a difference. They are human trash, husks of men that fate has spewed out. Wet with the spittle of fate, they stick to a wall, a lamp-post, leaving a dark, filthy trail behind them" (39).[28]

28. Agamben has suggested that Rilke's portrayal of the outcasts in *Malte* anticipates Primo Levi's reflections on the "Muselmann"—Levi refers to them as "husk-men"—a crucial point of refer-

In one of his longer portrayals of an outcast, Malte describes the moment he perceives a man finally succumbing to his fate, to becoming a "husk" of a man. Malte refers to him as a dying man, but what he witnesses in this scene in a Parisian crémerie is a man suffering not so much a biological death as an existential one—a dying to a world that has already abandoned him (in Agamben's parlance, this would be the moment of fully succumbing to the "ban" that already informs this life). As was the case with the epileptic pedestrian, the connection between Malte and this outcast is characterized as a nonencounter of peculiar intimacy and intensity: "But then I felt him, though he didn't move. It was precisely this immobility of his that I felt, and I understood it in an instant. The bond between us was established, and I knew that he was numb with terror" (51). The German conveys the intensity of this nonencounter still more powerfully. Malte grasps what is before him "mit einem Schlage," a phrase that suggests an electrical shock. This is equally true of the formulation that follows, suggesting the sudden establishment of an electrical connection: "Die Verbindung zwischen uns war hergestellt." But as I have also indicated, the word for terror, *Entsetzen*, carries as well the connotation of being *deposed*, of being cast out of one's symbolic identity. Malte serves as a kind of witness—offers a "deposition"—regarding this silent "event" in which nothing and everything happens. Indeed, the entire novel seems to be organized around a series of just such "events": "Yes, he knew that he was now withdrawing from everything in the world, not merely from human beings. One more moment, and everything would lose its meaning, and this table and the cup and the chair he was clinging to would become unintelligible, alien and heavy. So he sat there, waiting for it to happen. And no longer bothered to defend himself" (51).[29]

Here, too, Malte links the collapse of the space of meaning to the domain of corporeality, to something happening in and to the body of the man in the crémerie. The *Entsetzen* seizing his being seems to call forth or at least to be correlated to an excess of bodily substance, as if something within were *crowding out* his own subjectivity: "Perhaps one of his

---

ence for his conception of the biopolitical turn in modernity. See Agamben, *Remnants of Auschwitz: The Witness and the Archive*, trans. Daniel Herrl-Roazen (Cambridge, MA: MIT Press, 1999), 62.

29. Very early in the novel, Malte describes the silence that for him is far worse than the noises of Paris and compares it to the silence he imagines one "hears" in the midst of a great fire just before the burning structure collapses. The silence at issue here is, I would suggest, the silence that accompanies just such "events": "Soundlessly a black cornice pushes forward overhead, and a high wall, with flames shooting up behind it, leans forward, soundlessly. Everyone stands and waits, with raised shoulders and faces contracted above their eyes, for the terrifying crash. The silence here is like that" (5).

blood-vessels had burst; perhaps just at this moment, some poison he had long been afraid of was trickling into a ventricle of his heart; perhaps a large abscess had risen in his brain like a sun, transforming the whole world for him" (51). I will address other examples of this correlation of meaning—of the space where things matter—and bodily matter/materiality, particularly this peculiar state in which the problem of "crowds" seems to become more an internal, corporeal one, one that concerns "masses" in the sense of internal growths and pressures that crowd one out of one's own body. But I would first like to recall that *Malte* includes passages not just about people cast out from their houses but also about houses that have been emptied of their people, houses that have become natural-historical ruins or "husks."[30]

One thinks, for example, of the passages on the fate of the tapestries that have become museum pieces, now appearing by chance among "chance spectators" (131). One thinks as well of Malte's references to the manor-houses, the *Herrenhäuser*, of his childhood, houses now inhabited by strangers and so in some sense emptied of their proper inhabitants—forms no longer "organically" linked to their contents. They become dispersed into memory traces that endure with the persistence that Freud attributed to the contents of the unconscious. Writing of the home of his maternal grandparents, Malte writes: "As I find it in the memories of my childhood, it isn't a complete building; it has broken into pieces inside me. . . . In this way, it is still dispersed inside me . . . all this is still inside me and will never cease to be there. It is as if the image of this house had fallen into me from an infinite height and shattered upon my ground" (25).

Finally, Malte brings together the two sides of this chiasmus—people without houses, houses without people—in the long, stunning description of the missing house he "sees" on the streets of Paris, a description that focuses on the traces of lived life still stubbornly clinging to the

---

30. The theme of "people without houses" does not, of course, simply apply to the outcasts. In the second part of the novel, Malte recalls childhood visits to a neighboring family, the Schulins, whose manor-house had burned down. Neither Malte nor his mother is fully able to accept the disappearance of the house; it persists for them as a kind of revenant, one of many specters that haunt the characters in the novel. The Schulins, by contrast, are obsessed with the possibility of a new fire and periodically find themselves straining their senses to detect any traces of burning. And in this episode too we find a version of that now-familiar disproportion between outside and inside, container and contained content, that seems to infect bodies and structures at such moments of danger: "Behind the people in the room, the enormous objects from the old house were crowding in, much too close. The massive family silver glittered and bulged as if it were being seen through a magnifying glass" (143).

building's remaining wall. I have discussed this remarkable passage in previous work and won't cite it again here.[31] What is crucial is the way this and other sections of the novel serve to figure Malte as a kind of *medium*, and indeed one in a double sense. He registers with the immediacy of a technical apparatus—one thinks above all of photography—the "spectral materiality" of the lives that once filled the house and thereby becomes a medium in a second sense: one who communes with the dead or, rather, with the *undead* (the obstinacy pertaining to the enduring traces he "sees" in the missing house recalls the uncanny vitality of the dying Chamberlain Brigge, of the death drive that seems to colonize his body). It is in this double sense that Malte is able to say, at the end of the description of the missing house, that everything he saw was now "at home inside me" [*es ist zu Hause in mir*] (48). Immediately after this long sequence, we are introduced to the man in the crémerie, who, we might say, is not so much homeless as *an inhabitant of such a missing house.*

IX

In the latter half of the novel, Rilke takes up again the language of existential death, the "event" of falling from the space in which events can truly take place, unfold, extend out meaningfully into a world. The focus here is on the meaningful and expressive coherence of human gestures at the very point where that coherence collapses, where the jointure of bodily movement and meaning that constitutes a gesture comes apart. I am thinking above all of a passage in the midst of a long series of reflections on the precariousness of life in the fourteenth and fifteenth centuries. These are sections of the novel that critics have tended either to ignore or to treat as extraneous material that strains the unity of the work, as intrusions into the novel that disturb its focus on the complex subjectivity of the narrator as he struggles to maintain his footing in Paris by "learning to see" his new urban surroundings in conjunction with the working through of childhood memories. I will have more to say about these sections that deal, for the most part, with various sorts of suffering sovereigns. At this point I would simply like to note the brief description of an anonymous figure caught up in the political violence and chaos of "that heavy, massive, desperate age," one in which "the kiss of reconciliation between two men was just a signal for the murderers who were standing

31. See *On Creaturely Life* (Chicago: University of Chicago Press, 2006), 49–52.

nearby" (226).[32] The passage tries to capture the ways in which an atmosphere of real and potential enmity seeps into and dissolves the link between social sign and natural order seemingly manifest in (a still functioning) human gesture:

The eyes of the dogs, as they looked up at him, were filled with doubt, and they grew less and less sure of his commands. From the motto that had served him all his life, a secondary meaning quietly emerged. Many long-established customs appeared antiquated, but there didn't seem to be any substitutes to take their place. If projects came up, you managed them without really believing in them. . . . And then, before the late supper, this pensiveness over the hands in the silver washbasin. Your own hands. Could any coherence be brought into what they did? any order or continuity in their grasping and releasing? No. All men attempted both the thing and its opposite. All men canceled themselves out; there was no such thing as action [*Handlung war keine*]. (228–29)[33]

The passage is immediately followed by a description of profoundly disordered sovereignty, a portrayal of King Charles VI of France, who seeks in the Passion Plays performed by the mission brothers' church a last locus of coherence, a final bastion against repeated bouts of insanity: "There was no action [*Handlung*] except at the mission brothers' church. The King, when he had seen them move and gesture, devised the charter for them himself" (229). The king seeks to regain through the performances of the mission brothers a capacity to move through the world with conviction, "to learn these things: how to come and go, how to speak out and turn away, in a manner that didn't leave any doubt" (230). But in the midst of the performances there would inevitably come moments when the coherence of the fiction could no longer help to sustain that of "the great, anguished, profane passion play that he himself was acting in": "All these people were moving around meaninglessly. . . . He wanted to take part in the play: but nothing came out of his mouth, *his movements didn't result in true gestures*" (230–31; my emphasis).

These passages concerning gesture recall an observation Rilke made years earlier in his monograph on Rodin, the commission for which origi-

---

32. For a wonderful study of this "heavy, massive, desperate age," see Barbara Tuchman, *A Distant Mirror: The Calamitous 14th Century* (New York: Ballantine Books, 1978).

33. In his November 10 letter to Hulewicz, Rilke explains the pensiveness of this anonymous figure by his having been overwhelmed by "what is peculiarly empty and far and already somehow no longer valid about his continued existence" [*das eigentümlich Leere und Weite und schon irgendwie Ungültige seines Noch-Seins*]. Cited in Engel's notes to Rilke, *Aufzeichnungen*, 302. This "pensiveness" is, of course, a form of that melancholy that Benjamin associated so closely with the allegorical imagination, the form of mindfulness captivated by the natural-historical dimension of human life.

nally brought him to Paris. There Rilke suggests that the sculptor was able to use the force of gestures that enjoyed a kind of plenitude and coherence—those of mythic beings, of animals, of ecstatic dancers, the participants in cultic actions—as a background to investigate the new gestures, those that "had originated in the long period in which art was turned away from such things and was blind to their revelations." These new gestures, Rilke writes, were especially interesting to Rodin:

They were impatient. In the same way that someone who spends a long time looking for a lost object becomes ever more perplexed [*ratloser*], distracted, and hurried, creating disorder and destruction all around him, a pile of things he has pulled from their proper place, as if he wished to force them to search with him—so have the gestures of humanity which can no longer find their meaning grown more impatient, more nervous, more rapid and hurried. And all the questions of existence that one has rummaged through lie strewn about. But their movements have also grown more hesitant. They no longer have the athletic and decisive directness with which people of former times reached for things. They no longer resemble those movements preserved in ancient works of art, gestures in which the point of departure and the point of conclusion were what alone counted. Between these two simple moments countless transitions have inserted themselves and it has become apparent that the life of people today transpires precisely in these in-between-states, their acting and their inability to act.[34]

Finally, in a long passage dedicated to Ibsen, Malte suggests that his distinctive sort of naturalism was precisely one attuned to these countless transitional states, to the (mathematical) sublimity of what we might characterize as a *microphysics of the infinite*:

There you made the enormous decision to so magnify these tiny events, which you yourself first perceived only in test tubes, that they would be seen by thousands of people, immense before them all. Your theater came into being. You couldn't wait until this life almost without spatial reality, this life which had been condensed by the weight of centuries into a few small drops, could be discovered by the other arts. . . . You couldn't wait for that; you were there, and everything that is barely measurable—an emotion that rises by half a degree, the angle of deflection, read off from up close, of a will burdened by an almost infinitesimal weight, the slight cloudiness in a drop of longing, and that barely perceptible color-change in an atom of confidence—all this you had to determine and record. For it is in such reactions that life existed, *our* life, which

34. Rainer Maria Rilke, *Werke*, ed. Manfred Engel et al. (Frankfurt am Main: Insel, 1996), 4: 426–27.

had slipped into us, had drawn back inside us so deeply that it was hardly possible even to make conjectures about it any more. (82–83)

Malte suggests that Ibsen's efforts to "transform this capillary action all at once into the most convincing gestures, into the most available forms," to find "equivalents in the visible world for what you had seen inside" (83), is what ultimately shattered him.

X

Malte's reflections on theater are not limited to the passages on the Passion Plays and Ibsen's theater, both of which, as we have seen, address the relation between action, acting, and gesture. One thinks also of the passages in which Malte condemns his own earlier efforts at playwriting, in which, as he indicates, he was too impatient to allow the difficult, conflictual space between lovers to develop according to its own logic (one thinks here, perhaps, of Lacan's notion of the impossibility of the sexual relationship) and so introduced the figure of the third, the plot-device of triangulation that generates familiar but distracting patterns of tension and drama.[35] One might also recall Malte's reflections on Eleanora Duse, in whose gestures, once again, something like the real of appearance breaks through the trappings of theatricality and presses in on the spectator with something like an ethical challenge, one that recalls the final lines of Rilke's great poem "The Archaic Torso of Apollo": "You felt how your heart ceaselessly rose toward an immense reality and frightened, you once again tried to take their looks off you, as if they were gossamer threads—: But now, in their fear of the worst, they were already breaking into applause: as if to ward off, at the last moment, something that would force them to change their life" (235).[36] One thinks, finally, of Malte's

35. This figure of the third, Malte writes, "is the noise at the entryway to the voiceless silence of a true conflict. It could be said that every playwright up to now has found it too difficult to speak of the two whom the drama is really about. The third person [*der Dritte*], just because he is so unreal, is the easiest part of the problem; they have all been able to manage him; from the very first scene you can feel their impatience to have him enter; they can hardly wait" (21). These reflections on the figure of the third in theater lead to the long, lyrical passages on missed opportunities in history ("Is it possible?").

36. The *becoming-real of theatricality*—rather than the theatricalization of the real, its exposure as fiction or illusion—was manifest in the Passion Plays in a different fashion, namely in the expansion of the frame of the play to the point at which it seemed to coincide with life itself, an expansion that in some sense functioned as an "immanentization" of transcendence: "The fatal thing about these drama-poems was that they continually enlarged and extended themselves, growing to tens of thousands of verses, so that the time in them ultimately became real time; rather as if someone were to

invocation of the ruins of the amphitheater in Orange that lead him to Chandos-like reflections on the current state of theater: "Now plays fall in fragments through the coarse sieve of our stages, and pile up and are swept away when we have had enough" (233).[37]

But there is, I think, another significant reference to theater in the novel, one that is buried in plain sight, so to speak, in the order of the "signifier." I would like to suggest that the name Rilke gives to his young Danish protagonist, "Malte," could be viewed as an anagram of that more famous Danish aristocrat, "Hamlet" (the one missing letter could be explained by the fact that in Paris, where the novel takes place, the "h" is silent).[38] This would be a meaningless discovery, were it not for the fact that the novel is itself deeply preoccupied with the resonances between Malte's experiences in Paris and matters pertaining to the fate of sovereigns, questions of royal succession, the political theology of kingship, and the enigmatic physiology of the royal body. And as I have already suggested in my discussion of the death of Malte's paternal grandfather, the novel is furthermore haunted by the phenomenon we have already noted apropos of Schmitt's reading of *Hamlet*: the *dying of the dying voice of the master*.[39] Finally, once we recognize Malte as a kind of Hamlet figure, all the other discussions of theater, action, gesture, and *Handlung* in the novel begin to "communicate" with the Danish Prince's reflections on these matters.

We might, at this point, recall Schmitt's paradoxical claim about the critical situation at issue in Shakespeare's tragedy, that is, about the *Ernstfall* with respect to which what might otherwise have remained a *Trauerspiel* first becomes a truly modern *tragedy*. Schmitt argued that, to use Freud's phrase, the "excessive energies at work in the external world" during and after the Elizabethan succession need to be viewed in two ways: as an index of a certain *underdevelopment* (with respect to the classical

---

make a globe as big as the earth. The concave stage, with hell underneath it, and above it—attached to a pillar—the unrailed scaffolding of a balcony, representing the level of paradise, only served to weaken the illusion. For this century had in fact brought both heaven and hell to earth: it lived on the powers of both, in order to survive itself" (221–22).

37. Malte's recollections of the ancient amphitheater point, once again, to a kind of theater in which theatricality itself opens onto a higher order of reality, one that now persists in the spectral materiality of ruins: "Here, in this vast, inward-bent circle of seats, there reigned an existence where everything was expectancy, emptiness, absorption [*ein wartendes, leeres, saugendes Dasein*]: everything in the realm of happening [*alles Geschehen*] was there inside it: gods and fate" (232).

38. We should also note that Rilke takes pains to establish specific links between Malte's paternal and maternal ancestors and the Danish Crown.

39. As readers of *Malte* know, the novel is filled with stories of encounters with ghosts, mostly from Malte's childhood. As Schmitt emphasizes in his reading of *Hamlet*, one of the ways in which the religious strife of the period manifested itself was by way of reference to doctrinal conflicts pertaining to the meaning of ghosts.

sovereignty of the centralized state) as well as of a *premature development* (with respect to the revolutionary energies of seafaring venture capital). These two facets of what Schmitt characterizes as a certain Elizabethan *barbarism* "break into" the space of theatrical play and endow it with a dimension of *seriousness* that in some sense makes it more real than reality itself. According to Schmitt, what, during the distress of the Elizabethan succession, was urgently needful of theatrical elaboration was something that could not, in the end, be fully elaborated. It was a historical "experience" that became manifest in Shakespeare's play precisely as a surplus or remainder that spoiled the game—and the realm of play more generally—in *an aesthetically exciting way*. Shakespeare's *Hamlet*, we might say, "twitches" under the pressure of historical forces the play has taken in but cannot metabolize with aesthetic means. Rilke, for his part, creates in the figure of Malte a kind of medium for the "after-twitchings," or *Nachzucken*, of late medieval and early modern barbarism (here the focus is, above all, on the tumultuous fourteenth century and one of its most peculiar figures, Charles VI, called both *le Bien-Aimé* and *Le Fou*) as well as on the excessive energies of the "revolutionary" barbarism of a now fully developed capitalist economy. And, of course, standing between Hamlet and Malte stands the figure of Marat—called, as was his journal, *l'ami du peuple*—and all that he stands for with respect to the French Revolution and the real, imaginary, and symbolic transfer of sovereignty to the People and the Nation.

As I have noted, the key figure in Malte's meditations on the political theology of sovereignty is Charles VI, who at least officially reigned as king of France from 1380 to 1422. But before Malte turns to this psychotic king, he recalls, almost as a kind of preparation for his later reflections, a little green book he read as a boy, containing stories dealing with the fate of various sovereigns. Two of them he can still remember: "the End of Grishka Otrepyov and Charles the Bold's Downfall" (188). Although neither story contains anything like the deposition scene in Shakespeare's *Richard II*, they both concern themselves with the precariousness of sovereignty and the ways in which this precariousness itself comes to be incarnated as the flesh of royal remains.

The story of the so-called "False Dmitri" concerns the final days of Grishka Otrepyov, the man who in 1603 publicly claimed to be the youngest son of Ivan the Terrible (it had been thought that Dimitri Ivanovich had died or been murdered some twelve years earlier). After the death of Boris Godunov in 1605 (Godunov had assumed the throne in 1598, after the death of Czar Feodor I), Otrepyov, who had raised an army with the support of the Polish nobility, marched into Moscow, where he was declared to be the rightful czar. Malte's recollections focus on the uncertainty concerning the czar's true identity, suggesting that the question of imposture, of political masquerade, that in this instance seemed to represent an exceptional case, might have broader implications with respect to those invested with sovereign authority. Indeed, Malte wonders whether the czar's legitimacy might not itself be the product of the nation's desire, a desire that not only invests the sovereign with a symbolic status, a kind of public mask, but also generates the flesh of a surplus body.[40] Once Dmitri was disavowed by the Czarina Mother and overthrown by his enemies, what was *in* Dimitri that was *more* than Dimitri persisted as an object of fascination, as the carnal correlate of the people's desire. Malte frames his final reflections on this figure with the invocation of a storyteller who would be up to the task at hand:

Up to this point the whole incident proceeds on its own momentum; but now we need someone who knows how to tell a story; because from the few lines that still remain to be written, a force has to emerge which will transcend every contradiction. Whether or not it is actually stated, you must be ready to swear that between voice [of the Czarina Mother] and pistol-shot, infinitely compressed, there was once again inside him the will and the power to be everything. Otherwise people won't understand what magnificent sense it made that they pierced his night-shirt and stabbed him all over his body, to see if they would strike the hard core of a personality. And that for three days after he died, he still wore the mask which already he had almost renounced. (191)[41]

The second figure Malte recalls from his little green book is Charles the Bold, the last of the Burgundian dukes to resist with any success the hegemony of the Valois monarchy, which, by the end of the Hundred Years War in 1453 (during which Burgundy had largely allied itself with

40. Emmanuel Levinas refers to Pushkin's treatment of Otrepyov's "investiture" as an indication of a dimension of chosenness that surpasses and, perhaps, ultimately undermines sovereignty. Here the equivocal signs of Otrepyov's legitimacy become manifest in a *dream*: "In Otrepiev's dream, thrice repeated, in Pushkin's *Boris Godunov*, the false Dmitri catches sight of his future sovereignty in the equivocal laughter of the people. . . . Laughter at the bottom of the gesture that points me out, shame and fear of the ego, the 'accusative' where everything designates me and assigns me, awakening in a headlong fall—all this is the unconditionality of the subject behind its sovereignty." Emmanuel Levinas, *Otherwise than Being: Or beyond Essence*, trans. Alphonso Lingis (Pittsburgh: Duquesne University Press, 1999), 195.

41. The novel contains numerous references to the phenomenon addressed by Walter Benjamin in his essay "The Storyteller," namely the radical attenuation of the capacity to tell a story that would be able to live off of and to sustain the fabric of emphatic experience, of *Erfahrung*. As we have seen, Rilke's novel struggles to acknowledge the crisis of experience and storytelling without succumbing to the pressure toward a mere serialization of *Erlebnisse* or other avant-garde aesthetic experimentation. For a rather different—and quite compelling—view on Rilke's stance with regard to such pressures, see Friedrich Kittler, *Aufschreibesysteme, 1800/1900* (Munich: Wilhelm Fink, 1985).

England), had consolidated its hold on much of what came to constitute the territory of modern France. Malte introduces Charles (who is never identified by name) as a figure in whom this hard kernel, this bit of the real of sovereignty, assumes ever-greater density: "When I think about it now, it seems strange to me that in this same book there was a story about the last days of a man who remained, his whole life long, one and the same, hard and unchangeable as granite, and weighing more and more heavily on those who supported him" (191). A few sentences later it is the blood of lineage (Charles was the son of Philip the Good and Isabel of Portugal) that is seen as the locus of power and authority, an element that can endow any limb or organ with an unnerving capacity for a kind of sovereign *Selbst-Behauptung*, an element that both sustains and, in the end, undoes mastery:

The blood could shoot into these hands as it might rush to someone else's head; and when clenched into fists, they did seem like the heads of madmen, raging with fantasies. . . . It required unbelievable caution to live with this blood. The Duke was locked in with it, inside himself, and at times he was afraid of it, when it moved around in him, dark and cringing. Even to him it could seem terrifyingly foreign, this nimble, half-Portuguese blood, which he hardly knew. He was often frightened that it would attack him as he slept, and tear him to pieces. He pretended that it had been mastered, but he always stood in terror of it. . . . During his frenzied last years it would sometimes fall into . . . heavy, bestial sleep. Then it became apparent how completely he was in its power; for when it slept, he was nothing. Then none of his entourage was allowed to enter; he didn't understand what they were saying. Nor could he show himself to the foreign envoys, desolate as he was. Then he sat and waited for it to awaken. And usually it would leap up and burst out of his heart, bellowing. (192–93)

Malte's reflections focus on the Duke's death in Nancy at the hands of the combined forces of the Swiss and the Duchy of Lorraine, or more precisely, on the search for and discovery of his mutilated body after the battle. Here the "hard core" of the personality appears to merge with the "blood" of sovereign succession in the rigid flesh beneath the skin of the Duke's face: "But the face was frozen into the ice, and as they pulled it out, one of the cheeks peeled off, thin and brittle, and you could see that the other cheek had been ripped out by dogs or wolves; and the whole thing had been split by a large wound that began at the ear, so that you could hardly speak of a face at all" (196).[42]

42. Readers familiar with *Malte* will no doubt recognize in these passages elements of a sequence very early in the novel dealing with faces and, more importantly, with the flesh beneath the face.

XI

Working backward chronologically from the false Dmitri, who enters the political stage at the end of the sixteenth and the beginning of the seventeenth century, to Charles the Bold, who ruled Burgundy in the latter part of the fifteenth century, Malte's ruminations on sovereignty finally reach into the fourteenth century, certainly one of the most turbulent and brutal periods of European history. It is as if the "existence of the horrible in every atom of air" that Malte breathes in on the streets of Paris led him back to "that heavy, massive, desperate age" (226). The madness of King Charles VI, who suffered some forty bouts of insanity, is presented as a kind of nodal point, where the various disorders of the era—the mass death of the great plague, the schism in the papacy, the Hundred Years War with England—converge, creating a monarch who himself seems to be composed only of royal remains, of the decomposing flesh of sovereignty.[43]

Malte introduces the figure of the mad king while considering his own descent—his own "deposition" or *Ent-Setzen*—to the place of the outcasts, those whose only distinction is to lack every social distinction or status: "I know that I am destined for the worst [*zum Äußersten bestimmt*], it won't help me at all to disguise myself in my better clothes. Didn't he, even though he was a king, slide down among the lowest of men? He,

---

But now it is as if those "royal remains" persist just beneath the surface of every face, though in *Malte* it would seem to be the outcasts who most manifestly enjoy this peculiar distinction. Malte describes a poor woman sitting on a bench, face in hands, who is suddenly disturbed by some noise: "The woman sat up, frightened, she pulled out of herself, too quickly, too violently, so that her face was left in her two hands. I could see it lying there: its hollow form. It cost me an indescribable effort to stay with those two hands, not to look at what had been torn out of them. I shuddered to see a face from the inside, but I was much more afraid of that bare flayed head waiting there, faceless" (7). One might say that Francis Bacon's paintings constantly struggle to overcome just such fear.

43. As Barbara Tuchman has argued, "The cult of death was to reach its height in the 15th century, but its source was in the 14th. When death was to be met any day around any corner, it might have been expected to become banal; instead it exerted a ghoulish fascination. Emphasis was on worms and putrefaction and gruesome physical details. Where formerly the dominant idea of death was the spiritual journey of the soul, now the rotting of the body seemed more significant." Tuchman, *A Distant Mirror*, 506. See also Michael Camille's study of the work of the fourteenth-century illustrator Pierre Remiet, *Master of Death: The Lifeless Art of Pierre Remiet, Illuminator* (New Haven, CT: Yale University Press, 1996). Among the books Remiet illustrated was Eustache Deschamps's *Lays de la fragilité humaine*—Camille calls it "the little booklet of death"—which was presented to the young Charles VI after the death of Charles V, for whom it had originally been intended. About the latter, Camille writes, "partially paralyzed owing to a sickness contracted in his youth and constantly attended by doctors, he obsessed around one of his royal bodies—the earthly fleshly one. In this respect he would have enjoyed every worm and empty eye-socket in Deschamps's and Remiet's work" (60). I have been arguing that the obsession with flesh can be fully understood only if one takes into account the *second* royal body.

who instead of rising sank to the very bottom" (214).[44] One of the longer descriptions of the king's struggles with madness focuses on its impact on the state of the royal flesh; Rilke's language recalls Kafka's description of the wound on the side of the young patient in "A Country Doctor":

It was in those days when strangers with blackened faces would from time to time attack him in his bed in order to tear from him the shirt which had rotted into his ulcers, and which for a long time now he had considered part of himself. It was dark in the room, and they ripped off the foul rags from under his rigid arms. One of them brought a light, and only then did they discover the purulent sore on his chest where the iron amulet had sunk in, because every night he pressed it to him with all the strength of his ardor; now it lay deep in his flesh, horribly precious, in a pearly border of pus, like some miracle-working bone in the hollow of a reliquary. Hardened men had been chosen for the job, but they weren't immune from nausea when the worms, disturbed, stood up and reached toward them from the Flemish fustian and, falling out of the folds, began to creep up their sleeves. (215)

The king's condition only worsens after the death of the one concubine who could tolerate his proximity and soothe his disordered mind: "Then she died. And since that time, no one had dared to bed another concubine beside this rotting flesh. She hadn't left behind her the words and caresses that had given the King such comfort. No one now could penetrate the wilderness of his mind" (216).

The word Rilke uses that is translated as "this rotting flesh" is *dieses Aas*. It is a word that shares many of the connotations of that key word in Schreber's lexicon that designates, as I have argued, the breakdown products of his own investiture crisis: *Luder*. It is, moreover, the German word used to translate the title of one of Baudelaire's most famous poems, "Une Charogne."[45] Malte's ruminations on the *entsetzlich* decomposition of sovereign flesh in the fourteenth century (along with the psychotic episodes that had already "psychically" deposed the king, making it im-

---

44. One might recall that Charles's English rival was Richard II. The two reached a provisional and precarious truce in 1396 when Charles's six-year-old daughter was given to Richard in marriage, a marriage that was ultimately shattered by the rout of the French army at Agincourt in 1415 under the leadership of Henry V. Henry's father, Henry of Bolingbroke, had himself been aided by the Duke of Orléans, Charles's brother, in his efforts to displace Richard from the throne. Against this background, one might read Malte's descriptions of Charles VI in conjunction with Shakespeare's deposition scene in *Richard II*, about which Kantorowicz wrote so eloquently.

45. As I have noted, in the French translation of Schreber's *Memoirs*, *Luder* is rendered as *Charogne*. Schreber, for his part, also quotes Hamlet's famous "something is rotten in Denmark" to characterize the disordered state of the world he sees all around—and inside—him.

possible for him to recognize himself or anyone else) thus form a con-stellation with his earlier remarks on Baudelaire's poem. The remarks are presented as part of a draft of a letter, and much of the language was in fact rehearsed in a letter Rilke had sent from Paris to his wife, Clara, in 1907 (in the letter, Rilke refers to the poem by its German title, "Das Aas," and reminds Clara of the relevant passage in a draft of *Malte* that he had already shared with her). Once again we are faced with a temporal logic according to which something becomes truly legible only after a certain period of latency. Malte asks, "Do you remember Baudelaire's incredible poem 'Une Charogne'? Perhaps I understand it now. Except for the last stanza, he was in the right. What should he have done after that hap-pened to him? It was his task to see, in this terrifying and apparently repulsive object, the Being that underlies all individual beings" (72). He goes on to reassure his addressee: "But don't think I am suffering from disenchantment [*Enttäuschungen*] here—on the contrary. I am sometimes astonished by how readily I have given up everything I expected, in ex-change for what is real, even when that is awful" (72–73).[46]

The 1907 letter elaborates on the kind of aesthetic stance and practice Rilke admires in the poem, one he characterizes as the same sort of *sachli-ches Sagen*, or "objective expression," he and Clara had come to admire so much in the work of Cézanne: "I could not help thinking that without this poem the whole development toward objective expression, which we now think we recognize in Cézanne, could not have started; it had to be there first in its inexorability. Artistic observation [*das künstlerische Anschauen*] had first to surpass itself to the point where it could see even in the horrible and apparently merely repulsive that which is and which, with everything else that is, *is valid* [*das Seiende zu sehen, das, mit allem anderen Seienden, gilt*]." Rilke adds how important it was for him to have learned that Cézanne had valued Baudelaire's ode to rotting flesh, "that in his last years [he] still knew this very poem . . . entirely by heart and recited it word for word."[47] At the end of the letter, Rilke writes that he has only now come to understand the destiny of his novel's protagonist, namely to have *failed* to rise to the moral, aesthetic, and in some sense erotic challenges posed by the very things that call for *sachliches Sagen*: "And all at once (and for the first time) I understand the destiny of Malte Laurids. Isn't it this, that this test surpassed him, that he did not pass it in the actual [*daß er sie am Wirklichen nicht bestand*], though of the idea of

---

46. In the last stanza of the poem, the poet suggests that art can save beauty from the process of putrefaction described in the poem.

47. Letter of October 19, 1907, in Rilke, *Letters*, 314–15 (translation modified).

its necessity he was convinced, so much so that he sought it out instinctively until it attached itself to him and did not leave him any more?"[48]

XII

These last reflections return us to an even earlier section in the novel, where Malte, at a point of extreme psychic vulnerability, copies into his notebooks, word for word, the text of one of Baudelaire's prose poems, "A une heure du matin," followed immediately by short passages from the book of Job. These two acts of transcription follow closely upon the section on the man in the crémerie, who, as Malte sees it, is in the midst of dying to the world around him and assuming fully his being as an outcast who no longer belongs to the space of meaning: "One more moment, and everything would lose its meaning" (51). If I might bring Rilke's remarks about Baudelaire's capacity to see *validity* in what is *there*, however destitute it might be, together with Gershom Scholem's famous claim about the nature of revelation in Kafka, we could say that the man in the crémerie has come to embody that state in which his existence as a whole is *valid* but without *meaning*, the state I have characterized as creaturely life at its purest. There, as I have argued, the human subject succumbs fully to the injunction to *enjoy (bare) life*, which represents, so to speak, the "positive" aspect of the process of "deposition" that at some level *includes* him by placing him *outside* the set comprising the "People." Malte immediately compares himself with this quasi-*Muselmann* and finds himself wanting, lacking in the courage to assume explicitly what has in some sense already begun to happen to him: "And I am still defending myself. I am defending myself though I know that my heart has been torn out and that even if my torturers left me alone I couldn't live. I tell myself: 'Nothing has happened,' and yet I was able to understand this man just because inside me too something is taking place that is beginning to withdraw and separate me from everything" (52). He then imagines the moment at which a dying man is still there, still in the world, but can no longer recognize anything as familiar; he reproaches himself for failing (in a way not unrelated to Hamlet's indecision) to seize in this approach to what we might call the *neighborhood of zero* the possibility of new possibilities of living and writing. The apocalyptic tone of Malte's reflections reinforces the sense that he is indeed approaching something akin to that *Nichts*

---

48. Ibid., 315 (translation modified).

der Offenbarung, that nothingness of revelation, that Scholem saw as key to Kafka's universe:

> If my fear weren't so great, I would find some consolation in the thought that it's not impossible to see everything differently and still remain alive. But I am frightened, I am unspeakably frightened of this change. I have not yet grown accustomed to this world, which seems good to me. What would I do in another? I would so much like to remain among the meanings that have become dear to me, and if something has to change, I would at least want to live among dogs, who have a world that is related to our own, with the same Things in it.
>
> For the time being, I can still write all this down, can still say it. But the day will come when my hand will be distant, and if I tell it to write, it will write words that are not mine. The time of that other interpretation [*die Zeit der anderen Auslegung*] will dawn, when there shall not be left one word upon another, and every meaning will dissolve like a cloud and fall down like rain. In spite of my fear, I am like someone standing in the presence of something great, and I remember that I often used to feel this happening inside me when I was about to write. But this time, I will be written. I am the impression that will transform itself. It would take so little for me to understand all this and assent to it [*das alles begreifen und gutheißen*]. Just one step, and my misery would turn into bliss. But I can't take that step; I have fallen and I can't pick myself up. (52–53)

It is at this point that he begins to copy into his notebooks "A une heure du matin" and passages from the book of Job, something Malte indicates he has done before in moments of distress. By way of a strange sort of compromise formation, Malte writes words that are not his own in an effort to defend himself against the time when his hand will be writing words that are not his own.

In an original and compelling reading of these passages, Friedrich Kittler, who has emphasized a certain family resemblance between Schreber and Malte, insists that they both need to be grasped in their relation to epoch-making innovations in science, medicine, and, above all, technologies of inscription, which in turn generate radical transformations in such crucial concepts as *subject, author,* and *literature.*[49] At one point, Kittler tries to summarize the force behind these transformations by citing a short fragment of Kafka's: "They were given the choice to become

---

49. Kittler, *Aufschreibesysteme*, 344. Kittler goes so far as to suggest that *The Notebooks of Malte Laurids Brigge* should really be called *Memoirs of My Simulated Nervous Illness*, after the title of Schreber's autobiographical text. I have offered a critique of Kittler's reading of Schreber in *My Own Private Germany: Daniel Paul Schreber's Secret History of Modernity* (Princeton, NJ: Princeton University Press, 1996).

kings or messengers. Just like children they all chose to be messengers. For this reason there are only messengers; they race through the world and, because there are no kings, they call out to one another announcements that have become meaningless. They would happily put an end to their miserable life but because of their oath of office they don't dare."[50] For Kittler, the "death of the king" ultimately signifies one thing and one thing only: the death and displacement of the *author*, a figure understood to be a kind of sovereign of the space of meaning, by the *writer*, a figure seen more as a kind of stenographer who merely transcribes the inexhaustible flow of ultimately meaningless information from one medium to another.[51] For Kittler the epistemic shift in medicine and, above all, psychiatry, which was, at this point, already well on the way to becoming psychophysical *brain science* pure and simple, represents merely a further indication that the space of *meaning*, *soul*, and *spirit* was being displaced by the space of the medial inscription and circulation of the *letter*. As Kittler sees it, what Malte is still resisting has already happened: the rise of "psychophysics against the pretentions of meaning."[52]

Among the passages Kittler cites to make his case is the section in which Malte, overwhelmed by his experiences in Paris, finally seeks out professional help at the Salpêtrière hospital. There he has been scheduled to receive electrotherapeutic treatment. I will pass over some of the marvelous descriptions of the hospital that Malte provides. Suffice it to say that they offer a vision of the institution of medicine and, above all, of psychiatry that is uncannily similar to Kafka's descriptions of the legal system in *The Trial*. This is, indeed, a space in which things are in

50. "Es wurde ihnen die Wahl gestellt Könige oder der Könige Kuriere zu werden. Nach der Art der Kinder wollten alle Kuriere sein. Deshalb gibt es lauter Kuriere, sie jagen durch die Welt und rufen, da es keine Könige gibt, einander selbst die sinnlos gewordenen Meldungen zu. Gerne würden sie ihrem elenden Leben ein Ende machen, aber sie wagen es nicht wegen des Diensteides." Franz Kafka, *Beim Bau der chinesischen Mauer und andere Schriften aus dem Nachlaß* (Frankfurt am Main: Fischer, 1992), 235–36.

51. The canonical statement concerning the birth of the writer out of the remains of the author—think: "The Author is dead! Long live the Writer!"—is Roland Barthes's essay "The Death of the Author." There Barthes writes: "Having buried the Author, the modern scriptor can thus no longer believe, as according to the pathetic view of his predecessors, that this hand is too slow for this thought or passion and that consequently, making a law of necessity, he must emphasize this delay and indefinitely 'polish' his form. For him, on the contrary, the hand, cut off from any voice, borne by a pure gesture of inscription (and not of expression), traces a field without origin—or which, at least, has no other origin than language itself, language which ceaselessly calls into question all origins." Roland Barthes, *Image, Music, Text*, trans. Stephen Heath (New York: Hill and Wang, 1978), 146.

52. Kittler, *Aufschreibesysteme*, 337. To return to Lacan's terms of analysis of the Schreber material, the claim here is that Malte is struggling to disavow a disavowal or foreclosure (of the Name-of-the-Father and the discourse of the master, more generally) that has, at some level, already "objectively" taken place in the field of the Other.

some sense *valid*, normatively binding on the life of the subject, without thereby being meaningful. Toward the end of his afternoon at the Salpêtrière, Malte overhears the treatment of a patient in a room adjoining the waiting area. The scene, which brings into play the body, the machine, and the signifier, is staged before the gaze and on the command of experts whose very job it would seem to be to desemanticize signification, on the one hand, and to spell out the domain of the bodily real, on the other: "But suddenly everything was quiet, and a vain, condescending voice, which I thought I knew, said: 'Riez!' A pause. 'Riez. Mais riez, riez.' I was already laughing. It was incomprehensible why the man in there didn't want to laugh. A machine rattled, and immediately stopped; words were exchanged; then the same energetic voice ordered: 'Dites-nous le mot *avant*.' Spelling it: 'A-v-a-n-t.' . . . Silence. 'On n'entend rien. Encore une fois: . . .'" (60–61). It is at this point that Malte is overwhelmed by a sensation he has known since childhood, a sensation he refers to as "*das Große*." Stephen Mitchell translates "*das Große*" as "the Big Thing," though a better translation might be just "the Thing." It becomes clear that the failure of this group of "city doctors" is prefigured in the help-lessness of a "country doctor" from Malte's childhood:

And then, as I listened to the warm, flaccid babbling on the other side of the door: then, for the first time in many, many years, it was there again. What had filled me with my first, deep horror, when I was a child and lay in bed with fever: the Big Thing. That's what I had always called it, when they all stood around my bed and felt my pulse and asked me what had frightened me: the Big Thing. And when they sent for the doctor and he came and tried to comfort me, I would just beg him to make the Big Thing go away. . . . But he was like all the others. He couldn't take it away, though I was so small then and it would have been so easy to help me. And now it was there again. (61)

Malte goes on to describe in detail the return of this *somatic sublime* dimension of embodiment:

Now it was there. Now it was growing out of me like a tumor, like a second head, and was a part of me, although it certainly couldn't belong to me, because it was so big. It was there like a large dead animal which, while it was alive, used to be my hand or my arm. And my blood flowed through me and through it, as through one and the same body. And my heart had to beat harder to pump blood into the Big Thing: there was barely enough blood. And the blood entered the Big Thing unwillingly and came back sick and tainted. But the Big Thing swelled and grew over my face like a warm bluish boil, and grew over my mouth, and already my last eye was hidden by its shadow. (61–62)

As I have indicated, Kittler interprets such passages as evidence that the "time of the other interpretation" that Malte continues to resist has indeed arrived and that it is, furthermore, a time that opens to a *beyond of interpretation*, a time in which the ultimately enigmatic materiality of the signifier—we might say *the real of the signifier*—overwhelms all effort to make things make sense. Kittler's thesis thereby enters into a certain proximity to Schmitt's claim with respect to *Hamlet*. For Kittler, the time that breaks into the realm of play (an intrusion that dethrones, at the very least, the author-king along with the aesthetic ideology of his realm) is a time governed by a kind of pure writing in excess of meaning (and the pleasure and reality principles that govern it). What is, however, missed in this otherwise compelling analysis is precisely the *dimension of the flesh*, this substance of creaturely life that Malte struggles to invoke with his grotesque description of *the Thing*. Malte's exposure to what we might characterize as the validity (without meaning) of psychiatric power—its attempt to spell out, without interpretation, the real of the body—has clearly generated a kind of *flare-up of the flesh*. But as I have argued throughout this study—and as Malte's preoccupations with the "sad stories of kings" suggests—such flare-ups are ultimately symptoms that point to crucial shifts in the political theology of sovereignty, shifts that simply cannot be accounted for by the discourse of even the most materialist media theory.

In this context I would like to recall Clark's analysis of David's painting *The Death of Marat*. Clark's description of the "empty" upper half of the painting no doubt sounds at times very close to Kittler's media-theoretical language. To quote the key passage once more:

And yet the single most extraordinary feature of the picture . . . is its whole upper half being empty. Or rather (here is what is unprecedented), not being empty, exactly, not being a satisfactory representation of nothing or nothing much—of an absence in which whatever the subject is has become present—but something more like a representation of painting, of painting as pure activity. Painting as material, therefore. Aimless. In the end detached from any one representational task. Bodily. Generating (monotonous) orders out of itself, or maybe out of ingrained habit. A kind of automatic writing.[53]

But as I have argued, Clark's entire analysis serves to bring into view the spectral dimension of the flesh as it rises from Marat's chronically

---

53. T. J. Clark, *Farewell to an Idea: Episodes from a History of Modernism* (New Haven, CT: Yale University Press, 1999), 45.

diseased skin (Marat appears here as a distant relative of Charles VI) to fill the upper half of the canvas, where it circulates *as* the very stuff of this "pure activity," an activity generated precisely by the impossible task of representing the People's Body. What becomes visible in David's canvas is the stuff of a surplus, of a second body, that will, over the course of the next centuries, push up against the skin of all who come to be invested with, who come to be entitled to enjoy, political and national sovereignty. Against this background the entire scene in the Salpêtrière becomes legible as a kind of *biopolitical procedure* aimed at administering the royal remains that now persist as a fleshy excess of immanence perturbing the bodies that inhabit the spaces of modern states. It is this background that also allows us to make sense of the numerous examples in *Malte* of bodies that can no longer contain their own insides.

XIII

Before turning to Malte's various experiences with such bodies, I would like to say a few words about the narrator's final—and historically earliest—representative of that "heavy, massive, and desperate age" in which he so clearly recognizes himself. I am thinking of the remarks on Pope John XXII, the second of the popes to reside in Avignon not long before that city became the proper name of the schism within the Christian world and of the antagonisms between political and ecclesiastical power. As I have noted, Rilke later wrote to his Polish translator Witold Hulewicz that figures such as Pope John and Charles VI "vibrated" or "twitched" at the same frequency of vital intensity, with the same *Schwingungszahl der Lebensintensität*, as Malte's own being.[54] In his attempt to give Hulewicz some orientation in the dense web of personal, literary, and historical references and allusions that run through the novel, Rilke compares Malte's own singular distress, or *Notzeit*—his own private *Ernstfall*, or critical situation—with the *Notzeit* of the Avignon papacy. What Rilke suggests in the letter is that in Malte's case the disorder that in an earlier historical period was played out in broadly social and political terms now registers as personal and interior, as a series of psychological symptoms amplifying, in fateful ways, one's *Lebensintensität*: "His period of distress [*seine Notzeit*] and the great period of distress of the Avignon popes, where

---

54. Letter of November 10, 1925, in *Letters of Rainer Maria Rilke: 1910–1926*, trans. Jane Bannard Greene and M. D. Herter Norton (New York: Norton, 1972), 371.

everything broke out externally that now turns fatally inward [*heillos nach innen schlägt*], are equated."[55]

Pope John XXII assumed his office in 1316, some sixty-two years before the great schism. The entire section focuses on matters of embodiment, ensoulment, and the disorders that threaten both. At the very beginning of this section, Malte characterizes the papal palace John completed as "a last, emergency body [*Notleib*] for the homeless soul of all" (222).[56] He goes on to emphasize the pope's intense preoccupation with real and imagined enemies—an obsession bordering on paranoia—and a doctrinal decree that made him all the more embattled. Regarding the former, Malte records a not-surprising preoccupation with the Jews: "His shrunken body became even more dry with horror and more enduring. And now they were even daring to attack the body of his empire; from Granada the Jews had been incited to exterminate all Christians, and this time they had hired more terrible accomplices. No one, from the very first rumor, doubted the conspiracy of the lepers; already several people had seen them throwing bundles of their horrible decomposition into the wells" (223). In the paranoid fantasy of the lepers, it is as if a fundamental spiritual disorder had become manifest in a vision of the body's own decomposition: "It wasn't out of any light credulity that people thought this possible; faith, on the contrary, had become so heavy that it had dropped from those trembling creatures and fallen to the bottom of the wells" (223).

But the depth of the disorder at issue in this "desperate age" is expressed more clearly in the doctrine pronounced and then quickly and repeatedly recanted by John, namely, "that *before* the Last Judgment there could be no perfect blessedness, not anywhere, not even among the blessed," for, as the passage continues, "how much stubborn tenacity was needed to imagine that, while such dense confusion reigned here [*während hier so dichte Wirrsal geschah*], somewhere there were faces already basking in the light of God" (225).[57] The doctrine thus tried to establish as an article of

---

55. Ibid. Malte's evocation of this fourteenth-century pope brings to mind Francis Bacon's numerous paintings of screaming popes that all, at some level, take as their point of imagistic reference Velázquez's *Portrait of Pope Innocent X*.

56. Rilke elsewhere explains the formulation *Notleib* as a body quickly constructed out of necessity to give the soul a place or location and compares the phrase with the more familiar concept "emergency exit," or *Not-Ausgang*. The annotation comes from Rilke's correspondence with his Danish translator Inge Junghanns, cited in Engel's notes to Rilke, *Aufzeichnungen*, 275.

57. To his letter of November 10 to Hulewicz, Rilke appended short responses to specific questions raised by his translator. Regarding Pope John's doctrine, Rilke writes, "Consider *what* it meant for the Christendom of that time to learn that *no one* in the beyond had entered the state of blessedness, that that passage would take place only with the Last Judgment, that there just as here all stood in anxious wait! What an image for the distress of a time [*die Not einer Zeit*] that the leader of

faith what had already in some fashion been registered at the level of the *real*: that the traffic between immanence and transcendence had come to a standstill, that what belonged in the realm of the beyond was now experienced as an excessive and invasive presence in "ordinary" life.[58]

XIV

As I have indicated, *Malte* is full of examples of the workings of such an excess in the bodies of the people who populate the streets of Paris, an excess with which, as the memory of "the Big Thing" indicates, Malte was already quite familiar from his own childhood.[59] We have already seen, in the case of the twitch moving through the body of the Parisian pedestrian, how a certain "mimicry of the too big cities" works to transmit a quantum of energy from the crowd into the pedestrian, then into Malte, then back into the crowd. A similar event occurs immediately after Malte takes in the spectral impressions—or, to use Hamlet's phrase, the "form and pressure"—of the missing house and just before he describes the

---

Christianity used the power of his office to cast this period's uncertainty into the heavens themselves." Cited in Engel's notes to Rilke, *Aufzeichnungen*, 300. Here one might recall that Schreber, in his *Memoirs*, addresses a condition very similar to the one declared by the Avignon pope. Schreber reports that the exceptional connection God's nerves had, over a period of six years, established with his own body "led to the total loss of all the states of Blessedness which had accumulated until then and made it impossible for the time being to renew them; the state of *Blessedness* is so to speak suspended and all human beings who have since died or will die *can for the time being not attain to it.*" See Daniel Paul Schreber, *Memoirs of My Nervous Illness*, trans. Ida Macalpine and Richard A. Hunter (Cambridge, MA: Harvard University Press, 1988), 60–61.

58. Schreber understood his own messianic task to be to reestablish the orderly traffic between the planes of immanence and of transcendence, a task that demanded that he first fully identify with the surplus of immanence manifest in his *Ludertum*, an identification that transformed him into a kind of feminized Wandering Jew. For a detailed discussion of this transformation see, once more, my study of the case, *My Own Private Germany*.

59. The best essay I know on this array of symptoms—organs without bodies, bodies that fail to contain their own interiors—is Andreas Huyssen's "Paris/Childhood: The Fragmented Body in Rilke's *Notebooks of Malte Laurids Brigge*," in *Modernity and the Text: Revisions of German Modernism*, ed. Andreas Huyssen and David Bathrick (New York: Columbia University Press, 1989), 113–41. Huyssen's argument is that the surreal physiology of the Parisian bodies described in the novel points to Malte's failure to consolidate the boundaries of a viable ego over the course of his childhood. Huyssen suggests that Malte in some sense never fully surmounted the so-called mirror-stage of ego development that would allow for an image of the unified ego to "contain" uncoordinated bits of bodily and psychic impulses. In order to make his argument, Huyssen is compelled to refer to the biographical details of Rilke's difficult relationship with his own mother, a relationship he contrasts with what he characterizes—strangely, in my view—as the "successfully 'symbiotic' . . . thoroughly nurturing" relationship between Malte and his *Maman*, in which "the typical roots of later disturbances do not seem to pertain" (124). I am arguing that Malte's childhood experiences of unstable bodily boundaries are already registrations of a larger structural disorder in the matrix of entitlements to enjoyment and enjoyment of entitlements that constitute what Lacan called the field of the Other.

devastating impact of seeing the man in the crémerie.[60] One will recall from that description the somatic dimension of an "event" otherwise characterized as a process of dying to the space of meaning: "Perhaps one of his blood-vessels had burst; perhaps, just at this moment, some poison he had long been afraid of was trickling into a ventricle of his heart; perhaps a large abscess had risen in his brain like a sun, transforming the whole world for him" (51). Panicked by what he saw, he flees into the street, where he encounters a crowd of carnival revelers he experiences as "a viscous flood of humanity" and from whose mouths "laughter oozed . . . like pus from an open wound" (48). This "mass" that seems to emanate or metastasize from the masses of revelers does not leave Malte unaffected or, perhaps better, uninfected: "Perhaps everything was stationary, and it was just a dizziness [Schwindel] in me and in them that seemed to make everything whirl. I didn't have time to think about that; I was heavy with sweat, and a stupefying pain was circulating inside me, as if something too large were rushing through my blood, distending the veins wherever it passed" (49).[61]

Not surprisingly, the waiting room in the Salpêtrière hospital is a space in which the surreal physiology generated by such "masses" is especially concentrated. The room is filled with bodies that in some sense no longer fit themselves, in which the parts no longer belong together. Malte notices, for example, a young child sobbing in the corner: "It had pulled its long skinny legs in, onto the bench, and was now holding them tightly to its body in an embrace, as if it would soon have to take leave of them forever" (56). This is a world of bodies held together by bandages: "Bandages wrapped around a whole head, layer by layer, until just a single eye remained that no longer belonged to anyone. . . . Bandages that had been opened and in which, as if in a filthy bed, a hand lay now, that was no longer a hand; and a bandaged leg that stuck out of the line on the bench, as large as a whole man" (56–57). When he is directed to take his place on the bench, he seems to discern in the man next him something like the bodily residue of the man in the crémerie who has now fully died to the

60. About the spectral materiality of the missing house, Malte writes, "it passes right into me: it is at home inside me" (48). Malte also indicates that it was the exhaustion generated by the impact of the missing house that first led him to seek out the crémerie.

61. These passages should, I think, serve to call into question any attempt to view the various phantasms of fragmented bodies and partial objects as instances of what Mikhail Bakhtin theorized under the heading of the carnivalesque. See, for example, Manfred Engel's efforts in this direction in his afterword to Malte in Rilke, Aufzeichnungen, 335. Rather, Rilke's novel as a whole lays out the terms for an understanding of Massenpsychologie—the psychology of groups, crowds, masses—as one that tracks the vicissitudes of the substance that now circulates through the People.

world: "What was on my right I couldn't recognize for a few moments. It was a huge, immovable mass [*eine ungeheuere, unbewegliche Masse*], which had a face and a large, heavy, inert hand. The side of the face that I saw was empty, without features and without memories; and it was eerie to notice that the clothes were like the clothes a corpse laid out in a coffin might be wearing" (59).

But it is, finally, Malte himself who serves as the prime example of a body that no longer fully coincides with itself, a body in which some somatic "surplus value"—some *Thing*—pushes against the boundaries of the skin and threatens the integrity of personhood. After running from the hospital waiting room in an attempt to escape from the quasi-somatic memory of *das Große*, Malte finds himself flooded by other memories of childhood anxieties, among them an anxiety that brings together the mathematical and what I have referred to as the *somatic sublime*: "that some number may begin to grow in my brain until there is no more room inside for me" (64). Later, realizing his own inability *not* to breath in "the existence of the horrible in every atom of air" (73), his lack of *Reizschutz* with respect to the atmospheric anxiety permeating the streets of Paris, Malte writes,

Now you have pulled yourself together; you see yourself end in your own hands; from time to time, with an imprecise movement, you re-draw the outline of your face. And inside you there is hardly any room; and it almost calms you to think that nothing very large can enter this narrowness; that even the tremendous [*das Unerhörte*] must become an inner thing and shrink to fit its surroundings. But outside—outside there is no limit to it [*draußen ist es ohne Absehen*]; and when it rises out there, it fills up inside you as well, not in the vessels that are partly in your control or in the phlegm of your most impassive organs: it rises in your capillaries, sucked up into the outermost branches of your infinitely ramified being. There it mounts, there it overflows you, rising higher than your breath, where you have fled as if to your last refuge. And where will you go from there? Your heart drives you out of yourself, your heart pursues you, and you are already almost outside yourself and can't get back in. Like a beetle that someone has stepped on, you gush out of yourself, and your little bit of surface hardness and adaptability have lost all meaning. (74)[62]

---

62. The very fragile reassurance that Malte gains from monitoring his own bodily boundaries—on seeing himself end with his own hands—is shattered in yet another childhood memory in which, while crawling under a table to search for a crayon that had fallen while he was drawing, the young Malte encounters *a phantom hand*—a limb without body—reaching toward his own hand from the wall: "I felt that one of the hands belonged to me and that it was about to enter into something it could never return from" (94).

But it is, I would suggest, the very first description of a body no longer made to the measure of its own interiority that provides a crucial clue as to how to read all these other examples. It comes at the very beginning of the long description of the death of Chamberlain Detlev Brigge, to which I have already referred. The excess that in this case grows within Malte's paternal grandfather, causing him to swell "enormously . . . out of his dark blue uniform" (12), is, Malte tells us, the chamberlain's own death, a death that, however, is not simply his own but rather represents the death of a form of life and the kinds of social bonds sustained by it. One might say that in this late aristocratic society it is only now that the flesh fully exits from the house and figure of the master.[63]

XV

As we have seen, childhood figures as one of the central themes or clusters of experiences in Rilke's novel. We have also had a chance to see the ways in which Malte, in his childhood, absorbed anxieties that were already signaling the disintegration of the coherence and forms of sociality of the world of his aristocratic family. Even as a child, that is, Malte was deeply aware—without quite knowing it—that something was profoundly rotten in the state of Denmark. Indeed, the novel makes quite explicit the child's experience of absorbing and struggling to make sense of enigmatic messages emanating from the world around him. In the aftermath of one of his childhood encounters with the spirit world in the home of his maternal grandfather, Malte hears his father address the master of the house: "Then I heard him say something, syllable by syllable, though I couldn't understand the meaning of his words. Nevertheless, they must have fallen deeply into my hearing, for about two years ago I discovered them one day at the bottom of my memory, and I have known them ever since" (34). And regarding his father's "body language," Malte recalls,

63. The German word for "manor-house" is *Herrenhaus*, or house of the master/lord. What dies with Chamberlain Brigge is, thus, not simply the master of the house but also, more generally, the house of the master. That Malte's father had stipulated in his own will that his heart be pierced after his death suggests a need for complete certainty regarding the death of the master. After Malte witnesses the procedure, his notebook entry underlines this finality; his language interestingly recalls the peculiar rhythm of the epileptic twitch that so viscerally caught his attention on the streets of Paris: "and in that spot something like a mouth appeared, from which, twice in succession, blood spurted out, as if the mouth were uttering a two-syllable word. . . . But now the Master of the Hunt was dead, and not only he. Now the heart had been perforated, our heart, the heart of our family. Now it was all over. This, then, was the shattering of the helmet: 'Today Brigge and nevermore,' said something inside me" (158–59).

"I saw without comprehending, I experienced without understanding, how he struggled with himself, and how, in the end he triumphed" (36; translation modified). Yet another passage brings the theme of childhood enigmas together with that of bodily excess:

And then came one of those illnesses which aimed at proving to me that this wasn't my first private adventure [*das erste eigene Erlebnis*]. The fever dug into me and out of the depths it pulled experiences, images, facts, which I had known nothing about; I lay there, overloaded with myself, and waited for the moment when I would be told to pile all this back into myself, neatly and in the right order. I began, but it grew in my hands, it resisted, it was much too much. Then rage took hold of me, and I threw everything into myself pell-mell and squeezed it together; but I couldn't close myself back over it. (96)[64]

Against this background, I would suggest that the numerous references to the task of working through childhood once more, of "achieving" it as if for the first time, must be seen as efforts on Malte's part to muster the preparedness to feel the anxiety (an anxiety that did not simply belong to him but rather to his world and form of life) that in childhood could be registered only below the level of consciousness. After witnessing the perforation of his father's heart, Malte writes, "So my childhood too would still, so to speak, have to be achieved, if I didn't want to give it up as forever lost. And while I understood how I had lost it, at the same time I felt that I would never have anything else I could appeal to" (160).[65]

This motif is picked up at the very end of the novel, where Malte retells the story of the prodigal son as one dealing with the complexities, even impasses, of human and divine love, a section that begins with a kind of provocation: "It would be difficult to persuade me that the story of the Prodigal Son is not the legend of a man who didn't want to be loved" (251). In Malte's adaptation, the prodigal son returns home after years of hardship because he grasps that the only way he might begin to open to a new kind of *eros*, one in which love would no longer represent the threat of being trapped or captivated within a purely imaginary register, would be through the strange labor of "achieving" his own childhood:

64. The "first private adventure" refers to Malte's experience of the phantom hand under the table.

65. Malte mentions that during his stay in Copenhagen he lived at the Hotel Phoenix. Kantorowicz goes into some detail on the importance of that mythological figure for the tradition of the King's Two Bodies. The novel in some sense lives off the uncertainty as to what might rise up out of the ruins of the paternal master.

Indeed, his inward composure went so far that he decided to retrieve the most important of the experiences which he had been unable to accomplish before, those that had merely been waited through. Above all, he thought of his childhood, and the more calmly he recalled it, the more unfinished it seemed; all its memories had the vagueness of premonitions, and the fact that they were past made them almost arise as future. To take all this past upon himself once more, and this time really, was the reason why, from the midst of his estrangement, he returned home. (258–59)

But in the same way that Rilke, in his letter to his wife, raised the question of Malte's capacity to succeed in his task, Malte immediately introduces uncertainty as to the fate of this prodigal son: "We don't know whether he stayed there, we only know that he came back" (259).

XVI

The uncertainty Malte introduces here brings us finally to what many readers have seen to be among the most problematic themes of the novel, that of human and divine love. As the sentence that opens the final section of the novel indicates, Malte's—and Rilke's—preoccupations with love concern, above all, the constraints it introduces by virtue of its *transitivity*, the fact that love has an object. The novel returns with some regularity to the vision of an intransitive love, a love that would in some sense exceed or transcend the beloved—without thereby becoming some sort of objectless love of humankind and so directed nowhere in particular—and that would, in turn, resist the lure of soliciting a love that would thereby convert the lover into a love-object, the delimited, identifiable figure of the beloved. The novel makes the case that the resources for grasping the nature of such intransitive love are to be found in the example of a series of representative women lovers who left behind in letters, poems, and memoirs a crucial archive of such erotic strivings. The most detailed example that Malte provides is that of Bettina von Arnim, in whose semifictional *Goethe's Correspondence with a Child*, a book into whose mysteries he is initiated by his mother's younger sister, Abelone, Malte first recognizes the aesthetic, ethical, and perhaps even political resources of such love, one that, as Abelone and Malte agree, surpassed the understanding and capacities of Goethe.[66]

---

66. Kittler sees in this and other examples evidence that the displacement of the sovereign author by the "automatic" writer-stenographer needs to be understood as a displacement of the poetry of the male genius-master by a kind of *écriture féminine*. It would be worthwhile to place into this

Rather than entering into the thicket of scholarly debates regarding Rilke's long history of poetic, essayistic, and epistolary reflections on love or, for that matter, regarding his own erotic history, I would like to make a simple claim that emerges out of the analysis of *Malte* I have offered thus far. One needs to grasp the love that, as Malte puts it, *exceeds* the object of love not as one that simply moves beyond or over the object toward another destination but rather as a love directed precisely at the *excess* in the love-object itself, a love that does not *transcend* the object but is rather oriented by the *surplus of immanence* in the beloved. And as I have argued, this surplus represents a dimension that does not simply belong to the love-object but is, rather, one that acquires its urgency in the context of a radical shift in the framework within which meanings, distinctions, entitlements, and, ultimately, erotic values are established. To put it in the terms I have been proposing throughout this study, this is a love that is willing—that gathers the will and the courage—to endure the encounter with the flesh that twitches in an always singular fashion in the other. This would be a love that would serve to suspend, to render inoperative, that process of selection that guides what Roberto Esposito has analyzed as the immunological procedures of modernity. Those procedures are, as we have seen, always at pains to sort out the flesh of the *people* from that of the *People*, the *entsetzlich* flesh of creaturely life—a life whose only entitlement is to *enjoy bare life*—from the flesh that gives substance to the *dignitas*, the claim to belong to the set of those endowed with sovereignty.[67]

At various points in the novel, Rilke suggests that such love might be something that lies beyond human capacities, that it depends, in a word, on the resources of the divine; that only a love nourished by and responsive to divine love can sustain the sort of "neighbor-love"—love in the neighborhood of creaturely life—that would seem to be at issue for Malte. One thinks, for example, of one of the passages dealing with the outcasts, in this case a blind newspaper salesman in Paris. By way of a distinctive insistence on his own creatureliness, this figure in some

---

context Winfried Menninghaus's stunning reading of Friedrich Hölderlin's short poem "Hälfte des Lebens." Menninghaus discerns in the poem the metrical traces of the Sapphic ode, a form used by Hölderlin only very sparingly. These traces—we might think of them as a kind of metrical twitch—serve for Menninghaus as the index of Hölderlin's own strivings to move away from the Pindaric forms of his most famous hymns and toward a new kind of poetic diction. Sappho, of course, figures in *Malte* as another crucial representative of what we might characterize as the libidinal economy of "the time of the other interpretation." See Winfried Menninghaus, *Hälfte des Lebens: Versuch über Hölderlins Poetik* (Frankfurt am Main: Suhrkamp, 2005).

67. Rilke is, thus, at some level ultimately right about Malte's failure, but not because his protagonist fails to become a poet; his real failure is that he cannot help clinging to a minimal sense of entitlement that serves to distinguish and thereby *immunize* him against those forms of (creaturely) life he refers to as the outcasts.

sense shames Malte into acknowledging the existence of God. A first step involves a certain rupture of the imaginary: "Immediately I knew that my picture of him was worthless. His absolute abandonment and wretchedness, unlimited by any precaution or disguise, went far beyond what I had been able to imagine. I had understood neither the angle of his face [*den Neigungswinkel seiner Haltung*] nor the terror [*das Entsetzen*] which the inside of his eyelids seemed to keep radiating into him" (210–11). Malte experiences this moment as a kind of divine revelation, one that at least has the potential to "elevate" this *creature* to the status of a *neighbor*: "My God, I thought with sudden vehemence, so you really *are*. There are proofs of your existence. I have forgotten them all and never even wanted any, for what a huge obligation would lie in the certainty of you. And yet that is what has just been shown to me" (211).[68]

In the retelling of the story of the prodigal son that concludes the novel, Malte's version of this New Testament figure explicitly couples his strivings for a new way of loving, a new libidinal economy that would succeed in no longer disavowing the excess, the surplus of immanence that ultimately makes the other *other*, with a turn toward the divine: "I see his whole existence, which was then beginning its long love toward God, that silent work undertaken without thought of ever reaching its goal" (257). This invocation of love as a kind of *pure means* is followed by a further characterization of this turn, one that brings to mind the last lines of Hofmannsthal's *Chandos Letter*: "He was like someone who hears a glorious language and feverishly decides to write poetry in it. Before long he would, to his dismay, find out how very difficult this language was" (257). At the very end of this retelling of the prodigal son's story, Malte imagines his return home, where, as we have seen, he has vowed to take on the full force of his childhood once more, to "achieve" it in a way that would help to prepare him for the time of the "other interpretation," one implying, in turn, another libidinal economy, another mode of *jouissance*. The last lines of the novel suggest, however, that this process of working through itself depends on the vicissitudes of divine love: "He was now terribly difficult to love, and felt that only One would be capable of it. But He was not yet willing" (260). I would suggest that among Rilke's great achievements in *The Notebooks of Malte Laurids Brigge* is to have left uncertain whether such unwillingness represents a final impasse or, rather, the narrow gate through which something truly new might come to pass.

---

68. In *On Creaturely Life*, I cite this passage in the context of a discussion of Paul Celan's famous "Meridian" speech in which he seems to suggest that only an ethically rigorous attentiveness to the *Neigungswinkel* of our neighbor's creaturely life can elevate mere "art" to the level of "poetry."

Epilogue

I

At the cost of a bit of repetition, I would like to summarize my argument. I have attempted to show that the complex symbolic structures and dynamics of sovereignty that inform medieval and early modern European monarchies do not simply disappear from the space of politics once the body of the king is no longer available as the singular embodiment of the principle and functions of sovereignty; rather, these structures and dynamics migrate into a new location, which thereby assumes a turbulent and disorienting semiotic density previously concentrated in, to use Foucault's formulation once again, the "strange material and physical presence" of the king.[1] If we think of the flesh as the *übersinnlich* element that "fattens" the one who occupies the place of power and authority (and who thereby comes to figure as its naturally—because supernaturally—endowed caretaker), one of the central problems for modernity is to learn how to track the vicissitudes of these *royal remains* in their now-dispersed and ostensibly secularized, disenchanted locations. As I have been arguing, the discourses and practices that we now group under the heading of "biopolitics" come to be charged with these duties, with the caretaking of the sublime—but also potentially abject, potentially *entsetzlich*—flesh of the new bearer of the principle of sovereignty, the People. The dimension of the flesh

---

1. Michel Foucault, *Discipline and Punish: The Birth of the Prison*, trans. Alan Sheridan (New York: Vintage, 1977), 208.

comes, in a word, to be assimilated to the plane of the health, fitness, and wellness of bodies and populations that must, in turn, be obsessively measured and tested—or, in the extreme, thanato-political context, exterminated. Political theology and biopolitics are, in a word, *two modes of appearance of the flesh* whose enjoyment entitles its bearers to the enjoyment of entitlements in the social space they inhabit.

I have furthermore argued that the Freudian revolution in psychology, conjoined with certain practices in aesthetic modernism, offer us another point of access to, another mode of engagement with, this uncanny dimension whose "after-twitches" now circulate through everyday life. These alternative modes of engagement offer unique opportunities to intervene into the "immunological" history to which both sovereignty and biopolitics have until now belonged. I have also suggested that these alternative modes of engagement can, at times, assume the form of a *comedic* deployment of the "stuff" of anxiety that, in the realm of aesthetics, tends to call for other generic elaborations (such as *Trauerspiel* and *tragedy*) and, in the realm of individual and collective life, tends to call forth defensive postures of various kinds.

In this context I would like to recall that Kantorowicz concluded his monumental work on the King's Two Bodies with a series of reflections on what he referred to as "man-centered kingship." Just as Kantorowicz turned to literature (Shakespeare's *Richard II*) to "flesh out" his central concept of royal gemination, he returns to literature, in this case, Dante's *Commedia*, to develop this new conception of kingship, one that, as we have seen, already sets the stage for a radical transformation of the political theology of sovereignty. The scene in which Dante is "crowned and mitred" by Virgil represents for Kantorowicz a kind of purely *humanist rite* in which the poet is baptized "into the likeness of Adam, the purely human model of man's perfection and actualization."[2] Through this peculiar act of investiture that, as it were, installs Dante in the office of his own humanity, the dual nature of kingship is transformed into "the reflexiveness of 'man' and 'Man,' of *homo* and *humanitas*, of *Adam mortalis* and *Adam subtilis* . . . of body natural of man and body corporate of Man" (494). As Kantorowicz sums it up, "It remained . . . to the poet *to visualize the very tension of the 'Two Bodies' in man himself,* to make *humanitas* . . . the sovereign of *homo,* and to find for all those intricate cross-relations and interrelations the most complex, terse, and simple, because most human formula: 'I crown and mitre you over yourself'" (495; my emphasis).

2. Ernst Kantorowicz, *The King's Two Bodies: A Study in Medieval Political Theology* (Princeton, NJ: Princeton University Press, 1981), 492. Subsequent references are made in the text.

In the course of the modern history of this "reflexiveness . . . of *homo* and *humanitas*," this "most *human* formula" finds itself confronted with a different one, one enunciated by a figure who would seem, in the very bareness of his life, to embody not so much the tense unity of office and incumbent but rather *the gap between them*, the third dimension that figures their jointure, the "X" that marks the spot of their chiasmic relays. I am thinking of that most famous of all modern office workers, Herman Melville's *Bartleby*, who in some sense responds to the humanist rite of investiture with his simple *inhuman* formula: *I prefer not to*. From this point of view, the narrator's final enunciation, "Ah, Bartleby! Ah, humanity!" becomes almost as enigmatic as Bartleby's famous utterance.[3] We are left in a state of considerable uncertainty as to whether Bartleby and humanity are being equated here or whether Bartleby—the fact of Bartleby—is seen as calling into question the very notions of the human and of humanity, the possibility of ever sitting comfortably in the "office" of the human. I have been arguing here that it might just be that the only dignified way of enjoying the *dignitas* of being human is to learn to live with, to be especially alive to, the indignity of such discomfort and, perhaps, to experience its pressure—its twitching—as a *Lachkrampf*, a paroxysm of laughter that simply cannot—and ought not—be held down.[4] Bartleby could thus be seen as the harbinger of a new sort of "divine comedy" of creaturely life, one created out of the troubles that plague the office of the human.

In this context, I would like to cite once more Kafka's wonderful parable that, as we saw, was so central to Kittler's argument about modernity: "They were given the choice to become kings or messengers. Just like children they all chose to be messengers. For this reason there are only messengers; they race through the world and, because there are no kings, they call out to one another announcements that have become

---

3. Herman Melville, *Bartleby and Benito Cerino* (New York: Dover, 1990), 34. We might also recall the narrator's allusion to the book of Job upon discovering the dead Bartleby in the courtyard of the Tombs. He is asked by the prison cook whether Bartleby is asleep: "'With kings and counselors,' murmured I" (33).

4. Malte recalls one such *Lachkrampf* from a childhood visit to his maternal grandparents. It is occasioned by the comical dignity of a nearly blind butler who pauses to serve one of Malte's relatives who on this night did not come to dinner: "The old, almost totally blind butler nevertheless held out the serving-dish when he came to her seat. He remained in that attitude for a few moments; then, content and dignified, and as if everything were in order, he moved on. I had watched this scene, and for the moment, as I looked, it didn't seem at all funny. But a few moments later, just as I was about to swallow a mouthful of food, a fit of laughter rose to my head so quickly that I choked and caused a great commotion. And even though I myself found this situation painful, even though I tried with all my might to be serious, the laughter kept bubbling up in little fits and in the end completely took control of me [*behielt völlig die Herrschaft über mich*]" (32).

meaningless. They would happily put an end to their miserable life but because of their oath of office they don't dare."[5] I am suggesting that the laughter generated by this comedy of creaturely life can induce a kind of general strike against the various "oaths of office" that bind us to the places we occupy in the world. The time of this strike allows for a new thinking about normative authority and the strange sorts of pressures it generates in human life, pressures that would seem to become most extreme once the sources of such authority have been fully dispersed into the plane of immanence.

II

If I understand Benjamin correctly, at least part of what is at stake in his writings on Kafka is the claim that the latter had, without anyone quite grasping it, already produced some of the finest examples of this modernist comedic genre. In the course of Benjamin's and Scholem's correspondence on Kafka's writings, the two friends reached something of an impasse as to the status of Jewish learning and tradition in Kafka's work. I have already cited Scholem's famous formulation about the "nothingness of revelation" in Kafka, the persistence of something like the force of revelation as *valid* even if no longer *meaningful*. In his letter of July 7, 1934, Scholem scolds his friend for resisting the force of this insight, one he had already adumbrated in earlier responses to his friend's still unpublished essay on Kafka (as well as in what Scholem himself characterizes as a didactic poem about Kafka's *Trial*): "I can only reinforce the position taken in those initial remarks. Kafka's world is the world of revelation, but of revelation seen of course from that perspective in which it is returned to its own nothingness. I cannot accept your disavowal of this aspect."[6] Referring specifically to Benjamin's essay, Scholem continues:

The *nonfulfillability* of what has been revealed is the point where a *correctly* understood theology . . . coincides most perfectly with that which offers the key to Kafka's work. Its problem is not, dear Walter, its *absence* in a preanimistic world, but the fact that

5. Franz Kafka, *Beim Bau der chinesischen Mauer und andere Schriften aus dem Nachlaß* (Frankfurt am Main: Fischer, 1992), 235–36.

6. *The Correspondence of Walter Benjamin and Gershom Scholem, 1932–1940*, trans. Gary Smith and Andre Lefevere (Cambridge, MA: Harvard University Press, 1992), 126. The essay, "Franz Kafka: On the Tenth Anniversary of His Death," was eventually published in the journal *Jüdische Rundschau* in December 1934. Harry Zohn's translation of the essay may be found in Walter Benjamin, *Selected Writings*, vol. 2, *1927–1934*, ed. Michael W. Jennings, Howard Eiland, and Gary Smith (Cambridge, MA: Harvard University Press, 1999), 794–818.

it cannot be *fulfilled*. It is about this text that we will have to reach an understanding. Those pupils of whom you speak at the end are not so much those who have lost the Scripture . . . but rather those students who cannot decipher it. And it seems to me utterly compelling that a world in which things are so uncannily concrete and in which not a step can be fulfilled will present an *abject* [*verworfenen*] and by no means idyllic sight (which you, for some incomprehensible reason, seem to regard as an objection against the "theological" interpretation. . .).[7]

In his response, Benjamin first of all denies any disavowal of theology in his reading of Kafka; he writes that his "essay has its own broad—though admittedly shrouded—theological side" and insists that what his friend perceived as an objection against the theological interpretation was largely a polemic against "the unbearable posturing of the theological 'professionals' . . . who . . . have held sway over all Kafka interpretations to date and whose smuggest manifestations are yet to come."[8] In a letter written several weeks later, Benjamin tries to further clarify the differences between them: "You take the 'nothingness of revelation' as your point of departure, the salvific-historical perspective of the established proceedings of the trial. I take as my starting point the small, nonsensical hope, as well as the creatures for whom this hope is intended and yet who on the other hand are also the creatures in which this absurdity is mirrored."[9] It is in this context, he continues, "that the problem of Scripture [*Schrift*] poses itself": "Whether the pupils have lost it or whether they are unable to decipher it comes down to the same thing, because, without the key that belongs to it, the Scripture is not Scripture, but life. Life as it is lived in the village on which the castle is built. It is in the attempt to metamorphize life into Scripture that I perceive the meaning of 'reversal' [*Umkehr*], which so many of Kafka's parables endeavor to bring about. . . . Sancho Panza's existence is exemplary because it actually consists in re-reading one's own existence—however buffoonish and quixotic."[10] It is in his letter of September 20, 1934, Scholem's most explicit and aggressive response to his friend's views on Kafka, that we find the famous formulation about validity in excess of meaning:

You ask what I understand by the "nothingness of revelation"? I understand by it a state in which revelation appears to be without meaning, in which it still asserts itself,

---

7. *Correspondence of Benjamin and Scholem*, 126–27.
8. Letter of July 20, 1934, ibid., 128.
9. Letter of August 11, 1934, ibid., 135.
10. Ibid. The village in question is, of course, the setting of Kafka's novel *The Castle*.

in which it has *validity* but *no significance* [*in dem sie gilt, aber nicht bedeutet*]. A state in which the wealth of meaning is lost and what is in the process of appearing (for revelation is such a process) still does not disappear, even though it is reduced to the zero point of its own content, so to speak. This is obviously a borderline case [*ein Grenzfall*] in the religious sense, and whether it can really come to pass is a very dubious point. I certainly cannot share your opinion that it doesn't matter whether the disciples have lost the "Scripture" or whether they can't decipher them, and I view this as one of the greatest mistakes you could have made. When I speak of the nothingness of revelation, I do so precisely to characterize the difference between these two positions.[11]

I would at this point like to cite one of the final letters from this fevered archive; it is among the last communications Benjamin sent to Scholem before his suicide in 1940. I think it is here that Benjamin finally hits on what he was trying to say when he spoke about scripture becoming the sort of life lived in the village at the foot of the castle hill. It is a life in which the dimension of transcendence that Scholem insists on preserving, if only in the form of validity without meaning, has become that surplus of immanence that accounts for the peculiar—and peculiarly comic—rhythm of everyday life in this village:

More and more, the essential feature in Kafka seems to be humor. He himself was not a humorist, of course. Rather, he was a man whose fate it was to keep stumbling upon people who made humor their profession: clowns. *Amerika* in particular is one large clown act. And concerning the friendship with [Max] Brod, I think I am on the track of the truth when I say: Kafka as Laurel felt the onerous obligation to seek out his Hardy—and that was Brod. However that may be, I think the key to Kafka's work is likely to fall into the hands of the person who *is able to extract the comic aspects from Jewish theology*. Has there been such a man? Or would you be man enough to be that man?[12]

III

There is, I think, general agreement that Scholem was not up to this task. I would suggest, however, that Benjamin's question—one pertaining to the work of a Jew writing in German in Prague—was at least in part answered not by way of philology, philosophy, or any other sort of scholarly enterprise but rather through another literary oeuvre, that of a Protestant

11. Letter of September 20, 1934, ibid., 142.
12. Letter of February 4, 1939, ibid., 243.

Irishman writing largely in French in Paris: Samuel Beckett. It is beyond the scope of this study to pursue this line of thought, but couldn't one say that in Beckett's universe—and perhaps above all in his theatrical works—"scripture" becomes "life" by way of a unique kind of convergence of *language* and *physical comedy*? Aren't all those Didis and Gogos and Nells and Nags and Hamms and Clovs and Winnies and Krapps (all no doubt distant and not-so-distant relatives of Kafka's "Odradek") figures in and through which the verbal and physical twitches of creaturely life, of the surplus of immanence we have been tracking throughout this study, take center stage?

Such a view would, I think, go a long way in helping to account for the strange status of these figures who are unmistakably singular yet also utterly generic (we might say *singularly generic*).[13] One thinks here too of another coincidence of opposites that distinguish Beckett's theater. The characters, the settings, the dialogue, the time and space of the "action" are all strangely abstract; they no longer belong to a recognizable world or form of life. And yet they never cease to be utterly, even excessively concrete; everything has been brought irremediably down to earth. The singularly generic figures move through—or, perhaps better, are immobilized within—an abstractly concrete universe. Recalling Arendt's account of the stateless, one could say that Beckett's characters acquire their particular strangeness by being rendered *merely human*.[14] One could further argue that Beckett has gone the greatest distance among modern artists in the process of *figuring out abstraction*, of forming singular figures out of the abstract materiality of the royal remains that, as we saw in David's *Death of Marat*, fill the space of representation where the sovereign People struggle and fail to take viable shape. Or, to vary the formula Schmitt invokes in his reading of *Hamlet*, we might say that when, in Beckett's theater, the time of creaturely life invades the space of play, *Trauerspiel* is not so much elevated to the dignity of tragedy as it is "lowered" to the comedy of an *Endspiel* in which, in a rather new sense, flesh becomes word and words take on the agitations of the flesh.

By its very title, Beckett's play *Endgame* places us in the midst of the turbulence of sovereignty, the rise and fall of kings and queens (on the chessboard of battle). Of more interest is the way in which the associations generated by the names of the two main characters of the play—Hamm

13. This status is no doubt related to the response Bartleby repeats three times when his employer offers him various alternative employments or "offices": "*I am not particular.*" Melville, *Bartleby*, 29, 30.

14. As I have argued, Arendt's great insight was that being rendered "merely human" results in becoming something *less than human and yet not simply animal.*

and Clov—seem to encapsulate crucial aspects and dimensions of the aesthetic transformation in question, the various "stages" of the shift from *Trauerspiel* to tragedy to comedic *Endspiel*. One could, for example, argue that the entire play is at some level haunted by the dimension of flesh evoked by the "dish" the two main characters embody through their names—ham with cloves—a meal typically served on the holidays marking the birth and death of Christ. One might further note that by reversing its letters, Clov's name spells out the name of the new bearer of sovereignty in modernity: the *Volk*. The fateful constitution of nations (along with the violence that separates out the *people* from the true *Volk/ People*) is further evoked by the link to the biblical figure Ham.[15] But as many readers have also noted, Hamm could be read as a shortened form of "Hamlet," thereby returning us to the "barbaric" early modern history of the political theology of sovereignty along with the multiple ghosts and spirits that haunt it.

Against this background it comes as no surprise that the figure of Hamm, who remains bound to his large chair center stage (Clov moves the chair around at various points in the play), recalls all those seated figures—mostly screaming popes—whom Francis Bacon painted over and over. Riveted to their thronelike chairs as if to an infernal machinery of torture, they might, one could almost imagine, speak the words Beckett gives to Hamm in this typical bit of dialogue:

Clov: Do you believe in the life to come?
Hamm: Mine was always that.

I would like to suggest that the "afterlife" in question here concerns not so much what lies beyond the natural life of the biological individual, of the mortal body, but rather what lies beyond the death of the forms of life evoked by the figures and concepts the traces of which haunt the names of the play's two main characters. There is clearly a great deal more work to be done with respect to the implications of such a claim, but at this point in my investigations, my capacities lead me to say, with Bartleby, *I prefer not to.*

---

15. Stanley Cavell places the cursed figure of Ham at the center of his reading of the play. See Cavell, "Ending the Waiting Game: A Reading of Beckett's *Endgame*," in *Must We Mean What We Say?* by Cavell (Cambridge, MA: Cambridge University Press, 1995), 115–62.

Index

abject art, 111
abstraction, 94, 118, 126, 133–34
Acéphale, 104
Adler, Marcia, 65n6
aesthetics, modernist, xvii, xxi, 62, 124, 246. *See also* art, modernist
Agamben, Giorgio, xv, xvii, 7, 20–21, 31, 44, 54–55, 57–61, 75–76, 86, 173, 182–83, 216n28, 217
Agrippa, Menenius, 37
Alt, Peter-André, 61n33
Althusser, Louis, 20
ancien régime, 8, 32, 60–61, 97
Andreas-Salomé, Lou, 189
animality, 112, 116, 131n51, 135, 138
animal magnetism. *See* mesmerism
animation, 84, 101, 114, 118–21, 124, 136
animism, 116, 121
Aquinas, 40n7
archive fever, 52, 158
Arendt, Hannah, xvii, 31, 48, 50–59, 86, 138, 148, 156n16, 216, 251
Aristocrats, The (film), 107–8
Aristophanes, 66, 78–79, 209n20
Aristotle, 40n7, 72; *Poetics*, 209n20
art, modernist, 5, 103, 114–18, 122–23, 158, 206
authority, xii, xvii, 8, 39; of nature, 122n40; normative, 69, 114, 116, 119, 122, 173, 248
Axton, Marie, 44n11, 45n13, 142, 158

Bacon, Francis, 124–32, 135–41, 143, 161, 168, 173–74; biography, 175–76; paintings, 180, 227n42, 236n55, 252
Badiou, Alain, 106n24, 172n35, 210n21
Bakhtin, Mikhail, 238n61
Barbarossa (Frederick I), 36n2, 40
Barthes, Roland, 201n12; "The Death of the Author," 232n51
Bataille, Georges, 103–10, 113, 119
Baudelaire, Charles, x n4, 168n30, 228–30
Becker, Paula, 189
Beckett, Samuel, 251
Bellmann, Werner, 183n50, 185n55
Benjamin, Walter, xix–xx, 22n24, 47, 76, 115, 138n63, 148n9, 153–54, 162n22, 174, 177n43, 184–85; analysis of Baudelaire, 198–200; correspondence with Scholem on Kafka, 248–50; on excessive energies, 201n13; "The Storyteller," 200, 206, 212–16, 225n41
Bernstein, J. M., 114–25, 129, 133n53, 136, 140; account of modernism, 204–8; notion of fit, 115, 118, 208, 215n26
Bible: book of Daniel, 66n7; book of Job, 230–31, 247n3
biocracy, thanato-political, 53
biopolitical pantheism, 137–38
biopolitics, xi, xiii, xv, xvii, xxi, 7, 12, 15, 29, 34, 60–61, 81, 154, 245–46; modern, history of, 100, 114, 137
biotechnology, 137